A

HISTORY

OF

THE ISLAND OF MONA

MAGMA

YNYS MÔN 2007

Angharad Llwyd's prizewinning essay was first published in 1833.
Presenting a copy to Princess Victoria, she called it
" *My Mona, bound in Bardic green.* "

———————

The compilation of this second edition is based on
the work of T. P. T. Williams of Llandegfan, Ynys Môn.

Source material for the preface (written by
Philip Steele of Llangoed, Ynys Môn) includes
The Gwyneddion for the Beaumaris Eisteddfod
of 1832, edited by William Jones (London 1839),
and the paper about Angharad Llwyd's life
by Mary Ellis, M.A., published in two parts in
the Journal of the Flintshire Historical Society
(volumes 26/1973-74 & 27/1975-76).

The portrait photograph of Angharad Llwyd
is in the collection of the Denbighshire Record Office.

Designed & typeset by Robert Williams

Printed in Wales

LLYFRAU MAGMA

LLANSADWRN, YNYS MÔN

© MAGMA, 2007

ISBN 978-1-872773-73-5

PREFACE TO THIS NEW EDITION.

IN 1832 the thirteen year-old Princess Victoria visited the Isle of Anglesey. She and her mother, the German-born Duchess of Kent, stayed at Plas Newydd, Llanedwen, home of Henry William Paget, the first Marquess of Anglesey. During Victoria's stay, an eisteddfod was held amidst the ruins of Beaumaris castle, lasting from 28th to 31st August. It was a splendid occasion, with balls, regattas on the Menai Strait and royal heralds trumpeting fanfares. The eisteddfod was attended by Members of Parliament and other prominent figures. The President of the festival was Sir Richard Bulkeley.

The theme of the eisteddfod's English-language essay competition was the island's history, and the winning entry, submitted under the pseudonym 'Bronwen', was written by Angharad Llwyd. In delivering the adjudication, one of the judges, James Henry Cotton, rector of Llanllechid and later Dean of Bangor, made the claim—

> "Who that examined the Essay … and saw its correct and beautiful representation of the Island of Anglesey, but must be excused if he indulged in a flight of fancy, and imagined the author to have soared to the heights of Snowdon itself, to have plucked a quill from one of its own eagles, and to have described with it, in language of incomparable accuracy and taste, all the varying characteristics of the island."

Disappointingly, bad weather prevented the attendance in town of the royal party, and Angharad Llwyd herself was absent. However both Princess Victoria and Angharad Llwyd did manage to attend a ceremony held later at Baron Hill, the home of the Bulkeley family just outside Beaumaris. Here the prize-winners were presented with their medals. Angharad was formally presented to the royal party, and complimented on her achievement.

Angharad Llwyd was already in her fifties at this time. In retrospect she may be judged the leading woman of letters in Wales in her day. She was not a writer of fiction or poetry, but was inspired by Welsh literature and history. She loved to pore over genealogies, with their resonant naming of names, and she researched the pedigrees and heraldry of prominent Welsh families. She was fascinated by the history of her native land and was already well versed in the matter of Anglesey before starting her Beaumaris Eisteddfod task.

Angharad Llwyd, *c.*1863
(Denbighshire Record Office)

Angharad Llwyd (also known as Ann Lloyd) was born on 15th April 1780 at Caerwys, in Flintshire, one of the eight children of John Lloyd and Martha Williams. Her mother was from an Anglesey family. Her father, a graduate of Jesus College, Oxford, was rector of Caerwys. John had a keen interest in history, and accompanied Thomas Pennant on the travels which resulted in *Tours of Wales,* published in 1778 and 1781.

John Lloyd ensured that Angharad was well educated and she evidently grew up to share his interests. Her favourite book in her youth was Edmund Spenser's *The Færie Queene* (published in 1590 and 1596). With its Arthurian inspiration and its allegorical exaltation of the Tudors, a royal dynasty which had its roots in medieval Anglesey, it was bound to appeal to someone of her cultural interests and social background.

After John's death, at the age of sixty in 1793, the Lloyd family continued to live at Caerwys in a house called Siamber Wen. However Angharad travelled widely across Wales and kept in touch with fellow antiquaries. She was an inveterate letter writer. The Lloyd family was well connected and Angharad was all too aware of the great libraries, often put to scant use, in the houses of the gentry. She made use of these to immerse herself in medieval poetry and history. Already by 1825 she had to build a house extension to accommodate all her research papers. Many volumes of her documents and copious notes, together with those of her father, are today housed in the National Library of Wales, Aberystwyth. Some of her correspondence, relating to Welsh pedigrees, is in the collection of the Central Library, Cardiff.

Angharad Llwyd was a staunch defender of the Welsh language. In 1817 parishioners of Llanbeblig, Caernarfon, protested when a non-Welsh speaker was appointed as their vicar. Objections were raised too by the Gwyneddigion Society. Although the result was a compromise—the newcomer agreed to learn Welsh—Angharad commended the stand that had been taken and organised a subscription for the presentation of silver cups to the rebellious churchwardens.

In 1821 Angharad Llwyd became an honorary member of the Cymmrodorion Society, which had been founded in London in 1751 by Richard Morris, one of the remarkable Morris brothers of Pentre-eriannell, Anglesey. The Society was being revived at this time, with the principal aim of overseeing the provincial eisteddfodau, which from 1819 were being organised by the so-called Cambrian Societies. Angharad Llwyd had become a leading campaigner and fund-raiser in the promotion of eisteddfodau, and during the Powys provincial eisteddfod of 1821 she became one of the first women to be admitted to the Gorsedd of the Bards. As a regular competitor herself, she met with several successes, marked by the award of gold and silver medals and cash prizes. Her topics included a *Catalogue of Welsh Manuscripts, etc, in North Wales* (Welshpool Eisteddfod, 1824), the *Genealogy and Antiquities of Wales* (Cymmrodorion Society medal, 1826) and an *Essay on the Castles of Flintshire* (Denbigh Eisteddfod, 1828). In 1827 she edited a handsome new edition of *The History of the Gwydir Family* by Sir John Wynn, which had been first published in 1770.

The full text of Angharad Llwyd's successful Beaumaris essay was published in Ruthun in 1833, under the title *A History of the Island of Mona, or Anglesey; including an account of its natural productions, druidical antiquities, lives of eminent men, the customs of the Court of the Antient Welsh Princes, etc*. The book was prefaced with a dedication to Princess Victoria, drawing attention to the royal family's connection with the island through the Tudors.

This new edition reprints the whole of Angharad Llwyd's *History of the Island of Mona*. What is the modern reader to make of it? The book does not of course have the structure of a modern academic essay, nor the narrative style of modern non-fiction aimed at a more general readership. It suits its age, being leisurely and discursive, a 'Grand Tour' in the company of a knowledgeable and interesting companion.

Caveat lector, Angharad Llwyd's history precedes the hugely important archaeological and linguistic methodologies and discoveries that have intervened during the last two centuries. Of course her essay can no longer stand as a reliable work of reference. This is perhaps most noticeable in her association of prehistoric monuments with the much later druidic cults of the Celtic Iron Age. Likewise she readily accepts without evidence the local legend that the ancient burial site on the Afon Alaw really is *Bedd Branwen*, Branwen's grave, as its name suggests. Even some of Angharad's contemporaries urged her to be more critical in her historical assessments. However very often the author does get it right, and in the wide range of her interests is truly a spiritual daughter of the Morris brothers.

The *History of the Island of Mona* begins with a level-headed economic assessment of Anglesey in the author's own times, referring to agriculture and livestock, fisheries, quarrying, copper mining at Parys Mountain and coal mining on the Cefni marshes. The variety and self-sufficiency of local industry in the early nineteenth century impresses us in the age of globalised, services-based economics. Angharad Llwyd describes ports and harbours, ferries and rivers, roads, dwellings and population. This is all fascinating material for the modern reader, written in the age when the road from Porthaethwy to Beaumaris, and the Menai Suspension Bridge, were still novelties.

Scarcely drawing breath—there are no chapters—Angharad Llwyd then rambles off in search of the druids, citing Roman historians and the generally unreliable *Mona Antiqua Restaurata* (1723) of Henry Rowlands as her sources. (To be fair, the author does challenge the accepted wisdom of many such authorities in the course of her essay). She proceeds to *Brut y Tywysogion*, the 'Chronicles of the Princes', with characteristic side swipes at 'monkery' and a scathing assessment of Saxon intelligence in the early Middle Ages. She writes proudly of the great age of the Welsh princes and concludes with the rebellion of Owain Glyndŵr.

From here on the text takes the form of a gazetteer of Anglesey locations, including historical observations, economic information and general descriptions. The entry on Beaumaris includes an account of the Civil War years, and that of Penmynydd pays homage to the Tudors. All this section should provide valuable reading material for local historians today.

So too should the subsequent biographical sketches, which include such *enwogion o fri* as Siôn Dafydd Rhys of Llanfaethlu (1534–*c*.1619), David Hughes (*c*.1560–1610, founder of Beaumaris grammar school in 1603, which was forerunner of the modern Ysgol David Hughes in Menai Bridge), the aforementioned Henry Rowlands of Llanedwen (1655–1723), the mathematician William Jones of Bodafon (*c*.1675–1749), his son, the orientalist Sir William Jones (1746–94), Lewis Morris (1701–65), and the poet Goronwy Owen (1723–69).

Many of the quotations in Angharad Llywd's essay are attributed to '*J. Lloyd*'. In a Conclusion, she acknowledges the debt owed to her father—"It affords the compiler of this work much pleasure to have an opportunity of rendering this just tribute to the acknowledged historical accuracy of her highly gifted father, justly said by his friend and fellow traveller, Mr. Pennant, 'to be equalled by few in his knowledge of the language and the history of the Ancient Britons, and few so liberal in his communication'."

A final section to the book, 'selected from the Bangor and Chester papers', gives an account of the proceedings of the Beaumaris Eisteddfod, and then concludes with the reprint of a stirring speech given at the Wrecsam Eisteddfod of 1820 by a prebendary of St. Asaph, Reginald Heber. (Heber became Lord Bishop of Calcutta three years later, and was the author of some of the best known Anglican hymns). Heber's address, evidently much admired by Angharad Llwyd, showed his appreciation of the extent of ancient Celtic cultural influence in Europe, his understanding of the international importance of Welsh literature and of the pressing need for Welsh to be the subject of modern academic study. Most significantly Heber, himself an Englishman, deplored the 'systematic and persevering hostility' shown historically to the Welsh language by 'English Rulers'.

The *History of the Island of Mona* is well worth reprinting today. Its informal structure makes it ideal for the reader to browse through and it offers rich pickings. It is very much a work of its time. Angharad Llwyd was representative of her social class in the county where she lived, admiring the role of the more progressive aristocracy and politically conservative. She was a dyed-in-the-wool Protestant, and an opinionated opponent of Catholicism, which she called 'Popery'.

In other respects, however, Angharad Llwyd was a surprisingly modern figure. Her romanticism was generally tempered by down-to-earth common sense and good humour, self-evident in her surviving portrait photographs. Her letters reveal a lively, resilient and energetic mind. She was a woman setting her own agenda and determinedly pursuing her interests in an age dominated by men. She did not marry. She loved animals, especially stray donkeys and her own ponies and pet dogs.

In her forthright defence of Wales and the Welsh language Angharad Llwyd foreshadows the cultural and political agenda of nationalists in the late nineteenth and twentieth century. Antiquarian research in the days before modern transport, communications and electronic media needed considerable stamina, and she had plenty of that.

The *History of the Island of Mona* is generally regarded as Angharad Llwyd's best work. After 1833 she continued to pursue her various interests. In 1845 at Llanover for the eisteddfod she met up with some other remarkable women: Augusta Hall (1802-96) another enthusiast for Welsh culture, with an interest in costume; Lady Charlotte Guest (1812-95), renowned for her translation of the *Mabinogion,* and the musician and collector of folk songs Maria Jane Williams (1795-1893).

From 1846 Angharad Llwyd lived, still within Flintshire, at the seventeenth-century house of Ty'n y Rhyl, a suitably historic environment. In her final years she was widely celebrated, respected and regarded with much affection. Angharad Llwyd died at Ty'n y Rhyl on 16th October 1866, aged 86 years.

— • —

" Angharad Llwyd inherited all her father's antiquarian tastes, and distinguished herself as an authoress. ... Miss Llwyd was equally well known for more peculiarly feminine qualities, constant kindness, charity, cheerfulness, and great hospitality. "

From an obituary published by the Cambrian Archaeological Association in 1867.

AN EDITORIAL NOTE.

Some of the evident typographical errors of the first edition have
been corrected in this reprint, and the listing of errata, appended to
the first edition, has also been applied to the newly typeset text.
Many of the archaic and inconsistent spellings—characteristic of
the period—nevertheless remain, in both the Welsh and English. In
addition, some of the punctuation has been simplified. Students of
Angharad Llwyd's life and work, and those wishing to quote from
her writings, should therefore refer to the 1833 edition.

The arrangement of the index follows that of the first edition.

A number of the essay's Latin quotations are set, as for the first
edition, in 'record type', a notation that serves to reproduce the
abbreviated scripts of ancient manuscripts. During the course of her
research, Angharad Llwyd transcribed some of these original
documents herself, but more often quoted from the handwritten
copies of others. Perhaps inevitably, therefore, her essay's draft
contained a number of errors, and more were probably introduced
during the typesetting process.

No attempt has been made by the publisher of this new edition
to correct such errors. Serious researchers will no doubt want to
refer to the earlier manuscripts.

———————

Angharad Llwyd frequently makes reference to the 'Sebright' papers.
The fate of many of these manuscripts, originally the collection of
Edward Lhuyd (1660-1709), is described on page 90 of her essay:

" Mr. Lewis Morris says of Mr. Edward Llwyd, 'that he was inferior
to no man in Britain in natural history, and had a prodigious knack in languages'. Four years after Mr. Llwyd's death, his extensive and valuable
collection of Welsh manuscripts was purchased by Sir John Sebright, and
since designated as 'The Sebright Collection'. A singular and mortifying
fatality seems to have attended these celebrated documents, which were
afterwards sold and became the property of Sir Watkin Williams Wynn and
Mr. Johns [Thomas Johnes] of Havod: such as had fallen to the lot of the
latter gentleman were consumed by fire, which unfortunately destroyed
his mansion, and the moiety purchased by Sir Watkin met with a similar
fate at the house of a person in London, to whom they had been sent in
1810 for the purpose of being bound. "

A

HISTORY

OF

THE ISLAND OF MONA,

OR

ANGLESEY;

INCLUDING AN ACCOUNT OF ITS NATURAL PRODUCTIONS,
DRUIDICAL ANTIQUITIES, LIVES OF EMINENT MEN, THE CUSTOMS OF THE
COURT OF THE ANTIENT WELSH PRINCES, &c.

BEING THE

PRIZE ESSAY

TO WHICH WAS ADJUDGED THE FIRST PREMIUM AT THE ROYAL
BEAUMARIS EISTEDDFOD,
HELD IN THE MONTH OF AUGUST, 1832.

––––––––

BY ANGHARAD LLWYD,

––––––––

RUTHIN:

PRINTED AND SOLD BY R. JONES, CLWYD-STREET.

AND MAY BE HAD OF MESSRS. LONGMAN AND CO. PATERNOSTER ROW, LONDON, AND OF THE
BOOKSELLERS IN CHESTER AND IN THE PRINCIPALITY.

1833.

MADAM,

The following pages having been distinguished by the approbation and rewards of my countrymen, at their great literary festival, which was honoured with the presence of your Royal Highness, and your illustrious Mother, it is with feelings of the deepest gratitude, that I avail myself of the privilege, which has been conceded to me, of presenting them to the public, under the sanction of your Royal Highness's name. Could I hope, that by satisfying the demand of a rational curiosity, my labours would be instrumental in adding an interest to the scenes by which your Royal Highness has lately been surrounded, or, of cherishing their recollection in your bosom, it would constitute the highest ground of my obligations to the Patrons of the Eisteddfod who suggested the subject, and incited me to the work, and as it contains notices of your Royal Highness's ancestors, the illustrious House of Tudor, in connection with the Topographical account of the Island of Mona, I humbly hope, that at some future period, it may contribute to amuse your Royal Highness' mind, by being a means of recalling with pleasure, the various feelings with which you visited this part of the Principality.

That your Royal Highness may live to fulfil the high station that appears to be appointed you by Divine Providence, that you may be endowed with virtues out of the treasures of Divine Wisdom and Grace, and that your future destinies may be combined with the extension of blessings to millions of the human race, is the ardent prayer of

Your Royal Highness's

Most obedient and most humble Servant,

ANGHARAD LLWYD

INTRODUCTION.

"While Cambria shrinks, with boding fear,
" And dreads the tale she's doom'd to hear;
" Affliction wild with piercing cry,
" And dark despair, with downcast eye;
" Misfortune throngs on every side,
" Fallen is Mona's strength and pride,
" And Britain's sons in pain are brave. "

Llwyd's Poems, p.64.

A HISTORY[1] of Mona (with which the events of 2,418 years are associated) including an account of the men of eminence who were natives of that Island, is a task which it would be impossible to accomplish within the compass of an Essay, on however comprehensive a plan an author might proceed, a task which would require more years than the months which were allotted to the competitors on the present occasion—a task that has engaged the attention and employed the pens of a greater number of literary men than any other subject connected with the Principality. For any one following in the track of so many diligent enquirers to produce any thing new must be a matter of rare felicity, whilst the repetition only of what has been already printed can scarcely be in the view of those who have instituted a competition on the subject. I shall combine so much of what has been generally made known through the medium of the press, as to preserve the perspicuity and the integrity of my plan, whilst I shall rest the merit of my Essay upon original matter, culled from various libraries. I shall thus endeavour to bring together with the utmost care from amidst the obscurity of so many dark ages, all the scattered rays of information which are calculated to throw any light on the early history of the sacred Island of the Druids. The riches of our valuable MSS have not been yet exhausted, and it will appear by the result of my enquiries that the Black Book of Basingwerk Abbey in particular—the remains of the Sebright Collection—Mostyn—Combermere—Wynnstay and Caerwys MSS &c. will enable me to restore to the pages of History many interesting anecdotes which have escaped the diligence of the Saxon historian, and assuredly the interest, with which we view the mansions of our country and many a neglected spot, marked with no feature to attract the

---

1 Too much praise cannot be given to the distinguished antiquaries the Rev. Peter Bailey Williams, and Mr. Llwyd of Chester (author of a Poem on Beaumaris Bay, &c.), for the very able and accurate description of this island, which they have given in Cathrall's *History of North Wales* and Evans's *Beauties of England and Wales.*

attention of a stranger, is ten-fold increased by a moderate knowledge of them: by them, and by tra-ditional evidence, of which much remains correctly retained amongst our mountaineers, we can tell who once occupied our ivy-mantled towers, our ancient manors and houses, whose foundations are dimly traced by their prominence amidst the green-sward, or marked by remaining heaps of grey stones. To the antiquary and tourist such knowledge is always interesting, when good authority is annexed to the intelligence; and the world may obtain satisfactory evidence that the primitive atoms of the whole chronological system as subsisting in Wales, were formed by men of talent, genius and education, and their works inspire full confidence in their skill and fidelity.

The reflections which have occurred to the author of the following pages, upon the subject pro-posed to be discussed, have been productive of very painful feelings, as in such a disquisition it was impossible not to be interested in the fate of a gallant people struggling for independence—a peo-ple, according to Geraldus, "equally fitted for the sword, or the plough, brave and happy, till the am-bitious arm of conquest sought them in their peaceful retreat, &c". When, however, those disastrous times have been succeeded by an extended period of great national happiness, the writer cannot but gratefully acknowledge the over-ruling goodness of Providence, which, by allaying animosities, once apparently interminable, has formed of the several people inhabiting these Islands one British na-tion enjoying unexampled blessings, whose destinies, temporal and eternal, whether under the de-nomination of Cimbri[2]—Cornish—Celts—Scotch—Irish, &c., are bound up still in the glorious and awful events connected with this Country,—a Country that has witnessed the rise and fall of the oppressive sway of the Roman, Saxon and Norman Dynasties—a country, which, unless provi-dentially rescued from the attempts of Atheistical Demagogues, is NOW doomed to witness the rapid decline of our temporal grandeur.

---

2 From Cyn, first, or primitive, and Bro, a people, being the first race that colonized Europe. Celtæ, from Cêl, shelter, or concealed, originating in the circumstance of the Celts living in woods. Caledonia their country, so called by the Romans from Celyddon, the name Scotland is still known by among the Cambro-British race—*Rowlands MS; Mona Antiqua; Camden L.M. and Caerwys MSS.*

HISTORY OF MONA.

———

" Tra Môr—Tra Brython." [3]

The ISLAND of Anglesea, which forms the subject of this Essay, is situated at the Northern extremity of the Principality in the Irish Sea; it was called by the ancient Britons, according to Rowlands, Bôn,[4] signifying end, or extremity, also Ynys Dywyll, from its impenetrable darkness, and Ynys y Cedeirn, from its heroes, or powerful Druids; for upwards of 2,000 years it was only known among the people of Wales by its present appellation of Môn,[5] in allusion to which the inhabitants are called in our ancient poems Monwys, Monwysiaid, Monwysion, and Gwŷr Môn, and at the Roman invasion, by adding the letter 'a' in conformity with the Latin idiom, we find it called Mona. This alteration has caused much dispute among historians, many of whom suppose it to be one of the three primary Isles mentioned in the Triads, which were Orkney (then undivided), Manaw, and Wight (Chwith), traces of an Isthmus being still visible at Porthaethwy Ferry where this insulated tract of country originally joined the main land. I learn from the Caerwys MSS that owing to a line of rocks near Craig y Ddinas, jutting out from each side, forming a most dangerous passage during the ebb and flow of the tide by the meeting of two strong currents, this Ferry was originally called Porthcaeth-ŵy. A geological map of the Island was published a few years ago, by Mr. Henslow of Cambridge, who makes its length from east to west, i.e. Penmon to Caer-gybi (Holyhead), to be thirty miles, its breadth measuring from Llanelian in the north to Llanddwyn in the south, twenty-six, and its circumference about ninety miles.

The Irish mail-road and the roads connecting the principal towns and places of note, are in good repair. Lord Bulkeley, a few years before his death, and at his own expence, formed a new road along

---

3 While there is sea, there will be Britons.

4 Fin or Vin, in the Hebrew, signifies the end of a place. Also, the Arabians call the end of a land "Fhinal" ie "the end of land"—*J. Ll. MS, Notes to Mon Ant.*

5 Powel, in p.vi. says, "But here I cannot wink at that notable error of Polidore, which (after his accustomed fashion) denieth this Island to be called Mona, but Anglesea, or *Anglorum Insula*, because it is called in English Anglesey, and gives this Mona to Man, and so hath lost the name of both Isles, which ignorance might be forgiven him, if he had not drawn others to this error with him, which in their Charters, do daily wrong these Isles, which may be easily proved; first, because the Inhabitants of the Isle do know no other name but Môn, and it is called through all Wales Tir Môn, unto this day; so that neither by memory of man—neither by any writing in the British tongue can it appear, that ever it had any name but Môn for these thousand years there be yet manifest monuments of this; it is grown to a proverb through Wales for the fertility of the ground "Môn Mam Cymru".

Both Anglesea and the Isle of Man accordingly bore this designation, the first being called, as we find in our early poets "Môn Vynydd", the Môn of the Mountain; and the other "Môn-aw" the Môn of the Water, afterwards corrupted into Manaw and Man.

the beautiful bank of the Menai, from Bangor Ferry to Beaumaris. The lands on the sea-coast,[6] more especially to the western side where the ground inclines to a plain, are of a sandy nature; the low grounds are chiefly covered with a black soil, which in many places yields the inhabitants good turf,[7] the fuel of the lower class of people, who frequently meet with large bodies of trees, preserved entire and as black as ebony, though several feet under ground. These are supposed to be remains of timber cut down by the Romans, when they invaded the Isle, and brought it to subjection under their leader Suetonius, A.D.61. The greatest part of the soil, especially about the middle of the country, is a reddish earth, approaching the nature of clay, which, by being manured with seaweed, sand and lime, becomes relaxed from its dense quality and produces plentiful crops, fully justifying the ancient appellation of "Môn Mam Cymru". In 1770 upwards of 90,000 bushels of grain were exported from its several harbours, and during the late war a portion of land was brought into tillage by the free use of lime, &c. in consequence of which improvement in husbandry, the produce of corn is immense and yearly increasing. But respecting the cattle, the general opinion is, that although their number is not materially diminished, yet the breed has certainly deteriorated, as affects the milk and butter owing to the application of so much compost, which tends to sour the grass; marl, the manure used by the ancient Britons not having that effect. By a survey made 1795, when there was a great dearth of corn, we find that the whole produce of the Island was 59,770 quarters of the following kinds;—35,485 quarters of oats—22,700 barley—1,578 of wheat; and rye 7 quarters. It yields at present more than three times the quantity above-mentioned. Mona was in former times noted for honey of a superior flavour. It is said that Queen Elizabeth (who inherited this with other Tudor prejudices) had a fancy that metheglyn could not be brewed so well elsewhere as at Penmynydd, from which house her grandfather claimed descent. To these princes, when they swayed the sceptre of England, a large quantity of this beverage was exported annually from this Island, which also produces wax, tallow, hides and coarse cloth in abundance; but the chief trade is in corn and cattle, the latter are well known and much appreciated by the natives of the Principality as "Cattel duon Môn" from their black colour. Lewys Morris, one of the three self-taught brothers of Mona, forming a Triad[8] of genius, writes in 1740 to a friend, thus, "Roberts in his map of commerce, published about one hundred years ago, says that Anglesey sent to the English market about 3,000 head of cattle yearly; but they have improved so much in husbandry since his time, that they amount now to about 15,000, besides at least 5,000 hogs and a great number

---

6 Concerning the wonders of the Isle of Mona.—The first wonder, is a shore without a sea.—The second, is a mountain which turns round three times in a year.—The third is a ford, the water whereof ebbs and flows as the sea does, with the tide.—The fourth is a stone, which walks during the night, in the valley of Eithein, and, when formerly thrown into the whirlpool Carevus, which is in the middle of the sea, called "Mene", it was on the morrow found on the side of the aforesaid valley. Translated from the original Latin Copy of Nennius.—*Harleian MSS 3859.*

7 emp. Ed. 1st. "We find an acre of low land was at this time valued at 8d.—high land 4d.—a turbary valued at more than a colliery and quarry put together.—*J. Ll. Caerwys MSS.*"

8 William Herbert, Earl of Pembroke, who died in 1630, composed the Triads of the four Nations.
    1. Three things notable in a Cymro,—genius, generosity, and mirth.
    2. Three things in a Sais,—coolness, boldness, and industry.
    3. Three things in a Frenchman,—gallantry, courtesy, and inconstancy.
    4. Three things in an Irishman,—flattery, cunning, and ostentation.
    Three things that will make a man wise,—"The genius of a Cymro, the courtesy of a Frenchman and industry of a Saxon, &c. &c."

of sheep." "The hogs", observes Mr. Williams of Treffos (an intelligent gentleman and a native of the island), "have not increased, in proportion one year with another, their number amounting at this period (1832) to above 6,000, of the average value of from £4 to £5, but in much better condition than they were formerly, owing to their being fed with grains and potatoes, of which the old Monenses raised very little except for domestic uses"; and previous to the introduction of this valuable root by Sir Walter Raleigh, (the overplus of corn being exported) the pigs must have been in a starving condition.

The annual export of cattle averages about 8,000 head, from one to four-year old.[9] Annexed is the account given by Mr. Provis, of the export over Menai Bridge in 1830 and 1831.[10]

The sheep are of a larger size and not so wild as those reared in the mountainous districts of Wales. They are called "Devaid mawr Môn", averaging about 15lb. a quarter, and from 4,000 to 5,000 are annually exported. The natives well knowing the important situation of this Island, in regard to its being the granary of their country, disputed its possession with that determined spirit, which would have done credit to the purest feelings of chivalry. The society of ancient Druids belonging to Mona is said to be the oldest institution of the kind in North Wales, and has the credit of extending its patriotic views beyond mere agricultural interests. The philanthropic object of some of the premiums given, especially of that for saving shipwrecked sufferers on the coast of Mona, is a proof of this. At the meeting of the "Anglesey County Society" held at Llangevni, on September 7th in 1819, when there was a greater exhibition of stock than on any former occasion, it was determined to establish an annual sale for superior stock, amongst farmers and others, within the limits of the society.

This sea-girt Isle gives rise to very few rivers. The Alaw, so called, probably from the lilies which grow about it. Braint, with a township of the same name, so called, it is said, from Braint Hîr, a native chieftain and head of the thirteenth tribe; although Mr. Williams conjectures that the name originated in "Braint"—freedom—meaning a township free from impost; Cevni, so named as taking its course

---

9 "The number of pigs shipped from Anglesey during the past year is 5,137"—*John Provis*

10 Number of cattle, sheep, and pigs, which passed over Menai Bridge, in the years commencing May 1, 1830 and May 1, 1831.

	Cattle	Sheep & Pigs		Cattle	Sheep & Pigs
May, 1830	624	716	May, 1831	408	895
June	199	702	June	258	510
July	106	830	July	88	1027
August	1033	422	August	1186	662
September	920	540	September	1260	1205
October	1506	347	October	1330	1213
November	512	795	November	427	936
December	98	471	December	220	211
January, 1831	25	749	January, 1832	58	156
February	178	749	February	110	430
March	179	470	March	107	364
April	380	276	April	252	352
	5760	6728		5704	7961

No separate account is kept of the sheep and pigs, as each pay the same toll. Very few of the latter pass over the bridge; they are chiefly sent by sea.

The gate-keeper considers that about one half of the cattle which pass the bridge in the month of May are taken out of Carnarvonshire to graze in Anglesey. This being the case, only half of the above number for that month ought to be taken, otherwise they will be counted twice over.—*J Provis.*

through the parish of Llangevni; Dulas, from the colour, a deep blue-black. Rivers in Scotland are so called from the same cause; hence the origin of the Douglas name, a clan celebrated by the historian for its prowess in the field; and by the minstrel, for its accomplishments in the bower and the hall.

Leland observes "there is a good commoditie for fishinge, about Tîr Môn, but theire lacketh courage and diligence". Until the year 1800, the fisheries of Mona were a hidden treasure, of the importance of which the old inhabitants were ignorant. The late Mr. O. Williams, then residing at Llanidan, about that time introduced the Torbay system of trawling into Caernarvon Bay, and, on changing his residence to Craig-y-don, some years after he opened in a similar manner the treasures of Red Wharf and Conway Bays; since which time, trawl-boats from Dublin to Liverpool have resorted in great numbers to the shores of Mona, to supply their respective markets with seals, plaice and turbots. The herring fisheries on the north coast from Penmôn to Holyhead, are in some years, a source of considerable wealth to that part of the Island.

For many years past, vast quantities of Arklow oysters have been laid down on the shore, between high and low water mark in summer, to supply the Liverpool and Chester markets during winter. Those taken on the eastern cost of the Menai are claimed by the corporation of Beaumaris, in virtue of a grant from Queen Elizabeth.

Minerals and fossils[11] have been so well described by Cathrall, in his History (p.19 &c.) that I shall only add, that the marble quarries on the north side of the coast, have been of late very productive, and given employment to a great number of men. They first supplied stone for the pier at Holyhead; then for Lord Anglesey's column; then for Menai and Conway bridges. The new great piers in Liverpool, and Donghadee in Ireland, are now supplied from these quarries. A magnificent town-hall now erecting in Birmingham, is to have its richly-decorated front furnished from the Mona quarries, which produce a variety of beautiful specimens of native marble, mentioned in a description of the different parishes in which they are found. Mr. Lewys Morris, in his Book of Charts, relates the following circumstance, "In the year 1747, a plank of grey marble had been thrown out of its bed by the sea and found in Red Wharf Bay, measuring twenty-seven feet long, nine broad and three thick; six hundred and twenty-nine cubic feet—its specific gravity being two feet seven inches. It must weigh above forty-seven tons. Such planks sawed would have made fine columns for public buildings. How could they have escaped the keen eyes of the Romans?" The triumphal arch (commemorative of the landing of King George IV[12] in Mona, on the 6th of August 1821), is built entirely of marble from the Moelvrey quarry. Llangwyvan parish produces white marble, said to be fit for statuary purposes. Mr. Jones of Bangor had lately designed, and is now executing two tables of marble, very superior to any works of the kind ever produced in Wales. The one ordered by the late Lord Newborough, is of an oblong form, having a tessellated surface, formed of two inch squares of marbles, from Italy. It is to be surrounded with a border of dark coloured native marble, and supported by pillars of the same material. The other

11 p.416 Vol.1 Cambrian Register, contains a catalogue of the natural productions of Mona.—*From a MS penes. D. Thomas.*

12 For an excellent account of this visit, read p.42 in Cathrall's History.

table ordered by Sir Richard Bulkeley is circular, the top formed of Mona marbles only, in the same manner as the other, and the pieces so placed as to represent radii, spreading from the centre. As a complicated work of art, this table is even superior to the other; evincing good taste and true patriotism in Sir Richard Bulkeley. It is highly characteristic of the honourable name he bears, and the noble house he represents, thus to give to the productions of his own country a preference to those of a foreign land. The valuable qualities of the Mona marble for building have no where been brought into notice with such effect as at Penrhyn Castle, one of the noblest specimens of modern architecture in Europe. The castle is built of the black marble from Penmôn, which is admirably suited to the heavy Saxo-Norman style of the building. The interior is ornamented with grey and brown, found on the north-east coast, and the porphyritic red marble from Llanvechell. The worthy and liberal owner, Mr. Pennant, deserves the thanks and admiration of every friend of Wales, for the almost exclusive encouragement he has given to native artificers of every kind, in the erection of this splendid pile, as much to be admired for the beautifully elaborate detail of the interior, as for the stupendous magnificence of the exterior. Mr. Hopper, the architect, has testified his great approbation of the skill and intellect manifested by these native artists. In the parish of Llanvair-y'nghornwy is a noted marble quarry, resembling the well-known verd di Corsica, of Italy: it is of a darkish green colour, variegated with black, white and dull purple; it is a compound species, partly calcareous, and may be acted upon by aquafortis; in the green part, which partakes of the nature of jasper, is found the celebrated asbestos, so highly esteemed by the Romans, from its possessing the remarkable quality of resisting fire. We are told by Pliny,[13] that the ancients wove it into a cloth, which, when it became soiled or stained, was thrown into the fire, and thus rendered cleaner than ever; by repeating this method of purification, it was found to diminish materially in substance, each time. The bodies of their great men were enshrouded in this cloth; to preserve the ashes on the funeral pile, which were subsequently deposited in an urn. A curious specimen of the asbestos, both in flax, thread, and woven, also a piece in its native state, may be seen in the British Museum.

The writer of this history, when at Trentham, was shewn a beautiful chimney-piece, made of the Mona-marble found at Rhôs Colyn, which the Duke of Sutherland assured her was nearly equal to some ancient specimen of the verd antique, which he had recently imported from Rome. This acknowledgement by a nobleman, whose correct taste and classical acquirements are indisputable, was highly gratifying to a native, possessing a spirit most truly patriotic. As the Roman verd antique has not been discovered in any other part of the world, there seems to be strong grounds for supposing that it was obtained from Mona. These quarries were brought into notice by the late Mr. Bullock, who manufactured a magnificent table of green marble which was sent to Bonaparte, when at St. Helena. There is a great deal of spar and crystal to be found on the mountain above Holyhead, said to be the highest in the Island; and in the neighbourhood a large vein of fullers' earth, yellow ochre, umber, mineral black, and some copper ore, is dug up in the parish Llanbadwg.

13 Pliny's Letters, &c.

In 1768, on the 2nd of March (observed ever since as a festival by the miners) was discovered the great body of copper ore on Mynydd y Trysclwyn, i.e. Pary's Mountain,[14] which has been the cause of much productive industry, given bread to many thousands of poor families, and diffused comparative wealth throughout the Island. The projector of the plans which occasioned the prosperity of his native place, was the late Mr. Thomas Williams of Llanidan, M.P. for Marlow, whose life is written among the eminent men of Mona. The mines, when at the best, have been known to produce £300,000 worth of ore in one year. It was supposed that the Plasnewydd family alone, has received not less than a million, and all owing to "Twm chwarae teg",[15] the name by which Mr. Williams of Llanidan went among the miners.

The mines now produce little more than what is sufficient to pay the expence of working them; but a very considerable profit is made of the strong copper water, issuing out of the mines. Some hundreds of tons of old iron are brought annually from London and elsewhere, and deposited in small square pools. The sulphuric acid contained in this water, having a greater chemical affinity to iron, attaches itself to that, leaving the copper previously held in solution in the water, to be deposited in a kind of mud at the bottom of the pools. This is now the most profitable part of the mining. Timber impregnated with this water, is never affected by dry rot. Vessels frequenting the harbour of Amlwch, into which this water runs, are known to last longer than any other. A few years since, the Admiralty had it in contemplation to send navy timber here, to be soaked; but the expence of doing so was found to be too great an obstacle to the plan. In the appendix to Mr. Pennant's last edition of his "Tour through Wales" (with additions by his son, the present Mr. Pennant of Downing), may be seen an account of these mines, derived from most authentic sources, and Cathrall's Works p.30 contains very elaborate remarks on this subject.

The Mona mine belongs exclusively to the Marquess of Anglesey, and the Pary's mine jointly, to the Lords Anglesey and Dinorben.

It may be inferred from the following Triad, that the coast[16] of Wales abounded with shipping, equally with the other shores of Britain. "The three principal Harbours of the Isle of Britain, Porth Ysgewyn in Gwent; Porth Gwgyr in Môn, and Porth Gwyddno in the north."[17] There were three princes, celebrated for having fleets, whose names are recorded on that account in this Triad. "Tri Llyngeisawg, Ynys Prydain; Geraint vab Erbyn; Gwenwynwyn vab Nav, a March mab Meirchion."

The works of the bards who flourished in the days of our native princes, contain frequent allusions

---

14 So called from Robert Paris, who was Chamberlain of Chester and North Wales, in the reign of Henry IV. His widow Sionet, daughter of Sir William Stanley of Hooton, married William Griffith of Penrhyn, whose son, William Griffith, became chamberlain of North Wales; and by his mother's side became possessed of Tir Paris.

15 "Tom the fair Dealer"

16 See observations on the sea coast of Wales, by Lewys Morris, which is a work replete with information, and appears to be drawn up with his usual diligence and accuracy.

17 "Porth Wyddno, either Glasgow or Edinburgh in the North." Lewys Morris, who again observes, "Gwygur river comes to Cemmaes in Môn, and is a very poor harbour; so that I take Porth Wygur to be the old name of Beaumaris; and Porth Ysgewyn may be the old name of Portsmouth".

to their naval affairs[18] and subsequent to the period when Wales was annexed to the Crown of England, we may collect from the like source, many more hints respecting this subject. About the year 1370, Iolo Goch composed a poem, in which a ship is minutely described; and Robin Ddû in 1450, wrote a similar piece, by which we find, that returning from his pilgrimage to Rome, to Pope Nicolas V he took his passage in a ship, with a cargo of wine, bound to Mona, his native country. Rhŷs Nanmor, a contemporary, describes a ship going from Milford, having pilgrims to St. John of Compostella; on board of which was a cargo of wine, destined for Calais, and "this vessel had three coverings", by which most probably decks are meant. Although destitute of navigable rivers, the form of this Island, being irregular, is so happily indented as to possess numerous harbours, which from the remotest antiquity have been highly beneficial to the inhabitants.

The harbour of Beaumaris (the "Gwygyr" of the Triads) lies before the town, and has seven fathoms water, even at the ebb; here is a good anchorage in the bay, where vessels often find security in hard gales. This port had in former times considerable trade, but with the rise of Liverpool,[19] Beaumaris has declined. Caernarvon, Conway and Pwllheli are considered, in the Custom-house, creeks to Beaumaris. Two steam packets are constantly plying between Beaumaris and Liverpool. We will draw a veil over the disastrous events connected with the sufferings of those who perished in that ill-fated vessel, the Rothsay Castle, on the 17th of August, 1831, it being the subject of a Prize Poem; neither do I wish to revive the wounded feelings of sorrowing relatives, by noticing, or alluding to former shipwrecks, which have occurred on this coast, as detailed by Cathrall, in p.24.

The King's revenues are under the management of Mr. Hughes and Mr. Price; the latter is also collector of the salt duties, &c. added to these are a surveyor and six boatmen. The custom-house is situated near the water side and rented by Government of Mr. Sparrow.

The regular daily communication betwixt the Menai Straits and Liverpool, commences in May and continues till October or November; and during the winter months the communication is weekly.

To the north-west of Beaumaris, distant about five miles, is Traeth Côch, or Red Wharf, a good tide harbour in which large sloops lie safe during the greatest storms. It is much frequented by small shipping, on account of the limestone being of a superior quality in this neighbourhood; and which they carry to different parts of the united kingdom.—Many thousand tons are annually exported. The sand in parts of this bay is found to be so mixed with shells, that it is esteemed the best manure in the Island. The western horn of the bay, called Castell Mawr, is composed of lime-stone, and beyond this place, on the shore, are vast blocks of black marble impregnated with shells, coralloids and fugitæ. In

---

18 Cæsar in his account of a seafight, describes the ships of the Gauls as being built of oak, so strong that the iron prows of those he had to oppose to them made no impression; and so lofty as not to be assailed in the ordinary mode of fighting, but under great disadvantage.

19 Camden remarks on Liverpool (p. 790) "as a place convenient for shipping, but not so eminent for its being ancient, as for its neatness, &c." for the name does not occur in old writers. Notwithstanding what he says, we find by our ancient MSS that Liverpool harbour was a place of some note so early as 1278; for Prince Llewelyn's Ninth Item of Grief is concerning his "righte of shipwrecks" on his own coast. "The Justice of Chester, contrarie to all custome, tooke fiftie pounds of honey, and manye horses; imprisoning the prince's men, &c. and this he tooke of the prince's owne proper goods, and further tooke booties of bagiers, whyche came to Lyrpool with merchandize; and never redelivered the same untill he had taken so much mony for the same, as itt plesed hym".—*Welsh Chronicles.*

p.8 is an account given by Lewys Morris, of one of these blocks being detached and thrown up in this bay. On the east side of Traeth Gôch, and about three miles from Plâs Gwyn, near the shore, are two round mounds on each side of a deep gully, leading towards Llanddona church. These seemed to have been the works of the Danes, cast up to protect their vessels in their plundering excursions. Between this harbour and Amlwch is Dulas Bay; it runs about a mile and a half deep into the country, and is often visited by small vessels which come to take their freight of corn and butter, the staple commodities of these parts. Off the mouth of this bay, is Ynys Gadarn, a small Island. Proceeding round St. Elian's point, about two miles, in the north-west direction, is Amlwch harbour, a small cove, formed as it were, by an excavation of a large rock; the extension of which, as far as navigable, is computed to be forty perches, by Mr. Lewys Morris, who describes it as a small creek, and no more than a cove between two steep rocks, where a vessel hath hardly room to wind, even at high water: it is here a common event, he adds, "to see men fishing, while they stand on the brim of the cavation". Since then, the copper company, at their own expence, have considerably improved this natural creek, for the convenience of their shipping; and though the breadth is only sufficient for two vessels to ride a-breast, the length and depth are such as to receive thirty sloops and brigs, of from fifty to two hundred tons burden, off this harbour. The Liverpool pilot boats usually ply, to be in readiness to render assistance to such vessels as are unacquainted with the coast and the Mersey. Cemlyn is a small harbour, situated to the west of Amlwch, about six miles; frequented only by small vessels, sloops, &c. not having sufficient depth for large shipping. There is safe anchorage here, but it requires some fore-knowledge and caution to enter.

Aberffraw, was anciently a very excellent port, and by the erection of a pier, thirty or forty yards in length, would become so again. Malltraeth, distant from it about four miles, is more properly a creek than a harbour, and situated between Aberffraw and the Menai, at the mouth of the river Cevni. At this place the sea has been excluded since 1812, by an embankment, three quarters of a mile in length, and twenty-one feet high. The river Cevni is also enclosed by banks, and the water of the sea admitted into its channel, intended to be navigable. This work was first attempted in 1788, but after a large expenditure, the sea broke in and the works lay neglected till 1811-12, when they were resumed and completed at a further expence of upwards of £40,000. The land gained from the sea, and now producing food for men and cattle, is about one thousand acres; the whole inclosure and drainage extends to three thousand acres. On the side of Malltraeth marsh, are two collieries, in which excellent coal and culm are raised for the supply of the neighbourhood; but it is the opinion of men of experience, that these valuable products, are not to be found in such quantities, as to be spared for exportation. About the centre of Malltraeth marsh, it is not uncommon to find under six yards of sand, a perfect shore,—a certain indication of the sea having once come up so far.

Holyhead (at all times a noted and safe harbour) is guarded at its entrance from the winds by Ynys Gybi. The use of this port to "the Romans in their passage, from various places to the ports of Lancashire and Cheshire, is very evident. They could not find a better place to run into, in case of hard weather, than this, as it projected farthest into the vergivian sea; so that they could make it with less danger of being embayed than in any other place." Mr. Lewys Morris, in 1748, observes of Holyhead:

"this is a well sheltered dry harbour, with soft ground to lie on, except in north-west winds, which reader it dangerous for large shipping to lie here. If a pier[20] was run out to the south-east from the salt house, within which large vessels might lie afloat, the north sound and the sound of Pary's Island walled up, it would prevent the swell in the harbour; all this might be done at the expence of about £8,000, it would then be a safe harbour.[21] A friend of the author remarks in his letter, "The very spot pointed out by Lewys Morris, is the one which Mr. John Rennie selected for this great national work,[22] the first stone of which was laid in August, 1810, including a graving dock, that cost £12,000; the whole expence to Government was £142,000; an immense sum, when compared with the estimate made by Lewys Morris."

Corn is shipped at Gorad, about four miles from Holyhead. A description of a storm on this coast, is given by a French ecclesiastic, in the sixteenth century, "so furious and so contrary", he says, "that it split all our sails and obliged us to put out all our anchors, one of which broke; this, together with the horrid spectacle of surrounding rocks, which seemed to threaten our destruction, threw us into great terror; the sea seeming opening to swallow us up, without any resource. This lasted all night, but the dawn of day brought us a stark calm, attended with rain, which, for as we could not, for want of depth of water, pass the strait that lies between the land and the Isle of Mona, we turned round-about, to go to the village of Holyed, distance from Chester more than sixty miles, to embark the merchandize and passengers, who come to this place as a rendezvous from England to go to Dublin, the capital town of Ireland." This is the place at which the packets are stationed for conveyance of the English mails to Dublin. The establishment consists of six; i.e. Escape, lately commanded by the brave and gallant officer, Captain J.M. Skinner[23], who was unfortunately drowned, by falling overboard in a tempestuous gale, on his return from Dublin, within two miles of Holyhead. To him succeeded Captain Grey. Wizard, Captain J. A. Stevens,—Dragon, Captain J. Duncan,—Harlequin, Captain G. Davies,—Aladdin, Captain Waddle, and Cinderella, Captain E. Owen. Two of these sail daily from Holyhead and two from Dublin; i.e. one from Holyhead, at twelve at night, on the arrival of the London mail; the other at half-past seven in the morning, on the arrival of the Chester mail; one from Dublin at 9 A.M. the other at 4 P.M. The average length of passage across is six hours. The packet agent is Mr. Goddard.

---

20 In Cathrall, p.41, is a detailed account of Holyhead pier,—its first projectors, &c. &c.

21 Lewys Morris adds, "upon enquiry at the Custom-house for the reason of no returns being made from the harbours of Conway, Caernarvon, and Pwllheli, the answer was that Conway, Caernarvon, and Pwllheli were creeks to Beaumaris, and Holyhead a creek to Chester."

22 See Life of Lewys Morris at the end of this Essay.

23 Captain Skinner ably filled the station for which he was so eminently adapted, for a long series of years. This lamented individual was gifted with an heroic spirit, united to an honourable and liberal mind; the urbanity of his manners, so universally felt and acknowledged by the passengers confided to his care; the uniform and marked attention displayed by him for their comfort and accommodation, deservedly gained him the regard and esteem of those whom he had so often conducted in safety over the deep waters. This worthy man, like an expert pilot, steered his course through life to promote the happiness of his fellow men, and fellow passengers, and to render its passage smooth through the boisterous and tempestuous ocean.

It is not therefore to be wondered at, that a liberal and splendid subscription has been entered into, as a tribute to his memory; to record the worth and excellence of one who by his own life and actions, has erected a Monument "Ære perennius".

Robin Ddû,[24] an eminent bard, who flourished from 1340 to 1370, foretold in a prophetic englyn, the rapidity of travelling by means of steam power, being made subservient to the same purpose:

" Codais, ymolchais y'Môn;
" Boreu-bryd Y'nghaerlleon;
" Ciniawes yn y Werddon,
" Pryd-nawn—wrth dân mawn y'Môn."

There is in this Island, a noble institution, supported by subscription, in connection with the Royal National British one, for the preservation of life from shipwreck. They have four life-boats, stationed at Holyhead, Rhoscolyn, Cemlyn and Penmon, with captain Manby's apparatus and various other stores suited to the purpose. They give rewards to those who risk their lives in saving others; furnish support to shipwrecked persons who are cast upon shore; and give them the means of reaching their destination. The Rev. James Williams is treasurer and Sir James Sparrow is secretary.

On the straits of the Menai are established, within the distance of fifteen miles, six ferries,—Abermenai is the most southern;—three miles to the north of this and opposite Caernarvon is Tal y Voel, immortalized by Gwalchmai, the son of Meilir; in his Ode to Owen Gwynedd, after the battle called "Gwaith Tal y Voel" in 1158, when

" The vessels of the torrents bore
" Three legions from the hostile shore, &c &c
" — — — 'Gainst Mona's gallant lord. " [25]

I have taken the liberty of transferring the whole of this poem, with a translation:—[26]

ARDDWYREAF hael o hil Rodri,	I CELEBRATE the generous chieftain of the race of Rodri,
Ardwyad gorwlad gwerlin teithi,	Who is curber of the border-country, first in gallant deeds:
Teithiawg Prydain,	The paragon of Britain,
Twyth afyrdwyth Owain,	Buoyant is the wrathful energy of Owain,
Teyrnain ni grain,	The princely one who will not quail,
Ni grawn rei	Who will not hoard the pelf.
Tair lleng y daethant, liant lestri,	Three legions came in vessels on the flood,
Tair praff prif llynges, wy bres brofi;	Three ample first of fleets, him fiercely to assail:
Un o Iwerddon,	One from green Erin came;
Arall arfogion	Another full of armed ones
Or llychlynigion,	Of the Lochlinian revers,
Llwrw hirion lli.	The long burdens of the deep.

---

24 It is said that there is a prophecy of the same person, that an Irishman riding on a white horse should break his neck, at a spot near Ogwen Lake. The leading of the great Irish Road in the present century, by that very spot, seems to prove that Robin Ddû if not a prophet, was at least an able engineer.—The accident of the white horse remains to be fulfilled.

25 Original "Draig Môn": Dragon of Mona.

26 From the Myvyrian Archiaology, vol.1, p.197,—This is a version line for line.

A'r drydedd dros for o Norddmandi,
A'r drafferth anferth anfad iddi.
A draig Môn, môr drud ei eissiludd yn aer,
　　Y bu terfysg taer i haer holi,
A ragddaw rhewys dwys dyfysgi,
A rhewin, a thrin, a thranc cymri
　　　Ar gad gad greudde,
　　　Ar gryd gryd graendde,
　　　Ac am dal Moelfre
　　　　Mil fanieri !

Ar ladd ladd llachar,
　　ar bar beri,
Ar ffwyr ffwyr ffyrsgawd,
　　ar fawd foddi
A Menai heb drai o drallanw gwaedryar,
　A lliw gwyar gwyr yn heli;
A llurygawr glas a gloes trychni;
A thrychion yn dudd rhag rheiddrudd ri.
O ddygyfor Lloegr, a dygyfrang â hi;
Ac eu dygyfwrw yn astrusi,
Y dygyfod clod cleddyf difri;
　Yn saith ugain iaith wy faith foli!

And over sea from Normandy the third,
Fraught with untoward bustle, be to it bad luck!
Before the dragon chief of Môn, so bold his clan in war,
　　Arose dire tumult from insulting claims;
And before him wild confusion ran,
And ruin and toil, and of pre-eminence an end:
　　　With conflict after conflict, assuaged with blood;
　　　With shriek after shriek of dying anguish;
　　　And about the front of Moelvre
　　　　A thousand banners waving.

Slaughter after slaughter,
　　gleaming with the clash of spear on spear,
And drive on, drive, in pain extreme,
　　in drowning so to drown,
And Menai without ebbing from a flood of rippling blood!
　The brine discoloured by the gore of men;
And those in armour clad did writhe with pain,
And heaps of wounded lay before the crimson-lanced chief,
From stemming thus the Lloegrian hosts in war,
And overwhelming them with ruin;
Yes, thus the glory of a trusty sword,
　In seven score tongues to distant times will be proclaimed.

Here it may not be amiss to observe, that in no language does there exist nobler or finer specimens of Elegies and Odes than in the Cambro British, "which is" (to use the words of Mr. Cotton, an eminent divine and a member of the Bangor cathedral) "the language of scripture and of poetry". And this was the opinion of Dr. Percy, the learned bishop of Dromore, who writes to the Rev. E. Evans, in 1763, informing him that he had been collecting specimens of english poetry, adding, "I am ashamed to shew you what wretched stuff our rhimers produced, at the same time that your bards were celebrating the praise of Llewelyn, with a spirit scarce inferior to Pindar, &c. nor do I know that any of the nations of the continent (unless perchance Italy, which now about began to be honoured by Dante) were able at that time to write better than the English; the French I am well assured were not." This language, which Bishop Percy eulogizies "for its infinite superiority, harmonious effect in poetry, &c." appears to be deteriorating towards the latter end of the reign of Elizabeth. In Mr. Lloyd's Glossary of ancient British words, he records an address in Welsh, from Thomas Price to his countrymen, admonishing them to "cultivate the British language, history and poetry, &c.—earnestly wishes that more Eisteddvodau might be held, &c." This gentleman was a son of Sir Robert Price, chaplain to cardinal Wolsey and brother to Dr. Ellis Prys of Plas Iolin; he was a captain in the low countries, and fitted out a ship of war, at his own expence, to cruise against the Spaniards. He was an excellent poet, and says in his book, that he and captain

W. Middelton and captain Thomas Koet, first smoked tobacco in London. The Londoners flocking from all parts to look at them. They had no pipes, but smoked, or as he terms it "drank the leaves twisted together into pettwns", I suppose like the Indian cigars. Pipes, he says were afterwards invented by one Twytsburn. This tobacco, he and his companions took in a ship, which they found between the Canary Islands and Africa. Captain Thomas Price owns in another place, that he heard that Sir Francis Drake and Sir Walter Raleigh had brought tobacco into England before, but asserts that it never was smoked publicly before his time.—"*J. Ll.*"

After this, he enumerates the wonders he had seen in Wales. First, Pwll Ceris in the river Menai;—second, the Monocular Fish in a lake in Eryri. He asserts that he saw some of the fish which were very ugly, but he never saw the lake, &c. His ninth wonder happened on the 2nd of June, 1619. As he was returning from Spyttû, the weather being remarkably hot, there fell such a terrible shower of what he calls "hail and snow" that he had much ado to crawl to a house, to save his life; his horse and that of his servant were both killed. Their lives were saved by their cloaks, breaking in some measure, the violence of the strokes; and if a house had not been at hand, they must have perished, &c.—"*J. Ll.*" Caerwys MSS vol.3. p.86. He had some of the stones which were found on the ground still in his possession;—he sent a box full to Chester.

Four miles further on from Tal y Voel, is Moel y Don, so fatal to King Edward's troops, recorded further on; and three miles beyond is Porthaethwy, now the site of the Menai bridge, the common ferry between Môn and Arvon, and through which the cattle used to be driven. "Actuated by one impulse, they rushed up a cliff on the Caernarvon shore, to cast one parting look on the Island they had been torn from." This ferry was valued in the 26th of Edward III (when the extent of Tindaethwy was taken) at £4 10*s*. per annum; forty-five shillings belonged to the Prince of North Wales and the other moiety to the heirs of Griffith ab Madoc Gloddaeth. "The whole of this ferry belongs to the Lord Prince, but on the festival of the Blessed Virgin, to the market of Beaumaris entirely. This ferry is commonly called Bangor ferry. The fifth is a foot ferry, from Garth, near Bangor, to Borthwen in Mona. The sixth, and the longest at high water, is between Aber and the town of Beaumaris, called Lavan.

They were all (except that at Garth) originally the property of the Princes of Aberffraw, or North Wales, and latterly of the Crown, till Henry VIII granted them in the thirty-third year of his reign to Richard Giffard, one of the gentlemen of his bed chamber, who set them to William Bulkeley of Beaumaris. Since then every one has been transferred to other hands, except Tal y Voel and Moel y Don, which are still the property of the Crown, and are granted out on lease.

" Av i dir Môn er dwvr Menai. "

So sang Robin Leiav, in 1476. Rhys Nanmor, another of our bardic prophets, in a peep he took into futurity, 1460, fancied he saw a timber bridge rising from the rocks of Cribinau:

" Ac yna coed crai ar Venai vydd. "

The idea of a bridge across the Menai, is nearly as old as our annals. Edward I crossed it on a bridge of boats; a fatal expedient, for, at the rising of the tide, his army was cut to pieces, in attempting to return. At length the prophetic prediction of our bards, and the wishes of ages has been accomplished,

> " Dwy vlynedd *ar ôl* avlonydd
> " Pont ar Venai a vydd. " [27]

I will not injure, by abridging so faithful and clear a description of Menai bridge, as that one given by Mr. Cathrall, in p.134 of his History of Caernarvonshire. As a just tribute to Mr. Telford, I cannot resist noticing that he employed native artists, who did justice to his discernment, in embodying his splendid conception. The first stone of this stupendous work was laid on the 10th of August, 1820; and the opening of the bridge took place on January 30, 1826. The expence was estimated at somewhat more than £127,000.

The population of a country is (to borrow Mr. Sadler's judicious, and no less just, sentiments) in general as good a comparative criterion of its flourishing or declining state, as can, perhaps be obtained. By an account given on the 13th of August, 1565, there were 2,010 families in Mona,—allowing five to a family; the whole number of inhabitants in that period was 10,509. In 1794 they were computed to be 12,000. In 1776 the number of houses in Mona was about 3,956,—allowing five persons to each; the number of inhabitants would be 19,780, which wants only 340 of doubling the number of inhabitants in the intervening spaces.[28] By the return made to Government under the Population Act of 1811, it appears the Island contained 6,880 houses,—33,806 inhabitants,—18,631 females, and 15,775 males, of whom 2,614 were stated to be employed in trade and manufactures,[29]— 9,766 in the labours of agriculture; since that time, the increase has been still more rapid. The population amounting in 1821 to 45,063 persons;—males 21,784,—females 23,279;—men employed in trade, were 1,936,—in agriculture 1,702,—houses 8,737; and when the census was made last year, the Monenses numbered 48,325, including male and females. They are a hardy and a generous race, strong and active, healthy and long-lived, eighty and ninety being a period at which they frequently arrive. A bard

---

27 Robin Ddû.

28 Pennant's History, p.280.

29 With respect to manufactures, there are none of any considerable importance; the few linen and woollen cloths made in the Island, are for home use, furnishing instances rather of private industry, than sources of public profit. In 1623, Syr John Wynn of Gwydir attempted to set up a sort of manufactury, and writes to Humphrey Jones, then "beinge prime officer at Beaumaris", telling him "there was a letter shewn me, within this fortnight, written unto you, by the servant of one Roper, of Roper's Rest, in Ireland, beinge one of the Privy Council. The contents was, that his master would gladly set three hundred people here a work to spin wool, and desired your answer, to know whether it might be done: I say it may be done, and a more fittinge tyme there cannot be, then att this tyme of necessity, for if the tymes did amend, they will run out of their own country. It will require a great some of money to make them looms and other implements, fitt for the occupation; and also to make mylls, and tenters, whereof although we have some, wee have not sufficient. Wool is very cheap, and because it is so charitable a deed, and for the good of the country, I offer my furtherance, with all my heart, and the service of my people; it is fitt the gentlemen should send a sufficiente man, with full instructions concerning his intended purpose. Let me intreat you to send an answer as soon as possible. The letter sent to you, was of a date longe since. I mervail you kepte it in your hands so long &c. I praye you do your endever to sell my lead ore, that is att Beaumaris; methinks these foreigners have received soe much mony of the country, ffor the corn they brought in. Should be bound to leave some part thereof for our country commodities. That all the mony of the land be nott carried away, and this should be done by your beinge prime officer in your towne. I sowlde alwayes, for three pounds a tonne, allowinge the long hundred, but to take mony nowe I would sell it for somethinge lesst."

To Humphrey Jones, Att Beaumaris.   J. WYNN. Gwydir, August 2, 1623.

of the thirteenth century, celebrates their hospitality in this couplet,

> " Gorddu yw brig y Werddon,
> " Gan vwg ceginau o Vôn. "

> " Mona's fat kitchen smoke for many a mile,
> " Curls o'er the deep to tinge the Emerald Isle. "

to which the translator (the Warden of Ruthin) added

> " Indignant Erin spurns the stranger soot,
> " And sends it back in clouds of Lundyfoot. "

The winters in this Island are not so severe as in other parts of Wales; the air is keen and salubrious, but owing to the land being surrounded by the ocean "it must needs partake of the sea saltes" in a great degree. This acrimonious quality makes the western parts of it very prejudicial to the growth of timber, "At a small distance from Moel y Don, I entered (observes Mr. Pennant, p.236) into the fine woods of Sir Nicolas Bailey, skirting the Menai for a considerable way. Plasnewydd is protected on three sides by venerable oak and ash. The wooded part of the Island is on this side: it commences at Llanidan, &c. and except in this part, the Island is entirely divested of trees, and the climate so averse to growth, that in most parts, it is with great difficulty the gentry can raise plantations." Most of the trees in the south-western side of the Island, appear in a stunted state. This is rather singular that so great a change should take place in the climate of Mona, so noted by Tacitus for its dark groves, and long after their destruction, by Suetonius and Agricola. Sir John Pryse makes the following comment in his description of Wales. "As for what Polydore saith of the great woods, it is nothing, for both the Romans and after when the Christians did fall and root them out, for the idolatry and absurd religion, which was used there, the King of Man sent for timber to Môn (read the Life of Hugh, Earl of Chester) which also is evident by the great beeches and other trees, found in the earth at these days." When avenging the death of Roger Puleston, we find in the History of the Princes, an account of Edward I cutting his roads through the woods of Mona. This must have been in 1294. Perhaps cutting down woods might have been encouraged, with a view of clearing the land for agricultural purposes, when it became essential to make this Island the granary of Wales.

The exterminating system levelled against druidical superstition began very early in the first century of the christian era. For the "three branches of the duty of man, were devotion towards God, benevolence to his fellow-creature and the improvement of science": and the three primary purposes of a bard, "to do the will of God, to benefit man, to cultivate amiability". These principles, upon which the Druid's faith was founded, did not militate against christianity. On the contrary, they were highly serviceable to facilitate the adoption of the new doctrine, because it was one of the leading maxims of the bards to examine every thing without prejudice,—to draw a conclusion from the evidence, and to abide by the result only, as further investigation would support it, or otherwise. In confirmation of this remark, we have a notable instance of the influence of that Spirit of investigation, recorded by the historians, of the first planting of christianity in Great Britain, who testify that the Britons embraced it generally and with more openness than any other people. In treating upon the History of the Aborigines of Mona, I will take leave to dilate more fully upon the subject.

> "The harp is hush'd on Mona's shore,
> " And mute the voice of mystic lore,
> " And the deep woods lie low;
> "Who shall recall the druid seers,
> "They that could lift the veil of years,
>   " ———and trace with gifted eyes,
> "Their burning pathway through the skies. "
>
> *Mrs. Hemans.*

Anglesey is (as Mr. Rowlands observes) "that celebrated Mona", but I cannot agree with him in calling it the "principal seat of the Druids". I grieve to differ from so learned a man, who, as he himself says, was scarcely ever out of the Island; for there are more druidical remains in the single parish of Llanwyndec, joining Abergwaen in Pembrokeshire, than in all this Island. He infers from the name, that a farm called "Tre'r Beirdd" was the residence of the bards and Druids; whereas it was in fact the land held by virtue of his office, by the bard of the Prince's household, from time to time, under the Prince of Wales,—residing at Aberffraw, he being one of the twenty-four "Swyddogion y Llŷs".

The limits of an Essay will only allow me to touch upon what is most obvious and remarkable in the History of this extraordinary race of men, acknowledged by their contemporaries the Romans, to have been well versed in geometry, astronomy and natural history. Mr. Lloyd of Caerwys, quoting Diodorus Siculus, lib. 3; cap. 11, speaking of the Druids[30] in these words:—"Et Diodorus, &c. ex: Hecatæo refert eos (i.e. Druidas) habuisse modum Lunam exhibendi oculis humanis propiorem montibus et Rupibus horidam et diffissam", from whence he infers that Galileo was not the first inventor of telescopes, &c. They were also supreme judges in all causes, ecclesiastic and civil; from whose determination there lay no appeal, and whoever refused to comply with their edicts was excommunicated. Caesar, in his description of the customs of Gaul, gives the following account of the Druids. "They are the ministers and teachers of religion; to them the youth, in great numbers, apply for instruction, who shew them great respect; they decide in all controversies, public and private: if a crime be committed, if a person be slain, if succession to property, or the boundaries of land be in question, they determine the case and adjudge the rewards and punishments. If any one, whether in a private or public station refuses to abide by their award, they interdict him from the sacrifices, which is the greatest punishment. No one will admit them into society, or speak to them, for fear of contamination. One Druid who has supreme authority, presides over all the rest, and on his death, if there be one of pre-eminent estimation, he succeeds. At a certain season of the year, they hold an assembly in a consecrated place, esteemed the central place of Gaul: hither all who have any controversies repair from every part, and submit to their judgement and decrees. The Druids are not accustomed to engage in warfare, nor do they pay tribute, but are excused from military service and in every respect are privileged persons.

---

30 "Druid, from Derw—Hyd—the verb hudo.—*J Ll.*" "Come to the oaken Grove".

Many become voluntarily attached to them and others are sent by their parents and relations. The students commit to memory a great number of verses, and some of them continue their study for twenty years, for they do not think it allowable to commit their institutes to writing. Though in all other affairs, whether public or private, they make use of Greek characters: this rule, I presume, they have laid down for two reasons, i.e. because they wish to prevent a disclosure of their instructions to the public, and because they who learn, when they have recourse to writings, neglect the exercise of the memory. Their leading principle is, that souls do not perish, but pass after death to other bodies; a principle, which in their opinion is the greatest incentive to virtue and contempt of death. They also lecture on the stars and their motion; the magnitude of the earth and its divisions; on natural history; and on the power and government of God, and instruct the youth in these subjects. All the Gauls say that they are descended from Dis,[31] and that is the tradition of the Druids. For this reason, they reckon time by nights[32], and observe the times of their birth, and the beginning of years, so as that the day is reckoned from the eve. Caesar de Bello Gall. lib.6. The bards, who were poets, and the vates, eubates, or ovyddion, offered the sacrifices, and made natural history their study. The bards, who were also recorders of events, composed and sang devotional songs, while the ovates made the offering; and it became their peculiar province to depict the great and the virtuous,—to embellish and recommend the precepts of religion and virtue,—to transmit to posterity excellent and sublime actions and sayings,—to celebrate the works of the Deity,—his beneficence,—his wisdom,—to record the memorials of the past and the predictions of the future. In the works which they have respectively left for the instruction of mankind, in the arbitration of our taste,—in the improvement of our philosophy,—in the elevation of our moral ideas, they stand pre-eminently forward. Their common fame will survive the whisperings of faction and the jealousies of criticism, and brighten, rather than sink with the weight of accumulated years. Lucan says, that the Druids resided in the recesses of thick groves; and Pliny, that the derw (oak), prenawyr (mistletoe), were esteemed the most sacred by them. The Druids were well acquainted with medical botany. They are said by Mr. Lloyd, in his notes upon Mon. Antiq. to have made use of many herbs, in their rites. Of these, the chief were misletoe, i.e. "uchel-wydd", by pre-eminence; samolus symy'e (cowslip), vervain (y câs gan guthraul), selago (hedge hyssop), &c. He adds they might be no way disinclined to represent those herbs as sacred, which had powerful effect in medicine. Mr. Row-

---

31 The meaning of this Tradition is, that the Gauls came from the Black Sea, and were descendants of the ancient Cimmerians. Homer places the regions of Dis, or Pluto, in the country of the Cimmerians. Mr. Edward Lhwyd writes in 1703, to inform Mr. John Lloyd of Ruthyn, that "one Abbe Pezron, an Armorique Breton, has lately published "Antiq. de la Nation et de la Langue Gaulais" wherein he has definitely outdone all our countrymen, as to national zeal. He proves they were and *are* the only nation in the world, that have the honour to have preserved the language of Jupiter and Saturn, whom he shews to have been Princes of the Titans, the progenitors of the Gauls, and to have had an empire from the Euphrates to Cape Finisterre, in the time of Abraham. He makes the curates, who had the care of Jupiter in Crete, &c. to have been Druids, and to have first introduced the olympic games amongst the Lacedemonians; where he observes, "The Britons are still the most noted for the exercise of running, wrestling, &c." The Romans, he says, borrowed the names of their weekdays from the old Umbri of Italy, a Gaulish nation; the true name of Jupiter, he tells us was Iou, to which the Romans added Piter, i.e. Peter. He next adds three large catalogues of words.—First, of those the Aeolians and other Greeks derived from the Titans.—Secondly, of those the Romans borrowed from the Cimbri.—Thirdly, of those the Germans, &c., borrowed from the Greek colonies.—*Edward Lhwyd.*

32 Wythnos, week—Pymthegnos, fortnight.

lands says, "that the chief Druid, clad in white, ascended the oak, and with a consecrated knife, gathered the mistletoe, on the 6th of March". Most probably it was on the day of the vernal equinox. The species which grows on the oak, is much larger and of a deeper green, than the common uchelwydd we find on apple-trees, &c. The sprigs are so well adapted to the formation of the bardic alphabet (first printed by the ingenious and learned Dr. O. Pugh)[33] that this may be one cause of the esteem in which it was held: there is another, and perhaps a more important reason; the blossom falls off within a few days of the summer solstice, and the berry within a few days of the winter solstice, in the common plant; and perhaps those on the oak misletoe, may drop off nearer to those times. As druidism was so soon repressed, though not for some ages wholly extirpated in Gaul, and no doubt persecuted in the like manner as far as the Roman power extended in Britain, the classic writers could have little, if any thing more to communicate, than what could be casually observed. To their enemies, the Druids would not, under such circumstances, be forward to give information, and from others it could not be obtained. We cannot wonder that their punishment of criminals by fire, should have excited the horror of the Romans; but they had little reason to reproach the Gauls, for a more savage and unprincipled nation than they were themselves, never polluted the earth; what refinement of science they had, was borrowed from that truly refined and civilized race, the Greeks, and they used it, as savages always do, as means of gratifying vanity, and extending the mischievous effects of artifice and circumvention. The mode of criminal execution used by the Druids, was however, common to many nations of antiquity; to the Canaanites, Greeks, Scythians, &c. and even at this day, the auto da fé of the papists, and the burning of the widow of a Brahmin, in the East Indies, are in fact, human sacrifices. This manner of putting enemies and criminals to death, is alluded to in part of the Gododin, as a custom of the Saxons, and in another ancient poem as that of the Britons,

"Gwelais y dull o bentir Adoen,
"Aberth am goelcerth y dgsgynnin."

Gorchan Cyncvelyn

"I beheld from the high land of Done,
"The spectacle of the sacrifice to be consumed by fire."

"Mal coelcerth fy ngwerth a wnaethant,
"O aur pûr, a dûr, ac ariant."

"When I was devoted to the (sacrificial) flames,
"They ransom'd me with pure gold, steel, and silver."

The latter poem is attributed to Taliesin, but is probably of a much greater antiquity; though he may be the recorder of this and several others, certainly druidical, which are supposed to have been composed by him. The principal doctrines of the Druids, and their mode of instruction, have already

---

33 The Dictionary (of which another edition is just come out of the press) compiled from the laws, history, poetry, and manners of the Ancient Britons, and their descendants,—a Biographical Dictionary of remarkable persons in the early History of Briton,—and other works in the language of his country, will be lasting proofs of the learning, perseverance and ability of Dr. Owen Pugh.

been given from Caesar; but as he has not mentioned any thing of the peculiar forms of the verses in which their morality, &c. was taught, a few examples of them, may be acceptable. These druidical stanzas were triplets, and denominated "englynion milwr", or "warrior songs". The first line was merely a kind of key. The second part introduces some circumstance in natural history, or common life; and the third is a moral sentence, in the proverbial style. Thus natural history and morality were blended together, and the disciple taught to draw moral instruction from familiar objects, as for instance,

" Eiry mynydd, gwancus iâr,
" Gochwyban gwynt ar dalar,
" Yn yr ing—gorau iw'r câr. "

" Snow of the mountain, the bird is ravenous for food,
" The wind whistles on the head-land,
" In distress a relation is the most valuable. "

" Galangauaf garw hin,—anhebig i cynhevin,
" Namyn Dnw nid oes dewin. "

" The first day of winter,—severe is the weather,
" Unlike the first summer,
" None but God can foresee what is to come. "

Thus (says Mr. Davies), "whatever page of nature was presented to their view, their teachers, the Druids, had contrived to make it a page of wisdom". Those wise men were acquainted with the cycle of nineteen years, when the moon returned to the same order. This cycle is called the "metonic", from Meton, an Athenian. Some of the Druid circles consist of nineteen pillars, in commemoration of it. "The Druids are supposed, and not without reason", observes Mr. Lloyd, "to have been acquainted with the circulation of the blood". We learn from Caesar, that they had times and places, sacred, and separated unto holy uses; and they assembled at such places as Bryn y Cwyn, near Tre'r Dryw Môn, Bryn Cwyn Caerwys, Dymeirchion, Mold, &c. to hear causes and to determine all disputes, and controversies; and from this tribunal[34] there was no appeal. But the supreme seat of druidism, without a question, was Wiltshire. There are more remains of the Druids on the plains and downs of that country, than are to be found in all England, Wales, Scotland and Ireland. Abury was the most stupendous druidical work in the world, and is still so; nothwithstanding the devastations committed by the present race of barbarians. Twelve large stones, of from sixty to one hundred tons weight, were blasted about the year 1797. Stonehenge[35] is near, but that sinks to nothing, compared with Abury. The circle of the latter, is fourteen hundred feet diameter, being an area of twenty-two acres; having an avenue of

---

34 Mr. Lloyd, in his Description of Trelawnydd, alias Newmarket, remarks that a Cromlech stands near Gop-Golenni, and surrounding it are places bearing the following names:—Braech y Dadleu, Pwll y Crogwyn, Coed Caerorsedd, Pant Erwyn y Gwrachod.—*J Ll.*

35 "The inscription in lead, found at Stonehenge, which Mr. Lilye the schoolmaster and Syr Thomas Elliot could not read, might be druidical. What author besides Edward Lhuyd mentions it? Inigo Jones said that he found a Thuribulum at Stonehenge, three feet deep.—*J Ll*". From Mr. Lloyd's *MSS. Notes on Stonehenge.*

a mile and half from the east, and a similar one from the west, lined with large stones: and Silbury Hill, is perhaps the largest artificial mound in the world, after the Egyptian pyramids, forming the meridional index to the circle. There is also a fosse round the circle, the outside slope of which, is forty-five feet deep; the earth out of this, forms a parapet on the outside, from which perhaps half a million of people might have a view over the circle. To this great temple, every ancient road in Britain led, nay in Europe and even Asia, concentrated in Abury. In this opinion, the author is fully borne out by the MSS notes of Mr. Lloyd and Dr. Owen Pugh, who asserted this as his notion, after investigating the place minutely, in company with Syr R. Hoare. One of the old bards alluding to Stonehenge or Abury, calls it "Mawr Côr Cyfoeth", i.e. the "Great Sanctuary of the Dominion"; and in the very clever representation of it given by Syr R. Hoare, in his Antiquities of Wiltshire, as he conjectures it originally appeared; I could not but be forcibly struck with the analogy, which the disposition of the parts bears to that of the stations of the court of law, in the time of Howell Dda, as represented in his code; and from this analogy, I imagine that the order in the great national council, bore a certain degree of resemblance to that of the law court. The great druidical temple at Carnac, in Brittany, and the Egyptian one of Labor, near Carnac, in Thebes, form with Abury such a Triad of magnificent colossal temples, as perhaps have never been equalled in the world. The one in Brittany has been most admirably described by Mon. de Caubon, in a letter to a learned friend of the author. "This immense work is situated near Carnac, and supposed by the inhabitants of the neighbourhood, who have no idea or tradition of druidism, to have been a Roman work, originally intended as a barrier against the influx of the sea. But though this may have been suggested by a superficial notice of the more perfect part as it now stands; it must appear from the extensive remains, that this could never have been the purpose for which it was erected. The most perfect part consists of pillars, about fifteen feet high, set in sixteen rows; so that the spaces between the rows, form alleys, of which that in the middle is the broadest, being about forty paces wide. These pillars are in form, somewhat like a nine-pin, being larger in the middle than at the ends. These rows of pillars appear tolerably perfect for nearly a mile from Carnac; and at about this distance from Carnac there is a flat altar. From the remains visible, the rows appear to have extended from sea to sea, across the tongue of land on which Quiberon stands, about four miles to the north of this town. Near the middle of this line some pairs of stones are standing, so placed, as if intended to mark entrances, or gateways; and near the east end of the line there is a large spheroid, once about forty feet long, but now lying in three pieces; and near is a flat stone, about thirty feet long, twenty-four broad, and two thick. I could not learn that there were any traces of stones in a circle. In digging near Carnac, there were found twenty-four celts, of highly-polished jasper, arranged in a circle; in the centre of which circle, was another celt, of the same form and materials; but this was larger than the rest, and was moreover, distinguished by being pierced through the middle. The hole, was in diameter, about half an inch. Tumuli are frequent in Brittany; and near Carnac, there is a mound, wholly artificial, and so high that it is made a station to observe vessels at sea.

Mr. Lloyd's third volume, 4to. contains four curious letters: the first gives an account of the druidical monuments in Scotland: the second relates to the bards, and method of Clera; with an account of the voluntary mourners at funerals, &c. The two last are upon the subject of druidical antiquities; wherein the writer shews a great deal of ingenuity in supporting Mr. Aubrey's opinion, that those circular stone monuments in Scotland and elsewhere, are of druidical origin, &c. I shall make no more extracts, than what are useful, and bearing upon the subject treated. Mr. Lloyd enumerates thirty Cromlechau in Môn, which I shall notice when describing the parishes, in which they are situated. He says, that "where there is a Cromlech, there is a Carnedd; and where there is a Carnedd, there are pillars and stone coffins; and the rest of their companions and attendants are not far off, i.e. pointing or directing pillars; stones of reverence, &c, which constantly and uniformly keep their stated distance from each other, as well as from the principal monument they belonged to; especially the low arched stone, which always presents itself within three or four cubits of a Cromlech. The inclination of the Cromlechau is supposed to form an angle of forty-five degrees with the horizon;—this angle is of great importance in optics, &c." The Cromlechau have this inclination to all points, except the south; the Druids never exercising any of their rights, at mid or full day, or in the night time, but in time of the new moon, &c. Cromlech derives its name from its inclined position, "Crymmu" from the Cromlech at Bachwen. Mr. Ll. infers that the Druids used divination by birds, &c. The smallest cavities on the altar, held their consecrated crumbs.

Carneddau were burying places. He reckons three sorts: princes and nobles were deposited in the large Carnedd;—persons of less note, in the lesser;—and the Arch-Druid in the Carnedd Hir. Stone coffins, skeletons, bones, partly burnt, urns, ashes, &c. are often found in them. The direction of the Druids burying, run north and south, from the "loose and conic structure of the Carneddau", he reasonably argues, that they could not be intended for immolations and burnt sacrifices, &c. How could the victim be dragged up, or where could the priests and their attendants stand? "Meini Hirion being near Carnedda", he supposes to be sepulchral; especially those found within two or three yards of each other. Queen Zenobia was interred between two such columns. "The single pillars might be stations for the priests to harangue from." He enumerates the low arched stone at three several distances:—the first within three yards of a Cromlech, oval or Carnedd; with one of their flat sides to the east and the other to the west: a station he thinks, intended for the priests to make their observations upon the fall of the victims, &c. Another at thirty yards distance, supposed to be assigned for the worshippers; the third at eighty yards distance, supposed to be a stone of Denudelion, or a barrier to keep off the profane and excommunicated. The cirques and oval, Mr. Lloyd conjectures were temples, in case the area could not contain the congregation; and if there was not room enough for the sacrifices and sacrificers; whilst the priest performed his office within, the congregation performed their devotions without.—"J. Lloyd".

Mr. Lloyd ends his clever notes upon druidical remains, &c. in these words. "The most remarkable Carnedd in Great Britain, is the monument of Bronwen, verch Llŷr (i.e. daughter of King Lear), in the Island of Mona; it being a little crooked cell not far from Alw; and to the west "Bedd Petrual a wnaed i Vronwen, verch Llŷr, ar lan Alw, ac yno claddwyd hi." She was the wife of Matholwch, king of part of Ireland, whose uncourteous treatment of this lady is the subject of one of the Mabinogion Tales. A farmer living on the bank of the Alw, having occasion for some stones, in 1813, accidentally discovered the urn containing the ashes of Bronwen:—

—(which is nearly of the above shape)— under a heap of stones, or Carnedd. It is now in the possession of one of the most ingenious of the bards of Mona, who resides in Chester. The tumulus raised over the illustrious deposit, was of considerable circumference, elegantly rounded, but low, about a dozen paces from the river Alaw; and is still called "Ynys Bronwen". The urn was preserved entire, with the exception of a small piece broken from the top. It is rude and simple in its construction, having no other ornament than little pricked dots, in height about fourteen inches. A few of the ashes and half calcined bones are religiously kept in the urn. The lady to whom the ancient tale ascribes them was Bronwen, i.e. "White bosom", daughter of Llŷr Llediaeth (Lear with the foreign or latin speech) and sister to Bran the Blessed (as he is styled in our Triads), the father of Caractacus. By the romance, we find that her adventures are connected with Ireland, where she was ill-treated by Matholwch, the then king of that country; in consequence of which she left it, and landing in Wales she looked back upon Ireland, which freshening the memory of the indignity she had met with there, broke her heart. To confirm the fact of the affront given to Bronwen, one of the Triads (those ancient British Chronicles by threes) records it as one of the "three fatal slaps by the hand of the Isle of Britain. The slap of Matholwch the Gwyddelean on Bronwen, the daughter of Llŷr,—the slap given by Gwenhwyvach to Gwenhwyvar, which occasioned the battle of Camlan,—and the slap given by Golyddan the bard to Cadwaladar the Blessed." The discovery of this urn was a most fortunate event, as it serves to give authenticity to our ancient British documents, the Mabinogion, even though they be introduced to minister to romance, as in the present instance, and fixes the probable date of the interment in question, within a few years;—a desideratum we despaired of being ever gratified with; and a circumstance beautifully alluded to in the close of Mr. Bowles's "Barrow Poem". The border round the top of Bronwen's urn, is similar in all, and appears to have been impressed with a tool, such as is used in making pastry. The difference in the clays of which they are composed, warrants a supposition, that the urns were made where they have been found; and probably they underwent no baking, further than the effect of sun and the fire wherein the bodies were consumed, as they are all imperfectly baked. Harlech Castle was anciently called "Twr Bronwen". The Carneddau, &c. fell into disuse, when the light of christianity dispelled the mist and darkness of ignorance, which shrouded the incantations and superstitious delusion of druidism:—Then the Roman[36] came:

36 Who included this Island in the province of "Britannia Secunda"; before which period it was called "Cambria".

" O'er the blue waters with his thousand oars;
"Through Mona's oaks he sent the wasting flame;
"The Druid shrines lay prostrate on our shores,
" He gave their ashes to the wind and sea:
" ———Ring out thou harp, he could not silence thee!" [37]

Roman ambition knew no bounds; the quickness, as well as extensiveness of glance, by which it perceived, and was enabled to execute with rapidity and precision, any plan of political aggrandizement, showed that it possessed an eye like its own eagle, whose outspread wings indicated unbounded love of conquest. We find Suetonius made an attempt to take this Island; and Tacitus, in his Life of Agricola says it was very populous, and a receptacle for thieves, criminals and deserters, &c. perhaps the city of refuge to our ancestors, from wrath or judgement; and the last asylum to which the distressed Britons fled for succour, from the victorious Romans, who after subduing the adjacent country, effected a landing in flat bottomed boats over the straits of the Menai; when they were arrested in their progress, by hearing of an insurrection under the conduct of Boadicea, Queen of the Iceni. It was but a momentary triumph; she being soon overpowered and taken, &c. We will pass over the savage and barbarous death[38] which this heroic and distinguished princess was doomed to suffer, by a cruel and unrelenting enemy: every generous and honourable sentiment seems to have been extinguished in a determination of conquering these brave but unfortunate people.

There is something peculiarly affecting and touching, in the manner in which Tacitus describes the conquest gained by Agricola, about fifteen years after this event,[39] over a race of "unarmed victims", voluntarily exposing themselves to the fury of the enemy;—running about as if distracted, with their hair dishevelled,—carrying torches in their hands and clad in mournful habits, &c. At a little distance from the army, stood the Druids, defending their sacred groves, and lifting up their hands to heaven, imploring the protection of their God, against these lawless invaders of their rights and Liberties. After an unequal though desperate struggle, the Druids and the remainder of the inhabitants fell a lamentable sacrifice to the most extreme outrages and fiercest cruelties ever practised, even by that nation. "As for the place of their landing, and of their routing this religious army, we have no exact certainty of it; but there, are probable grounds to conclude, that it was near Porthamel, between Pwll y Vuwch and Llanidan: for Tacitus says, that the horse swam it at the ford, which is just under Llanidan; and it seems that their foot landed from their flat bottom boats, near the said Pwll y Vuwch, where there is a place called "Pant yr Yscraphiaid" to this day. The Romans calling such boats, scaphoe, and we from them, "Yscraphiaid". Indeed the Tumulus in one of the fields near, about three bow shots, from the sea, seems to have been the place of that great sacrifice; whence they took up firebrands, in their hands, brandishing them like furies about the invading army, and where they involved the taken and slain Britons in the devouring flames of their own sacrifice. There are the ruins of two or three small British towns near

---

37 Mrs. Hemans's beautiful Lines "to the Harp".
38 On an unhewn upright stone, called "Carreg Bedd Buddig", used as a gate-post, within a mile of Caerwys, is a latin inscription, cut in rude letters to this effect:—HIC JACIT MULI ERBO .... OBIT. Multitudes of Tumuli are scattered over the neighbourhood, and one very near it.
39 A.D.59. *Tacitus Annals. 14. c.30.*

this place of battle; one near Bryn Siencin, called "Hendre"; another on the top of Bryn Gwydd Vryn, called "Cader Idris", and a third on the top of a hill, near Porthamel House, whose name is lost. These were in all likelihood then demolished; and it is probable, that on the top of Gwydryn Hill, the Romans built a fort: it being a place of great strength and conspicuous to the whole Island.—Rowlands's Mona Ant. p.98. The Druids who escaped the massacre, fled to the Orkneys, Norway; Ireland, &c.

> " To chaunt their Maker's praise,
> " And keep their language and their lays.
> " Mona's guardian powers are fled,
> " Her oaks have bowed their crested heads; "

and in return for all this outrage and devastation, the Romans erected here no public building, excepting two forts. The remains of one is not far from Rhosvair; and the other at no great distance, Segontium, being their principal station; yet coins, vases and domestic utensils have been found, sufficient to manifest it was once occupied by a colony[40] of that keen and ambitious people, then residing at Caernarvon[41]. On the decline of their government in Britain, early in the fifth century, we find that hordes of Irish encroached upon the Monenses and contrived to make a permanent settlement in this Island, as appears evident from hillocks or entrenchments of earth, to be seen in many places at this day, called by the natives "Cwttiau'r Gwyddelod", the most remarkable are in a wood, near Llygwy, once the property of the Lloyd's, but now by purchase it belongs to Lord Boston.

The period of time immediately after the Saxon Conquest is the darkest and most intricate of all the History of Britain. The Saxons could not then write and the Britons had not leisure. When their oppressors were converted to christianity, then monkery came into vogue; and it was the chief act of the clergy to keep the laity in darkness; so that the bards are the only persons that can be said to have left us any memorials of those days. The Saxon conquerors being the successors of the Romans in that part called England, were but then scarcely initiated in letters; their business was war and the maintaining of their conquests. We find nothing of the literary production of that nation, that we can attach any credit to, more ancient than Bede; though they had most of the libraries and colleges of the Britons in their possession.

From "Brut y Brenhinoed" we learn that about this time the land was divided into four parts, of which the chiefest was Môn (where the Prince's chief palace was at Aberffraw), which is an Island separated from the main land by an arm of the sea, called Menai; and had in itself three cantrevi, or hundreds, which were subdivided into six comottau,[42] enumerated in the following Englyn,

> " Menai a Malltraeth-wyr mwynion—Twrcelyn,
> "Tir caled Talybolion;
> " Llawen iw cwmmod llivon,
> "Tindaethwy nid oes mwy ym Môn "

40 Segontium, called by Nennius "Caer Cystenydd". Hugh, Earl of Chester, built a castle at "Heu Gaer Gwstenyn". Matthew of Westmynster says that the body of Constantius Chlorus was found here, A.D.1283, and interred in the Church of the new town, by the order of Edward I.—*J Ll. Caerwys MS.*

41 Mr. Pennant in p.71, 3rd vol. gives a description of two Roman bracelets, a bulla, and an amulet, all of pure gold, being dug up in 1775 or 1776, in the parish of Llanflewyn. p.301.

42 A Description of Cambria, by Syr John Price, Knight; and augmented by Humphrey Llwyd, temp. Elizabeth, p.v. has something of this account.

By the Hengwrt MS[43] I find that "from the most remote periods, Môn has been divided into seven districts, called 'cymmydau', or communities, being the usual subdivisions of the cantrev or hundred; and it is probable that the expression of 'saith aelwyd Môn', or the seven hearths of Anglesey, has reference to these divisions of the Island." But the extent taken in the 26th of Edward III makes only six comots, and Cemmaes, which is the seventh, is there called a manor. The natives being left to themselves by the Roman invaders, it was natural that they should resume their ancient form of government, under which they had lived previous to the arrival of the Romans,—Britain was once more divided into Petty sovereignties. About A.D.443, Caswallon made choice of Mona for his residence; he, representing the elder royal branch, consequently possessed pre-eminence in dignity;—the other Cambrian Princes paying homage and deference to him as their superior Lord. In the Triads of the Isle of Britain, he is mentioned as being one of the three "Banded Tribes". The tribe of Caswallon Llaw Hir, who put the fetters of their horses on their feet, by two and two, in fighting with Serigi Wyddel, in Môn, at a place called at this day "Cerrig y Gwyddyl", where he slew the Irish champion with his own hand; for which signal bravery, he had the privilege of wearing golden bands; and in the Chronicle of the Kings (Brut y Brenhinoedd), Caswallon is said to have reigned sovereign of Wales from 443 to 517, when he died, after a reign of 74 years. His son Maelgwyn succeeded; he was a great character and said in the the Black Book of Basingwerk Abbey[44] to have been sagacious, bold and rigorous; subduing many kings. He was the first sovereign after Arthur who gained possession of six countries, dependant upon Britain, i.e. Ireland, Iceland, Scotland, Orkney, Norway and Denmark. Maelgwyn kept his court at Diganwy.[45] Gwyddno, one of his distinguished courtiers, lived in the neighbourhood, and had a fine weir there, which to this day is called Gored Gwyddno, and belongs to Bodscallon. Elffin ab Gwydno was always at court, where he exhausted all his finances, so much, that he was constrained to become a petitioner to his father for the benefit of the weir for one night. He obtained his suit; but the only fish he found in the weir was Taliesin, the bard. When Maelgwyn was surrounded by all his courtiers, his twenty-four chief bards, heralds, &c. in the christmas holydays, they all strove who should flatter the king the most. They agreed that he was the handsomest, the wisest and the most powerful of monarchs; and that his queen surpassed all women in beauty and accomplishments;—in short that his troops were the bravest;—his horses and dogs the fleetest;—his bards the best and the most learned in the world, &c. Elffin very modestly said that no body should enter into comparison with a king, but a king, otherwise he would venture to affirm that his bard Taliesin was the chief of poets, &c. When Maelgwyn heard this, he ordered Elffin to be bound and thrown into prison, till the truth of these as-

43 Parthau Cymru.—"Llyma y modd i mesurwyd a rhanwyd cantrevydd a chymydau holl Gymru, yn amser Llewelyn ab Gryfydd, y Tywysawg diweddav o'r Cymru; tair talaeth a vu yn Nghymru, un yn Aberffraw yn Môn &c. Cantrefi Môn a'i Chymydau.—1. Cantrev Aberffraw,—Cwmmod Llivon,—Malltraeth; 2. Cantrev Cemmaes,—Talybolion a Twrcelyn; 3. Cantrev Rhosir.—Cwmmwd Tindaethwy a Menai.—Yn Llyvr Hengwrt.
44 "Llyvr Du Dinas Basing", written in that House, by Gyttyn Owain, a celebrated bard and genealogist, genealogist "who beinge of the time of Edward IV wrote (Powel, p.206) the beste and moste correcte copie of the actes of the Princes." It is in a good text hand; and contains Dares Phrygius.—The Chronicles of the Kings of Britain. The Chronicles of the Princes, better known as their History, by Caradoc of Llancarvan, which is continued down to his own time by Gyttyn Owain; the last entry being in 1433. The use of this valuable MS the author had by the favour of Mr. Thomas Taylor Griffith of Wrexham, in whose possession it is.
45 Diganwy, or Gannoc Castle, was an ancient fortress in the time of the Kings of Brytagne; for Maelgwyn lived there; and lieth buried at Priestholme.—Hanes Helig ap Glanawg. Caerwys MS.

sertions should appear. Taliesin resolved to set his friend at liberty, in order to which, he goes to Mael-gwyn's court, where he was not known, and by his superior skill he overcomes all the laureats of the palace, and does some other wonders, which restored Elffin to liberty and the favour of his prince. After this, Taliesin advises Elffin to make a wager with the king, that he had a horse fleeter than all his horses; upon which a course was marked upon Morva Rhianedd, and twenty-four of the fleetest horses in the stud were started, and every one beat by Elffin's horse. After the race was over, Taliesin took Elffin to a spot where there was dug up a cauldron full of gold; when the bard addressed his pa-tron and said, "Elffin, lo! here is your reward for taking me out of the weir; and for rearing me from that day to this". This spot is now a pool of water and called Pwll Paerie, "Pool of Cauldron."—"*J. Lloyd*".[46] Maelgwyn[47] died in the church of Rhôs in Creuddyn, from having seen the Yellow Spectre, "Vad Velen", i.e. Plague, through a hole over the door of the church, which gave rise to an adage, "Hûn Maelgwyn yn Eglwys Llanrhos." "The sleep of Maelgwyn in the Church of Llanrhôs." He was buried in Ynys Seiriol.

"Rhûn, the son of Maelgwyn, reigned from 560 to 586. He is the subject of a Triad, as being one of the three golden-banded sovereigns of Britain. St. Beuno wrote the account of the battles of Rhûn ab Maelgwyn; and Elidr Mwynvawr lodged it in the college of Bangor.—*J. Lloyd*."[48] In 620, on ac-count of Môn being infested by the Irish Picts, Cadwallon removed the court from Aberffraw to Caernarvon. At this time, a Bishop Austin, sent by Pope Gregory, came from Rome to preach to the pagan Saxons of Britain; for they were ignorant of the faith and had destroyed it in their territories; but the Britons maintained it, as they had done from the days of Electherius. The preaching of Austin was attended more with ridicule than conversion to the faith. He heard that there was an archiepiscopal church, at Caerlleon, having seven bishops under it; besides the great monastery of Bangor, having Dunod, the most learned man of his age, as head: with him Austin disputed the pope's supremacy, &c. Dunod answered him in the following words; "know and be assured, that we, in all humility are ready to defer to the Church of God, the Bishop of Rome, and every one according to his station, &c. so to love every pious and sincere christian, and to assist them all by word and deed, so that they may be-come children of God; but as to farther deference than this; I know of none which he whom ye call pope, or father of fathers i.e. bishop of bishops, can claim or demand", &c.[49]

This dispute was the cause of the battle of Bangor, fought between that place and Chester. Mr.

---

46 Caerwys MS transcribed by Mr. Lloyd, out of an old book that once belonged to Mr. Jones of Gelli-lovdu. Mr. Ll. concludes "there is probably some truth in the above curious account about Maelgwyn Gwynedd, Elffin, &c. as some of Taliesin's Poems, or at least what pass for his, relate some of the facts mentioned. A Poem translated by Evan Evans, alludes to this Legendary Tale, entitled "Dyhuddiant Elffin".

47 From the battle of Camlan to the death of Maelgwyn, ten years, A.D. 506.—From the death of Maelgwyn to the battle of Arderyd, when Gwrgi and Peredur were slain, seven years, A.D. 593.—*Red Book of Hergest*.

48 Caerwys MS.

49 Transcribed out of a MS in the Mostyn Collection, written in Welsh, and not later than the tenth century, "Even to the time of Geoffrey of Monmouth, the British and Romish Churches were distinct."—*ib*. This last remark is in a much more modern writing. The original MS from the orthography, which is a criterion of very considerable importance, I cannot consider to be later than the tenth century; and many think that it is of higher antiquity.—*John Lloyd, Caerwys MS*. And that the British possessed the Bible in the native tongue, so early as 380, we learn from Cephilos, Bishop of the Goths having about that time "translated the four evangelists—a precious monument of the ancient Celtic mixed with the Tudesque". The MS was preserved in the Library of Upsal Maseau.—viii. 4/0.

,

Jones of Gelli-lovdu,[50] out of whose books the following extracts are taken, contradicts some of the English historians, relative to this bloody affair. They say that "Ethelfridus", or Elidr Mwynvawr, fought the battle of Bangor in the time of Cadvan, Prince of North Wales, whereas he proves, that Elidr Mwynvawr was slain by Rhûn ab Maelgwyn, who was Cadvan's great-grandfather, at a place called Abermhedus, in Caernarvonshire; and says that Ethelbert, King of Kent, was the person that fought the battle of Bangor and not this Elidr, who it seems was a Cambrian Briton; and after his death, several chieftains from the North came to Arvon, to revenge it, amongst whom were Cludno,—Eyddin,—Nudd,—Hael, vab Serill,—Mordav,——Hael, vab Servari and Rydderch Hael, vab Tuddwal Tutclud. These burnt Arvon: after this Rhûn gathered his forces and went to return the compliment in the North; and upon that account he granted the men of Arvon particular privileges. They are fourteen in number and styled "Breintiau Gwyr Arvon". They are dark, and in a great measure, I believe unintelligible. St. Beuno wrote the account of the battles of Rhûn and this Elidr, and lodged it at the college of Bangor. At the end of these historical records, I find this remark, "Has notas ex Historia Britannica Dñi Johñs Jones excerpsit David Parroeus apud Dolgelleu merviniæ oppidam, mense, Februarii, A.D.1689".[51]

Cadwallon reigned forty-two years paramount sovereign of Wales and England; and after his death, which happened in November, the Welsh embalmed his body, and deposited it in an image of bronze, of curious workmanship, which they placed over a gate in London, so as to appear to rush on the Saxons. At this gate was built a church, dedicated to God and St. Martin. Edelfrid,[52] the father of Edwyn, quarrelled with his wife, who applied to Cadvan, the father of Cadwallon, to mediate between her and her husband: in the mean time (she being in Cadvan's palace) gave birth to a son, whom she named Edwyn; and about the same time Cadvan's wife was delivered of a son, named Cadwallon. Both were reared together until they grew up; then they were sent for their instruction in the manners of a court and to the use of arms, to Solomon, King of Bretagne, and were by him gladly received. Here they improved so much, as not to be surpassed by any in accomplishments. When Cadvan and Edelfrid died, their sons succeeded them, and renewed the amity agreed on by their respective fathers. But at the end of two years, Edwyn demanded permission of Cadwallon, to make a crown for himself (that is, to be acknowledged as an independent king), that he might wear it on the other side of the Humber, &c.

The first mention of Mona, by Powel, in his Chronicles is, when its possession was disputed by the sons of Roderic Molwynog, in 810. "Howel, the younger son, did claim the Isle of Mona for part of his inheritance, as Prince of North Wales;[53] which Cynan, who began his reign over the Brytagnes in 755, refused to give up to hym. Each prepared for battle: victory deciding in favour of Howel, who re-

50 John Jones of Gelli-lovdu, distinguished as one of the most indefatigable collectors of Welsh literature that has appeared amongst us. He continued transcribing old MSS for a period of about forty years, it appears from some of his volumes, which are dated variously from A.D.1590 to 1630; and of whose work in this way, upwards of fifty large volumes still exist.

51 Caerwys MS.

52 Black Book of Basingwerk

53 Powel Chronicles p.21.

tained it till 817, when Cynan again levied an armie and chased his brother out of the Island, who was faine to flie to Manaw, where he died in 820." The conflicts between these princes, are thus recorded in the Black Book of Basingwerk.—

"Oed Crist, 810, y duodd y lleuad, dydd nadolig, ag a llosges Mynyw, ac a bu varwolaeth ysgrybl drwy holl Gymru; ar vlwyddyn honno y bu varw Owain ab Meredydd, ac y bu ymladd Hywel a Chynan, ac a goryg Hywel Ynys Vôn, yr ûn vlwyddyn a llosces Diganog, gan dân mellt. Oed Crist, 815, y bu daranau mawr, a mellt yn llosgi llawer, ac a bu varw Gr. ap Rhun, ac a llâs Griffu ab Cynen ab Cadell Deirnllig o dwyll Elisau, ac gorfu Hywel o Ynys Vôn, a Chynan i vrawd, ac ai deholes ev ai lû. Oed Crist 817, y deholed Hywel i Vanaw, ac a bu varw Cynan Dindaethwy, Brenin Gwynedd, ac y dyvethwyd y Saeson ynysoedd Erryri, ac a dynant Ryvoniog i ar y Cymru. 818 y bu ymladd y Môn, yr hwn a elwyd Gwaith Llanvaes."

This was a battle fought by Egbert, King of the West Saxons, who invaded Wales with a powerful army, seized the Lordship of Rhyvoniog, in Denbighland, desolated the country as far as Snowdon, and crossing into Mona,[54] took possession of it, after "sore conflicte" with the Britons, at Llanvaes, near Beaumaris; and although this Island was soon recovered by Mervyn, Prince of Wales (in right of his wife Essyllt, daughter and heir of Conan Dindaethwy), and the Saxons were driven out, yet from this period it lost its ancient name of Mona among the English, "whose King, Egbert, called it Anglesey,[55] when he wan the cittie of Caerlleon,[56] at Dowrdwy, which was then the chieffe cittie of Venedotia,[57] outt of the hands of the Bryttaynes, in whose possession itt remayned untill that tyme. He caused alsoe the brazen image of Cadwallon, Kinge of Brytaine, to be throwne downe and defaced; comandinge that no man upon paine of death, should set up anie such againe, forbidding this land to be called Brytaine, anie more, but Englande, and the people Englishmen, &c[58]. He also made proclamation, "That no Brytaine should remain within the confines of England, commandinge that al and singular, whiche were of the Brytish blood, should within six monseths, avoide with their wives and children outt of hys kingdome, upon paine of losinge their heads." There was something in the Saxon character, so little susceptible of those impressions which humanize and polish the rudest nations that even at this period, the middle of the ninth century, they retained their natural barbarism. Egbert added injury to insult, by making another law, as savage as it was unavailing, which affixed the penalty of death to every Briton who passed the limits of Offa's dyke, and should be taken on the English borders. More coercive restraints were necessary, than such a feeble barrier and futile law; though the hand of power had drawn an arbitrary line, which insulted the feelings and entrenched on the rights of a warlike and bereaved people. 843 is a memorable era in the annals of Cymru, when Roderi the Great, son of Mervyn Vrŷch, succeeded to his father's throne with a greater extent of territory, than had fallen to the share of any Cambrian sovereign. "This prince divided all Wales into three territories; i.e. Aberf-

---

54 Welsh Chronicles p.22.
55 Island of the Angli.
56 Chester on Dee.
57 North-West Wales.
58 Powel Chronicles p.27.

fraw, Dinevor and Mathroval. He had greate warres with Burchred, King of Mercia, whoe by the aide of Ethelwulfe, entered North Wales, with a strong armye, and advanced as far as Mona which they cruelly devastated by fire and sword; "they fought with the Welshemen dyvers tymes", and slew Meuric, "a great prince amonge them", &c. There is a turn in human affairs, arising out of existing circumstances, which neither sagacity can foresee, nor power prevent; and which, if taken up with spirit, and wisely conducted, leads to prosperity. The Kings of England and Mercia, were fortunately for the Britons, employed in the protection of their own dominions from the ravages of the Danes;—the inroads of those people increasing every day. The English fully employed in attending to their own safety, left the Britons unmolested. In this favourable juncture, if Roderic had made a proper use of the leisure, which the troubles in England had given him, by fortifying the passes, where every mountain was a natural fortress, he might have secured his territories, and by this wise and judicious act have prevented the battle of Bangoleu. "Oed Crist,[59] 872, y bu gwaith Bangoleu ym Môn", where the invaders, "y Paganiad Duon", i.e. Grim Pagans, "mewn brwydr galed" in two hard fought battles; one at Bangoleu and the other at Menegid, received a most spirited opposition from Rodric; "ac ev a ddivethwyd y Paganiaid Duon. Ac yr un vlwyddyn y bu waith Bangor, lle y lladdwyd y Saeson wrth y niveroedd, a cherrig a dreiglwyd arnynt oddiar y Brynniau, ac yn mlith y rhai hynny, Escob Bangor a lâs"[60]. Sometime in the following year Roderic changed the royal residence back to Aberffraw from Caernarvon.[61] From this time, Mona formed part of the Principality of North Wales, and the chief seat of government to that dynasty. In about three years after this, an interval of quiet from the Danes, gave the English an opportunity in 876 of making another descent upon Mona, where the king, with his usual promptness and gallantry of spirit, met him in a "sore battel". He there fell, bravely fighting in defence of his country. "Dydd Sûl y bu y waith Môn, ac yno y llâs Rodri mawr, ac Gwriaid ei vrawd, a Gweyrydd ab Owain Morganwg, gan y Saeson, ac yna yn ei llawn angerdd y cymmerth gwragedd Môn arvau, ac a ruthrasant ar y Saeson, au lladd yn greulon, oni orvu arnynt ffo."[62] This heroic spirit seems inherent in the women of Cambria, who in our own time, and without the aid of husbands or brothers, overcame and made prisoners, some hundreds of Frenchmen, who had landed at Milford Haven.[63] In the following year, Anarawd amply avenged his father's death, in the battle of Camryd, which he designated by the term of "Dial Rodri" and "where was a great slaughter made of the Danes and Saxons", who united their forces to make war against Wales. Roderic, agreeable to the custom of Gavelkind,[64] divided his extensive dominions into three distinct sovereignties, which he left to his three sons, "under[65] theire meares and boundes, with a princely house in everie of them, which he named 'y Tair Talaith', and his three sonnes were called 'y Tri Tywysog Talaethog', that is 'The Three Crowned Princes', because everie of them did weare upon his bonnet or helmet, a coronet of gold; beinge a broade lace or head-

---

59 Llyvr Ieuan Brechva.
60 Llyvr Dû Ddinas Basing.
61 From "Caer Segontium" alias "Caer yn Arfon". ibid.
62 Llyvr Basing p.72—"Ei vab Gwriad. Oed Crist 955, a bu hav tessoc, ac y llâs Gwgan ab Gwriad ab Rhodri Mawr".
63 This occurred during the last war in 1800.
64 Gavel is a British term, signifying a "hold".—*Blackstone.—Welsh Chronicles.*
65 Welsh Chronicles p.38, 35.

band, indented upwards, set and wroughte with precious stones, whiche in the British language is called 'Talaeth', and soe to thys daie nurses doe name that broade bande, wherewith a child's head is bound, 'Talaeth' ".[66] According to the Chronicles of our Princes, Anarawd the eldest, succeeded to that of North Wales. The residence of the sovereigns of this district was at Aberffraw, "the chiefe house of the Prince of Gwynedd", whose dominions was therefore called "Talaeth Aberffraw", in Môn, in a palace which had been erected during the life time of King Roderic,[67] and who regarding Anarawd as the immediate heir of the Cynethian line. He left to him and to his successors the title of "Brenhin Cymru oll", i.e. King of all Wales; he also ordained, that if any difference should arise between the Princes of North and South Wales, they should meet at Bwlch y Pawl, and the Prince of Powys was appointed umpire. If the Princes of Aberffraw and Powys should be at variance, they were all to assemble at Morva Rhianedd, on the banks of the Dee; and the Prince of South Wales was to determine the controversy. If the dispute should arise between the Princes of Powys and South Wales, the meeting was appointed to be held at Llŷs Wen, i.e. White Palace, upon the river Wye; and the matter in contention was to be decided by the King of Aberffraw,[68] &c. Roderic, when he ordained these laws, must have been little acquainted with human nature, to imagine that such regulations were sufficient to counteract, at a distant period, the wild passions and ambition of princes.

"Oed Crist 900, y daeth Igmwnt ai Baganiaid Duon i Vôn, ac yna Gwaith Rhôs Meilion", &c.[69]

"There be some" (says Powel in p.42) "Brytish copies of this historie, whiche affirme that this battel betweene Igmond, captaine of the Blacke Nations, and the Brytains, wherein Mervyn was slaine, was fought at a place called Meilon, of the whiche, it was called Maes Rhôs Meilion." In 915, according to the Black Book of Basingwerk, "a divethwyd Môn gan wŷr Dilyin" (i.e. 'Men of Dublin'); in 958[70] was a wonderfull hott summer, when Gwgan the sonne[71] of Gwriad the sonne of Roderic died. Affter the whiche heate there followed a greate plague in March following; and in those daies Iago and Iefa by force and strength ruled all Wales; and yet ffor all their power, Abloic, King of Ireland landed in Mona, having burnt Holyhead, 'divethwyd yr Ynys yn gwbl gan veibion Bloic, Brenin y Werddon'. At which time this king of the 'Green Island', assisted by his sons, carried the shrine of St. Cybi to Dublin."[72]

---

66 Welsh Chronicles p.35.—The Three Bandlet-wearing Kings of the Isle of Britain,—Cadell, Brenin Dinevor.— Anarawd, Brenin Aberffraw.—Mervyn, Brenin Mathraval.—2nd Series of Triads.

67 "Rodri Mawr a ddoles drevn newydd ar lywodraeth Cymru hyd y cerddai ei vraint ev, aid amgen Ceredigion a Cadell ei vab hynav ai cavas, ac iddaw ei Lŷs yn Ninevwr. Gwynedd i Anarawd ei vab, ac iddaw Lŷs yn Aberffraw ym Môn. Powys a roddes i Verfyn ei vab, ac Lŷs ym Mathraval. Ac yr hynav o honynt deyrnged i Vrenin Llyndain; ac i'r hynav deyrnged gan y ddau ereill. A'r Tri Tywysog Talaethiawg au gelwid, am iddynt yn anad vu ou blaen hwynt wisgaw Taliaethiau am eu coronau, val y gwnelei vrenhinoedd yng Ngwynedd: eraill ni wisgynt namyn hualen euriaid." —Brut y Tywysogion, i.e. Chronicles of the Princes.

68 Wynn Hist. of Wales p.35; Rowlands Mon. Ant. pp.174, 175.

69 Llyvr Ieuan Brechva.

70 Welsh Chronicles p.35.

71 See a note taken from Llyvr Du Basing, referred to in p.32.

72 Llyvr Dinas Basing.—For the year following there is the death of Edwy recorded, accompanied by this curious allegory:—"Ag megis y dwe yr un tir y llysie da, a rai drwc, ac weithiau yn emyl y ddanhaden y tŷf y rôs; velly o'r un Edmwnt dda, wirion, y daeth Edwyn ddrwe ac Edgar dda."

In 961 Edgar the King of England invaded North Wales, and as he marched through the country, spread around the usual devastations; the people then were just recovering from the sad effect of Abloic's invasion. "The cause of this warre was the nonpaiement of the tribute thatt the King of Aberffraw, by the lawes of Howel Dda, was to paie to the King of London."[73] And the more ancient, but no less impolitic and imprudent institution of King Roderic the Great, who ordained that the Princes of South Wales and Powys, should each of them pay yearly to the Sovereign of North Wales, a tribute called Maelged of £63, as a mark of subordination, but the royal tribute, or teyngred, which was due from Cambria to the imperial crown of London, agreeable to the original old laws, was to be paid by the Princes of North Wales.[74] When these laws were framed by Dyvnwal Moelrnud, he never contemplated the possibility of "the sceptre departing from his house". Reflecting, perhaps, upon the unreasonableness of this demand, and hearing of the injuries both countries had received from wolves, Edgar remitted, with some degree of liberality, the ancient tribute, and only exacted the yearly payment of the heads of 300 of those animals. This demand, so singular in its nature, was paid by the prince "untill he had never a wolffe left in Wales".[75]

The Black Book of Basingwerk notes this event as occurring in 962. "Oed Crist 962, y diffethawdd Cadbrig ab Eyrlaid Vôn, ac ev a wnaeth dravael vawr yn yr Ynys, ac yna y daeth Edgar; Brenhin y Saeson, a llû dirvawr yn erbyn holl Gymru, ac a dodes ev wyr Denmarc yn Ynys Vôn, lle y gwledychasant er gwaetha gwyr y wlad, ac y denvones ev wyr i ysbeiliaw yr wlad, ac nid arbedynt na llŷs na llan, eithr dwyn daoedd, a thlysau eglwysi, ac y gwrthladdodd Iago vab Idwal o'i gyvoeth, ac a roddes Wynedd i Hywel Ddrwg ab Ioan, ac nid oedd drwg o'r byd, nac gwnelai hwnnw o ladd a thynnu llygaid, ac yspeilaw, a thwyllaw." &c.

In 966, Aberffraw, the royal seat of the Princes of North Wales, was destroyed by the Irishmen, "when Rodri the son of Idwal, was slain in Aberffraw".[76] The union, so long subsisting between the Princes of North Wales, Ieva and Iago, was at this period fatally dissolved by force of arms. Iago seized the person of his brother Ievaf and consigned him to a tedious imprisonment. In 968, Howel, son to the captive prince, raised an army to deliver his father out of prison. It was an evil peculiarly fatal to the independency of Wales (and produced by its civil dissentions), that the weaker party usually fled for protection to the Kings of England. We learn from the Black Book of Basingwerk, that Howel was accompanied by a strong body of English,[77] who overran and destroyed Llŷn and Mona, taking possession of the lands of Iago, from which they were never fairly extirpated, and this was the occasion of calling the Island of Môn, Anglesea, that is, the Island of the English.

And to augment the miseries of the poor harassed natives, Malctus, son of Harold, entered

---

73 Powel Chronicles p.61.

74 British Ant. Revived by Mr. Vaughan of Hengwrt, p.8, 25, 40. This tribute was sometimes paid in honey and flour.— *Humphrey Llwyd* p.64, 65.

75 Powel Chronicles p.62.

76 Black Book of Basingwerk Abbey.

77 A llu dirvawr o Saeson, a difethiaw Llŷn a Môn, a dodi Saeson yn holl diroedd Iago, a chadarnhau y tiroedd hynny iddynt, a hanped gwaeth i Ynys Vôn o hynny, can nas galled ei gwared vyth wedi hynny; ac achaws hynny y doded enw Anglisei ar Ynys Vôn, sev hynny iw, Ynys y Saeson.—*Llyvr Du Dinas Basing*.

Mona[78] with an army of Danes, and shortly after this we find that the whole Island was subdued by Godffrit, vab Harallt, who made it tributary to him, "ac ev ai gorescynodd iddaw yn drethawl", but he did not enjoie itt long,[79] for Howel having driven his uncle Iago into England, "notwithstanding he set his father Ieva at libertie, yett took upon himselfe the whole rule of the lande ffor his lifetyme".[80] Being too much enamoured of power to relinquish it easily along with the rest of the principality, he regained possession of Mona. Fired with the deepest resentment, and with the hopes of dispossessing him of the crown, Cystenyn Ddû (Black Constantine), son of Iago, collected an army of "y Paganiad Duon"[81] who invaded North Wales and again laid waste the Isle of Mona: for these Danes had leave from Edgar to settle there. But Howel, who was not deficient in bravery, though destitute of other virtues, collected his forces and gave the Danes a signal overthrow in the conflict called the "battle of Heibarth, where Black Constantine was killed". "A châd dost a vu cyn no hynny rhyngddynt. A chydag ev a ddaeth lû o o'r Danead Duon; y chedag ev y codasant y Saeson a wledychant yr Ynys a divethiawr yr wlad honno yn dost aruthrawl, a Gottffrid ab Harallt oedd evo Cwstenyn."[82]

In 986, Meredydd, the youngest son of Owen ab Howel Dda, disregarding the rights of his two nephews the sons of Eignion, assumed the reins of government, but before he could be well confirmed in his dominions, Godfrid the son of Harold, a third time entered the Isle of Mona, and having taken his brother Prince Llowarch ab Owain prisoner, with 2,000 of his men, he, with great cruelty, put out Llowarch's eyes, to gratify a mean revenge; unworthy a great mind to injure those, whom his arms had not been able to subdue, and that too, in a manner so wounding to sensibility. This inhuman custom of Asiatic sovereigns, was too frequently adopted by the princes of the Saxon race, tinging more deeply, by such a cruel measure, the native barbarism of their manners. Meredydd, shocked at this disaster, and terrified by the fate of his brother, fled into South Wales, leaving his new subjects exposed to the ravages of the Danes; and to heighten their calamity, a distemper fell upon their cattle, which raged with so much fury as to leave very few remaining in the Island. This distressing event is thus noted in the Black Book of Basingwerk,[83] by the Chronicler, in his usual pithy and comprehensive style.

"Oed Crist 986, y tynwyd llygaid Llywarc ab Owain, ac y diffethwyd Môn gan Gottffrid ap Haralt, ac ev a ddileodd ddwy vil oi gwŷr, ac gweddill a ddug Mredydd ab Owain y gantho i Garedigion a Dyved. A'r vlwyddyn honno y bu varwolaeth ar yr ysgrybl drwy holl Gymru. Ac wedi gwybod a gweled o Elfridas Frenin, amled gwŷr Denmark yn Lloegyr, ovni a oruc; kanis o ddauddec Iarllaeth ar hugain oedd yn Lloegyr, yr oedd gwŷr Denmark yn gwladychu un ar bymtheg o naddynt; ac yna y gwelwis y brenin atto holl ieirll i gymryd cyngor am wŷr Denmark; ac yn eu cyngor y kowsant ladd, au pennau

---

78 "Yn y vlwyddyn 968, y daeth Macht ab Harallt i Ynys Vôn, ac ai ddivethwys Benmon, lie ydoedd decav, cyn no hynny, yn holl Ynys Vôn. Ac ebrwydd wedi hynny, y daeth Gottffrid vab Harallt yn erbyn Ynys Môn, ac ai diveithas; ac Edgar a roddes gennad i wŷr Gottffrid aros ym Môn yn gavaneddawl, ac ymunaw yno â gwŷr Edwyn a wnaethant yn un ormes, ac nid aethant vyth o honi, ac nis gellid vyth gwedi hynng gwared brâd o'r Ynys."—*Brut y Tywysogion. Llyvr Mr. Williams o Aber-pergwm.*

79 Powel Chronicles p.62.

80 Ibid. p.63.

81 Black Pagans, alias Danes.

82 Llyvr Du Dinas Basing.

83 Confirmed in Brut y Tywysogion by Ieuan Brechfa, with some curious additions.

oll yn oed un dydd; kanis pawb oedd yn eu kynnal hwy ai Meirch wrth ei bywydr: nid amgen, gŵr o bum punt a gynhalia un gŵr; gŵr a deg punt a gynhalia ddau; a phob gŵr kyvoeth awg oedd yn eu kynnal hwy, herwydd eu kyvoeth ai gallu; ac yn oed un dydd ac un nôs y llâs hwynt oll, wrth orchymmyn y brenin." Consequently, in 988, the Danes, at Hampton, having broke their league with the English king, sailed towards the west, annoying the inhabitants on the coasts of Cornwall and Devonshire and at last landed in South Wales, ravaging and laying waste that country with marked animosity and cruelty. To such a pitch of misery was Prince Mredydd ab Owen reduced, that he was obliged to purchase peace on ignoble terms, and "was faine to agree to give them a pennie for everie man within his lands, whych was called the Tribute of the Black Armye".[84] But this tribute, so delusive and dishonourable, a miserable substitute for valour and exertion, was never paid (it may be recorded to their credit) by any of the Princes of North Wales. During a contest in 990 and 991, between Edwyn, the eldest son of Einion, and rightful heir to South Wales, and his uncle Mredydd, the reigning prince of both principalities, North Wales had been left without a sovereign, exposed to the ravages of every invader "whyche thing, when the Danes perceived, they arrived in Mona and destroyed the whole Isle".[85] In consequence of famine, which was caused by this "Cenedl Ddu", the Grim Tribe of Marauders, the islanders were constrained (for the first time) to eat shellfish.

"Naw cant a phedwar ugain a deg,[86] y diffethwyd Môn, gan y Genedl Ddu. Bu am yr un amser ryfelu, a lladdgarwch mawr rhwng pendefigion Gwynedd a Phowys; ac bu rhyfel rhwng Mredydd ab Owain, Ithel ab Morgan, Brenin Morganwg, achos anrhaith gwyr Mredydd yn eu newyn. Gan drudaniaeth a'r amser hwnnw y dechrewyd bwytta cregyn y môr". And in that year Edwal, son of Meuric was elected sovereign, by the men of Mona for there was no prince to lead the army of North Wales against the "Grim Tribe of Pagan Danes" y Paganiad Duon, who had laid waste the country.[87]

On the accession of this prince, Eidwal ab Meuric, he began to regulate the affairs of his kingdom, and to place his subjects in such a posture of defence, as might secure them from the incursion of the Danes (Cenedl Ddu). He soon experienced the salutary effects of such a spirited conduct; but his prosperity was of short duration. In 993, the Black Book of Basingwerk informs us, that the principality was visited at this time by accumulated calamities in the shape of famine: "a llawer a vu varv o haint y Saeson, sev y haint chwyslyd", and to complete the misfortune, Mona was destroyed, and Idwal, vab Meuric was slain by Swayn, the son of Harold. The Chronicles of the Princes are still more diffuse in noting down these lamentable events.—"Yr un vlwyddyn y daeth y Dainiaid Duon i Ynys Vôn,[88] ac a ddiffeithiasant yr holl Ynys val y mynynt; canys nid oedd ar Wynedd, yr amser hynny, na phen, na pherchen, na llŷs, na llywodraeth; na neb a savai yn mhlaid y wlad, rhag estron, ac anrhaith, am hynny cymmerasant y Cymru attynt Eidwal, vab Meyric, ac ai dodasant yn Dywysawg arnynt, ac a cawsant

---

84 Welsh Chronicles p.71.
85 Ibid.
86 Llyvr Ieuan Brechva.
87 Ac yr amserodd hynny y gwnaethpwyd Eidwal ab Meuric yn Dywysawg gan wŷr Môn; lle nid oedd na Thywysawg, na neb, a elai ymlaen gwŷr Gwynedd: achaws hynny y diffeithwyd y wlad honno gan y geuedyl Paganiaid Duon yn avived.—*Llyvr Ieuan Brechva.*
88 Brut y Tywysogion.—Llannerch MSS.

borth gan Ithel, Tywysawg Morganwg, a gyrru ffô, a lladdva vawr, ar y Dainaid Duon a wnaethynt. Ac Eidwal a vu yn Dywysawg clodvawr, a chyviawn, ag a wnaeth lywodraeth ar Wynedd, a threvn a weddai ar heddwch a rhyvel, canys ev a dysged gan Hywel ab Morgan Vawr, ac eve yn ben doethion Cymru, yn y gwybodau y ddylai tywysawg ei ddeall, ai cynnal. Oed Crist, 994, y daeth Swayn ab Hallt ar Dainiad Duon gydag ev, a diffeithiar wlad o Wynedd, hyd Ynys Môn, lle y bu Câd Penmynydd, ym Môn, y lle y llâs Idwal, vab Meyric, y Tywysawg Gwynedd, ac a divethwyd Matharn, gan y Saeson, ag hwy ai llosgasant oll."

This part of our Chronicles is only a recital of reciprocal inroads and injuries; a series of objects unvaried and of little importance, which pass the eye in a succession of cold delineations. The characters and events are not sufficiently explained to enable the historian to trace the connection of causes, with effects, by leading incidents or the general springs, which direct human affairs. In pursuing details, there is nothing gained towards clearing up the obscurity of those times of turbulence.

We hear nothing more of Mona till 1074, soon after the accession of Trahaiarn ab Caradoc to the throne of North Wales. Gryffydd ab Cynan, the right inheritor, came from Ireland with "succour whiche his brethren Encumalhon King of Ultonia and Ranaltt and Mathawn had delivered him, and landed in the Isle of Mona, and brought it to his subjection. This yeare also Grono and Llewelyn the sons of Cadwgan ab Bleddyn did join theire powers with Caradog, against Rhys ab Owen and Rhydderch, to revenge theire grandfather's deathe. They foughte att a place called Camdhwr, where the sonnes of Cadwgan obtained the victorie. Shorttlie after Gryffydd ab Conan passed over the water ffrom Môn to the maine lande, and Trahaiarn; met with hym att Bronyr-Erw; where Gryffydd was put to flighte, and retired backe to the Ile."[89] The same account (but much more circumstantial) is given by Mr. Lloyd in his comments on the life of Gryffydd ab Cynan, which I will here take leave to insert verbatim.—

"The life[90] of Gryffydd ab Cynan is full of disastrous incidents. It seems to have been wrote by some ecclesiastic near his time, and has been translated from Welsh into Latin by Nicolas Robinson, Bishop of Bangor. It seems to be sensibly, and soberly written; his pedigree in the beginning is a little extravagant. I believe Dr. Powel was not acquainted with this history. It says, that his mother was Racwel, daughter of Aelodd, King of Dublin, and of the fifth part of Ireland; and amongst other great possessions, that he had formerly some footing in North Wales, particularly Mona; and that he built there a strong castle, with its tommen and fosse, extant in the author's time, who says it was called 'Castell Aelodd Frenin', but the country people commonly called it 'Bôn y Don'. Query:—Whether there be any traces of it now to be seen? This Aelodd is called Alffed in Powel's History. Gryffydd ab Cynan, upon his first landing from Ireland at Abermenai[91], was assisted by Asser, Meriawn and Gw-

---

89 Welsh Chronicles p.112.

90 "Ystori Gruffydd ab Kynan, Brenhin Gwynedd.—E. cod. msto. Chart. penes Dom. R. Davis de Llannerch convenit cum cod. anti quo. membr. penes. D. Jo. Wyn de Watstay".
"Nicholas Robinson, Bishop of Bangor's Latin translation of the life of Gryffydd ab Cynan, was in the possession of the Rev. Hugh Hughes, Vicar of Bangor, in 1760; whose father and eldest brother were successively agents at Gwydir. The MS is said to be now (1788) at Wîg, Llandegai."—*J. Ll. Caerwys MS.*

91 "Odd yna Gruffydd a esgynnws oi long, ag ymchoelodd i'w daith oi reidwyf hyd yn Abermenai, a chaffael porth yno; ag yno Ruffydd anvones gennadeu at wŷr Môn ag Arvon, a tri meib Merwydd o Lŷn, oeddynt yn ffoi rhac Cynwic, vab Rhiwallon, Breninyn o Bowys."—*Caerwys MS.* These three gentlemen were in sanctuary, &c.

gawn, sons of Merwydd ab Collwyn ab Tangno. These three had been obliged to take sanctuary at Ce-lynog, for fear of the Powys men. He, Gryffydd, paid a visit to Robert of Ruddlan, to solicit his assistance, which he obtained. Whilst he was there, he was visited by his relation Tangwystl, wife of Llowarch Holbwrch, who presented him with the finest shirt and a coat made of the robe of Prince Gryffydd ab Llewelyn ab Seisyllt, whose treasurer and prime minister her husband had been, &c. He had afterwards a bloody battle with Trahaiarn ab Caradoc, in a narrow glyn. The place was afterwards called Gwaederw, or Tir Gwaedlyd, i.e. Bloody Land. From this circumstance, I believe that this battle was fought near Gwydir, and that the place was so denominated. After this, Gryffydd ab Cynan attacked Robert of Rhyddlan, in his castle, took and burnt the Baili; killed a great number of his men, both horse and foot, so that very few of them escaped into the tower. N.B. This was long before the building of the castle, in the form its ruins now present. After some more conflicts, Gryffydd, chiefly by the treachery of his own men, was again obliged to take refuge in Ireland; and during his absence, his country suffered all the horrors of war. For as (the author says) Hugh, Earl of Chester, with many other chieftains, Robert of Rhyddlan, Warren, Earl of Salop, Walter, Earl of Hereford, with an immense number of horse and foot, together with Gwrgeneu ab Seisyllt and the men of Powys, marched over the mountains as far as Llŷn, where they destroyed most unmercifully all before them, insomuch that the country was a perfect desert for eight years afterwards. Those that escaped with life fled to other countries, and few of them ever returned back. The author observes that this was the first time that Gwynedd felt the dreadful plague of the Normans, after their coming into England, &c.

"Gryffydd returned the second time from Ireland, and landed at St. David's, in South Wales; soon after (in conjunction with Rhys ab Tewdwr, Prince of South Wales), he fought the battle that decided the fate of the principality upon 'Mynydd Carn', where Trahaiarn[92] ab Caradoc was slain, &c. This place was called 'Mynydd Carn', because there was a large carnedd upon it, covering the remains of some heroic chieftain, that was buried there in times of yore. Gruffydd's prosperity was but of short duration, for soon after he returned to North Wales, he was betrayed by one Meiriawn Gôch, into the hands of Hugh, Earl of Chester, in the following manner:—It was agreed between the parties, that Hugh, Earl of Chester, i.e. 'Hugh Vrâs', and Hugh, Earl of Shrewsbury, i.e. 'Hugh Gôch', should bring a strong force of horse and foot to Rûg, in Edernion: when in the mean time, the traitor Meiriawn informs the prince that those two earls desired a conference with him at that place. He went there, attended, it seems, by some of his strange followers, who came with him from Ireland, and he was immediately seized, conveyed to Chester, bound in irons, and cast into prison. There he remained full twelve years, until he was released by the bravery of one Cynric Hîr, a young man of Edernion, who attended by a few followers, went to Chester, upon pretence of buying some necessaries. Cynric took an

---

92 A Gryffydd ab Cynon y ddaeth a deg llong ar hugaint llawn o Wyddyl a gwŷr Denmarc, ac yn Abermenai i dyscynant, ac yna i cawsant Trahaiarn yn gwleddychu yn y wlad. A phan gigleu Trahaiarn ddyvod y llynges vrenhinawl honno, tristau ac ucheneidaw a oruc, ac ergryn ac ofn ai dygyrchws, a mudaw gwŷr Llŷn sc Ardadwy sc eu dâ, a oruc, attaw hyt yng Cantrev Meirionydd, a gavas o naddynt; a Gryffydd ynteu ae lu a ddugant y rhan arall o Leyn ac Arvon, hyt ym Môn, val i gellynt bot yno yn ddiogel dan ei amddeffin ef. Oddy yna i llidws y Danawyssyeit ev a gwŷr ei dŷ, ai dylwyth ei hun, can ni cheint eu gorddyvneit mal ir, addawdod iddunt, ac ir anrheithiassant gan wyav Môn o dreis i arnaw, ac ymchoelyt i eu gwlat, ac eu llongeu yn llawn o ddynion a goludoedd, ae ddwyn ynteu ganddynt, ac nit oe vodd.—*Arch. vol. 2, p. 591.—Buchedd, neu Hanes Gryfydd ab Cynon, o Hên Lyvr Syr Risiart Gwyn.*

opportunity at the edge of night, when his keepers were feasting, to convey the prince away in his irons, upon his back, and got clear off with him. The prince underwent a variety of concealments and hardships before he recovered his princedom, or rather his kingdom, for he was always stiled king. During which time, and that of his imprisonment, his country was most miserably harassed by that monster of cruelty, the Earl of Chester, who in order to carry on his ravages with greater security, erected several castles and garrisoned them strongly with horse and foot, i.e. Aberllienawg in Môn; another at Hên Gaer Cwstenyn[93] in Arvon; another at Bangor, and another in Meirionedd, which in process of time were all taken by Gryffydd ab Cynan. But some time after this, the two earls landed in Môn, and while these two invaders were exercising their cruelties upon the poor inhabitants, it happened most fortunately that Magnus, King of Norway, the son of Olanus, having made a conquest of the Isle of Man, directed his fleet to Mona, and when he would have landed, Hugh Gôch, with a great army opposed him. In this engagement the earl fell, being shot by an arrow, which Magnus aimed at him from the prow of his ship. The king seeing him fall, thus insolently exclaimed in the Danish tongue, 'leit loupe' (let him dance). He died on the seventh day, after he had used unheard of acts of torture, more savage than ever stained the annals of any country, upon one Cenred, a priest. After a great number of victories and defeats, Prince Griffydd ab Cynan enjoyed a little of the blessings of peace, in his old age. He died, aged eighty two, and was buried in a shrine, on the left side of the great altar in the church of Bangor.

"It is to be noted, that this prince experienced a great deal of revolting and treachery from his own subjects. By the tenor of the history, I guess it must have been occasioned by their aversion to the strangers he employed, for he was obliged several times to go to Ireland, and once as far as Denmark, for aid; and I find that the Cambro-Britons had but little cordiality for those gentry. He had a number of them with him when he was seized at Rûg, who had every one of them the thumb of his right hand cut off, and then sent about his business. This no doubt was done at the instigation of Meiriawn Gôch, &c.

"There is another copy of this history in the Gloddaeth MS No.39; which, from the orthography, seems to have been taken from a more ancient MS than that from which this was transcribed: the original of that one at Gloddaeth appears to be a MS at Plâs y Ward, which was there in 1683.—J. Lloyd".[94]

When Gryffydd ab Cynan first landed in Mona (as related in page 37), he sent messengers to the chief men of Môn and Arvon, and amongst the rest to Asser, Meriawn and Gwgan, the sons of Merwydd Gôch of Llŷn. These three gentlemen had taken sanctuary at Celynog, for fear of the men of Powys. Headed by Cynric ab Rhiwallon, they adopted the cause of Gryffydd, acknowledging him their lawful prince, who sent them, and what men they could muster, together with sixty choice warriors, sent him by Robert of Rhyddlan, and eighty men from Môn, to Llŷn, then ravaged by this Cynric, styled "Brenhinin o Bowys", whom they slew. If he claimed any such title, it must be by usurpation, as

---

93 Caernarvon.
94 In the Myvyr Arch. Vol.2, p.583, is another Bugedd Gruffudd ab Cynan, o Hên Lyvr Syr Richard Wyn o Wydr; this being the MS most probably which Mr. Ll. says was in 1683 at Plâs y Ward.

he was not the son of Rhiwallon ab Cynvyn, Prince of Powys, but of Dungad ab Tudyr Trevor, and is in our pedigrees called "Lord of Bromfield", i.e. "Arglwydd Maelor". Indeed the term "Brenhinin" may mean no more than Baron, of which word it is the origin. "Pan ddaeth y Saeson gyntav ir Ynys hon, a chael y Cymru yn galw pob Arglwydd yn Vrenin: Mal, Brenin Gwent; Brenin Morganwg; Brenin Dyved, &c. a wnaethynt air Saesnec iddaw, sef Barwn, a oddi wrth hynny y cawynt nhw ar Cymru y gair Barwn, ac wrth hynny, yr ûn yw Brenin, Brân, a Barwn, yn Cymreig, ac nid iw Dinas Bran, amgen na Dinas y Barwn.—*J. Lloyd*" [95]

William Rufus, to resent the depredations committed by the Cambro-Britons on the borders, entered Wales, invaded Mona, and punished this devoted country with the full force of his vindictive vengeance. After this, it seems to have enjoyed a long period of tranquillity, till the year 1151, when Cadwaladr escaped out of his nephew Howel's prison, and subdued "parte of the Ile of Môn or Angleseye to himselfe"—*Powel Chronicles, p.203.* "Ac ev a ddug rann vawr o'r Ynys Vôn y danaw; eithr Owain ei vrawd wedi clywed hynny, a gynhullawdd lu yn ei erbyn, a chan vyned i Vôn, efe ai gyrrawdd ar ffô, ac a ddug yn ol yr Ynys iddaw ei hun."—*Llyfr Du Dinas Basing.* "Ei vrawd" was the celebrated and puissant Owain Gwynedd, Prince of North Wales, who, hearing of his brother's escape, and the prosperous situation of his affairs, sent (as the Book of Basingwerk says) against him a body of troops, which proving too formidable, that prince was obliged to fly into England, to solicit assistance from the relations of his wife, a daughter of the Earl of Glare, a powerful house. Aided by their interest, his own solicitation and representations, Cadwaladr succeeded in persuading the English king to attempt the subjugation of the land of his fathers. The glory to be acquired, and the importance of the object, with the apparent facility of the enterprise, determined Henry to exert himself, and every means which his power afforded, for the conquest of Wales. But this was happily counteracted by the skill and bravery of Owain Gwynedd, the reigning sovereign, as related in the Black Book of Basingwerk.—

"1151 y duc Harri Vrenin i lu hyd morva Caerllëon ac yno gosod i bebill; ac yn i erbyn yntau y daeth Owen Gwynedd, Tywysog Cymru, ai lu, hyd yn Ninas Basing *(Basingwerk Abbey)*; ac yno mesuro lle castell, a dyrchavel cloddiau mawrion; a gwedi clywed o'r brenin hynny, anvon tywysogion, ierill, a barwniaid, a llu mawr ganthynt, hyd yno; ac yn i herbyn y daeth Davydd ab Owain Gwynedd, ai hymlyd hyd ar draeth Caer, gan eu lladd. A gwedi gweled o'r brenin y lladdva, kynullaw llu a oruc, a myned dan y traeth hyd yn Rhyddlan; ac yno yr aeth Owain Gwynedd i Dal Llwyn Pennant, i vesuro castell, ac o ddyno gwneythyr koddiant yr brenin ai wŷr. Yna y daeth Madoc ab Mredydd, Tywysog Powys, a llawer o lu y brenin gyd se ev, a'r llongau, hyd yn Abermenai y Môn, ac yna ysbeilio eglwys Vair a Phedr, yn Rhosvair; a hynny a ddangoses Duw uddynt drannoeth, pan ddaeth ieunctyd Môn i ymladd ac wynt, ai gyrru ar ffô arnynt, a lladd llawer, a gyrru eraill yw boddi, y llâs Harri vab Harri Brenin, a thywysogion y llongau oll; ac yna yr heddychwyd y rhwng y brenhin ac Owain Tywysog Cymru, ac y cavas Cadwaladr i vrawd i dir", &c.

"In this viage of King Henrie, he was put in greate danger of his life in a strait at Counsyllt, nott far from Flint, where Henry, Earl of Essex, whose office by inheritance, was to beare the standard of England, caste downe the same and fled; whiche thinge encouraged the Welshmen in such sort, that the kinge beinge sore distressed had much adoe to save himselffe (and as the French Chronicler saithe), was faine to fflee, of whose parte Eustace Fitz John and Robert Curcie, two worthie knights, with diverse other noblemen and gentlemen were slaine." Powel in his Chronicles, p.207, who again says, in confirmation of Llyvr Du, that all the strength of Mona set upon the men of Powys and their auxiliaries, when they returned to their ships after spoiling the churches of "Pedr and Mair, at Rhosvair", "so that none of those which robbed within the Ile, broughte tidings how they sped".[96] Considering the triumphant success of his arms, Owen is not justified in concluding a peace with Henry upon terms so dishonourable to himself and to his country; besides restoring Cadwaladr his lands and admitting him to his friendship. By this treaty, as recorded in our Chronicles; Prince Owain and his chieftains submitted to do homage to Henry, &c. The patriotism of the Welsh prince sunk under the influence of a little generosity shewn by the king, in remitting the payment of tribute, claimed by his predecessors, according to the laws of Cadwallon and Howel Dda. The gallant and independent spirit inherited from a long line of ancestors, and which had so eminently and invariably distinguished Owen's conduct in his late rencontre with the invader of his country; all that the terror of Henry's arms, and a series of hostilities could not shake, was now done away, by a few acts of welltimed courtesy. His son, Davydd ab Owen succeeded to the throne, and in 1173, owing to family feuds, he imprisoned all his brothers, excepting Madog and Maelgwyn. To the enterprising spirit of this Madog, we owe the discovery of America.[97] He was the admiral of his father's fleet, a considerable one, since it could face the fleet of Stephen, King of England, and those of the Irish and Scots, at Abermenai, in 1142. Upon the death of Prince Owen Gwynedd, to avoid the dissentions of his brothers respecting the succession to the throne, Madoc set sail with five or six ships from Mona, in 1170 (16th of Henry II), with so prosperous a gale towards the south-west, leaving Ireland on the right, that after some weeks he descried land, and having spent some time in putting matters in order in the country, somewhere about Florida, he returned back to his own country, leaving about 120 men; and being directed by God's providence (the best compass) and the benefit of the polar star, arrived safely at home, where recounting his marvellously successful voyage, fruitfulness of the land, &c. he persuaded his countrymen not to strive with the English, or kill one another, about so barren a country, for that he had found a better, &c. And upon this, about eleven ships went away full of Britons, which were never heard of; therefore the disappearance of this fleet was ranked with the three voyages of Gavran and Merddin in the Triads.—John Lloyd."[98]

96 Powel Chronicles p.203.
97 Columbus discovered America in 1492, about 321 years after the Cambro-Britons had established a colony there. A spirit of enquiry and enterprise is characteristic of this nation. William Penn, when he settled in America, was accompanied by several intelligent and well educated Welshmen, who recognized among the Indians (from their language and custom) a tribe of Madogians residing on the banks of the Missouri.
98 Caerwys MSS. Syr Thomas Herbert's Book of Travels to the East Indies, Smollet's History of England, p.143. Dr. Plott's Account of an Ancient Discovery of America, &c.

To return to my history, Maelgwyn[99] was at large, and kept possession of Mona for three years, against Davydd, who collected all his forces, and again usurped the government of this Island, imprisoning Maelgwyn, who soon escaped and succeeded in giving liberty to his brothers and friends: they dispersed, some, into South Wales, and others into Ireland. This was a most flagrant instance of injustice and rapacity on the part of the prince. Mona being then the property of Roderic ab Owen Gwynedd, who in 1177, broke out of his confinement, and by the help of Gothric, King of Man, "entered Mona",[100] where he was universally received by the people as their sovereign, "a phawb yn ei gyfnerthu, achaws nid oedd a garai Ddavydd ab Owain ei vrawd; a Chadwaladr ab Owain a ddinilles Nant Gonway a Rovoniog; ac a daeth Maelgwyn yn ei ôl or Werddon".[101] "This Roderic ab Owain married a daughter of Gothric, by whose assistance he invaded and recovered Mona."—*J. Lloyd.*

Llowarch, y Prydydd Môch, in a spirited poem, recounting the battles of Rodri,[102] describes his going with his host from Porthaethwy

> " ———— on the steeds of the torrent,
> " Gliding over the raging tumult of the waves ", &c.[103]

Thus Prince David[104] had rendered himself odious by cruelties to his brothers and kinsmen, seizing upon their lands, banishing them, &c. having grown bold in the exercise of tyranny, by his alliance with the English King, Henry II, whose sister Emma he had married. The young Prince Llewelyn,[105] lawful heir to the throne, was at this time entertained in the court of his uncle Roderic in Mona. When arrived at the years of maturity, we find him claiming the principality. Aided by his various accomplishments and popular manners, this claim was allowed, and in 1201, upon the deposition of his uncle David, he was restored to the throne of his ancestors. After having with much dignity settled a peace with England, he had an opportunity of exerting the native vigour of his highly cultivated mind. He convened an assembly of his chieftains, re-edified the laws, &c. and during a long period of an unexampled prosperous reign, brilliant in military career, the tranquillity of the times afforded him leisure to give some attention to the order and interior government of his kingdom and people, by which means, he elevated their minds and multiplied their comforts; he also reestablished the rules of the royal suite, made in 914, consisting, of the following officers and domestics.—

The officers of the household and twelve gentlemen, composed the royal guard, and were

---

99 Maelgwyn a gadwadd Môn Ynys yn ei erbyn dair blynedd, gwedy aeth Tywysog Davydd ai lû cadarn, yn ei erbyn, ac ynnill yr Ynys, ac a garcharawdd Maelgwyn; ac yn ebrwyd wedi hynny, efe a dorres ei garchar, ac a dorres garchar ei genedl ai vrodyr, a ffoi i Vorganwg, rhai o naddynt, ac eraiil i Werddon.—*Lyvr Dinas Basing.*

100 Powel Chronicles p.243.

101 Black Book of Basingwerk Abbey.

102 Rodri lies buried at the College of Caer-Gybi.—*Ibid.*

103 In Vol.2, Myv. Arch. are several Poems celebrating the magnanimity of this Rodri.

104 In 1197, fighting on the side of David, Prince of Wales, in Mona, was slain Robert Fitz Henry, base son to Henry II by the beautiful Nest; she afterwards married Gerald de Windsor, and was mother to Gerald Fitz Gerald, the principal person in reducing the Irish, and by whose assistance, Henry II made a conquest of Ireland; thereupon he had a grant of large possessions in that countrie; he built Wexford, and from him descended four distinct Earls—of Kildare,—Desmond,—Kerry, and Plymouth.—*Holinshead's Conquest of Erin.*

105 Afterwards Llûn the Great. "He was then in the court of Aberffraw".—*Caerwys MS.*

mounted on horses, furnished by the king.

THE MASTER OF THE PALACE was always of the royal blood. When any person of the court fell under the prince's displeasure, this officer protected him till restored to favour. On three festivals in the year he was obliged to deliver the harp into the hands of the domestic bard;—he was also treasurer.

THE DOMESTIC CHAPLAIN was to say grace, read prayers, &c. He was also secretary, and with the judge of the palace and steward of the household, exercised the royal authority in the prince's absence.

THE STEWARD OF THE HOUSEHOLD superintended the inferior domestics. He was the king's taster,—drank, but did not eat at the royal table. He paid the household their wages, and assigned them their proper seats in the hall of the palace.

THE MASTER OF THE HAWKS slept near the birds, and had his bed in the king's granary, where they were kept, and not in the palace, lest they should be injured. He was restricted to a certain measure of metheglyn and ale that he might not neglect his duty. In spring he had the skin of a hind, and in the autumn, that of a stag, for gloves to guard his hands, and thongs for the gesses of his hawks. The eagle, the hawk, the raven, crane, and falcon were considered as royal birds. When any of these were killed without authority, a fine was paid to the prince. If the prince were not in the field when his huntsman killed a royal bird, he rose from his seat, to receive him in the hall, when he returned; if he did not rise, he gave him the garment he then wore.

THE JUDGE OF THE PALACE presided at the principal court of Wales. He always lodged in the hall of the palace. The cushion on which the prince was seated in the day, served for his pillow at night. On his appointment, he received an ivory chess-board from the prince; a gold ring from the princess, and another gold ring from the domestic bard, which he always kept as the insignia of office. When he entered or departed out of the palace, the great gate was opened for him, that his dignity might not be degraded by passing through a wicket. He decided poetical contests, and received from the victorious bard (whom he had rewarded with a silver chain, the badge of poetical pre-eminence) a gold ring, a drinking horn, and a cushion, &c. The person whom the prince designed to make chief judge, was required to reside a whole year in the palace, that he might obtain from the other judges, who resorted hither, from the country, a competent knowledge of his duty and profession. If complaint were made to the prince, that the judge of the palace had pronounced an unjust sentence, and the accusation were proved, he was then for ever deprived of his office, and condemned to lose his tongue, or to pay the usual ransom for that member.

THE MASTER OF THE HORSE.—His lodging was near the royal stables and granary; to him belonged the riding caps, saddles, bridles, and spurs, which the prince had laid aside. The spurs, we are told, were of gold, silver and brass.

THE CHAMBERLAIN was obliged to eat and sleep in the prince's private apartment, which he was appointed to guard. It was his duty to fill and present to the prince his drinking cup, and to keep all his plate, jewels, &c. When the bed, furniture, and wearing apparel were laid aside, they were given to the chamberlain. If a person walking in the royal bed chamber at night, without a light in his hand, happened to be slain, the laws gave no compensation.

THE DOMESTIC BARD was next in rank to the chief bard of Wales. He was obliged at the queen's command, to sing in her own apartment three different pieces of poetry, set to music, but in so low a voice that the court might not be disturbed in the hall. At his appointment he received from the prince (or king) a harp, and a gold ring from the queen. He accompanied the army, and when they prepared for battle, he sung before them an ancient poem, called "Unbeniaeth Prydain", or the "Monarchy of Britain", and for this service was rewarded with the most valuable beast of the plunder.

THE OFFICER TO COMMAND SILENCE.—This he did, first by his voice, and afterwards, by striking with his rod of office a pillar near which the domestic chaplain sat; and to him a fine was due for every disturbance in the court. He was collector of the royal revenues.

THE MASTER OF THE HOUNDS.—He was entertained in the hunting season, together with his servants and dogs, by the tenants who held lands from the prince. On the first day of November he brought his hounds and hunting apparatus for the royal inspection. A little before Christmas he returned to the court, to support his rank, and to enjoy his privileges. His bugle was the horn of an ox, valued at a pound. Whenever his oath was required, he swore by his horn, his hounds and leashes. Early in the morning, before he put on his boots, and *then only* he was liable to be cited to appear before a court of judicature.

THE METHEGLIN, OR MEAD BREWER.—This wine commonly used in Wales, is made with honey and spices, mixed in a vat of boiling water. The wax separated by the process from the honey, was applied to the uses of the hall (which was the refectory) of the palace, and to those of the queen's dining apartment.

THE PHYSICIAN OF THE PALACE.—He was entitled to a bond from the family of his patient, by which he was indemnified, if death ensued from his prescriptions. He was also a surgeon, and attended the army on its march.

THE CUP BEARER had charge of the mead cellar,—he filled and presented the drinking horns.

THE DOOR KEEPER.—His duty was to carry messages to the king and his court. He lodged in the gate-house, and was required to know personally all the officers of the household, that he might not refuse admittance to any of them. He cleared the way before the prince, and with his rod kept off the crowd. He did not sit, but knelt in the royal presence. The door-keeper of the palace and the door-keeper of the royal chamber lodged with him in the gate-house.

THE COOK, to whom belonged all the skins of the animals killed for the use of the kitchen. He always carried the last dish out of the kitchen and placed it before the king.

THE SCONCE BEARER held wax tapers when the prince sat in the hall and carried them before him when he retired to his chamber.

THE STEWARD OF THE QUEEN.—This officer was always her taster: he superintended the domestics, and was entertained at her table.

THE QUEEN'S CHAPLAIN, who was also her secretary, and received a fee for every grant which bore her seal. He was also a guest at her table, sitting opposite to her. He was entitled to the penitential robes, which the queen wore during Lent. He lodged together with the king's chaplain in the sacristan's house.

MASTER OF THE HORSE TO THE QUEEN, was in every respect upon the same footing with the king's officer of the same rank.

QUEEN'S CHAMBERLAIN transacted every business between her and the hall;—kept her wardrobe. His lodging was near the royal chamber.

WOMAN OF THE QUEEN'S CHAMBER, whose office was to sleep near her, so as to be able to hear her speak, though in a whisper. She was entitled to the queen's linen, hair-laces, shoes, bridles, and saddles, when laid aside.

THE DOOR-KEEPER TO THE QUEEN lodged in the gate-house.

THE QUEEN'S COOK.

THE QUEEN'S SCONCE BEARER.

THE GROOM OF THE REIN, who when the master of the horse was absent, supplied his place. He led the king's horse to and from the stables,—brought out his arms,—held his stirrup when he mounted or dismounted, and ran by his side as his page.

OFFICER TO SUPPORT THE PRINCE'S FEET AT BANQUETS.—He was the footstool of his throne, and the guard of his person. There was one in every cantrev.

THE BAILIFF OF THE ROYAL DEMESNE.—He punished the prince's vassals; to him the heriots and amercements were paid. By him the royal household was supplied with provisions.

THE APPARITOR was an officer who stood between the two pillars in the hall, and had the charge of the palace, that it might not suffer any damage from fire, or otherwise. He carried a rod or wand of office. He conveyed summons or citations to the court of justice, and claimed entertainment at every house to which he was sent.

THE GATE-KEEPER claimed by custom, a share of several things carried through the gate to the palace. State prisoners were committed to his custody, and he took care that the fires were lighted in the palace.

THE WATCHMAN OF THE PALACE was a gentleman who guarded the prince's person, while he slept. When the household retired to rest, a horn was sounded, which was a signal to the watchman to go upon duty.

THE WOODMAN procured fuel and slaughtered the cattle.

THE BAKER WOMAN made the bread.

THE PALACE SMITH was obliged to work without a reward for the household, except when he made a boiling-pot; the point of a spear; the woodman's axe.; the iron-work of the palace gate, or royal castle. It was his duty to knock off the shackles of prisoners released by the prince in court of justice and for which he received a fee.

THE LAUNDRESS washed the royal linen.

THE CHIEF OF SONG was chosen and seated in the chair of music, for his superior skill in that science, by the session of the bards. At the end of every third year, when his term was expired, if he maintained his superiority, he was re-chosen. He was lodged in one of the common apartments belonging to the heir apparent. In the hall he sat next to the judge of the palace. When the prince desired to hear music, he sung two poems, one in praise of the Almighty, and the other in honour of princes, and of their exploits. The bards accompanied the songs with the harp, the crwth, and flute.

These were the officers of whom the royal household was composed. They were freeholders by their offices. They received for their wearing apparel, woollen cloth from the prince, and linen from the queen. They were all called together by the palace horn.

We have room to infer that Aberffraw was a favourite residence with Llewelyn and his Princess Joan of England, who was, agreeable to her desire, buried upon the sea-shore at Llanvaes; the prince building over her remains a house of barefoot friars. In 1237, early in the spring, and soon after the death of his princess, Llewelyn's character, which had hitherto appeared with so bright a lustre, shewed symptoms of declining vigour. In a moment of weakness, and perhaps the desire of repose, he put himself under the protection of Henry III King of England, naming his youngest son David (nephew to that ambitious monarch), heir to the principality, when Gryffydd, his son by a former marriage, was still alive, possessing many qualities, which, among a people like the Britons, were held in high estimation, i.e. very brave in war, tall and comely in person, &c. and being the eldest son of Llewelyn, was heir apparent to the crown. Taking advantage of his father's infirmities, David entered his brother Gryffydd's territories, seized him when in company with the Bishop of Bangor, and confined him in the castle of Cricciaeth (Matthew of Westminster, p.118; Holinshead, p.226), a fortress situated on the verge of the sea, in Caernarvonshire. The treatment of this popular prince excited the greatest emotion, and North Wales, for some time was deluged in blood, of the "beste of her people". In this state of affairs died Llewelyn, after a prosperous reign of fifty-six years. His talents and virtues, with the fortunate direction of both, have given this prince the illustrious title of "Llewelyn the Great".

In 1240, within a month of his succession in this year, Davydd ab Llûn now Prince of Wales, having secured the allegiance of his subjects, attended by all his barons, proceeded to Gloucester, where having done homage to the king, his uncle, a peace was ratified, and a general remission also took place of offences, which either party, at any time had committed. (Rymer, pp.389-90). Gryffydd, the real heir of the crown, together with his son Owen, was given up to Henry, who confined them in a tower in London, a conduct full of duplicity and meanness, unworthy of a great monarch, the king ordering a noble a day for his maintenance; Sir John de Lennton having charge of these princes. In this situation, they were not deserted by friends: Gryffydd's faithful adherent, the Bishop of Bangor went up to London, to intercede with the king for his liberty, but humanity and justice "not mingling with Henry's councils", all solicitations made in his favour were unsuccessful. In Mr. Lloyd's MS notes upon Carte's History of England, is the following observation: "Senena, Gryffydd ab Llewelyn's wife offered King Henry 600 marks, and £200 a year, for procuring the release of her husband and son. This Gryffydd was exceedingly beloved, and was not illegitimate, as the author says, but the true heir to the principality.—J. Lloyd". A harder fate awaited him, says the chronicler of Basingwerk Abbey.

"Oed Crist, 1244, yn y vlwyddyn honno y torres Gruffydd ab Llûn i wynwyl wrth ceisio diane dros y Tŵr Gwyn, yn Llundain, o garcher y brenin, ac i canhiadaodd I Hari vrenin, i Abad Aber Conwy ddwyn ei gorff o Lundain i Aber Conwy." Confirmed by Powel, who says, in p.307, "when Prince Gryffydd saw how all things wente, and that he was nott like to be set at libertye, he began to devise waies and meanes to escape outt of prison; therefore deceivinge the watch one night, he made a long line of hangings, coverings, and sheets, and havinge gotten out at a window, he let himselfe downe by the same from the topp of the towre; but by reason that he was a mightie personage, the line brake with the weighte of his bodie, and so fallinge downe headlonge of a great heighte, his necke and head was driven into his bodie with the fall; whose miserable remains beinge found the morrowe after was a pittiful sighte to the beholders." After languishing in the tower two years, thus died this unfortunate prince, the victim of state policy, condemned to be shut up for life in a foreign prison. We must feel emotions of sorrow at the fate of this brave man, who in obedience to the first law of, nature, was killed by attempting to escape. His son Owen and Senena, who had shared his tedious captivity, were witnesses of this melancholy spectacle. This disaster, instead of raising Henry's pity, was a reason with him for treating Prince Owen with greater rigour. He drew aside the veil that concealed his ambitious views, acknowledging Gryffydd as the right heir; and upon his death directly gave to his own son Edward, the title of "Prince of Wales". At this intelligence, David, revolted from his allegiance, alive at last to a sense of shame for the ignominious situation of his country, which he unwittingly placed under the protection of Rome, the most corrupt court in Europe, promising to pay the Pope annually 500 marks; who having received a large sum of money from the Welsh prince, invested the Abbots of Conwy and Cymer with full power to sit as a court of enquiry, summoning Henry to appear before them at Caerwys.[106] He, well acquainted with the venality of the Pontiff, made larger offers, which agreeable to the versatile, avaricious, unprincipled conduct of Rome, turned the scale in favour of the English. Summonses were sent to all the barons, knights and others, throughout the realm. Orders were likewise sent to the justiciary in Ireland, that a diversion should be made from thence on the Isle of Mona; and for that purpose he was to provide "the choicest soldiers"; he was also to furnish the necessary provisions for the army employed in the Welsh expedition. A nation like that of the principality, small in extent, and scattered over a few barren mountains, rises in importance as we view these mighty preparations. It was about the middle of August that Henry entered the confines of Wales, "a holl gadernid Lloegr ac Ewerddon, ar vedr distrywio holl Gymri".[107] Powel calls this host "a huge armye of Englishmen and Gascoignes, intendinge to destroi the countrye". At that time (1245) the Irish had effected a descent on Mona, and had dreadfully ravaged that Island; they were however powerfully assailed by the infuriated inhabitants, when loaded with plunder, and driven back with great slaughter to their ships. Everything was totally destroyed and laid waste, causing great dearth in the country. The people thus injured and reduced to want, by a set of invading barbarians, were prevented recriminating in predatory excursions towards Chester, by the garrison at Diganwy Castle, then being rebuilt; the king strictly forbidding any kind of provisions to be brought into Wales, from any part of England or Ireland, on pain of forfeiting life, lands, and goods. This occasioned great scarcity, not only to the wretched natives, but his own army suffered great distress. "Of this viage", says Powel, p.310, " a certaine noble-

---

106 Caerwys, one of the three places of judgment, is now a decayed town, in Flintshire, and one of the seven contributory boroughs, in sending a member to Parliament. The first item of greefe sent by the men of Tegengl to the Archbishop of Canterbury, in 1280, "That they were spoiled of their righte and privileges and costumes of the countrey, and were compelled to be judged by the laws of England whereas the tenor of that their privilege was to be judged according to the laws of Wales, at Trefedwyn, (in Caerwys parish) at Rhyddlan and Caerwys, &c. and Grono ab Heilyn, they (Robert Crevcoeur and Godfrey Marlieney) called hym ... againe to answere att Caerwys, but hee durst not go thither, but by the conduct of the Bishop of St. Asaph, ffor that Reginald Grey was there with his men in harness."
107 Llyvr Dines Basing; Carte's History, vol.2, p.82; Rymer, p.432, 433; Matthew Paris, p.599; Welsh Chronicles, p.310, &c.

man, beinge then in kinge's campe, wrote to his friende, about the ende of September, 1245. The kinge with his armye lyeth att Gannoc, fortifyinge of thatt strong castle (Matthew Paris, p.924), and we lie in our tents thereby, watching, fastinge, praying, and friezinge with cold. We watch for fear of the Welshmen, who are wonte to invade, and come upon us in the nighte tyme. Wee faste ffor want of meate, for the halvepenny loaffe is worth ffive pence. Wee praie to God to sende us home againe speedilie; we starve for colde, wantinge oure winter garments, and havinge no more than a thin linen clothe betwixte us and the winde", &c. Things were in this situation, when the rage of contending parties, was for a time suspended.

In the spring of the year 1246, in the month of March, Prince David ab Llewelyn, sinking under the weight of sorrow, broken in spirit, and lamented by his subjects, died at his palace of Aber. He was buried (observes the chronicler of Basingwerk Abbey) in great magnificence, with his father, at Aber Conwy; "ai gladdu yn anrhydeddus iawn gyda ei dad, yn Aber Conwy". (Llyvr Dinas Basing.)

In this season of common calamity, the Welsh nobility immediately elected his nephew, the last prince Llewelyn ab Gryffydd to succeed; giving him the strongest assurance of perpetual allegiance. The justice he did to the appointment, displayed itself in the noble stand he made in defence of the liberty of his country. The firmness of his mind, when betrayed by one in whom treachery was hereditary, dignified him in the eyes of his enemies; and extorting their respect, when bereaved of all but Snowdon, he spoke the language of a freeborn soul, to him who tyrannized over the dominions of his ancestors. "Llewelyn was with Henry (when he had been for some months in London) and upon hearing the news of his election to the principality, he stole privately away."—From the Sebright papers; which also informs us that, "in 1251, an arbitrary grant of lands from Chester to Conwy, not within his realm or jurisdiction, was given by Henry III as an appendage to his son, and made to appertain to the sword and dignity of Chester", of which place he was earl: Prince Edward farmed it "to Alan de la Zouche, an English baron, for 100 marks". Oppressed by the hated laws of England, the natives at this time, had neither opportunity nor spirit to carry on commerce, nor to cultivate their lands; for by this grant they were deprived of the usual pasturage for their cattle, and in consequence, were perishing by famine. It was not in the nature of Llewelyn, when the dearest concerns of his people were mingled with his own, to remain inactive, or unmoved by their repeated solicitations, to attempt once more to throw off the English yoke. In the most solemn manner, and with an affecting, though manly spirit, they declared that they would rather die on the field, in defence of their natural rights, than be subject any longer to so cruel and oppressive an enemy. Virtue, necessity, and despair, determined Llewelyn to rescue his country from its vile dependence on England, or bravely perish amidst the ruins of its freedom. Accordingly in 1255 on the feast of St. Kenelm, hearing that Prince Edward was examining his father's castles in North Wales[108], which he justly thought foreboded no good; Llewelyn, by a rapid and decisive movement, recovered the inland parts of his territories, and in 1257 we find him at the head of 60,000 men, equipt in all points, and armed agreeably to the cus-

---

108 "Oed Crist, 1255, y doeth Edwart (vab Harri) Iarll Caerlleon, i edrych cestyll Yngwynedd; ag Awst nesa ar ol hynny, y daeth Twysogion Cymru I gwyno att Llewelyn ab Gryffydd i halldudo o'r Saeson, a dywedyd wrtho, vod yn well ganddynt veirw yn y rhyvel na dioddev i sathru gan estronion drwg gaethiwedig", &c.—*Llyvr Du Basing.*

tom of the country, attended by a squadron of 500 horsemen, "elegantly appointed, and entirely covered with armour". With this formidable force the Welsh Prince laid waste, all the frontier on each side of the river Dee to the gates of Chester. Edward, said to be an eyewitness of the glorious appearance of his rival in fame, unable to resist the impetuosity of this army, retreated into England. The English king at this time, became entangled in dispute with his subjects; a fortunate event to the Prince of Wales, who resolved to take every advantage of the present conjuncture; for the chance of war at the battle of Lewys, had thrown the king and his son into the hands of the potent Earl of Leicester, who in 1264, met Prince Llewelyn at Hawarden castle, where they established a peace between the two countries, in order to promote their respective designs. The prince demanded a full restitution to the inheritance and dignity of his ancestors—the sovereignty of Wales, &c. under the sanction of the king's name.—All that Llewelyn required was restored to him. To strengthen the union, and to render it more lasting, the Earl of Leicester made an offer of his daughter, Ellen de Montford, then educating in the French court, to Llewelyn, an alliance which coincided too well with his present views, to be refused by the Prince. A victory soon after, gained by Prince Edward, at the battle of Evesham, gave liberty to Henry, who now had leisure to look back on the part acted by the Prince of Wales, and was determined therefore that he should feel the whole weight of his resentment, before the army was disbanded. Llewelyn, without an ally to support him, thought it more prudent to appease Henry[109] by an early submission than to encounter him in the field. A treaty in consequence took place, by the mediation of Ottobani, the legate; and I learn from the Caerwys MSS that the £32,000,[110] stipulated to be paid by Prince Llewelyn to Henry III were not solely for purchasing peace,[111] but for the confirmation of his ancient right to the castles in the cantrev of Ellesmere, the castles of Hawarden, Montgomery, Whittington, the cantrevi of Rhos, Rhyvoniog, Dyffryn Clwyd, and Tegengl, besides the homage of all the inhabitants. The following relates to the ceded cantreds;— "vol.6, Sebright MS a thick 4to. containing charters, inquisitions, and a variety of other things. Page 263 contains the articles of agreement between Henry III and Owen, and Llewelyn, our last prince. It is observable, that as well in these articles, as in some other instruments of the like kind, where the two princes were concerned, I always find the name of Owen before that of Llewelyn; from hence and from an ancient poem, that I have quoted upon the same occasion, I have no room to doubt, but that Owen was the eldest brother, &c. By these articles, the two brothers cede to the king and his heirs for ever, the cantrev of Rhôs, Ryvoniog, Dyffryn Clwyd, and Englefield, all the river of Cunewy, and the country of Montalti. The king confirms to Owen and Llewelyn all the rest of the principality; but upon condition of their supplying him, at their own expence, with one

---

109 "Henry III was so noted for his charities, that Llewelyn, Prince of Wales was wonte to say, that he more dreaded the power of his alms, than all his forces and clergy together."—*Echard*, p.126.

110 Llewelyn, Prince of Wales, who had greatly supported Earl Montford's rebellion, for £32,000 was restored to four cantreds, which the king had taken from him in the war and fully reconciled."—*Ibid.* p.125.

111 "It appeareth by the recordes in the Towre, that about thys time, to wit 43 Henry III, there was a commission to William, Bishop of Worcester; John Mansel, Treasurer of Yorke; The King's Chaplaine, and Peter de Montfort, to conclude a peace with the Welsh Prince. *Math. Paris, p.*284. "I reade also in the same author, that the Bishop of Bangor was this yeare, about Michaelmass, sente from Llewelyn the Prince, and all the Barons of Wales, to the Kinge, to desire peace, and to offer him the summe of £16,000." &c.—*Welsh Chronicles,* p.325.

hundred foot and twenty-four horse, while he was employed in any wars in the marches; and in his wars in England, they engaged to supply him with five hundred foot soldiers, well armed, &c. N.B. This reward is not complete in the original, owing it seems, to the devastation of time, and what is still remarkable, that though the names of the two eldest brothers are often repeated, the name of the other brother Davydd, does not once occur." [112] Most probably this was the truce of 1264 which lasted only one year.—Page 396, 4th vol. Sebright Collection, "yn y Tŵr". Ex bundello Literarii de Anno 48 Henry III in Turr. London. (Tŵr Llundain.)

This page and the following contain four letters from the last Prince of Wales to Henry III complaining of the breach of a truce then subsisting between them by some of the lords marchers, and others. The first sets forth that a day being fixed to settle the damages and to make satisfaction for the same, between him and the justiciary, [113] with other barons, and the sons Dñi, &c. laid waste his lands, and those of Gryffydd de Maelor, &c.

Dñi Estranei plures incursiones ā insultus fecerunt in terras dilci ā fidelis, nri Dñi Grifini de Bromfeld, villas comburendo predas diripiendo homines quosdam occidendo quosdam capidendo. Et nunc ultimo die lun ꝑbook of chartsxima post festum v̄i Māth apli cū dies ille essct constitus ad heñdum ꝑliamentū inter nos exuna ꝑte et dim̄ Justū ex altera hominibus nr̄is, et hominibus dc̄i Griff. congregatis ad dc̄m ꝑliam̄entū dc̄us Justic cum sua sequela magnam predam in alia pr̄e terre dc̄i Griffin. cepit ā abegit, &c. &c. Here we may see how unjustly this justice, whom I take to be Reginald de Grey, acted.

The second letter sets forth, that a day was fixed to meet "apud vadu mangūr" to adjust damages on each side between the king and prince.—The latter solicits the king to prolong the day till after the then Easter, as it was impossible for him, on account of the shortness of the time, to be at Montgomery, and bring with him the persons necessary for such a negotiation, by the day already fixed, &c. and he further desires the king to fix upon the "Album Monasterium" for the place of treaty, and requires him to prohibit the marchers and others, from molesting him and his subjects in the mean time, &c.

The third, chiefly complains of Roger Mortimer, and Humphrey de Bohan, for seizing one of the prince's castles, and refusing to give it up, until he compelled them by a siege, &c. The fourth contains a like complaint against the barons of Leicestershire, Staffordshire and Salop, and the Bailiff of Montgomery, whose bailiwick, the prince declares he would have destroyed to the very walls of the castle, if the great respect he had for Henry had not prevented it.—*J. Ll.* The prince writes with great moderation and firmness, insisting that the truce had never been infringed on his part, but that it was continually so on the part of the kings, barons, and the marchers. In all his letters, he desires his highness to interfere, and put a stop to these outrages. The spirit of a free constitution, in restraining the will of an arbitrary monarch, runs through the whole of these interesting letters; in one of which the prince says that he is unacquainted with the language, the laws, and the manners of England.

112 Caerwys MS.
113 Reginald de Grey, mentioned in a note to p.47.

It does not appear what answer Llewelyn received to this manly and just remonstrance; I suppose not of a satisfactory nature. Soon after this, we find the noblemen of Moldsale making similar complaints againste Roger de Montalto, the king's lieutenant, and his deputy, Roger Scroghil, for their rapacity and unjuste exaction of talliage, &c. Princes may be taught the danger of tearing up by the roots those habits that are grown venerable by time, and that by long usage are become dear to a people. For some years, the natives, dispirited and inactive, had lost, with their freedom, every trace of their national character till the demon of discord, rousing their spirit and reviving their genius, called at once into action, all their energy of character.

Early in the year of 1276, Ellen de Montford, who was cousin to the king of England, and the affianced wife of Llewelyn, was "sente by her mother, the Countess of Lecester,[114] who remayned att a nunnerie at Montargis in France, intoe Wales, to marrie the prince, as it was agreed betwixte them in her father's tyme, &c., and with her came her brother Almeric, and a goodlie companie, who fearing the coast of England, kepte theire course to Iles of Sylle, where they were taken by four ships from Bristowe, and brought to the king, who entertained the ladie honorablie, sendinge her brother to be kepte prisoner in Corffe Castel," &c. In this part of Edward's character we see no traces of heroism, no resemblance of the courteous manners which distinguished the better period of the feudal age, when kings were noted for such sayings as, "If faith and truth should be banished the rest of the world, yet ought they to be found in the mouths of sovereigns."

It is only to personal dislike we are able to attribute the insult which was offered to Llewelyn in detaining the Lady Ellen de Montford, in the English court. After so decisive a conduct, lenient measures, and the arts of expediency, were delusive, and of no avail: Llewelyn resorted to arms, and ravaged the English borders, resenting the conduct of Edward, and alive to the feelings of an injured prince, deeply wounded by the captivity of his expected bride.

In Midsummer we find, by the Black Book of Basingwerk, Edward, at the head of a formidable army, had arrived at Chester, intending to penetrate into the heart of Wales. During this time he rebuilt his castles of Flint and Rhyddlan, &c. The English advanced through the level part of the country as far as Conwy, landing some forces in Mona. With a fatality which had usually attended the princes of his house, Llewelyn had trusted the safety of Wales to the chance of war. A powerful enemy, pressing by slow degrees, and decisive in their operations, became masters of the country below Snowdon, to which he had retired, waiting the result of Edward's seeming determination of starving him into submission. A magnanimous prince like Llewelyn, the freedom of his country being lost, would scarcely have wished to survive its ruin, if the sufferings of his people—crowding round him, and perishing by famine, had not inclined him to hazard his personal safety and interest, from a tender regard to theirs. In this state of affairs the Prince of Wales sent to propose accommodation with the English king. There was little generosity to be expected in terms offered by Edward: of this transaction, Holinshead and Echard give the following statement.—

114 Powel Chronicles p.332.

"Prince Llewelyn finding himself unable to resist so potent an adversary, desired peace, which was granted him upon very hard conditions; the principal of which shews the Welsh to have had greater riches in possession at this time than after-ages would believe: for one article was that Llewelyn should pay £50,000 at the king's pleasure; and another, that he should hold the Isle of Anglesey in fee farm of the king, for himself, and his heirs, upon the payment of 5,000 marks ready money, and 1,000 marks annual rent", &c.[115] This treaty, observes Mr. Lloyd, was concluded at Aberconwy, and must have taken place in the month of November, by this entry in the Chronicle of Basingwerk.—"Oed Crist, 1277, 7d Octobris i llosgi Môn gan llu Llewelyn; a'r 19eg o vis Novembris, heddwch rhwng Llewelyn a'r brenhin, a'r tywysoc aeth I Lundain i gadw i wiliau;—rhyddhau Owen Gôch, brawd Llewelyn, ac Owen ab Gryffydd Wenwynwyn gan y brenhin; ac Owen Gôch a gavodd Gantrev Llŷn gan ei vrawd Llewelyn y tywysoc." Carte has recorded the following anecdote on this occasion.—"The barons of Snowdon, and other noblemen of the most considerable families in Wales, had attended Prince Llewelyn to London, when he went thither in the Christmas of 1277, bringinge according to custom used, large retinues with them. They were quartered in Islington, and the neighbouring villages. These places did not afford milk, for such numerous trains. They liked neither the wines, nor the ale of London, and though plentifully entertained, were much displeased at a new manner of living, which did not suit their taste, nor perhaps their constitutions." They were still more offended at the crowds of people that flocked about them, when they stirred abroad, "staring and laughing at their garb, appearance, and language". They were so enraged on this occasion, that they engaged privately in an association, to rebel on the first opportunity, and resolved to die in their own country, rather than ever come again to London, to be held in such derision. They communicated their resentments to their compatriots, who made it the common cause of their country.

The year following, 1278, was celebrated at Worcester, the marriage "betwixte Elen de Montford and Prince Llewelyn; when the kinge, the queene, and the moste part of the nobilitie of England were presente". In a style of simplicity, that carries persuasion to the heart, Prince Llewelyn details, in his Eighth Item of Greefe, how the king had taken advantage of his situation: "when he invited the prince to his feaste, at Worcester, with everie faire words, that he shoulde have his kinswoman to him to wife, and enriche him with much honor; neverthelesse, when he came thither, the selfe same daye theye shoulde be married before masse, the kinge required a bill to be sealed by the prince, conteininge amonge other thinges, that he never would keep man againste the king's will, nor never maintaine any, whereby it mighte come to passe, that the prince's force shoulde be called from him. The whiche letter he delivered the kinge by juste feare, whiche mighte move anie constante man, whereas the kinge was not to require anie thinge that was not conteined in the peace."[116] As soon as the ceremony was over, the king remitted the payment of the £50,000.—*J. Lloyd.* Out of the Sebright Papers.

Llewelyn with his princess returned into Wales, to soothe the asperity of adverse fortunes, in the enjoyment of private felicity, but her death in 1280, loosened the only tie of union subsisting between

115 Echard's History; p.128. Holinshead p.278.
116 Welsh Chronicles p.348.

the two nations. The calamities of a public nature, which then surrounded Llewelyn, were rendered more poignant in this domestic affliction. The mild influence of Ellen de Montford had been hitherto the means of preventing hostilities, by restraining the angry spirit of these princes. The Chronicler of Basingwerk relates the cause of the princess's death. "Oed Crist, 1280;—ag o Elinor y dywsoges bu verch a elwid Gwenllian; ag yn escor y verch honno, y bu varw y dywsoges, ac y claddwyd yn anrhydeddus iawn, y mynachlog y brodyr yn Llanvaes y Môn; ar Wenllion honno wedi marw i thâd, a ddycpwyd i Loegr, ai rhoi oi hanvod yn vynaches." Most probably this princess died at Aberffraw, and consequently was, as the Black Book records, buried at Llanvaes.

We have seen in the preceding pages, the Cambro-Britons subject to the most distant extremes of fortune; a people, proud and irascible, who though vanquished, were still alive to injury and insult, to a sense of their own valour, and to the fond idea of their native independence. What efforts then might not be expected from this brave people, who were bred on their own mountains, the indigenous children of freedom, to protect those mountains, and to preserve that freedom. "My pen" writes Giraldus, in 1188 "shrinks with abhorrence from the relation of the vengeance exercised by those hordes of barbarian invaders, against this once happy race, compelling by force the owners to give up their lands"; &c. and this is termed *conquest*, by the English historians. Our annals, in rapid succession, are marked with striking vicissitudes, and as the renown of the North Wales Dynasty began, so it ended in Mona.

The era now is at no great distance, which is to mark the close of the Cambrian Monarchy, which for more than 800 years, had resisted the utmost efforts of the Saxon and Norman Princes.

The Cambro-Britons, in the lately ceded cantrevi, early began to taste, in the conduct of their new masters, the bitter fruits of the English government. Edward had thrown his portion into districts; appointed sheriffs, and sent judges, who had the temerity to summon Llewelyn before them, at Montgomery, to attend the issue of a trial, pending between him and Gryfydd ab Gwenwynwyn, respecting some lands held of the king, which highly exasperated the prince. The idea of this demand being in future drawn into a precedent, awakened, at last, Davydd ab Gryffydd to a sense of his own situation, as heir male to the principality, added to the insult which he had recently received, by being sued for the village and castle of Hope, by William de Venables. The Welsh chieftains besought him to be reconciled to his brother Llewellyn, calling on him by every incitement, which could act on a brave, or angry spirit, to desert the cause of a merciless ravager. This appeal was not made in vain, and to retrieve the honour he had lost, by having so shamefully betrayed his country, he was the first found at his post, shielding her in the hour of danger. A plan being made for a general insurrection, Davydd opened the campaign by a gallant exploit, performed late in the evening of Palm Sunday. "1281[117] y gorescynodd ev gastell Pen yr Halawg, &c. Yn y nos, &c" which was dark and stormy, he took by surprise, the castle of Hawarden, the key of North Wales, the governor of which, Robert de Clifford, justiciary of Chester, was taken in his bed, mortally wounded, and carried away to Snowdon. Several knights residing in the fortress, were put to the sword, in the fury of the attack; among them was Fulke Trigald, who appears to have been a great favourite with King Edward, for he afterwards condemned Prince David

---

117 Llyvr Basing.

to be hanged for having murdered Fulke Trigald.[118] Wearied with reiterated acts of oppression, we cannot wonder, that a spirit of patriotism, once more animated every bosom, no longer able to bear the yoke, imposed upon them by the English. Numerous parties of natives, fired with enthusiasm, burst upon the marches, ravaging the country as they spread along. Animated with the same feeling, Llewelyn poured upon the terrified borderers, a full measure of retaliative justice. "Y torres Llewelyn Tywysoc ar Brenin Duwsul y Blodeu, 1281; ar cynhaiav gwedi y daeth y Brenin i Rhyddlan, a anvon llynges i Môn, dan Howel[119] ab Gryffydd ab Ednyved Vân, ai gorchymyn oll."[120] When men meet and deliberate with a resolution to revolt, decisive conduct should then take place of feeble and temporising measures. Llewelyn and Davydd having joined their forces, invested the newly repaired castles of Flint and Rhyddlan, the only fortresses then in the possession of the English.[121]

The bold step taken by these princes determined the conduct of the King of England; he once more resolved to make an entire subjugation of the Principality;—all other concerns were laid aside;—the credit of Edward was staked;—his talents, and the military strength of his kingdom were rendered subservient to this great design. In the mean time, he sent part of his forces to the relief of the besieged castles, and appointed all his knights and their tenants by service, to meet him at the castle of Rhyddlan, which had been regarrisoned. In July, 1281,[122] we find him issuing orders to the sheriffs of the neighbouring counties, to send him, in proportion to the extent of each, a number of hatchet men, who were to cut down woods, and open passages for his army, &c. On the approach of Edward, the princes retreated slowly towards Snowdon. The retreat of Llewelyn, for the present, was of little advantage to the enemy; like that of a lion, it was slow and full of danger. It is with pity and admiration, we see a band of heroes and patriots, stationed on the only mountain that was left them, sending to their oppressive invader, memorials of their griefs,[123] ending in these emphatic words; "ffor whiche greefes, we believe ourselves free before God, from the oath whiche wee have made to the kinge". Thus calmly and with firmness, asserting their rights, and making their last struggle for freedom. "The archbishop, John Langley, to whom these "greefes" are addressed went in person to the prince, to Snowdon, that he might move him and his brother David, to submit themselves, together with the other companye", &c.[124] The Prince of Wales answered, "that he was readie to yeelde to the kinge, reserving two rights; that is to say, hys conscience, whiche he oughte to have the rule of, for the safeguard of his people, and alsoe the decency of his callinge", &c. at which the king said, " that he woulde not anie other treatie of peace, than that the prince and his people, should simplye submit themselves"; whereupon the archbishop besoughte the kinge againe, that the Welsh princes might have free access to his grace, to de-

---

118 Caerwys MS.

119 Howel was knighted by Edward, and for acting the part of a traitor, had Henglawdd bestowed on him. His daughter Catheine was married to Syr P. Dutton, and she was mother to Syr Piers Dutton.—*Hengwrt and Wynnstay MSS.*

120 Basingwerk Chronicle.

121 Henry de Knighton, de event. Angl. 2464.

122 Guthrie's Hist. VI. 1, p.895. J. Rossi p.165. Welsh Chronicles, p.338, 340. Annales Waverleinsis, p.235.

123 Welsh Chronicles p.360.

124 It was proposed in secret to the Prince of Wales, that he should throw himself upon the mercy of Edward; resigning the Principality, &c. and in return, £1,000 a year, with an English county, besides providing for his daughter, suitable to her rank and station, were offered him in compensation.—*Welsh Chronicles, p.365.*

clare theire greefes. The kinge answered, "they shoulde freely com and departe, if it should seeme that by justice, they deserved to departe",[125] &c. Llewelyn's answer to this dark and evasive promise of safe conduct, is worthy of that great and magnanimous prince:—"That as the guardian of his people's safety, his conscience alone should direct his submission, nor would he consent to any compliance, which mighte derogate from the dignity of his station", &c. In this critical situation, the caution of the Welsh prince was justified on the principle of expediency, as well as self-preservation. The treaty being ended, and Edward not able to bring the enemy to action, he ordered a strong detachment of marines, and other forces, in the vessels of the cinque ports, to take possession of Mona. The manoeuvre was wisely planned; the success of which, would not only deprive the Welsh of the advantage of this Island, as a source of provisions, but would also confine them within the range of Snowdon. This service was effected; the Island was easily taken, Howel being in command of part of the fleet, the chief persons there (his connections) siding with Edward, agreeably to the oaths they had taken, when in London, at the last peace.[126] With a view of getting possession of part of Caernarvonshire, to form a junction with the other part of the army, preparation was made at a point of land, nearly opposite Bangor called "Moel y Don", where the water is much narrower than in any other part of the straits:—"ac yno gwneythyr pont ar Venai, a thorri a wnaeth, a boddi aneiriv o'r Saeson,[127] a Howel ab Gryffydd oedd yno o'r blaen, gwedi goresgynu Môn oll dan y lynges; ac wynt a vynesynt oresgyn Arvon, ac wneythynt bont o ysgraffau, ai gosod ar Venai, a phan dorres honno gan y ffrwd a llanaw, y boddes aneiriv o'r Saeson. Ac amser hwnnw y gwnaethpwyd brâd y Tywysog Llewelyn, ynglochdu Bangor, gan ei wyr ehan; canys yr amser hwnnw y gydewes Llewelyn, Davydd ei vrawd i gadw Gwynedd, ac yntau aeth ai lu i orescyn Buellt."[128]

As soon as the natives saw the design of the English, they raised entrenchments on their side of the river, to check the enemy's advance, and to secure a retreat to the mountains. Some Gascon lords; with some spanish troops then in the service of Edward, despising them for the easy conquest of Mona, and fancying that Caernarvonshire would have made no greater resistance, passed over the Menai at low water, to examine the works then erecting. Riscart Walwyn, who commanded this post, knowing that the tide would soon flow, kept quiet within his entrenchment, neither opposing their passage or advance into the country; but as soon as the Menai began to rise, the Welsh rushed down the mountains, assaulted the invaders with loud outcries, and drove them into the water, in which they were drowned, encumbered with the weight of armour. Fifteen knights, thirty-two squires, and one thousand soldiers were slain or drowned.[129] Among others who fell this day, were Lucas de Tang, leader of the foreigners; William de Dodingeseles, and William de la Zouche. Lord Latimer, who com-

---

125 Welsh Chronicles, p.371. These Memorials were taken from the Records of John Peckham, Archbishop of Canterbury, who was Edward's ambassador on this occasion, ending in this observation, made by David Powel. "Thus farre out of the Records of John Peckham, Archbishop of Canterbury, written about three hundred yeares agoe, whiche are extante att this daie to be seene.—*David Powel.*"

126 John Rossi, p.165. Chron. T. Wyke, p.110. Holinshead, p.281. Polyd. Virgil, p.323.

127 Llyvr Du Dinas Basing.

128 Ibid.

129 Welsh Chronicles, p.372. Holinshead, p.281. Annales Waver, p.535. Polyd. Virgil, p.324. Hen. de Knighton, 2464. Carte, vol.1, p.193.

manded the English, had the good fortune to regain the bridge by the stoutness of his horse. This bridge was constructed "soe that three-score men could well pass over in a fronte; itt was made of boates and planks, and put where the land is narroweste, and the place is called Moel y Donn, where before Julius Agricola did the like, when he subdued the Ile of Môn; and nott betwixte Man and Brytayne, as Polydore Virgil ignorantlye affirmeth."[130]

Edward set out from Rhyddlan about the 6th of November, 1282, threatening to extirpate the whole nation; and arriving at Conwy, he heard of the defeat of a part of his army. This disaster was a severe check to the views of Edward, whose situation was now become dangerous and humiliating. In this state of things, unable to advance, he returned back to Rhyddlan; and from that place, on the 21st of November, he issued out summonses to the sheriffs of England, to send all who were able and fit to bear arms, to assist in repressing the "rebellion of Llewelyn ab Gryffydd and other Welshmen his accomplices".[131] Such was the colour he gave to his lawless invasion of another's territory. But an event happened soon after, sudden and unforeseen, which closed with glory the life of Llewelyn, and decided the fate of this country. The prince[132] was betrayed, and fell by the sword of Adam de Francton:—"Ai ladd, a llawer oi lu, dydd gwyl Damasens y Pab, yr unved-ar-ddeg o vis Rhagfyr, Duw-gwener; ac yna bwriwyd holl Gymru i lawr." This was at Buellt, where he had appointed Roger Mortimer to meet him.

This base act of Edward needs no comment.[133] In the elevation of our moral thinking, Llewelyn must rise superior to his rival in arms, and his uncompromising character and fame will survive future ages.

"Oer galon dan vron o vraw—allwynin,
"Am Vrenin Dewin Dôr Aberffraw."

Thus died Llewelyn ab Gryffydd, after a reign of thirty-six years; leaving two daughters. The eldest was confined in a nunnery, much against her inclination, "oi hanvodd"[134] by the order of Edward, who wrote seven years after the death of her father, to Thomas de Normanville, to enquire minutely into the state and safe conduct of this princess. Owen Glyndwr claimed descent from the youngest. Gratitude could pay no tribute to the memory of Llewelyn, so expressive as the tears which his country shed upon the tomb of this fallen prince.

We are told by the English historian, that Edward received his head "joyfullye" from the hands of Lord Edward Mortimer, at Rhyddlan, where the king was then lodged, "whoe sente itt into London, appointing thatt theire shoulde be an ivy crowne sett upon itt, in token that he was a prince".[135] His

---

130 Welsh Chronicles, p.372.
131 Rymer, vol.2. p.429.
132 The Black Book of Basingwerk Abbey.
133 One Madoc Min, then Bishop of Bangor, is said to have betrayed Prince Llewelyn's plans, at Buellt. This treason was got up in the belfry of Bangor cathedral.—*D. Jones's MS.*
    A deed, dated at Kenilworth 3rd of January (no year specified), mentions the name of a sister of our last Prince Llewelyn, and how the conqueror took possession of her lands in Llŷn: as they are mentioned to have *fallen* into his hands upon *her death.* I am afraid she had not fair play for her life.—*J Lloyd, Caerwys MS.*
134 Black Book of Basingwerk Abbey.
135 Holinshead, p.281.

bereaved subjects, confounded and in dismay, fled on every side, and were slaughtered without mercy. One victim remained to feel the weight of Edward's severest vengeance. Prince David, all this time, in possession of the castles and strong-holds of the country, had kept within his posts, regarding himself however as the Sovereign of North Wales. On the death of his brother, he summoned the chieftains, to hold a consultation on public affairs, and seemed fully determined to vindicate his rights. Before they had time to emerge out of the state of insensibility, into which they had been thrown by the death of Llewelyn, the king ordered his forces to make a further advance, and to beset them more closely on every side. His own army invested Snowdon, on the side of Conwy. His troops in Mona, not having hitherto dared to make good their passage over the Menai, had now leisure to finish the bridge, and to penetrate the country on the side of Caernarvon. The people who inhabited Snowdon mountains, were now entirely surrounded by this immense body of troops. In this state of consternation, all union was dissolved, by the death of the late prince, who was the central spring that had kept them together and had given energy and force to all their plans of emancipation. In the present situation of Prince David, it became an easy matter for Edward to corrupt some of his retainers; these are supposed to have been Einion ab Ivor, and Grono ab Davydd y Penwyn, of Melai, who in the night of the 21st of June, 1282, surprised[136] the prince and his family, in a morass, into which they had fled for security. Himself, his wife, two sons, and seven daughters, were brought prisoners to Rhyddlan Castle. When Prince Davydd was taken, a relic was found on him, called "Croes Enych", held in superstitious veneration by the Princes of Wales, which was delivered to the king by the above named chiefs, together with the crown of the celebrated Arthur, and many other articles of curiosity and value, consisting of precious jewels, &c.[137]

When at Rhyddlan, the prince repeatedly petitioned that he might be admitted into the king's presence, but this indulgence was denied him. Inflexible in the design he meditated, Edward refused his solicitations; not choosing perhaps, that his firmness should be put to the test, which the recollection of former intercourse might have softened. He was tried as a peer and subject of England. A feeling of interest influenced the judges decision, and silenced the claims of humanity and justice. We will pass over the barbarous and horrible death which this prince, the last of a brave and honourable line, was doomed to suffer. With him closed the only sovereignty, which remained of the ancient British empire;—an empire which had withstood the arms of imperial Rome. The fall of this people, as an independent nation, who had been forced into a long and unequal contest, in defence of their rights, with no other resources than valour, and a fond attachment to their mountains and liberties, will be entitled to a tribute of admiration and esteem, as long as manly sentiment and the love of freedom shall remain.

136 "Am un bunt ar bymtheg,
    "Ag again o wartheg,
    "Gwerthodd y Penwyn Davydd Deg."—*Hen Ddywediad Rûg MS.*
      "For thirty marcs and twenty head of kyne,
      "A prince descended from the royal line,
      "Was, sold by Penwyn base."
137 J. Rossi. Ant. Warw. p.202. Rymer, vol.2, p.247. J. Rossi, p.166 Annaleiensis p.338. T. Wyke, p.111.
    In an account of the Parish of Rhosvair, there is given a list of the remainder of the regalia.

Edward having finished the affairs of North Wales, to gratify a martial nobility, he, in 1283, ordered a tournament to be held at Nevyn, Caernarvonshire; and on the 2nd of January, he issued a writ from thence, of a conciliatory nature, by which the inhabitants of Rhyddlan, Conwy, Caernarvon, and other towns, were freed from talliages for ever.[138] And to secure the obedience of his newly subdued country, and to fix its government on a solid bases of equal laws, Edward took up his residence at Rhyddlan, where we find him in 1284, instituting a body of laws, under the title of "The Statute of Rhyddlan"; from hence he issued a proclamation, assuring the inhabitants that they should enjoy their lands and properties, and hold them under such tenures, as they had done heretofore under their native princes; the king reserving to himself the same duties and services, which had always belonged to the princes of Wales. "The rents paid by the Monenses, were much reduced; they had yielded 1,000 marks annually to Llewelyn, but only paid afterwards £450 to the king of England. Edward reserved to himself the seventh part of all the lead mines, with a promise to buy as much as he should want of the remaining six parts, towards his works."—Out of the Sebright Papers.

At this castle of Rhyddlan, in April the same year (1284), Edward acted the farce of giving to the natives a Prince[139] "born in their own country, who could not speak a word of English, and whose life was free from stain", &c. The Welsh nobles, who were then surrounding Edward (having been summoned for the purpose), eagerly assented to acknowledge such a person for their sovereign. Their surprise and disappointment, may be imagined, when the King exclaimed "eich dyn", at the same time presenting to them, his son, lately born at Caernarvon. On the treachery and chicanery, which was shewn in this transaction, the reader will draw his own conclusions. But the natives have ever since been faithful to the oath of obedience, into which their unsuspecting ancestors were thus cajoled. We see them fighting[140] with their wonted bravery, under the banner of a Prince of Wales, whose brow was wreathed by the fatal words that first betrayed them, still clinging to, and animated by the fond name on which memory loved to dwell, and following up by deeds of valour, the manly declaration of Syr David Gam, at Agincourt, who with a party of valiant Welshmen, having been sent to review the strength of the enemy, made this gallant report to his royal master: "There are enow to be killed, enow to be taken prisoners, and enow to run away."[141]

An insurrection by Madoc, the illegitimate son of Prince Llewelyn, with the revolt of Syr Griffith Llwyd,[142] in 1322, and the rising of Owen Glyndwr, were the last efforts which the Cambrians made to recover the freedom they had lost. This Madoc was a brave man, and to his naturally well-endowed mind, is said to have been joined very extensive views, and a very aspiring ambition. Some events

---

138 Sebright Collection, p.603, vol.7. Caerwys MSS.

139 Welsh Chronicles p.377. Matthew of Westminster, p.178. Henry de Knighton, p.2465 &c. Sebright papers.

140 6,700 Cambro-Britons joined the Black Prince, at Portsmouth, in his expedition to France; and he commanded 3,800 of them at the Battle of Crécy. "The success of that day was entirely owing to this corp of Britons."—See Corte, vol.2, p.462. And at the Battle of Poictiers, in 1356, the majority of the English troops were Britons, at which battle "Syr Howel y Fwyall took the French King prisoner, and did great acts of prowess with his battle axe", &c.—*History of the House of Gwydir, by Syr John Wynn.*

141 Holinshead. Rapin. Echard &c.

142 In p.409 of the 1st vol. Myvyr Archiology, is an ode to "Syr Gryffydd Llwyd, pan oedd yngharchar ynghastell Rhyddlan". Gwylym Ddû o Arvon, ai cânt.

seemed calculated to cherish this ambition; he was hailed by his countrymen as their deliverer, and greeted with the title of "Prince". He headed a party of insurgents in 1294, seized and hanged Syr Roger Puleston, who was a favourite with Edward, and had been, by him, appointed sheriff and keeper of Mona[143] in 1294, which was one cause of this revolt among the inhabitants. Madoc[144] proceeded with a chosen band to Caernarvon at the time of the fair (about the middle of July), setting fire to the town, killing all the English who fell in his way; he attacked and took the castle, and soon after he gained possession of Mona. Edward marched against them in person, and with great difficulty reduced the country to submit again to his yoke. Finding no enemy to resist him, he entered Mona, "and builded there a castle, and called the same Beaumaris,[145] as a check upon the natives of that Island, " causing roads to be cut through the woods; [146] and having punished all who were concerned in the murder of Syr R. Puleston, he carried the gallant Madoc with him to London, where he was doomed to perpetual imprisonment in the tower.[147] On this disaster, all the chieftains and nobles of Wales, submitted themselves to the king, whose conduct, on this occasion, was politic; no victim being offered to the severity of his justice, and he gave to the heirs, the estates forfeited by their fathers. Their wild spirit of independence, and their enthusiasm for liberty, from this period, gradually declined. We see this remnant of the ancient Britons uniting in interests; and mingling in friendship with the English, fighting their battles, &c. The pages of Troissart and the English historians, recording the events of the continental wars,[148] are rich in brilliant feats performed by this "brave and happy people", "if they had" says Giraldus "but one prince, and him good". Giraldus was himself a native of the principality; and a great traveller. He gives the following description of his countrymen. "Both sexes exceed all other nations in cleanliness; pay great attention to their teeth, &c. The men shave all their beard, except a little on the upper lip; leaving whiskers. They as well as the women, wear cloaks, and cut their hair short. The women, after the manner of the Parthians, cover their heads with a large white veil, folded like a turban. The men of North Wales are remarkable for spears, so long and well pointed, that they can pierce a coat of mail. The men of South Wales are accounted the best archers, &c. They are not given to excess in eating or drinking. There is not a beggar to be seen among them", &c. This account was written at a period, when the native manners and habits were pure and unadulterated, by foreign in-

143 Matthew of Westminster p.190. Carte, vol.2, p.237.

144 Caerwys MS.

145 Welsh Chronicles p.381.

146 Holinshead, p.294. Powel &c.

147 Matt. of Westminster p.423.

148 The Sebright MSS contained a great number of commissions of array from Edward II. For his wars in Scotland;— Edward III and Henry V for their wars in France. Page 396, 16 Edward III 7th vol. Sebright, "The king acquaints his chamberlains of North Wales, i.e. Robert de Hanbury, William de Shaldeford, Gryffydd ab Caddr. and Thomas de Compegne, that the 500 men which were sent to Winchester, out of Angleseye and Caernarvon, were 'debiles and insuffentes', and commands them forthwith to raise another 900 ablebodied man (over and above those already sent) within the said districts, &c. to be conveyed to Plymouth by Gryffydd ab Caddr. and Thomas de Compegne, 'servienti suv ad armia', &c. and to be there by the feast of Allsaints." Dated 7th of October. He directs his Cameranis of North Wales, to pay the expences of their cloathing, and to be answerable for their other expences on their march, &c. Another follows, directed to his chamberlain of North Wales, to defray the same expences for 650 men, raised by his son, in all amounting to 3,100 archers.—ℐ Lloyd. 6,700 Welshmen went with the Black Prince. The success of the Battle of Cresey was owing to the Welsh.—Carte's History, vol.2.

tercourse. He describes them as extremely hospitable, and devoted to arms, which the peasant, as well as the courtier was prepared to seize, on the shortest summons. The pithy address of Galgacus to his followers, fully justifies the opinion formed by the Romans of their valour, "Britons, when you march to the combat, think of your ancestors and descendants." Colonel Pascal, a Breton, in the last continental wars, led on his troop of Bretons with this emphatic war-cry "Tor ei Pene". By the Red Book of Asaph,[149] I find, that in the 29th of Edward I and on the 30th of March, his Son Edward of Caernarvon, styled "Prince of Wales", was in Mona, receiving the homage of the principal inhabitants i.e. Tudyr Vychan of Penmynydd, Llewelyn ab Gryffydd, Davydd Vychan ab Davydd, Madoc Gôch, Gryffydd ab Howel, Davydd ab Owen, Llewelyn ab Iorwerth, Gryffydd ab Ednyved, Llewelyn Gethin, Tegwared Vychan, Iorwerth Gôch, Bleddyn Gôch, Madog Llwyd, Grono ab Madoc ab Trahayarn, Madoc ab Gronw, Madog ab Owain, Tydyr ab Gronw, Iorwerth ab Madoc Sais, Gryffydd ab Philip, Davydd ab Rotpert, Iorwerth ab Llewelyn, Gryffydd ab Davydd, &c.

Hotspur having had the following ample grant, 1st of Henry IV, may be one reason of the islanders taking so active a part with his ally Owen Glyndwr. "Sebright Papers, yn y Twr."

"Pat. Henr̄ IV ā°. 1°. pars. 4. M.Y. Pro. Henr̄ de Percy." R. oib⁹ ad quos &c. sciatis quod de grā nr̄a spāli et ex certa Licencia nr̄a Concessim̄ Carissimo et fid nr̄o consanguin̄ Henr̄ de Percy fil Comitis Northumbr̄ totū Com̄ et dnı̄u de Anglesey in North Waḥ cū Castro de Beaumarreys in eodm̄ Com̄. Commota, Maneiria, terras, Teñ, feodi firmas, redditus servicia libōr et nativōr tenentiū, reversiones, feoda militū, advocacōes prioratuū, ecctiar, hospitaliū, Curo turna, vicecomitū, visus francipleḡ cū omnimod ₥fic eordem Raglorias, ringeleias, senescalsias, amobragia cū feodis ₥fic et allis rebus quibusc̃uq₈, ad dc̄as raglorias, Ringelias, Senescalsias et amobragia qũq₈, modo spectantib⁹ escaetis, Thesaūru inventū vel inveniend̄ forisfacturas, deodandas wreccū maris et piscis regalis, Custumas, prisas Vinōr et aliār mencandisar et rerū quārcunq₈ applicanōr et puceñdor in Com̄ prsdc̄o sūp costeras maris ejūsdm quocunq₈, modo venı̄nt cū feriis mercatis Franchesiis libertatibus minerā plumbi et quorcuñq₈, aliōr mettalōr et petrār una cū chaceis Warrenis, Stagnis, Vivariis, Mariscis moris, boscis et allis rebus que infra Com̄ et dñui predc̄a aliquo modo emₑ₂q₂ₑe poterunt una cū Catellis felonū et fugitōr et illorū qui obierūt intestati escapia felonū et convictōr de felonia vel ₥dicōe, fines extus et amerciamenta et fines ₥licencia concordandi duellum prisoñe fines et redemcōes ₥ feloniis murdris et ₥dicoib⁹ si eedm̄ ₥dicoes nos, statū ñm aut regnū ñm non tangat, &c. &c.

This ample grant, which seems to constitute Henry Percy absolute Lord, if not sole proprietor of the Island of Mona (for life only), is dated the 12th of October. The king, however (if I understand it

---

149 "Llyvr Côch Asaph, in the year 1828 belonged to Mr. Athelstan Owen, who was then a schoolmaster at Llangedwyn. This register was compiled in the time of Davydd ab Bleddyn, who became bishop, according to Willis, in the year 1314. What is here presented chiefly refers to the time and acts of his two immediate predecessors, i.e. Anian de Schonaw, and Leoline de Bromfeld. It is all in latin (except a little at the end in Welsh), and so full of abbreviations, besides being badly wrote, that it is very difficult to make any thing out of it.—*J Lloyd.*"
The copy Mr. Lloyd alludes to, and parts of which he has transcribed is the one mentioned in the following letter by Edward Llwyd, dated "Tal y Cavn, May 25, 1693". "One John Evans of Ysgwyvrith Lâs communicated an olde MS of William Llewelyn, augmented, &c. by Thomas ap William, containing an exposition of the obsolete Welsh words, &c. Mr. Watkyn Owen of Gwydir shewed us a copy of Côch Asaph (but you need not speak any thing of this) together with a large Book of Pedigrees, written by one Syr Thomas ab Ievan, who tells us; he was made a priest, at Rome, in 1500", &c. This Book of Pedigrees is now in the possession of Mr. Davies Cooke of Gwaesnau.

right), reserves to himself "Ligeanica oppũ officiis regalibus Justiciatus et Cancellaritus nõb et heredibus nr̃is plene et integre semβ salvis"; otherwise (observes Mr. Lloyd) the whole revenue of the Island, if I mistake not, was given to Hotspur for life.[150]

He must have been a popular governor, or the Monenses would not have sided with him, in Owen Glyndwr's rebellion, as a partizan of that injured chieftain. Considering circumstances with the provocation which he had received, and his natural vehemence of character, it cannot be a matter of surprise, that Owen Glyndwr, should from defending his paternal estate from ravage and sequestration, advance a claim to the principality.

Fol.39, Cotton MS in the British Museum, contains a curious letter, written by Reynald de Baylon to William Venables, constable of Chester, giving him to understand "That all Caernarvinshire purposin hem, in al the haste that thae mae for to go into the Yle of Anglesey; for to have owte al the men, and al the catel there, and for to bring hit with hem unto the mountaine, leste Englishemen shulde bee refreshyt therwith, &c. Better to mak levy and to take wagys of the sam dette for my lord, than ffor to lett the rebel Owin Glynder hav al, &c. more I can nott. Wrytten in haste at the ton of Conowy, the Sattordey next after the ffeste of Epiphannie. Yr. por sevte. Reynold, keeper of Conowy."

In p.80 of "Memoirs of Owen Glyndwr", written by Mr. Thomas Ellis, Rector of Dolgelleu, a MS[151] in Jesus College Library, may be seen the names of "the several persons and inhabitants of the county of Anglesey, who were indicted and fined for being in arms and rebellion with Owen Glyndwr, and to appear at Beaumaris, the next day before the feast of St. Martin the bishop, being the 11th of November, 8th of Henry IV before Thomas Toncul, Phillip Manwaring, Robert Paris the younger, commissioners, by virtue of a commission from Prince Henry; son and heir, Prince of Wales", &c. "To indite and fine the several persons, inhabitants of the said County of Anglesey, whose names are here written, being in arms and rebellion with Owen Glyndwrdwy." N.B. Many of them being persons of ordinary condition, to write out their names is of little or no use.

"CWMMWD LLIVON.—Men amerced—411; amercement, total—£100 18s. 8d. Amongst them of the clergy were, Cynric, offeiriad; Madoc, offeiriad; Davydd ab Evan ab Tudor Llwyd, offeiriad and Davydd, offeiriad."

"MENAI.—Men amerced—308; sum total—£65 10s. 8d. Clergy,—Davydd, vicar of Llanidan; Davydd ab Evan Goch, rector of Rhosvair; Hwlcyn ab Davydd, offeiriad; Gronw, rector of Seyviog Howel Gloff, rector of Rhoscolyn; Gryffydd ab Howel, offeiriad Llangevni; Deicws ab Evan ab. Davydd, offeiriad."

"TAL-Y-BOLION.—Men amerced—399; sum total—£123 16s. 4d. Clergy,—Gwyn, offeiriad Llanvairynghornwy; Iorwerth ab Madoc, offeiriad; Davydd ab Leicy, offeiriad; Evan ab Gryffydd, offeiriad; Howel, vicar of Llanbadric; Bedin, person Llanbabo; Iorwerth, person Llantrisaint:; Davydd, person Llanvachreth; Morrys, person Llanvaithley; Madoc ab Ithel, person Llanvwrog; Evan ab Owen offeiriad."

---

150 Caerwys MS.
151 Published in 1776.

"TWRCELYN.—Men amerced—279; sum total—£83 5s. 8d. Three clergymen."

"TINDAETHWY.—Men amerced 389; sum total—£79 19s. 8d. Clergy,—Evan ab Ednyved ab Howel, offeiriad; Gryffydd, offeiriad Pwllgwyngyll; Einion ab Iorwerth, offeiriad."

"MALLTRAETH.—Men amerced—326; sum total—£83 16s. 0d. Clergy, Gryffydd, offeiriad; Tudor ab Madog, offeiriad; Ievan, offeiriad; Rhys ab Davydd Ddu, rector of Penmynydd".

"The persons undernamed were men of note that were outlawed for that rebellion,—Llewelyn ab Rhys, clericus et prebendarius in Ecclesia de Caer Gybi; William Jenkin ab William, rector Ecclesiae de Llanddyvnav; Iun ab Bleddyn ab Grono, clericus qui se vocat archdiaconum Angleseae."

The parishes in Mona, are at present seventy-four, in former times there were probably more, as appears evident from ruins of churches found in different parts. A list of the monasteries, abbies, and chapels, demolished in this Island, is given in p.286, 1st vol. Cambrian Register.

BEAUMARIS is the principal town in Mona, and so named from French words, signifying its situation,—marshy and a beautiful sea, it is sometimes called Bonover in old MSS.

Beaumaris is distant from London 249 miles and 27 from Holyhead, and owing to its celebrity as a watering place, excellent houses are built annually for the accommodation of visitors. I do not know any tract of country, in which, within the same compass, may be found an equal variety of beautiful scenery, with its romantic and sylvan banks, the Menai fronted by the fine old castle of Caernarvon, and that again backed by the magnificent range of Snowdonian mountains, headed by the cloud-capped monarch of this truly sublime landscape.

Beaumaris possesses more attractions than any other marine residence in the kingdom. Mr. Pennant, in p.243, says "there is even a strong tradition, that one Helig ab Glanawg had great possessions, &c. all which were suddenly overwhelmed, and it is pretended, that there may still be seen, at very low ebbs, ruins of houses, and a causeway from Priest Holme, pointing towards Penmaen Mawr", &c. In vol.3, Cambrian Magazine, p.39, may be read extracts out of the Caerwys MSS giving an account of the awful inundation of Cantrev Gwaelod; little doubt, however can be entertained, that the present town originated from a "castell being built there, as a check upon the natives", in 1295, upon private property belonging to Einian ab Mredydd, Gryffydd ab Tudor Llwyd, and Einion ab Tegwared, who were amply recompensed by having a grant of lands elsewhere.

> " Llydan oedd castell Edward,
> " Ai dyrrai gwych, ai dair gwrt,
> " Caerau Edwart, cwncwerwr,
> " Tyrrau oedd ar gaerau'r gŵr." [152]

The two castles of Conwy and Caernarvon were completely finished in the space of two years, by the indefatigable labour of the peasantry of the country, "magnoque primorum hominum sumptu". This seems to refer, to the great men of Wales. In the Gloddaeth MS. [153] No. 39, I find this anecdote,

---

152 Caerwys MS.

153 This MS contains an account of a strange shower of hail fallen in Mona, on Monday, the 3rd of May, 1697. This curious event, if I mistake not, is published in the Philosophical Transactions. It is written by Mr. Henry Rowlands.— *J Lloyd. Caerwys MSS qu. 3. p.75.*

"De Belli marisci origine situ nominisque Relione. After King Edward had made the said castles to the forme they be of nowe, and devised romes and dykes for the towns, he made Henry Ellerton, master-mason of the saide castle of Caernarvon", &c. Probably this man was the great architect who planned and built these castles. Caernarvon, according to this MS was built in the first, and Conwy in the second year after the subjugation of Wales. Edward thought these castles sufficient for the keeping of all that part of the country in awe and subjection, but he found himself mistaken, and that it was necessary to have such another fortress in Mona; accordingly the castle of Beaumaris was erected about nine years after the other two. The MS says, that it was surrounded by water, and had its communication with the sea, by means of a canal; that the marsh was formerly much larger than it is now, and covered with fine bullrushes, &c. the name derived "a Bello marisco", rather than from Bimaris. Probably the Britons might call the place "Morva Teg", hence the Norman Beaumaris; they might afterwards make use of "Mariscum", to signify a marsh. The author brings several arguments to prove that some sort of a town stood here before this period. That the chapel of Meugan stood near the place of the present church; and he supposes that the place was at first denominated from Meugan, but he stumbles upon another, i.e. "Bon-over, Quasi, Pen y Gaer, Vel Potius, Bon y Gover." He proves from the extent of North Wales, that several persons had lands assigned them in other places, in lieu of the lands taken from them to build this castle and town upon. "From this time we have no more mention of Diganwy;—Conwy supplied its place, and together with that of Caernarvon on one side, and Beaumaris on the other, put an effectual bar to any hostile design of the Welsh nation."[154] By an extent taken the 26th of Edward III, I learn that the lands given by Edward to Einion ab Mredydd Gryffydd ab Ievan and Einion ab Tegwared (in lieu of that which he took from them to build his castle upon), were in Erianell and Tre'r Ddol. This extent of North Wales, is a curious and valuable record; there is a copy of it in the British Museum. The purpose of making it by Edward III was for ascertaining different rents, services, and customs, claimed by the native Princes of Wales, in order that a commutation should be made, by paying the value of those claims, in money, into the English exchequer. At the time this extent was taken at Rhosvair, 26th of Edward III lands in the township of Erianell and Trev-Ddôl, were found to be in the possession of the descendants of Einion ab Mredydd, Gryffydd ab Tudor Llwyd, and Einion ab Tegwared, "granted to them free from rent and service, by Edward I in lieu of certain lands of theirs, on which the castle of Beaumaris is built". It does not appear how the king came into possession of lands in Erianell; those others in Tre'r Ddôi, which he granted to Gryffyddd ab Tudyr Llwyd, are said in this extent to have been forfeited by Howel ab Iorwerth. The castle stands on the north-east side of the town, and covers a considerable space of ground, but wants height to give it dignity. It consists of an outer ballium, or envelope, surrounded with a broad ditch, (supplied with water from the sea) and flanked by ten round towers, and has on the north side an advanced work, called the gunner's walk. The east and west sides are built with stones of different colours, so as to have the appearance of chequers; within this building stands the castle, which is nearly square, having a round tower on each angle, and another in the centre; it encloses a court of fifty-seven yards from north to

154 Caerwys MS.

south, and sixty from east to west. The hall, notwithstanding its neglected state, still retains striking evidence of its former magnificence. Within the walls, on one side, are the remains of a beautiful chapel,
in form of a theatre; the sides ornamented with gothic arches; and the roof supported by ribs, spring-
ing from pilasters, between each of which is a narrow window, and behind some are small closets,
gained out of the thickness of the wall, probably allotted to the officers or persons of rank.[155] To this
chapel was an ascent by some steps, now demolished or taken away; it was arched[156] and ribbed, with
pointed intersecting arches. Beneath this chapel, is a kind of vault; its floor has been dug up in search
of treasure,[157] there being a tradition that "in troublesome times, much money was hidden there". And
a tale is told, that a large brass mortar, full of gold, was found not many years ago. There is a communication round the buildings of this inner court, by a gallery of two yards broad. In the centre was a
drawwell, which is now filled up with stones, rubbish, &c. Edward also cut a canal, in order to permit
vessels to discharge their ladings beneath the walls. As a proof this, there were within the last century,
iron rings fixed to them, for the purpose of mooring the ships and boats.

    The first governor appointed by Edward I was Sir William Pickmor, a Gascon, who was also cap-
tain of the town, his annual fee being 40 marks (afterwards increased to £40) as governor, and £12 3s.
4d. as captain. The porter of the gate of Beaumaris had £9 2s. 6d. annually: adjoining Porth Mawr, i.e.
the south gate of the town, stood his lodge, which in the time of Charles II was converted into a
bridewell.

    The constable of the castle, I find by a MS in the Harl. Collection, was always captain of the town,
except in one instance;—in the 36th of Henry VI; when Syr John Botelar of Bewsy, near Warrington,
held the first office, and Thomas Nones the other. In a thick 4to. containing "grants, charters, inquisitions, esscheats, &c. (relative to Wales) "yn y Twr" and which was burnt, with a moiety of the Sebright
Collection,[158] in 1810, was the copy of an inquisition taken, in consequence of this castle and others
belonging to the king, being robbed, &c.

    Page 383, vol.6, Sebright Collection.—"Inquisitiõ capta coram Johñ Aleyn locum tenente
Justic̃ Dñi Regis North Waɫɫ apud Carnarñ die Lune px̃a post ffñ Apostolm̃ Petri et Pauli, Anno R. R.
Edwardi tertii post conquestum quinto."

    This inquisition was taken in consequence of a writ directed by the king for that purpose, setting
forth, that the victuals, arms, and other goods and chattels, belonging to his castles in North Wales,
had been stolen, or otherwise squandered, since the time that Adam de Whitford was Chamberlain,
&c. The jury, which consisted of men from the aggrieved places, i.e. Conwy, Caernarvon, Beaumaris,
and Harlech; all with English names, excepting Gronough ap Madoc of Beaumaris, say, that "all things
remained in the same state that they were in when they were received by the said Adam from his predecessor Niclas de Acton; excepting what the said Adam de Whitford had sold in his time, but for what,

---

155 Pennant p.224 and Caerwys MS.
156 Grose's Antiquities.
157 Ibid.
158 In the 2nd vol. Cambro-Briton, p.201, may be seen an account of the Sebright Papers. The moiety belonging to the
    Wynnstay library, was burnt in 1810, when at the bookbinder's shop, in London.

they could not tell." &c.[159]

The castle was extremely burdensome to the country, the garrison continually harassing the natives and committing unheard of acts of barbarities. In the time of Henry VI quarrels were very frequent; "one bloody fray happened, in which Davydd ab Howel of Llwydiarth was slain, with many others".

A MS in the Harl. Collection, marked 433, records that King Richard III, in the 1st year of his reign, granted to Syr R. Huddlestone, "the constableship and captainship of the castle and town of Beaumaris"; and in December, in the 2nd of his reign, there is the following entry:—"Sir Ris. Huddelston hath twenty-four souldis in Beaumares, th' ordinary charge, paide duringe halfe the yeare, with the wages of 4d. by daye, for everye soulder". I find by the Lleweny Papers, that in the 1st of Henry VII he appointed his illegitimate son, Sir Roland Velville, alias Britany,[160] constable and captain of this place, but the conduct of the garrison was so offensive to the neighbourhood that the king gave orders for its removal. Lord Combermere of Combermere Abbey is in possession of the original grant of the constableship to his maternal ancestor, Syr R. Velville, dated "apud Caernarvon, Julii 3, 1st Henry VII". He died in 1533, describing himself in his will, made in that year, as "constable of Beaumars castell". Nothing more is said of this as a military post till 1642, when the loyalty of Thomas Cheadle, deputy to the earl of Dorset, then constable, caused him to furnish it with men and ammunition, for the service of Charles I. By "a shorte acconte of the rebellion in North Wales, in Olyver Cromwell's tyme", a curious original MS belonging to Mr. Wynne of Penniarth, I find on the 14th of July, 1648, the men of Mona, from sixteen to sixty, signing a memorial drawn up by Syr John Owen, "againste the wickedness of rebellion". The natives acted up to this loyal feeling, by taking every opportunity of harassing and surprising their opponents. "Whilst Captain Sontley and his men were in Dolgelleu, in July, certain men of Anglesey, understanding that a company of Parliamenteers lodged at Bangor, came over in the night, and in the morning took of them between thirty and forty, near Aber; then Sontley and his men went towards Bala on Sunday morning." "In Caernarvonshire the soldiers of the parliament did plunder Clynene, and a great number of gentlemen's houses in Llŷn. Shortlie after, Anglesey men came over to Caernarvon, and took some men and horses about Clynog, and hearing that General Mytton and Colonel Jones were at Pwllheli, they made that way, but those men having intelligence of their purposes, went their way, and returned to Anglesey."

"About the midst of August, Sir Harry Lingen, Knight, of Herefordshire, came with horse and foot, and advanced towards North Wales, intending to join with Anglesey men, but being narrowly watched by the troops of the counties adjacent, who gave General Horton intelligence of Lingen's de-

---

159 Caerwys MS, signed "J. Lloyd".

160 From the circumstance of being born there. Sir Roland Velville's daughter and heiress married Tudor ab Robert of Beren. By an extract here, taken from a letter in the Combermere Collection, so late as 1636, his descendant, Sir John Salusbury, could only hint at Sir Roland's *demi-royal* birth. "I have searched for records at Denbighe, att the commande of my Lord Presidente of Wales, but coulde not fynd anye. Thomas Salusbury, the then deputye steward of the Lordshipp of Denbighe, and Tudor you name, was no wayes allyed, or of kindred, for three descents after. Sir Thomas Salusbury, my grandffather, was the matche betwixte Llewenyie and Beraine: and I doe ffreelye thinke, that the afforesayde Tudor, was hee that married with Sir Roland Vellwell's daughter and hayre, and *whose reputed sonn* Vellvell was, I doubt not you have heard", &c. &c. "Lleweni, March 6, 1636. John Salisbury."

sign, whilst they followed after him, Horton came from Pembroke crosswise, and met Lingen's men near Llanidloes, took Sir Harry, sore hurt, and —— prisoners; the rest fled, whereof about thirty horse and some few foot came to Mallwyd, 17th day, and lay there that night. The next day they came to Dolgelli, where they rested till the morrow, being Saturday, for they were bruised; and thither came Sir Arthur Blaeney, and they went to Harlech and to Anglesey."

"Another company of them (or from the north) to the number of sixty, came to Bala, intending to go to Anglesea; but they had no sooner lighted, but Colonel Jones, and —— soldiers came after them, and after some struggling, they took about fifty of Lingen's men, some few escaped:—it is reported they had £300 in money and booty."

"Colonel Horton followed as far as Pool, and returned, and in his return burnt Havod Uchtryd, Morgan Herbert's house, for that one of his men had been there murdered by Morgan Herbert's men, but without the privity of Morgan, who was then ★ ★ ★ ★ [text lost].

"September 26, at night, the parliament forces entered Anglesey, and with fifty or sixty boats, put over both horse and foot the 27th day.

"1649, passed an act for the propagation of the gospel in Welsh. Lords Worcester and Holland were beheaded, and by the grace of God, Syr John Owen was preserved." &c.

There is a force in these recitals, thus arranged and authenticated, expressive of the situation of the suffering natives, in those days of anarchy and confusion, when they were subject to the depredation of both parties, a set of lawless men, whose "brief authority" was that "of a day", the power of the mighty over the weak.[161] In 1643, Thomas Bulkeley (soon after created Lord Bulkeley) succeeded Thomas Cheadle, as governor of Beaumaris castle. He must have resigned in favour of his eldest son, for Mr. Pennant says "Richard Bulkeley, son of Lord Bulkeley and several gentlemen of the country, held it for the king till October 1648, when it was surrendered upon honourable terms to General Mytton. King Charles's subsequent captivity produced, in 1648, together with partial insurrections in other parts of the country, a general revolt of the inhabitants of Anglesey, and which gave rise to the parliamentary expedition for the reduction of this Island.

"As soon as the parliamentary forces, under the command of General Mytton, appeared on Penmaen Mawr, the greatest demonstrations of defiance were made by the inhabitants of this place, by whom they were descried from Beaumaris Green; but, after a slight skirmish near Cadnant, with Major Hugh Pennant's troop of horse, General Mytton advanced with his forces, with out further opposition, to Orsedd Migin, where they held a rendezvous the morning after their landing, and whence they marched immediately upon Beaumaris, by way of Red Park, and drew up in order of battle upon the hill. The islanders, commanded by Colonel Bulkeley and Colonel Roger Whiteley, drew up in the fields below the hill, assisted by the town's company, commanded by Captain Sanders. The Parliamen-

---

161 Mr. Lloyd of Caerwys used to relate an anecdote; told him by his maternal grandmother, that her parents preserved their house of Llannerch y Medd, from being ransacked by a party of Oliver Cromwell's men, on their return from Bodidris, by causing the feather beds to be ripped open and scattered on the premises; this ruse de guerre succeeded, for the men were overheard to say, as they passed on, "It is useless to call here, for some of our people have been before hand with us."

tary forces began the attack, but were resolutely repulsed by the town's company, and, at the same time charged by the cavalry; but the rest of the infantry on the side of the royalists soon fled in disorder, and the remainder being overpowered by numbers, and the town being closely pressed, the islanders were dispersed, and the royalist commanders, with most of the officers, retired into the castle. Captain Lloyd of Penhênllŷs, who had been ordered to defend the church, locked his men within it, and ran away, taking the key with him; but the men, notwithstanding, climbed upon the roof and the steeple, and, firing upon the assailants, killed a considerable number; among whom were three of the parliamentarian officers. General Mytton, having at length entered the town, immediately despatched a messenger to the castle, to demand the persons of Colonels Bulkeley and Whiteley, threatening unless they were given up to him, to put to death all the prisoners he had taken in the course of the day, about four hundred in number; and these officers, to prevent the effusion of blood, immediately surrendered themselves, and remained prisoners at the Old Place, in Beaumaris, the seat of the Bulkeley family, till they were ransomed. The garrison, unable to withstand the superior force of the enemy, soon after capitulated on honourable terms; and General Mytton, who was appointed governor by the parliament, made Captain Evans his deputy-constable of the castle, and lieutenant governor of the town. In consequence of this capitulation, a quarrel ensued between Thomas Cheadle, and his relation Colonel R. Bulkeley. A duel was fought by them, which ended fatally; Colonel Bulkeley was slain, and Thomas Cheadle fled, but was taken at an inn, at Nantwich. A "Cywydd Marwnad", written in the best of our elegiac style, tempts me to give a specimen of the original, with a translation. This sad event that caused the "Death Shriek in the Ynys", happened on February 19th 1649, upon Traeth Wylovaen.—

> " Pa lais yw hwn ?—pa arwgdd yw ?
> " Pa oernad ⋆   ⋆   ⋆
> " Mae tònau o'r dagrau dwys
> " Môr du affaith mawr diffwys;
>
> "   ⋆   ⋆   ⋆   ⋆   ⋆   ⋆   ⋆ "
> " The sea beats waves of tears !
> " Black is the sea, and terrible to behold !
> " O sea ! thy rocking-cradle is the nursing-mother of death,
> " And many a brave man has found his grave in thy bosom.
>
> "   ⋆   ⋆   ⋆   ⋆   ⋆   ⋆   ⋆ "
> " What murmuring noise is that I hear ?
> " What plaintive voice is that which floats the midnight air ?
>
> "   ⋆   ⋆   ⋆   ⋆   ⋆   ⋆   ⋆ "
> " The sea groans in pity, weeping rivers of tears;
> " And in those tears the sheet-anchor of Mona is lost for ever.
>
> "   ⋆   ⋆   ⋆   ⋆   ⋆   ⋆   ⋆ "
> " Weep, Mona, Queen of Isles,—weep seas of tears,
> " For the blossom of three ages is cut down on thy shore,—
> " The promising heir of Beaumaris is numbered with the dead,—
> " The chiefest branch of Gwynedd is gone,
> " And in this stroke each house mourns the loss of a son.
>
> "   ⋆   ⋆   ⋆   ⋆   ⋆   ⋆   ⋆ "

" A death-shriek is gone through the Isle.
" Fiercely in his circles did the sun of Mona set this night.
"The birds of prey are hovering over the Isle,
" And the moon of Mona beams dimly this night.
" A mournful shriek is heard in the blast,
" And wrathful beat the waves of Mona this night:
" Cold and death-like will be the smile of his mother."
"T'rawyd y wlad trwy dy loes,
"Torwyd blodeuyn tair oes—

"   *   *   *   *   *   *   *   "

After the death of General Mytton, the constableship was given to Hugh Courtney, who was succeeded in that office by Colonel Jones, the regicide, and he was superseded by Sir John Cartar, possessor of Cinmael, by his marriage[162] with the heiress, Miss Holland; he seems to have been a moderate
man; General Monk knew this, and appointed him, preparatory to the restoration of Charles II who
reinstated Lord Bulkeley, as constable of the castle, in 1661. In 1653, keeping this garrison, cost government £1,703. According to a MS account of the expences incurred annually, A.D.1696:—

	s.	d.	
The constable (besides a captain's pay)	2	0	per day.
A gunner	1	8	
A mattrosse	0	10	
A captain	8	0	
A lieutenant	4	0	
Two sergeants, each 1s.—Two corporals ...	2	0	
A drummer 1s. and 80 soldiers	0	8	

With an allowance of 1s. per diem for fire and candles for the guard.

This Castle was purchased from the crown by that genuine patriot, "the humane and charitable"
Lord Bulkeley, who died universally lamented, in June, 1822, leaving this, together with his other possessions, to Sir Richard Bulkeley; who with the property and name, seems to inherit all the popularity,
patriotism and loyalty of his distinguished race.

Beaumaris anciently possessed, with Rhuddlan, extensive commerce, but since the rise of Liverpool, both places have greatly declined. The traffic here must have been considerable, for Sir John
Wynn of Gwydir, in his noted Triad characterising the inhabitants of the three castellated towns on the
Menai, says, "The lawyers of Caernarvon,—the gentlemen of Conwy—and the merchants of Beaumaris." The wealth of this country must have been enormous, when we consider that Prince Llewelyn
agreed to pay £50,000, and an annual tribute of 1,000 marks for the Isle of Mona (which is more than
equal the value of the land-tax of the whole county, when it pays 4s. in the pound). In addition, the

---

162 This marriage caused a wit of the day to say, that Colonel Carter "had carried off the best piece of Holland in the
country".

prince paid £5,000 on his being admitted into quiet possession; and in 1544, I find by the Lleweny Papers, that when a loan was demanded by Henry VIII Mona paid £195; and by an inquisition, taken the 44th of Elizabeth, 1602, it appears that the revenue drawn from this county amounted but to £425 per annum, whereas it produced, 50th of Edward III (1376) £832. In Charles I time, the ship-money paid by this Island, was only £462, when Rhuddlan paid £800. Annexed is a note,[163] containing an account of the money paid in the time of Oliver Cromwell, by the gentlemen who compounded for their estates. Edward, when he built the town of Beaumaris, surrounded it with a wall; made it a corporation, with great privileges; endowing it with lands to a considerable value, and it is still governed by a mayor, recorder, two bailiffs, twenty-one chief burgesses; a town-clerk, and two sergeants at mace, in whom only are vested a right to elect a member for the borough. The first return was made 33rd of Henry VIII. Richard ab Rhydderch of Myvyrian, being chosen representative; the mayor and bailiffs are the returning officers. Sir Richard Bulkeley was elected member for Beaumaris, in 1831, and in 1832; Sir F. Paget was elected under the Reform Bill, member for the united boroughs of Beaumaris, Holyhead, Llangevni, and Amlwch, when Sir R. Bulkeley became representative of the county. Towards the latter end of this volume, may be seen, a list of the members who have served in parliament for this Island; and also the names of the sheriffs, from the time of Henry VIII when Rhys ab Llewelyn of Bodorgan was knight of the shire, during his life.

The site of the chapel of St. Meugan,[164] is still shewn in a field, near the new battery; this was the chapel of ease to Llandegvan prior to building the present church, which is dedicated to St. Mary and Jude (their vigils celebrated on the 8th of September), and is a handsome gothic building, repaired by the late Lord Bulkeley, who added a towerclock,[165] &c. The most remarkable monument in this church, is that of a knight in armour, recumbent, with a female by his side, well sculptured in alabaster; his head rests on a helmet, and at his feet is a lion. The female is habited in a long robe, richly ornamented round the neck. The hands of each are uplifted. Various small figures, dressed like knights and monks, decorate the pedestal of the tomb, which is said to have been brought from the religious house at Llanvaes, at the time of its dissolution; but the names of the persons to whom it was erected are now lost. On the south side of the altar is a stone with a latin inscription, commemorative of the following gentlemen,—Sir Henry Sidney, Antony St. Ledger, Francis Agard, Edward Waterhouse and William Thwaytes.[166] "2nd and 3rd of Philip and Mary, Henry Sydney, father to Sir Philip Sydney, was made governor-general of all the kinges and queenes revenues within the realm of Irelande, and about two

---

163 The gentlemen compounded for their estates as follows: the first instalment was paid to Colonel George Twistleton £7,000. By a MS account, the second appears to be greater, £9,000. Lord Bulkeley and son Colonel Bulkeley, £1,000. Hugh Oweni £700. Owen Woode £500. Dr. Whyte, £1,000. Mr. Bod and his nephew, £500. Mr. Pierce Lloyd, ditto. Owen Holland, £200. William Trefarddw, £50. John Owen, Maethlu, ditto. William Owen, Trefeilin, £50. Lewis Llwyd, captain of Menai, £60. Henry Llwyd of Penhenllys, captain of Tindaethwy, £16. Henry Davydd, captain of Twrcelyn, £50. Richard Bodychan, £80. Henry Owen Mosoglen; £50. Dr. Williris, £50. Mr. John Bodivel, at Mr. Thelwal's £600. John Wynn, Chwaen, £50. William Bulkeley, Coedon, first, £200. 5s. 2d. Richard Prydderch and his son, £200. Major Pugh, £20.—*Thomas Williams, Collector.*

164 Page 286, vol.I, Cambrian Register, contains a list of Monasteries, Abbeys, and Chapels demolished in Mona.

165 Cathrall, p.52.

166 Pennant, p.247, and the Caerwys MSS contain the inscription at full length, which is in latin.

years after Lorde Justice thereof." In the 2nd of Elizabeth, he was appointed Lord President of the Marches of Wales. Holinshead says, that at "eache severall tymes" he was sent deputy into Ireland, he was furnished with a new secretary.[167] "The ffirste was Master Edward Waterhouse, nowe knighted, and one of hys majestie's council for Ireland." The same author adds, "he made speciall choice of two worthy counsellors, whom ffor theire faithefulnesse in counsel, ffor the state, good-will and friendshipp towards hym, and ffor their integrity and sincerity every way, he entirely loved and assuredly trusted; one of these was Master Francis Agard, whome he commonlie called his "Fidus Achates", &c. I can find no biographical information respecting William Thwaytes, the era of whose death is recorded on the tablet, as having occurred on January 20, 1565.

In page 251 of Browne Willis's Bangor, may be read a copy of the grant of Llandegvan[168] advowson, with its chapel of St. Mary's at Beaumaris, by Henry VIII to his kinsman Sir Richard Bulkeley and his heirs for ever; valued then at £23 6s. 8d. The present incumbent is Dr. Richard Howard, rector of Denbigh, to whom it was left by the late Lord Bulkeley. The resident population amounted in 1821 to 1,975 persons, and in 1831 to 2,497. The parish rates were, in 1803, £287 0s. 5d. (at 4s. 6d. in the pound), and £689 10s. in 1831. The school was founded in 1603, and liberally endowed with certain tenements in the Island, by David Hughes, who in 1613, founded also the almshouses for six poor persons, to whom he granted small annuities; the late Lord Bulkeley added four more. Agreeable to the kindhearted testator's wishes, "a lofty and spacious schoolroom" was built, with small but suitable apartments for the two masters, who on a vacancy occurring, are chosen by feoffees, who meet once every year, when a sermon is preached by one of the masters, in memory of the worthy benefactor. Owen Hughes, M.P. for Beaumaris, married Margaret, the rich widow of the Rev. Goronwy Davies, a celebrated scholar. The birch was the bay of the bards, and this idea is ingeniously expressed in a copy of congratulatory verses, which Henry Bulkeley (son to Thomas, the first Viscount Bulkeley), addressed to his tutor this Goronwy Davies, on his promotion to the head mastership of Beaumaris school, in 1650.

> " But if you chance the rod to use,
> " For to quicken our dull muse,
> " I know your birch another day
> "Will prove unto our heads a *bay.* "

The Rev. Hugh Davies Owen, and his brother Briscoe Owen, A.B. Fellow of Jesus College, Oxford, are the masters. These gentlemen, by their great attention to the moral, as well as classical education of their pupils, do ample justice to the trust reposed in them. Bishop Rowland left lands in this Island for the maintenance of one Fellow at Jesus College, Oxford, to be chosen out of this school. The national school was built by public subscription, on lands given by Lord Bulkeley, who undertook to pay a salary of £100 a year to the master and mistress.

---

167 A system kept up to the present day, to the infinite detriment of good government in that country.
168 For Ecclesiastical Church Government, read p.15, of Cathrall.

THE TOWN HALL is a commodious modern edifice, built by the munificence of the late Lord Bulkeley. The lower story including a prison, butcher's shambles, &c. is secured with iron grates and railing. This hall is erected on the site of one built in 1563, under which were kept the stocks and ducking stool, with a pillory near. The markets are held twice a week (Wednesdays and Saturdays) and are well supplied. The fairs are held on the 13th of February, Holy Thursday, September 19, and December 19.

THE COUNTY HALL is a small low building. A curious trial[169] took place here in 1672. Plaintiff, Owen Hughes, M.P. for Beaumaris, originating in a libel, written by a neighbour, reflecting upon the characters of himself, his wife, and wife's mother; accusing them and others named, with being concerned in a murder, committed at the house of one Ann Goodman, "whiche place hathe had a brand of infamie attached to itt, above a hundred years agoe, when one Ralffe Goodman dwelt theire, ffor when dame Agnes Nedham, alias Bulkeley was charged with poisoning her husband, the goode Syr Risiart Bulkeley (the great-grandfather of the Lorde Bulkeley now livinge) about the yeare 1569, itt was proved thatt the metheglin wherewith the noble knighte was poisoned, came ffrom Ralffe Goodman's house, &c. Thys Owen Hughes ys the sonne of Thomas Hughes of Porth y Llongdu, parish of Llanbedr, Môn; Thomas Hughes married the sister of Michael ab Rhys Wyn, and having manie children, and a small estate to maintaine them, i.e. about £14 a yeare, was forced to sell his house att Porth y Llongdu to Hugh Morgan of Beaumaris, Esq. but itt was hys good ffortune to sell it att the beste price, i.e. £400, ffor £14 per annum. Margret, the wiffe of Owen Hughes was the daughter of Evan Wynn ab Robert ab John Wyn of Penllech, by Grace, verch Owen ab Ris ab Llewelyn of Llandegvan, alias 'cell' that is a sort of sly rogue. Be itt observed thatt Owen and Margret were of decent and honeste descente on the paternal side, butt both of them of the worste generation of the maternal side. Owen Hughes was a poor boy, the sonn of a landsellinge ffather; yett he contrived to keepe hym att schole, and when he attained enoughe of latin, bounde him clerke to Owen Wynne of Llandaniolen, councellor att lawe, with whome he lived as servante sixteen years, wipinge hys shoes and bootes, ridinge affter hym, then scribblinge bondes and faringe on hard dyett. &c. The said Margret lost her ffather when verie yonge; her mother married a second husbande, i.e. Robert ab Rys Wyn of Tinllwydan, county of Môn. These had noe better livelehood than to keepe a public house att Beaumarys. Ffrom her youthe, Margret was the servante of the tapp-room; and ffrom her youthe covettous, and extremely addicted to playeing with cardes, and with a shewe of religion, soe thatt George Glover, the mercer, used to saye "thatt Margret y Bont (theire house being near itt) carried a 'Practice of Pietye' in one pocket, and a pack of cards in the other. Att thys tyme, Mr. Grono Davies, a verye clever scolar, an ingenious companion, A.M. and sometyme principall of St. Marye's Hall, at Oxford, was headmaster of Beaumarys school, by companye keepinge, fell into low estatte; and to gett himselffe outte of difficulties, married thys woman, who had by cheatting, &c. scraped together three or four hundrede pounds. This happened in 1649 or 1650. Dr. Robert Cheadle, makinge a copye of verses ffor a schol

169 Transcribed from a folio MS now in the possession of Mr. Madocks of Glan y Wern.

boy, to Mr. Gronow Davies, to beg leave to playe (itt was in latin), wherein he told hym, that hys wyff played cardes, &c. Mr. Grono Davies ledd a sad liffe with her til 1654 when he died, levinge her all his effects, together with Carddwr, worth about £18 yeerlye, &c. Owen Hughes, had by the intereste of hys olde master, sett up ffor himselfe, and soon gott £120, and had the good lucke to oblige Lorde Bulkeley, whoe wanted itt; and in consideration, sett and lett to hym, the farm of 'Cemlyn Heylyn', valued att £36 yearly, within a mile of Beaumaris, ffor that somm, ffor the terme of eightye years. Affter thys bargaine was strucke, Owen Hughes thought himselffe noe small gentleman, ande the countreye thoughte Lord Bulkeley noe small foole, &c. The saide Margret, affter seven yeares widowhoode, married Owen Hughes, &c. On Assension Daye, A.D.1664, beinge the fayre day att Beaumaris, one Humphrey Thomas was murdered, &c. Hee was seene att Baron Hill, att foure o'clock in the eveninge, and att Ann Goodman's, att ffive, the last houre he was seen alive." Owen Hughes was agent to Lord Bulkeley, and sheriff of Mona, in 1683, and M.P. for Beaumaris, the 10th of King William.

If the reader should complain that the quotation is too long, neither important, nor interesting, I can only plead in excuse my inability (at this hurrying moment) to make any selection that would obviate this remark, without being liable to the weightier objection of exhibiting an imperfect picture of the characters implicated.

BEAUMARIS FERRY lies near the town, and is passable at low water. In the time of Edward I it was royal property; but Elizabeth, in the 4th of her reign, granted it by charter to the corporation. In the 4th vol. Sebright Collection, I find the following order to Robert Power, then chamberlain of North Wales, to inspect the boat, which was out of repair, &c. It appears by this, that the inhabitants paid 30s. annually into the exchequer, the king finding the boat. Escheats,[170] from the Sebright Collection continued, vol.4, p.484, clause 18, E.2, M.2.

"Pro Rege de battell repandis. R. Dilco ilico suo Robto Power Camerar suo North Wall saltm quia datum est nobis intelligi q̃o battellus nr̃ apud villam nr̃am de Beaumareis ultra aquam ibidem deputatus adeo inveteratus et comfratus q̃u ꝑ passagio illo non potest ulterius deservire ꝑ quod hoīes dc̃e ville qui 30 solidos ꝑ passagio pr̃dicto pcipiunt ā nobis inde ad s̃iem nr̃m de Kaernarvon annuatim respondent ꝑficum illud de cetero pcipe non possint nisi de alio Batello eis ibidem prideatur mãnd q̃o Battellum pr̃dictum supervideatis et si Batellus ille ꝑ passagio pr̃dicto com̃ode repari possit tunc eum de exitibus Ballie vr̃e repari fac̃ et si ppter vetustatem ejusdem repari non possit tunc unum alium Batellum ꝑ passagio illo competentem eum fac̃ et nos vobis inde in compoto vro debitam her̃e allocacoem faciemus T. R. apud Wesf, 6to. die Julii pr̃ ip̃m Regem."

The other battellus to be repaired or new constructed, was that of the village of Aberconway, for the use of which, the inhabitants paid eight marks. It was directed to the same person and at the same time. This battelus, I suppose means a ferry boat.—John Lloyd."

In the same volume of the Sebright Collection, p.427, pat 1.2, R.2, pt.1, M.1 P. Priorissa et monĩcal Cestr̃. "R. omnibus ad quos &c. Saltm sciatis q̃o nos considerantes paupertatem dilectãr, nob

170 Caerwys MS.

in x͠ti Priorisse et monalium Cestͬ et q̊ ipse ꝑ pͣitencia sua ultra panem et clvissiam non hen͠ nisi quͣelt ipsarum unum obulum ꝑ diem ut accepimus, de grã nrã spaͭi dedimus et concessimus ꝑ nobis et heredibus eisdem Priorisse et monialibus advocacͦoem ecclie sīc Beblicii in Arvon, in North Waͭt cum Capella de Caernarvon eidem Ecclie anexa hend ͞et tenend eisdem, Priorisse ͞et monialibus ͞et succes-soribus suis inpꝑm. Et concessimus ͞et licentiam, dedimas ꝑ nobis ͞et heredibus ñris quantum in nobis est eisdem Prioriesse ͞et monialibus q̄ipse dcãm eccͭeam cum capella prͭdicta appropriare ͞et eccͭeam illam cum capella prͭdicto sic appropriatum in pprios usus tenere possint sibi ac successioribus suis in relevacͦoem et emendacͦoem status et sustentaccͦoeis earum impꝑm statuto de terris et Teñ ad manum mortuam non poneñd edito non obstante saluis semper nͦob et heredibus ñris serviciis de odvocacͦoe dͨca Eccͭlie cum Capella prdicta debitis et consuetis. In cujus &c. T.R. apud Westͫm 20 die Novͬ ꝑ brͤ de privato sigillo." N.B. the presentation to the church of Llanbeblig and Caernarvon, is in the gift of the Bishop of Chester to this day. Mr. Lloyd's extracts[171] from the Sebright Collection, enhanced by his valuable comments, tempts me to transcribe largely from them, though not always bearing on the sub-ject in question.

THE BULKELEYS OF BARON HILL.—The first of this distinguished family that settled in this country was William Bulkeley, constable of Beaumaris, in 1440. He was the grandson of Richard Bulkeley of Eyton, Davenham parish, Cheshire: which Richard married in 1327 Agnes, fil. Thomas Cheadle, and William Bulkeley, constable of Beaumaris, married Ellen, daughter to William Griffith of Penrhyn, relict of Robert Paris. The family, previously to their occupying this spot, resided at Court-mawr, in the town. Baron Hill was built in 1618, by Sir R. Bulkeley, the most celebrated personage of his day for accomplishments and liberality; possessing, with his great wealth, a heart willing to dispense it to the advantage of his country. His estates in Mona let for £2,500 a year; in Caernarvonshire, £800; and those in Cheshire for £100. He was deservedly a great favourite with Queen Elizabeth, who nobly protected him from the machination of Leicester, when he wanted to implicate the "worthy olde courtier" in the Babington conspiracy. His mother was maid of honour to Queen Mary, and might have done good services to Queen Elizabeth in those days, which her majesty amply requited by heap-ing favours on her son, whom she appointed Deputy Lieutenant of Mona, in opposition to Leicester's wishes, who then "lorded it over the country" as constable of Denbigh, including the rangership of Snowdon. In the Caerwys MSS is a correct and interesting account of Sir Richard Bulkeley, and his un-compromising character, to which, under providence, he owed his life, liberty, and ultimate success in withstanding Leicester's tyrannous conduct. The greatest test of genius, is the manner in which ex-traordinary difficulties are surmounted, such as that by which Sir R. Bulkeley counteracted all Lord Leicester's plans of aggrandizement at the expense of the freeholders of Mona and Caernarvonshire, assisted by his base accomplice, that renegade to his country Dr. Ellis Price of Plas Iolyn. Mr. Lloyd's comments upon these gentlemen's conduct, as recorded in the Sebright Papers, together with the copy of a letter in the Harl. Collection, I will take leave to insert here as a valuable contribution to this work;

171 J. Lloyd Caerwys MS.

which letter gives another instance of Lord Leicester's oppression and cruelty to Walter Lord Essex, whose son Robert, the celebrated favourite of Elizabeth, was brought up in Mona, living "there a contented and quiet life".

"Attempts[172] of the Earl of Leicester when made ranger of the forests of Snowdon to dispossess the freeholders of their estates. Dr. Ellis Price of Plas Iolyn, was made sheriff of Môn, to serve the earl's purposes, though he had not an acre of land in the county. Three grants belonging to the royal forest of Snowdon, now extant; one from the Duke of Suffolk, dated April 30th, 1532, and another in the 1st of Queen Elizabeth, signed by Robert Townsend, and a third in 1561, by Henry Sydney. The second was addressed to 'the master of the game, ranger, and keeper of the queen's highness' forest of Snowdon, in the county of Caernarvon." The last extended the forest into the counties of Merionydd and Mona, with the view of gratifying the rapacity of the favourite Dudley, Earl of Leicester, who had by letters patent, been appointed chief ranger of the forest. In consequence, he tyrannised over the counties with great insolence. A set of informers immediately acquainted him that most of the freeholders' estates might be brought within the boundaries. Commissioners were appointed to enquire of the encroachments and concealments of lands within the forest. Juries were empanelled; but their returns were rejected by the commissioners as unfavourable to the earl's designs. The jurors performed an honest part, and found a verdict for the country. Leland, who no longer before than the reign of Henry VIII had gone over this tract, as he did most of England, under the royal commission, yet reports that all "Cregery", i.e. Snowdon, is in Caernarvonshire, and no part in Merionethshire, though, says he that shire be mountains.[173]

A new commission was then directed to Sir R. Bulkeley of Baron Hill, Mona, Sir William Herbert and others; but this by the firmness of Sir R. Bulkeley was likewise superseded. But in 1578, another was appointed, dependent on the favourite. A packed jury was directed to appear at Beaumaris, who went on the same day to view the marsh of Malltraeth, ten miles distant, and found that marsh to be in the forest of Snowdon, notwithstanding it was in another county, and divided from the forest by an arm of the sea, because the commissioners had told them, that they had met with an indictment in the exchequer of Caernarvon (which they had broken open and ransacked), by which they had discovered that a stag had been roused in the forest of Snowdon, in Caernarvonshire,—was pursued to the banks of the Menai,—that it swam over that branch of the sea, and was killed at Malltraeth, "infra forestum nostram de Snowdon". The jury appeared in the Earl of Leicester's livery, blue, with ragged staves on their sleeves. They were ever after branded with the title of "the black jury who sold their country". Sir Richard Bulkeley, not the least daunted with this decision, continued steady in his opposition to the tyrant, and laid before the queen, the odiousness of the proceedings, and the grievances her loyal subjects, the Cambro-Britons, laboured under by the commission, insomuch that in 1579, she was pleased, by proclamation, to recall it.

172 Vol.2 Sebright Collection.
173 Itinerary, v. p.437.

Sir R. Bulkeley served in parliament for the county of Mona, the 2nd and 3rd sessions of Queen Mary, the 3rd of Elizabeth, and the 1st of James. "He was a goodly person, fair of complexion, and tall of stature. He was temperate in his diet,—not drinking of healths. In the last year of Elizabeth, being then somewhat stricken in years, he attended the council of marches at Ludlow, in winter time. When the Lord President Zouch went in his coach to church or elsewhere, Sir Richard used to ride on a great horse; and sometimes he would go from his lodging to church, in frost and snow, on foot, with a short cloak, silk stockings, a rapier and dagger, tarry all prayers and sermon, in very cold weather; insomuch that Lord Zouch was wont to say, he was cold to see him. Sir Richard was a great reader of history, and discourses of all estates and countries; of very good memory and understanding in matters belonging to housekeeping, marytime affayres, building of ships and maintaining them at sea. He drew his own letters, and answered all letters with his own hand; and being complained of at the council of the marches for breach of an order of that court, he drew his own answer, that he could not be evicted out of his possession but by course of common law,—pleaded magna charta, and demanded judgment; which answer being put into court, the chief-justice Sir Richard Shuttleworth, called for a sight thereof, and after perusal, said to the councillors at the bar, "look my masters, what a bone Sir R. Bulkeley hath cast into court for you to tire upon"; and the matter being argued, it was referred to the common law. He was a great housekeeper, and entertainer of strangers, especially such as passed to or from Ireland. He nobly entertained the Earl of Essex in his way to be lord lieutenant. He made provision of all necessaries for his table before-hand. He sent yearly two ships to Greenland, for cod, ling and other fish, which he did use to barter in Spain, for malaga and sherry wines, and always kept good stock of old sack in his cellar, which he called amiable, besides other wines. He kept two parks, well stored with red and fallow-deer, which did afford such plenty of venison, as furnished his table three or four times every week, in the season, besides pleasuring of friends. He kept several farms, besides his demesne in his hands, which furnished his house with fat beef, mutton, lamb, &c. He was an excellent horseman, and an expert tilter, keeping two or three stables of horses, one in Cheshire and another in Beaumaris, and a great stud of mares. His estate in Mona was £2,500, in Caernarvonshire £800, and in Cheshire £1,000 a year, having always a great stock of money lying in his chest. He kept many servants and attendants, tall and proper men. Two lacqueys in livery always ran by his horse. He never went from home without twenty or twenty-four to attend him. He was a great favourite of Queen Elizabeth. He had powerful friends at court, and had the gentry and commonality of the county of Mona at his service, except the Woods of Rhosmore, who were always his enemies. Sir Richard being one of the deputy lieutenants of Mona (upon intelligence of the Spanish armada threatening England) was to cesse the country in arms, and cessing Mr. Wood of Rhosmore, he was highly offended and thought himself too heavily loaden, therefore went up to court to the Earl of Leicester, carrying a false tale with him, that Sir Richard Bulkeley (a little before the attainder and execution of Thomas Salisbury, son of Catrin y Beren, by her first husband John Salisbury of Lleweney, and one of the accomplices of Antony Babington, the traitor, 1585), had been in the mountains of Snowdon, conferring with him, and that at a farm of Sir Richard's called Cwmligie, they had layn together two or three nights. The Earl glad of this information, presently acquaints the queen and council therewith. Sir Richard being called before

the council and examined, absolutely denied the whole matter; and when the Earl, at that time president of the queen's council, did severely enforce it against him, he told the Earl to his face, "your father and the very same men as nowe informe againste me, were like to undoe my father; for upon the
death of King Edward VI by letters patent from your father, he was commanded to proclayme Queen
Jane, and to muster the country, which he did accordingly; and had not my mother been one of Queen
Mary's maids of honour, he had come to great trouble and danger." Hearing these words, the council
hushed and rose, and Sir Richard departed. The Earl hastened to the queen, and told her, that the
council had been examining Sir Richard Bulkeley about matters of treason, that they found him a dangerous person, and saw cause to commit him to the tower, and that he dwelt in a suspicious corner of
the world: "What! Sir Richard Bulkeley", said the queen "he never intended us any harm. We have
brought him up from a boy, and have special tryal of his fidelity! you shall not commit him." "We" answered Leicester, "have the care of your majesty, see more, and hear more of the man than you doe. He
is of an aspiring mind, and lives in a remote place." "Before God", replied the queen, "we will be sworn
upon the holy evangelist, he never intended us any harm", and so ran to the bible and kissed it, saying,
"you shall not commit him, we have brought him up from a boy". Then the lords of the council wrote
a letter to Dr. Bellot, Lord Bishop of Bangor, to examine the truth of the accusation layd to Sir
Richard's charge, which the bishop found false and forged, and so certified to the council; whereupon
he was cleared, to the queen's majesty's great content,—to the abundant joy of his country, and to his
own great credit and reputation. And afterwards, divers of the lords of the council wrote letters to the
justices of assize of North Wales, to publish Sir Richard's wrongs, and to notify to the Queen's subjects, his clear innocence. But that Sir Richard might not rest in peace, one Green, belonging to the
Earl of Leicester, in the name of one Bromfield, a pensioner, came to him to challenge him to meet
Bromfield in the field. "Have you no other errand?" quoth Sir Richard, "No", says Green. Then Sir
Richard drew his dagger, and broke Green's pate; telling him to carry that as an answer, he scorning
to meet such a knave as Bromfield. This treatment of Green, highly increased the anger of the earl.
Bromfield, Green, and others of his retainers, plotted mischief to the person of Sir Richard, but he
stood upon his guard, keeping always twenty-four stout men, with swords, bucklers, and daggers, to
defend him from their attempts. They hired boats and wherries upon the Thames, with a design to
drown Sir Richard as he went from Westmynster to London: but he being privately informed thereof,
borrowed the lord mayor's barge, furnished with men, musquets, billets, drums, and trumpets, and
rowed along the Thames, shot the bridge, and went down to Greenwich, where the queen kept her
court at that tyme; and at the landing place, over against the palace, caused his companie to discharge
their musquets, to beat their drums, and sound their trumpets. The Earl of Leicester hearing thereof,
repaired to the queen, and informed her, that Sir Richard Bulkeley, more like a rebel than a subject,
had come with barges, men, musquets, drums, and trumpets, and had shot several pieces over against
her majesty's palace, to the great terror of her court, a matter not to be suffered. The queen sent for Sir
Richard, and after hearing his apology for himself, made the earl friends with him. Within a while after,
the earl sent for Sir Richard to his chamber, who coming thither, the earl began to expostulate with
him on several wrongs and abuses, he pretended to have received at his hands, and that he had lost

£10,000 by his opposition; but the discourse ended in milder terms, and Sir Richard was bidden to dinner, but did eat or drink nothing, save of what he saw the earl taste; remembering Sir Nicolas Thogmorton, who was said to have received a fig at his table. But the Earl of Leicester dying in October, 1588, Sir Richard Bulkeley and his country, enjoyed peace and quietness from his tyrannical oppressions, his devices and wicked practises, and Sir Richard Bulkeley survived to the 28th of June, 1621, when he died, aged eighty-eight. He had attended the coronation of Mary, Elizabeth, and James. His cloak at the last coronation, cost him £500. His second wife, Alice Needham, was implicated with the Goodmans in attempting to poison this "good olde knighte in a cuppe of metheglyn". Mr. Pennant gives the same account of Lord Leicester's conduct, as the above, which is quoted from the Caerwys and Plâs Gwyn MSS.

The life of the illustrious Robert, Earl of Essex, &c. written by Mr. Coddrington, Harl. Miscellany, p.155.—"Sir W. Devreux was created Viscount Hereford and Earl of Essex, about the 12th of Elizabeth, because he was descended by his mother's side from the ancient and honourable family of the Bourchiers, some tyme Earls of Essex. It was the deliberate pleasure of the queen and state, to increase his honours by the knowledge of the fullness of his merit, and to make him Governor of Ireland; and this place being preferred unto him (for indeed he was a gentleman of incomparable endowments) he did manage the affairs of that kingdom with great honour and judgment; by a secret power of attraction, which is natural and inherent to that family, he gained the approbation and applause of all men, and did much advance the affairs of England in that kingdom. But the ambition and policy of the Earl of Leicester, who would have no man more eminent than himself, did so prevail at court, that upon no cause at all, but that Lord Essex was as good as he was great, he must needs be dishonoured from his dignity, and the government of Ireland conferred on Sir Henry Sidney, a deserving gentleman indeed, and the more meritorious because he was the father of Sir Philip Sidney. This indignity did stick such an impression on this noble earl, who had now only a charge of some empty regiments of horse and foot, that his melancholy brought a fever on him; and the sooner because his *friend* was the author of this injury; for the Earl of Leicester did pretend to no man greater affection than to himself. After some days his sickness did confine him to his chamber, and afterwards to his bed. His dying words were remarkable: he desired that his son who was then not above ten years of age, might refrain from the court, and not trust his ear with the flatteries, nor his eye with the splendour of it; and above all things, that he should be mindful of the six and thirtieth year of his age, beyond which neither he, nor very few of his forefathers lived. His instructed son did obey his father's will, and for many years did lead a contented and retired life in Anglesey; until (I know not by what spell) the Earl of Leicester did work him into the fatal circle, and betrayed him to destruction. Being condemned to the block, he remembered his father's prediction, which now he could not avoid. And which is indeed wonderful, on the same hour (and as it is believed, on the very same minute) that he was beheaded, his son, who at that time was a student in Eton College, did suddenly and distractedly leap out of his bed, where he was fast asleep, and to the amazement of all, he cried that his father was killed—his father was dead! And not many hours after, the sad news was brought, which, so early in the morning, and so strangely he presaged."

To return to the Baron Hill family. Richard, the fourth viscount Bulkeley, was a noted jacobite, and to him are addressed these curious letters, signed A.B. The writer feigns to be of the royal side, calling James the Second's son "Pretender and Chevalier",—directing his letters to John Richards, Beaumaris.

London, January 21, 1715.

SIR,

This day His Majesty came to the House, and gave his assent to the Habeas Corpus Bill being suspended till the 23rd of May next; and then made a speech to both Houses, and told them, that it was now certain that the Pretender was in Scotland, to head the rebellion there, and that he and those with him certainly expected reliefe from abroad, and therefore recommends to them to take such measures as may effectually disappoint all invasion of papists, &c. ——t certainly all good protestants who have regard to their civil or religious rights, but what will exert themselves in such a juncture.

Some say that it is expected that the Regent of France will declare himself openly in favour of the Pretender.

And 'tis said that the mob in Paris run after Lord Stair's coach and insult him, by crying out "assassin, assassin !"

Mr. S. S. said in the house, that there is six or seven hundred officers in and about Dunkerque, ready to imbark for Scotland, The D. of Argyle was to march as yesterday, without further delay, to attaque Lord Mar, let it cost what it will.

I am, as ever, with all just respect,

To John Richards, at Beaumaris,   Your most faithful Servant,
    In the Isle of Anglesea.   A. B

February 4, 1715.

SIR,

General Cadogan marched with the vanguard from Stirling, on Friday last week, and the D. of Argyle followed with the body of the army, the day after, so that in all probability the greatest part of the action is over ere now. I hope to tell you next post, how all is gone with the rebells. Our army consists of 9,000 or thereabouts; and that under Lord Mar about 7,000 strong, and that the latter intends to dispute his grace's passage over the river Em. Three ships are arrived in Scotland, with officers, &c. A great deal depends upon what this march will produce. God's will be done.—Adieu.

To John Richards, at Beaumorce, Anglesea.

February 9th, 1715–16.

SIR,

This day the Lord Chancellor was Lord High Steward for this day, and pass'd sentence on six of the Preston lords.

The Pretender left Perth on Tuesday last week, and he and the army under Lord Mar retired to Montrosse, some thirty miles north-east from thence; and it is said, that he and Lord Mar are imbarked there and gone, tho' I believe he may make a stand at the bridge upon Dee, near Aberdeen.

I am, as ever, Sir,

For John Richards, att Beaumorise,   Your most faithful Servant,
    Anglesea.   A. B.

February 23rd, 1715–16.

SIR,

There has been great disputes yesterday in both Houses. The lords disputed and divided severall times about the receiving the petition of the condemned lords, and tho' it was caryed in the House of Lords by twenty majority, to petition His Majesty: accordingly this day the lords carried their add—— on this day (tomorrow being appointed for the day of execution). Their answer was, I will no this, as on all other occasions, do what is most for the honour of the government, and the safety of my kingdoms. But notwithstanding of all this, I do believe Lord Nithsdale, Viscount Kennore, and Lord Widderington will suffer tomorrow. I am told that 600 of the guards are ordered to be on Tower Hill tomorrrow, at eight in the morning.

The Comons did choose rather to agourn themselves, than receive the petition.

I am, Sir,

To John Richards, at Beaumorise,   Your most humble Servant.
    Anglesea.

February 28th, 1715–16.

SIR,

Yesterday I had the honour of your's, with your handsome undeserved present, of such an uncommon sort, that I could never have expected. However I pretend not to give you any other return than to tell you, I shall long for having it in my power to make you a more suitable satisfaction, than in words or writing.

Pamphlets of late are all of one side, either for the government, or on account of taking the oaths, or poetry, panegyricks upon our king, or this or t'other minister, and to tell you the truth, the army, &c has knock'd down all our paper war.

I have reason to believe that Lord Notingame and his brother, with their children—even Sir R. Mostyn will all be turned out.

Lord Windsor will out soon, and Orrery and Orkney, I hear has orders to sell.

The three condemned lords are reprieved till March the 7th, at which time, I am afrayd they must suffer. Lord Nithsdale was to have suffer'd on Friday last, made his escape over night, in a ridinghood which his lady brought in on purpose; so now we calle a woman's riding hood, a Nithsdale.

All the gentlemen, we are told, will suffer death, without doubt. The chevalier and several of the Scotch nobility are at Barledue.

I am, without compliment, Sir,

Your most obliged and most faithful Servant,

Direct to me at Will's Coffee-House, in Bo.-street.   A.B.
    Coven Garden, London.

For Mr. John Richards, &c.

April 10th, 1716.

SIR,

This day the D. of Devonshire proposed the taking off the triennial bill, and Lord Notinghame and his brother opposed it with all their might; but it being carried against them and the bill was read for the first time. No doubt it will pass both Houses, yet it is brought in by the lords, in hopes to cast off all the odium from off the Comons, thereby to save their interest amongst their electors. This day the prince of your country, treats all the loyal Irish gentlemen, in Somersett House, by reason, the university of Dublin have chosen him their chancellor. So soon as our court knew of the chevalier being landed in Scotland, then the king writ to the Earl of Marr, and promised him £100,000, a general pardon for all that was past, life, fortune, and honour, &c. and any places and preferments, he would ask if he would deliver up the chevalier. This letter was sent by an express to the D. of Argyle (who by the by is in disgrace) and his grace was to send it forward to his lordship, and be sure to have it delivered into his lordship's hands, which was done accordingly. This letter the Earle of Mar never show'd it to the chevalier, nor made the least mention of it to him, till they landed in France. Mr. Walpool is in a fair way of recovery.

I am, Sir,

For John Richards, at Beaumarice,   Your most faithful Servant,
    Anglesea.   A.B.

March 3rd, 1715.

SIR,

Lord Notinghame was turned out, whereupon his brother, son, and nephew, layd down, seeing they were to be turned out, and Sir R. Mostyn will follow very soon, 'tis believed.

There was like to be a great division in both Houses, but our vigilant ministers do always contrive some thing to divert them till their heat is over, which is commonly very soon. "Twas given out in both Houses yesterday, at noon, that a messenger had come in that minute from Lord Stairs, to acquaint the court that the Regent of France had resolved in council, to declare war against England. This will not only divert the Lords and Comons, but they will agree to raise more forces, and even to bring over more foreign troops to—inslave the —
— .

I am, with all due respect and esteem,

For Mr. John Richards, at Beaumarice,   Your's, most faithfully,
    Angelsea.   A.B.

March 10th, 1715.

SIR,

We are credibly informed that the seals are taken from Lord Bollinbrook, for having kept up a letter, from the chevalier his master, which was writ to him by Lord Marr, which letter was to this purpose:—"The Marquess of Huntley and Seaforth have deserted your cause, so that we are like to be in the utmost confusion; therefore seeing you have delayed your coming hither till this time, I do beg it of you not to venture at this desperate juncture." But instead of giving him this letter, he kept it up and hurryed him as much as possible to venture through all the difficulties imaginable. Others do add that he has divulged all he knew to Lord Malborow. The seals were given to Lord Marr.

I am, with all truth, Sir,

For Mr. John Richards, &c.   Your most faithful Servant, A.B.

London, March 24, 1716.

SIR,

The private news at present is that the courtiers have had severall meetings with their cronies, in the House of Comons, in order to settle all things, to bring in a bill to take off the triennial billes for calling of parliaments. And the plausible reason that is to be given for the absolute necessity for so doing is, that the emperor, the states of Holland, and several other potentates, will not come in to any new league or alliances with Great Britain, until such time as they are very well assured that they shall not be abused, and left in the lurch, as they were of late by the late ministry.

'Tis very confidently reported, that the Bishop of London has lost his reason, and is actually gone mad.

Whither the Chevalier de St. George is gone to the Principality of Deux Pontris (in Germany) belonging to the King of Sweden, or whither he is gone to Avignon, belonging to the Pope, tho' within the territorys of France, 'tis somewhat uncertain to us, as yett.

One thing I am certain of, which is, that I am with all truth and sincerity, as well as with all duty and respect,   Sir, your most obliged,

And most faithful Servant,

For John Richards, &c.   A.B.

March 16, 1715-16.

Sir,

Letters from Paris, from pretty good hands, tell us that no doubt you at London hear a great deal of the Lord Bullenbrook. I must tell you in short that he is ten times a greater villain than you there can imagine. We are told that he has not only betrayed all the chevalier's concerns, but that of the French court, as far as he could; and thus he actually settled a correspondence with the D. of Malb'orow, before he went hence.

The Duke of Argyle met not with an agreeable reception, however we hear that he declares open war against the gest Duke of Malb'orow, and that one or t'other shall certainly fall. Argyle intends to bring in an Act of Indemnity for a general pardon over both kingdoms. There was a prospect of calling all the lords to town, or that they should send their proxys, in order for a general pardon, and that the two archbishops should bring it in. But that is dropt, and his grace is to do it.

I am, Sir, your most obliged
and most humble Servant,
A.B.

Lord Strangford and Mr. Manering have renounced the Church of Rome. Lord Winton's tryal is not yet over, but he will be certainly tomorrow, or on Saturday at farthest.

Lord Nithisdale is certainly arrived in France.

To Mr. John Richards, &c.

LLANVAES.—About a mile north of Beaumaris, is that memorable spot, Llanvaes, "the church of the field or plain", from a memorable battle said to have taken place here early in the ninth century, between Egbert, King of the West-Saxons, who had effected a landing in Mona, near the site of the present town of Beaumaris, and a body of Welsh forces, whom he totally defeated in a sanguinary engagement; although he was shortly after compelled by Mervyn Vrych, the Sovereign of North Wales, to retreat into England. This victory was the cause of the ancient name of Mona being abandoned by the Anglo Saxons for its present appellation, Anglesey. This parish is of a small extent; the soil is fertile, and on the whole well cultivated, consisting of rich meadows, corn fields, and a few acres of woodland. The living is a perpetual curacy, endowed with £400 private benefactions, £800 royal bounty, and £600 parliamentary grant, and in the patronage of Sir R. Bulkeley. The church, dedicated to St. Catherine, is an ancient and spacious structure, in the early style of English architecture, with a lofty square embattled tower, which was built in 1811, at the sole expense of the late Lord Bulkeley. The Rev. John Williams is the present incumbent. The population in 1821 was 213, and in 1831, 271. Lady Bulkeley bequeathed £1,000 in trust to the Archdeacon of Anglesey, and the minister of Llanvaes, to distribute the interest annually, among the poor of this parish. The rates in 1803 were £70, at 3s. in the pound, and in 1831, £124 8s. 8d.

All that remains of the ruins of the priory, once so "splendidly endowed"[174] is now a barn. "Llewelyn ab Iorwerth, Tywysog Cymru a wnaeth brodordu Llanvaes",[175] which was consecrated by Howel, Bishop of Bangor, in 1240, over the remains of Joan, daughter of King John, "Princesse of Wales, who

174 Sebright Papers.
175 "Llewelyn ab Iorwerth Drwyndwn, a wnaeth mynachlog Aberconwy, a brodordu Llanfaes, er coffadwriaeth am y dywysoges, a vu varw 1231."—LIyvr Du Dinas Basing.

was buried upon the sea-shore, within the Isle of Mona, att Llanvaes, as hir pleasure was where the Prince dyd build a house of Barefoote Freers over hir grave";[176] a testimony of respect which may, in some degree, take away the stain that history has cast upon her character. Gryffydd, the son of Ednyved Vychan, was obliged to fly into Ireland, to avoid Llewelyn's wrath for his lampoon "am y Dywysoges Siân",[177] In the Black Book of Basingwerk she is praised for her good sense and *discretion*, thus corroborated by Powel, in the Welsh Chronicle, p.265:— "Then Prince Llewelyn seeinge all England and Wales againste hym (1211) thoughte itt best to entreat with the kinge, and thereupon sente Jone hys wiffe, the kinge's daughter to hir father to make peace; who beinge a discreete woman, found means, that upon pledges given ffor safe conduct, the prince came to the kinge and made peace, and dyd homage", &c. Black William de Breos (Gwylym Ddu) Earl of Pembroke, is said to have been one of the hostages sent by King John. Mr. Lloyd observes, that in the wars afterwards, when this nobleman fell into the hands of the Prince of Wales, he had, ransomed himself for 3,000 marks, but was afterwards taken and hanged by Llewelyn, at Aber. This gave rise to a supposition that the princess was partial to him, and tradition says, that a bard of the palace met and accosted her in the following manner:

> " Diccin, doccin, gwraig Llewelyn,
> " Beth a roit am weled Gwylym ? "

To which the princess answered—

> " Cymru—Lloegr—a Llewelyn,
> " I gid y rown i weled Gwylym."

On which the bard pointed to him suspended on a tree opposite the palace windows. The extent of Tindaethwy, taken 26th of Edward III contains the following notice:—"Here in former times was a Priory of Barefoot Friars; and Davydd ab Madoc, and Madoc ab Ievan and other bond servants, do suit att the Lord Prince's mill, at Llanvaes, at two-pence per diem. In this township there is one water mill, which is now let to Gronw Bron, for 26s. 8d. and which used to be let for 18s." &c. This priory was dedicated to St. Francis, whose head, Mr. Lloyd says, was seen by him on a carved stone in a wall, at Beaumaris. Within its precincts are buried several persons of note; a son of the King of Denmark, besides other knights[178] who fell in (Gwaith Llanvaes) the battle of Llanvaes, 818. By the Black Book of Basingwerk Abbey, I find that in 1280, the Princess Eleanor was buried here "yn anrhydeddis iawn" with royal pomp and honours; and several of King Edward's leading warriors slaine in the action of the Menai rest in this place. Here also were deposited the remains of Gryffydd Grûg, the bard, who flourished from 1330 to 1370, and an able opponent of Davydd ab Gwyllym, as appears from his monody, written by that generous rival. The Lord Clifford, whose death is recorded in a note to p.112, was buried at Llanvaes, which must have been a favourite place of interment, in those days of superstition

---

176 Welsh Chronicles, p.293.
177 Hengwrt MS.
178 Powel Chronicles, p.66.

and ignorance.[179] The will of Sir Poland Velvelle leaves £5 to the friars to celebrate mass for his soul. The items being curious induce me to give a few extracts. He begins by saying he was squier of the bodye to Henry VIII &c. "I, Sir Roland Velville, constable of Beaumaris Castle, knighte, &c. My wille is to bee burried in the monastery of Llanvaes, leaving £5 to a chaplain to celebrate masses ffor my soul; alsoe I bequeath to the said Monasterye of Minor Friars 13s. 8d. and to the Chapel of the Blessed Mary att Beaumaris, 15s. To the Monastery of Preachinge Friers att Bangor, 13s. alsoe I bequeath to the Church of St. Eistyn, 6s. 8d. To the "fabric of the Bangor Cathedrall" 6s. 8d. the same to the Church of St. Tegvan, and to St. Catherine, 6s. 8d. alsoe I bequeath to Agnes, my wiffe, all the landes, burgages, fines, houses, &c. lying in Beaumaris. The residue of my goodes I leave to my wieff Agnes Gryffydd, alias Velville, whome I alsoe appointe sole executrix. Dated to the place of my habitation, the Castel o Beaumares, in the presence of Mr. Thomas Grono Canter, Mr. William Rhys, Rector of Beaumarys, John Gryffydd, son and heire of Edmund Gryffydd, Richard Johnson, Burgess, William ab Grono, Medici." This will of Sir Roland Velville's was proved before Archbishop Cranmer, "in his court of Canterbury, in the third year of his consecration, 1533".

There must have been a town here of some note in the time of Llewelyn the Great, for in a chronological table[180] compiled then, there is the following entry for 1211:—"on the vigil of St. Simon and St. Jude in this year, the steward of the household of the King of Denmark, by name Harold Pig, came to Lanvaes with six privateers, and despoiled the town, and burnt it; and there he and the best of his followers were slain."[181] The friars in this monastery sided with Madoc in his rebellion (as related in p. 59) and consequently they were great sufferers, their church and priory were destroyed by the English. Edward II. In consideration of their misfortunes, remitted to the friars the payment of taxes, due to him, which before the war, were levied at £12 10s. annually. This king at the same time granted, or rather renewed a charter of Prince Llewelyn ab Iorwerth.

Page 793, vol. 4, Sebright Collection, Claus 12, E.2 M.8 "P. Decano & capitto Ecclie Bangoren." This is directed to the treasurers and baron of the exchequer, and sets forth that the dean and chapter of Bangor, "colltor decime epãtus Bangoreñs", i.e. if I mistake not, collectors of the tenths of the clergy, in the diocese of Bangor, had represented that the Church of Lamas "nũp in gueᷓia Madoci ap Llewelyn, contra celebris memorie dñm E. quond Regem Añgl prẽm nr̃m motam ꝙ combustionem & destrucioẽm, maneni & ville ibidem ac translacõem ꝙochianõr ejusdem ecclie de mandato & ordinãcoe dc̃i patris nr̃i ad villas de Bello Marisco & Rosphair quo ad redditus & ꝙovᷓ̃as in tantũ minorata existat quod valorem 20 solidõr a tempore combustionis destrucõis & translacõis pr̃dictõr non excessit nec adhuc excedit, sicut ꝙ inquisioᷘ ꝙ dilc̃m et fidelem nr̃m Rogerũ de Mortuomari de Chirk Jusᷓc Watt ad mandatũ nr̃m, &c. It further set forth, that before this period pr̃dicta eccᷓia ante guarra illã ad 12 lĩbr & 10 solid taxata fuit põne deciar & aliõr auxiliõr tam dc̃o pri qm̃ nõb a teᷘpe pr̃dicto ꝙ clerᷓ regni nr̃i concẽssor." &c. The king in consideration of their impoverished state, exempts them from the

179 Lleweny Papers.
180 Page 256 of the Red Book of Hergest, Jesus College, Oxon.
181 "1211, Nos Wyl Symon a Jude, y vlwyddyn honno y daeth sytiwart Llys Llychlyn, Herallt Pig, oedd ei enw, a chwech herw llong gantaw, hyd yn Llanvaes, ac espeiliaw y drev, ai llosgi, ac a llas Harallt yno, ai oreu gwyr".

payment of the tenths. Dated York, 22nd of May.

The church here mentioned to be laid waste, is Llanvaes, alias Friars, in Mona. The war here alluded to, was an insurrection made, if I mistake not, in favour of Madoc, the infant son of our last Llewelyn, in which he perished. I have read somewhere, that he was taken and murdered, in cold blood. Query.—What is said in this instrument to be translated from this church to Beaumaris and Rosphair, a corruption of Rosvair, alias Newborough, pochîanor for parochaniorum, i.e. parishioners.—*J. Lloyd.*[182]

These brothers, i.e. friars, were likewise strong favourers of Owen Glyndwr. Henry, in his first march against Owen, plundered the convent, and put several of them to the sword, and carried away the rest; but afterwards set them at liberty, and made restitution to the place, and peopled it with English recluses. It was again reduced to ruin; and I find by the following grant, that Henry V relieved them, provided that there should be always in this monastery eight friars, and that *two only* should be natives.

Vol.4, Sebright Collection, pat. 2 Henry V. m. 29. "P. Fratribus minôr de Llamaysi. R. omnibus ad quos, &c. Saltm̃ monstraverunt nobis diſti nobis in x̄tio. Frẽs ordines patrũ minorũ qualiſter domus fr̃m minôr de Llamasi infra Insulam nr̃am Anglese in North Waꝉ, in qua quidem domo divinũ ſerv̄m ab antiquo honeste factũ fuit & usitatũ ꝑ rebellionẽ Wallensiũ & guerrar̃ ibidem jam tarde factar̃ & continuatar̃ totaliter desolata & obsequiũ divinũ in eadem diminutũ et substractũ existunt. Nos. considerantes quod domus pr̃dicta de fundacoẽ ꝑꝑgenitôr nror̃m quondam. Regũ Angl & nr̃o patronatu existit & similiter quod in eadem domo corpus tam filie Regis John ꝑgenitoris nr̃i quam filii Regis Dacie nec non corpora dñi de Clifford & aliôr Dnôr militũ & armiger̃or qui in guerris Wallie tẽporibus illustriũ ꝑꝑrogentôr nrôrm oc̃isi fuerant sepulta existunt ac volentes ꝑinde servicũ divinu in ꝑfata demo manuteneri & ibidem de cetero continuari. Concessimus ꝑ nobis & heredibus nris quantũ in nobis est quod in eadẽ servicia celebratur̃ & Deũ ꝑꝑ salubri statũ nr̃o ac carissimorum̃ fratrũ nror̃um & aliom̃ de sanguine & ꝑꝑgenie ñris & ꝑꝑ animabus ñris cũ ab hac luce migraverimus & similiter ꝑ aiãbus pr̃is & matris mortũ & ꝑꝑgenitôr nrom̃ & eôr qui in domo ꝑꝑdicta ut ꝑdictũ est sunt sepulti & omnia fideliũ defunctor̃m exoratur̃ imꝑqm̃ quorũ quidem octo fratrum exoratur̃ imꝑꝑm̃ quorũ quidem octo fratrum volumus quod duo sint de natione Walliensi rône victus sui & aliorũ ad sustentacõem suam necessariom̃ adquirẽnd. In Cujus, &c. T. R. apud Westm̃ tercio die Julii ꝑ b̄ve de privato sigillo."

It appears from the above patent, that the Friary of Llanvaes had suffered considerable damage in the wars of Owen Glyndwr. I presume that the number of friars minors in this house, was greater before this period; and that they were now obliged to be reduced to eight, on account of the desolation hinted at. In the patent, only two Welshmen were admitted of the number.[183]

Page 185, Sebright Collection of vol.4, a thick 4to. bound in calf containing grants, charters, inspeximas's, &c. all in latin. In the beginning are some instruments relative to Scotland. Page 183 (observes Mr. Lloyd) contains a charter granted by Edward I to Vale y Crucis Abbey, dated at Llanvaes.

182 Caerwys MS.
183 Caerwys MS.

The first part is wanting, by a leaf being either lost or misplaced. The first that is entire, is a confirmation of his former grant by Madoc ap Gryffydd of Maelor, the founder, dated 1205. The second is a grant from all the freemen of Llangollen, by name of a fishery, in part of the river Devrdwy, near their town, and for want of a seal of their own, they made use of that of Madoc the founder, by his affixing it to the instrument himself. After this, a dispute arose about erecting the said fishery. It seems the freeholders of Llangollen were unwilling that the monks should construct any new works upon the river, for the purpose of taking fish. After many quarrels and disputes, they at last referred the matter to the abbot and five of his monks, of their own choosing, who should, upon oath, adjust the affair. Madoc who is here styled prince, and his seneschal, J. Parous, appoint a day for this purpose. The abbot and his monks, in the presence of the prince, seneschal, and several others, after taking their solemn oaths, make a decree in their own favour, affirming that they had purchased from the heirs of Llangollen, a right of erecting and repairing their fishery, in what manner they pleased, &c. The prince ratifies and confirms this decree, and the donation of the fishery, &c. Dated 1234. The third is a confirmation of all the grants of his father, by Gryffydd, the son of the above Madoc. "Scriptum confirmacois q⁹ Griffinus filius dc̃i Madoici fecit Abbati et Conventus cisterciensis ordinis apud Vallem Crucis deo et bẽ marie ibidem servientibus", &c. He confirms Dona ives etiam coheredum ejusdem Madoic Videlt Owini Ponkintonm filienin etiam Owini parvi de Gwaenmevoc eisdem monachis confirmari. Dated 1237. The fourth is of Fulca filius Gwarini. He grants and confirms to them Domum hominum meorum de Porkingtyn scilt totam terram de Ceymluesteu Regis Henrici Anglorum in totis terminis suis, &c. Et sunt istius terre termini de Karreg henant majori usq⁹ ad minorem et de minori carregnant dum durat gweble usq⁹ ad nand Gorsedde et deinde usq⁹ ad Heleck Correloet &̄ usq⁹ ad mordaf." Then follows a general confirmation of the whole, by Edward I dated at Lammays, 24th day of April;—no year specified.

I find (the 25th of Edward I) by the same volume, that John de Havering held his court at Llanvaes. P. 216.—Eschaeta de Anno 25th Edward I. "Inquisitio cãpt apud Lamays Cõr John de Haveringe die Jovis px̃a ante festum Invencios st̃e Crucis Anno R. R. E. 25 ꝓHowell Chwith, &c.

By this inquisition it appears that the lands of Iorwerth Gôch and Davydd Chwith, in "Glasgrug and Thleghok in Turkelyn" were charged annually to Prince Llewelyn, at the rate of 24s. 8d. in lieu of all services. But after his death, the king sent Dn̄s Gocelinus de Badlesmere &̄ "frater Leolinus" to make an extent of the whole Isle of Mona, who unjustly charged the villains of the above named Iorwerth and Davydd with 24s. 6d. over and above the said sum of 34s. 8d. In this record we have the names of the very persons who made the survey of Mona. Temp. Edward I.—*J. Lloyd.*

In an extent of the County of Mona, taken by John de Delves, A.D. 1352, I find that the heirs of Iorwerth Gôch, and Davydd Chwith, were in possession of Glasgrug and Llechog, in that year. "Melin Isaf", in Amlwch, belonged to Iorwerth Gôch; this mill, "besides plough lands, yielding on account of escheat, three pounds annual rent". By the following englyn, I discover that Iorwerth Gôch resided at Bodavon.—

> " Mae deigen y Glaslyn, mae digon—o dottes,
> " O ddae tu Bodavon,
> " Mae tir Iorwerth, serth, heb sôn,
> " Gwych—heb gael—Gôch ab Gwion."

At the dissolution, Henry VIII sold this house and its possessions, to one of his courtiers. In his rage for reformation, the church of the convent, was converted into a barn, and the coffin of Princesse Joan was taken up, and placed near a brook, from which ignominy (after being used for 250 years as a water trough) it was rescued by the late Lord Bulkeley, who erected a suitable gothic mausoleum for its reception, in his grounds at Baron Hill, where it is now to be seen, with a suitable inscription in British, Latin, and English. Here are still remaining the gothic arches, door-ways, and carved roof of the old monastery, in a tolerable state of preservation; in the yard is a carved stone coffin lid, with no inscription, and in the flower garden is a plain stone basin, which has the appearance of having been a baptismal font. In digging foundations for buildings, in and near the gardens, yards, &c. the workmen frequently discover human bones, ornamented tiles, &c. Over an archway, close to the House of Friars, are the arms of Whyte (sable, a chevron between three fleur de lis, argent) cut in stone, with the initials R. W. 1623, L. B." A short extract, accounting for the name, taken out of the Salusbury Pedigree, may be interesting to some of the readers. "John Wyn (so called by his nurse) was third sonn to Robert Vychan, of Plâs Hên, in Evionydd, from Collwyn ab Tangno, and served the Earl of Pembroke, in 1565, who having another servant, called John Wyn, ffor distinction sake, hee desyred thys John Wyn ab Robert Vychan, to call hymself by the surname of Whyte, whych hys posterity have continued, sayth Mr. William Whyte of Shrewsburie's Genealogy, and is soe entered in Mr. Dugdale's booke ffor Salop, A.D. 1663. Ievan Whyte, the eldest sonn of John Whyte, lived at Llanfair, in Môn. Dr. Robert Whyte was a physician in London. Sir Richard Whyte, another sonn, lived in London, and married Elisabeth Adgar of Gloucestershire. Gryffith Whyte lived and married in Salop; and Rowland Whyte, another sonn of the above John Whyte, lived at Friars, in Môn, and in 1623, built there a goodly mansion", which was purchased by the late Lord Bulkeley, from his brother (by the mother's side) the late Sir Robert Williams, Bart. whose son Sir William Bulkeley inherits it from Lord Bulkeley; and his mother Lady Williams, lives at this beautiful marine residence, displaying much taste in improving the house and grounds, and dispensing comforts to the neighbouring poor, by relieving their wants with a liberal hand and feeling heart.

The MSS copied by the industrious compilers of the "Salusbury Pedigree" (out of which book the above document was taken), were an authority, be it remembered, sufficiently high to induce a Tudor of Pen-mynydd, in Mona, successfully to claim the throne of England, who in the Battle of Bosworth stood under the ancient colours of Britain, i.e. a banner of green and white silk, displaying the Red Dragon of his nation, thereby appealing to that union of local attachment, innate honour, and perhaps prejudice, which constitutes (as Mr. Lloyd aptly observes) what is called nationality; and when his kindred and country were objected to, as vile and barbarous, "sente a commission to make out his paternal ancestors, to the twentieth degree, to the Abbot of Vale y Crucis, Dr. Owen Poole, Canon of Hereford, Sir John Leiaf, &c. in the search of British MSS of pedigrees, out of which they drew King Henry VII's perfect genealogy, from the ancient kings of Britaine, and Princes of Wales.[184]

---

184 Powel's Chronicles. Wynn, &c.

ABERFFRAW,—"A elwir velly o'r avon sy'n i hymyl lle rhoedd gynt Lŷs enwog i Ddwysog Gwynedd ar avon honno a elwir Ffraw; ac ewyr pawb mae Aber cyn y Vrutanet a arwydd ocha yn gyffredin gyhurdhiad a thrawiad avon yn a môr Tegaingl, sev Tanaet. Gaer Segont, herwydd yr y savai garllaw avon a elwid yn gyffredin Avon y Saint. Ac a elwid hevyd Caer Euda; ac o achos i bod yn agos i Vôn, elwid y wlâd Ar-Vôn.[185]

Aberffraw is now reduced to a village, containing about 179 houses, with a population in 1821 of 1,204, and in 1831 of 1,367;—in 1831 the poor-rates amounted to £583 19s. 0d. It is situated in the Comot of Malltraeth, and distant about twelve miles from Holyhead;—is a rectory in the gift of the Prince of Wales, and valued temp. Henry VIII at £20 15s. 10d. The present incumbent is the Rev. Hugh Wynne Jones. The church is dedicated to St. Beuno, who founded Clynog Vechan, in 616. The wakes celebrated on the 21st of April. This Beuno, was son of Hugi ab Gwynlliw, he was founder of the Monastery of Clynog, in Arvon.[186] In p.9, vol.3, Cambro-Briton, may be seen more about this saint.

An old ruin, called "Eglwys y Baili" was repaired in 1729, by Sir Arthur Owen of Bodowen, for a school, who endowed it with £4 per annum, very sensibly prohibiting all foreign languages, thereby ensuring to the "six poor children" a knowledge of the scriptures (as wisely enacted by the rubric) in the vulgar tongue.

Excepting the walls of a barn and Gardd y Llŷs, at the west end of Aberffraw, not a vestige remains to mark the spot where once stood the princely residence of the Sovereigns of North Wales.[187]

The chiefest of the three royal domains,[188] established by Roderic the Great (as related in the acts of the princes), and his eldest son Anarawd, one of the three coronetted kings of the Isle of Britain kept his court here, in 877, the acknowledged Sovereign of all Wales, "Brenin Cymru oll"; the other two princes paying him "Maelged", in token of homage, and the ancient Teyrnged to the King of London, was to be paid by the Princes of Aberffraw,[189] &c. The "non-paimint" of this tribute was the cause of Edgar's invasion of Mona, which is given in p.34 of this history, which also records the death of Rodri ab Idwal, and the devastation of this royal palace by the Irishmen. In this court was kept one of the three copies of the codes of laws regulated by Dyvnal Moelmud and Howel Dda; consequently Aberf-

---

185 "Llyvr Côch Asaph", which book is now in the possession of Mr. Athelstan Owen who lent it to the author in 1828.

186 Clynog, from Clun, and awg, water.—J Lloyd, Caerwys MSS.

187 About the year 1818, some amateur artists on a visit at Bodorgan, painted a full length portrait of Prince Llewelyn, in full armour, for a sign for the small inn in the village, kept by a widow of great celebrity, with the following lines under it:
" Where dwelt of old brave Prince Llewelyn,
" Betty Williams now is selling
" Bread and cheese, and good strong beer;
" Pri'thee traveller enter here ! "
        THUS TRANSLATED INTO WELSH.
        " Lle bu trigfa gynt Llewelyn,
        " Prif rëolwr, barnwr, brenhin,
        " Cewch yn awr gan fwynlan Betty,
        " Goreu bwyd a glanaf letty. "

188 Triad CXI. "The three royal domains, Aberffraw, Mathraval, and Dinevir. There was a prince wearing a diadem in each of the three dominions."

189 Mon. Ant. p.275. "Howell Dda's Code of Laws, establishing this tribute after the Britons had ceased to rule in England."

fraw was one of the three courts of justice for the principality, at which all causes were tried; and one of Prince Llewelyn's items of certaine greefes, sent by him to Edward I alludes to that king persisting, contrary to an article of agreement, "to sende justices to Mona, whoe presume to judge there the men and subjects of the prince; setting fines upon them, contrarie to the lawes of Wales, seeing neither this, nor anie like was ever heade in tymes paste; imprisoninge some, outlawing others, when the prince in at all tymes, readie to doo justice to all men, thatt complaine upon anie of his men; and at the laste, Prince Llewelyn was called to divers places, whither he ought not to have been called, neither coulde he obtaine justice, nor anie judgement, unlesse it were, according to the laws of Englande, contrarie to the saide articles of peace; and the kinge himselfe, at London, denied hym justice, unlesse he would be judged according to the English lawes in the said matter", &c.

The following being the extent of Aberffraw, shews in some measure, how the prince's rents were paid. Sebright Collection, vol.5, p.1 a thick quarto containing escheats, &c. "Yn y Twr." Aberffraw, &c ₽tin. Esch. aº 13, Edward III, nº. 58.

Extenta maneri de Aberffrau in North Wall facta apud Kaern die Sabbat px post frn sci Gregori aº R.R. Edward III post Conquest⁹ 13º Cora Wilo de Shaldeforde locu tenente Dni Rici comitus arundel justi Dni Reg in North Wall virtute cujusdam lris eisdem justic vel ejus locu tenent de Cancellor Angl direct ₽ sacom Kenwrick ap Gryffyth, Ievaf ap Iorward, Gryffydd ap Davydd Vaghan, Howel ap Llewelyn, Gryffydd ap Davydd Gethin, Ievan ap Howel, Eignion Temoc, Ednevet Gôgh, Howel ap Davydd ap Rotpert, Ievan ap Philip, Blethin ap Madoc, et Kenwric ap Eignion de Com Angles qui dicunt sup suâ quod sunt in maneris de Aberffrau quinq⁹ carucate terre de quibus, magr Rojr de Heytone tenet unâ carucatâ terr & dimid et sic remanent iii. Camicate terr et dimid et que valent ₽ annu £cv. viz:—quelibet camucat xxxs. Item dic quod sunt ibidem iii. molend que valent ₽ annu ixli. Item II.—que valent ₽ annu xiiis. iiiid. Item 1 piscaria que valet iis. Item de redditu libere tenentiu ibid xxixs. viiid. Item de reditu teneniiu de Bodoneyck.—Eodem manerio xvs. xid. Item de redditu libere tenentiu de Hamelto, de Traws y Park, xs. Item de Villanis ejusdem ville de tunk, vs. viz. Item de eisdem Villanis ₽ farma butiro catle et opratinb⁹ xiiis. viid. ob. Item de Hamelleto de Teplerwych huic man añexo De reditu a 6|iȝ villanor—ixs. viiid. Item de iiiiº or cronicis farine ordei vs. iiiid. Items de ix inbrambȝ iiis. vid. Item de ix agnis xviii. Item de eisdem villanis ₽ butiro iis. iiiid. Item de cxx ovis viid. Item de ix gallinis ixd. Item de dcis noibs ₽ opratinb⁹ de clxi dur xxxviis. iid. ob. Sma xxili. xvs. vid." &c.

The above being the extent of the manor of Aberffraw, shews in some measure, how the prince's rents were paid; thus one paid 13s. 7d. instead of butter, milk and services in work; and another district rendered civ. sheep, ix. hens, and 37s. 11d. in lieu of the labour of a 161 days.—(The copy was not very correct.)" "Another extent taken 28th of Edward I. By the above extent, it appears that the king had a domicile, three oxgangs of escheat lands, which belonged to Gwaith Goeth, and mills, friths, or lands, which are now a frith in the lord's hands for want of tenants, &c. There he claims, no doubt, as having been the inheritance of Prince Llewelyn, especially as we find the like claim laid to the estates of five freeholders who had sided with him. An acre of low lands, at this time, was valued at 8d. and the high lands at 4d. Indeed there are ten acres of moor or rough marshy land mentioned, which were valued at half a mark per acre. The mill is valued at £6 per annum, which is equal to 180 acres of land, at 8*d*. per acre. In all these records, I observe that mills bore a very high value in proportion to land, &c. What appears most extraordinary is, that there was a turbery (that had belonged to the prince) at this time, which was valued at more than a colliery and quarry put together.—*J. Lloyd*". In the 26th of Edward III the heirs of the domicile of Porthorion, Howel and Davydd the sons of Meilir, were to pay every quarter 5*s*. 3*d*. to grind with the other tenants, all their wheat, malt and other grain, at the prince's mill, at Aberffraw, they shall make and repair one portion of the wall of the Palace of Aberffraw, on one side of the gate of the same, and one other portion on the other side; and if the Lord Prince should be within, they shall receive from him meat and drink for nine men employed in making the above wall", &c. The heirs of Ceyvnerth ab Hwva and others pay annually £2 14*s*. 0*d*. besides suit and service. They work at the Lord Prince's manor-house at Aberffraw."

Edward I did not foresee the restoration of the ancient British line to the throne of their ancestors. I am tempted here to insert a prophecy concerning this, and said to be one of Merlin's; it was published in Welsh and English by Thomas Pugh, in 1658; foretelling the troubles of the rebellion—the restoration of Charles II &c. as follows:—"Then shall a king come to England from a princely race, with his noble descent from Aberffraw in Anglesey, the ancient seat of the Princes of North Wales; then, or in such time when this cometh to pass, let the Britons sit still at home and be quiet, while the great ones of England contend; for the crown shall go at the disposal of the subjects", &c. The last extract shall be one quoted by John Pugh, from "Goronwy of Môn", who fancied that an angel foretold him the regal succession, till the restoration of the British line in the Tudor race, and afterwards in the Stuarts. Rowlands, in his MS notes, is very diffuse and clear upon this point of Walter Stuart, who he says (p.176 Mon. Ant.) was born in the palace of Aberffraw. In my account of Rhosvair, will be seen Mr. Lloyd's opinion concerning this palace, which he thinks must have been at Rhosvair. But there is no such lake in that neighbourhood to justify the bard's admiration (in his englyn) as Llyn Coron, which is two miles in circumference, and very near to Aberffraw. From the plenty, as well as variety of fish it contains, many amateur anglers are induced to visit it during the summer months.

Near the barn, at Aberffraw, were found glass rings called "Glain Naidr"; the author has an old druidical one, with the appearance of a snake, having its tail in its mouth (emblem of eternity). This curiosity, together with a singular looking shell, was discovered in an ancient barrow, by the late Mr. Lloyd of Caerwys. In this neighbourhood, and not at Caerhun (as stated by Mr. Pennant) was found the curious mass of copper which is now in the Library at Mostyn, probably smelted from the ore of Pary's Mountain; it is in the shape of a cake of bees wax, weighs 42lbs. and is impressed (in raised characters) with the words "SOCIO ROMÆ". This curiosity was presented to Lady Mostyn (Mary, daughter of Sir John Wynn of Gwydir) by archbishop Williams, who found an asylum at Gloddaeth, "where he died"; (as Hacket his chaplain remarks), " well nursed by her tender care, shee nott quitting him till he had breathed his last breath", &c. Edward Llwyd, in a letter which he wrote to Mr. Mostyn of Penbedw, quotes part of one he had received from Mr. George Davies, Rector of Newborough, calling the cake "Corinthian brasse". This letter is printed in the third volume of the "Cambrian Quarterly", a work containing much valuable information, under the patronage of Lord Ashley, a nobleman of great erudition and literary accomplishments, who discovered, by his study of the ancient British language, that it forms the root of all others. In another letter not published, written the year after by Edward Llwyd to the same gentleman, he describes it as a copper *plate*.

HONOR'D SIR, Oxford, January 8th, 1694–5

  I oughte to have returned my thanks ere this, for the favor of your lettre of December 7th, wherein, as in the rest I have received from you, appears your obliged civility and readinesse to promote whatever bears even upon some shadow of learning. Sir Roger is pleased to grant me the favor of a draught of the Torch Aur, though it bee too late for Camden. The table of antiquities for Wales, being long since engraven and printed off, and the book now completely finished, and dedicated by Mr. Gibson to the Lord Keeper. I hope you have received ere this, that county I made bold to trouble you with, as also the plate wherein all the figures are much less than I expected, because they would not be at the charges of two plates.

  I think I never mentioned to you, that Mr. George Davies, Rector of Newborough, in Anglesea, informed me that the great copperplate, inscribed "SOCIO ROMÆ", was found about fifty years ago near Aberffraw in that county, and there can be no doubt of it, in regard a gentleman now living in his neighbourhood saw it when first found. I conclude he meant the very same with yours; because he says Mr. Owen Wood of Rhôs Môn gave it Archbishop Williams. However I have mentioned it at Caer Hun. I must beg your pardon if I have committed a mistake in the place where the brasse axes were found, for Mr. Stodhart the school-master of Wrexham, having given me one of them, soon after they were discovered, told me as I find by a memorandum on the paper I kept it in, that they were dug up at, or near Diganwy Castle. I was unwilling to trouble you at the time, therefore ventured to place it at Diganwy, having an opportunity of adding an annotation on that place.

                      "Edward Llwyd."

Mr. Lewis Morris says of Mr. Edward Llwyd, "that he was inferior to no man in Britain, in natural history, and had a prodigious knack in languages". Four years after Mr. Llwyd's death, his extensive and valuable collection of Welsh MSS was purchased by Sir John Sebright, and since designated as "The Sebright Collection". A singular and mortifying fatality seems to have attended these celebrated documents, which were afterwards sold, and became the property of Sir Watkin Williams Wynn, and Mr. Johns of Havod: such as had fallen to the lot of the latter gentleman, were consumed by fire, which unfortunately destroyed his mansion, and the moiety purchased by Sir Watkin met with a similar fate at the house of a person in London, to whom they had been sent in 1810, for the purpose of being bound. The Mr. Mostyn of Penbedw, to whom Edward Llwyd addressed his letters, was Richard, a younger son of Sir Roger Mostyn of Mostyn; he was a celebrated antiquary, and collected together an excellent library, adding to it (by his marriage with Charlotte, co-heiress of John Digby of Gothurst) the finely illuminated volume, called the "Digby Book of Genealogy", which is written on vellum, and executed by some celebrated artists, in Paris, at the expence of £1,000 paid to them by Sir Kenelm Digby; and for the same sum it was purchased in 1828, by the Earl of Digby, from Mr. William Wynne, the heir and representative of the Penbedw property.

Sir Roger Mostyn above-named, was a noted royalist, and a great sufferer by the civil wars of Charles I. Colonel Whitelock in his memoirs of those disastrous days, says "This Colonel Mostyn is my sister's son, a gentleman of good parts and mettle; of a very ancient family, large possessions, and great interest in Wales, so that in twelve hours, he raised fifteen hundred men for the king, at his own expense, whom he also maintained." I may add from two Welsh MSS, in the Mostyn and Hengwrt Libraries, that he took the castle of Hawarden, repaired the castle of Flint, at his own cost, of which he was appointed governor; kept it for the king, enduring a long siege, with great privations, and although reduced to the last emergency, did not deliver it up until he had the king's special order. He spent £60,000 in the service of the crown; had his house at Mostyn so plundered and stripped, that he was obliged to desert his family seat, and live several years in an ordinary farm house, in the neighbourhood.

In the Mostyn Library is an illuminated pedigree of the family, not less than forty-two feet in length, which, after passing through the British and Saxon race of monarchs, pursues its progress through the kings of Israel, reaches Noah, and the Ark, and finishes with Adam and Eve. Descended maternally from this long line of British Worthies, is the present possessor, the Honourable Edward Lloyd Mostyn, who has learned early to value the beauties of his native tongue, by speaking it fluently from his childhood.

AMLWCH[190] is situated within twenty miles of Beaumaris, and two hundred and sixty-six from London. "The little village of this port" observes Mr. Pennant, in 1781, "is increasing fast" and the market which is on Friday is considerable, owing to its vicinity to that mountain of wealth, "Mynydd y Trysglwyn" afterwards called Pary's Mountain, from having belonged to Robert Paris, Chamberlain of Chester and North Wales, in the reign of Henry IV. A copy of his commission granted at Beaumaris, in the 3rd of Henry IV is among the Caerwys MSS. He left his property to his widow Jonet, daughter of Sir William Stanley of Hooton, who afterwards married William Griffith of Penrhyn; by him she had Sir William Vychan Griffith, who by his mother's will became possessed of "Tir Paris", in 1440. This gentleman was made chamberlain of North Wales, and created a knight in the 18th of Henry VI upon condition that he did not marry a lady belonging to the principality; consequently he took to wife, Alice, daughter and heir to Sir William Dalton of Apthorpe, in Northamptonshire.[191] Nothing could more effectually weaken the ties of the aristocracy to their native country, as intermarriages with those who were ignorant of their language and customs. In my description of Carreg Lwyd in Llanvaethlu parish, may be read two curious letters bearing upon this subject, written in 1632, by Sir John Maynard, and Sir Thomas Salusbury, the young heir of Lleweney, ancestor to the present Viscount Combermere of Combermere Abbey, the gallant conqueror of Burghtpore.

Amlwch is in the hundred of Twrcelyn, and with the hamlets of Garthur and Bodvarthan, Glas-

---

190 "Sandy Beach." *Evan Evans.* "Bending, or Winding Loch, very descriptive of the place." *Lewis Morris.*

191 Transcribed out of an old illuminated MS of Genealogies, written in the time of Queen Elizabeth, containing all the marriages, armorial hearings, &c. belonging to the crowned heads of Europe, South & North Wales, with an account of the ancient British banner, &c. by William Smyth, now in the Library, at Llannerch, in the County of Denbigh.

grug, Llechog, &c. consisted of eight domiciles in 1352; seven of these were free tenants, having right to grind at the Lord Prince's mill, "at Melin Adda", &c. "They the heirs and tenants of these seven free-holds make a part of the manor-house of Cemmaes. The Lord Prince providing timber, iron, and all necessaries for the hall, chamber, and chapel of the same manor-house, and shall bring them to the nearest port, and from thence they are to carry them, and make the repairs at their own expence."

This "little hamlet of six houses"[192] has increased so much as to contains a population of 5,293 persons, according to the government return in 1821, and in 1831 to 6,285. Lewis Morris describes the port of Amlwch as only a small creek, two miles to the west of Elianus's point, in the north of Angle-sey, and no more than a cove between two rocks, where a vessel hath not room to wind, even at high-water", &c. The copper companies, at their own expence, have considerably improved this natural creek, for the conveniency of their shipping; and though the breadth is only sufficient for two vessels to ride a-breast, the length and depth are such as to receive thirty sloops and brigs, of from fifty to two hundred tons burden. Here are always two Liverpool boats on duty off Ynys Badrig, or "Middle Mouse", and occasionally they anchor in Bull Bay, or "Porth Llechog".

The reader is referred to the chapter on minerals, for a detailed account of Pary's Mountain, and its celebrated mines. There were formerly two chapels of ease in this parish, both of which are now in ruins; one, four miles to the west of Amlwch, called Llanlleianau, or "Church of the Nuns", and the other the same distance to the south, called St. Cadog. The church, a spacious handsome structure; was erected by the Pary's mine company, in 1800, at the expence of £4,000, and dedicated to St. Elaeth ab Meuric ab Idno. "Cyngogion Elaeth" are ancient moral verses, said in the Myvyrian Ar-chaiology, to have been composed by him. He flourished from A.D.640 to 700. The living is a perpet-ual curacy, with that of Llanwenllwyvo annexed, and endowed with £200 private benefaction; £200 Queen Anne's Bounty, and £1,100 parliamentary grant, valued in 1809, at £114 per annum. The bishop presents, and the Rev. William Johnson is the incumbent. Edward Kynnier, Esq. in 1689, gave by deed £311, directing the interest to be appropriated to the payment of a master to teach poor chil-dren of this parish. This gift has been incorporated in the national school, established at Amlwch, in 1821, in which are gratuitously educated 120 boys, and the same number of girls. The school room was erected at an expence of £1,200, defrayed by subscription. The interest of several charitable donations and bequests, by various benefactors, amounting in the aggregate to £44 per annum, is distributed among the poor at Christmas. The average annual expenditure for their support, amounts to £1,043 5s. 0d. Near the extremity of the parish, and bordering upon that of Llanbadrig, are the remains of the monastery of Llanlleianau, situated near the sea-shore, consisting principally of some traces of the foundation and ruins of sepulchral memorials, scattered over the extensive cemetery. Near this spot are the remains of the British fortress of Dinas. The ancient well, called Ffynnon Elaeth, in this parish, was formerly in high estimation for the efficacy of its waters, in the cure of various diseases, and is still held in some degree of repute. Amlwch is now one of the contributory boroughs.

192 Lewis Morris's Description of Amlwch.

BODEDEYRN[193] is about eight miles from Holyhead, and called a hamlet in the twenty-sixth of Edward III when an extent of the Comot of Llivon was taken, in which comot or hundred this parish is situated. "The township of Conisiog, consisting of nine hamlets, including Bodedeyrn, was enjoyed then by the heirs of Hwfa ab Cynddelw, "un o tri tywlwyth Môn", owing suit and service at the county and hundred courts, having a moiety of the mill, called Melin Clegyrgwynion, exempted from "suit at any of the prince's mills". The owners of these hamlets had shares in Melin Caer-gybi, Melin Owain, and Melin Tyndir. They "make part of the prince's chamber and hall, at Aberffraw", &c. Considering what high value the mills bore at that period, this township and other great possessions in Mona, made the Llwyth of Hwva ab Cynddlew, the most distinguished in rank and the wealthiest in the Island, "hyna llwyth a ddewr iawn oedd".[194] Hwva hwn a'i etifeddion a wiscant y dalaith am ben y tywysoc gyda Escob Banger." He resided at Presaddfed, and held his estate in fee, by attending on the prince at his coronation, and bearing up the right side of the canopy over the prince's head at that solemnity. This parish, in 1821, was computed to contain 1,117 inhabitants, and in 1831, 1,085. The rates at 1s. 6d. in the pound were in 1803, £156 13s. 1d. and £309 12s. 0d. in 1831. On the demesne of Presaddved, are the scattered remains of two Cromlechau, situated about a mile from the church, eastward. The village which is one of the most extensive in Mona, is pleasantly situated on the old Holyhead road. Tre' Iorwerth, the residence of Mr. Wynne Jones, is in this parish, a good family mansion, beautifully situated in the midst of thriving plantations. Near this place is Llyn Llwennyn, a fine lake. The spinning of woollen yarn is carried on in the village, for which purpose there are two manufactories, together with dye-houses, and a fulling-mill. There is a branch establishment under the post-office at Bangor, and fairs for cattle are held on March 13, April 16, May 5, June 9 (Whit. Tuesday for hiring servants), August 16, September 14, and December 1 and 22. The petty sessions for the hundred are held here once a month. The living is a perpetual curacy, endowed with £400 Queen Anne's bounty, and £600 parliamentary grant, in the patronage of the principal and fellows of Jesus College, Oxford, valued at about £70 a year. The Rev. James Hughes is the present incumbent. The church, dedicated to St. Edeyrn, the son of Nadd ab Beli ab Rhun ab Maelgwyn Gwynedd, is a small ancient structure, displaying some good architectural details, and containing some fine monuments to the memory of deceased members of the Pre-

---

193 Bodedeyrn, the habitation of Edeyrn. Upon the etymology of the word Bôd, Edward Llwyd observes thus:—"I take it for granted that the word Bod in vulgar speech, signifies the same with Esse; so that at other times it signified the same with Esse a nounsubstantive, i.e. a being, and by degrees it came to mean a house, or place,—thus Hafod, from Bodhav, a summer residence up in the mountains, made use of only at that time to make butter and cheese, as they do at present about Snowdon and elsewhere in Wales; and also in Switzerland and many other places, amongst the Alps. It is very clear to me that we never borrowed the Welsh word Bod from the English abode; it being one of the most primitive words in our language, and being but a monosyllable is more radical and simple than the English word abode."—E. Llwyd.

194 Llyma henwau pymtheg Llwyth Gwynedd, a pha leoedd y doeddynt y Môn: —Yr oedd nid amgen Llowarch ab Bran, arglwydd Menai, ag aer apparens i Gryffydd ab Cynon, ac o'i ddewrder yr ynillodd amlyoedd; a'i gar oedd.—Hwva ab Cynddelw vy aer apparens i Owen Gwynedd, a llwyth hyna oedd yn Môn. Yr Hwva hwn ai etifedd a wiscant y dalaeth ar ben y tywgsog", &c Lewys Dwn,—Gloddaeth MS &c. "Gweyrydd ab Rhys Goch a gyvodes y tywysog yn bendevig." —Transcribed from a MS in the possession of the Rev. T. Wynn Edwards of Rhyddlan, being one of the collection that belonged to his ancestor, "Foulc Wyn, Prydydd Nantglyn".—Davies of Llansilin, p.46, 47; Pennant's Whitford, besides 2 volumes of the Cambrian Register, contain, upon the whole, a very fair and correct history of the Tribes.

saddved and Tre'orwerth families. A national school was erected in 1822, where about seventy children of the parish receive gratuitous instruction. Dr. Gwynn gave a portion of tithes, producing £2 10s. 0d. per annum. Mr. Edmund Griffith and Mrs. Jane Wynne, gave certain portions of land; and Mrs. Jane Roberts assigned the moiety of the interest of £100 to the poor of this parish, the produce of which benefactions, together with that of other charitable bequests, is annually distributed, according to the directions of the several benefactors.

BODEWRYD. "Bod"—residence, "Ewryd"—by the ford, is ranked as a township, in the extent of Twrcelyn, taken the 26th Edward III. "There is in this township, one ploughland free, called Rhingynllaeth, belonging to the heirs of Iorwerth ab Trahaiarn, Mredydd Ddû and others, paying quarterly rent of £1 8s. 2d. They owe suit at the prince's mill, "Melin Adda", for their lands in Bodewryd, and suit besides at Melin Dulas, county and hundred courts. They do a part of the prince's manor-house, with the other free tenants of this court", &c.

Bodewryd is a perpetual curacy, detached about thirty years ago, from Llanelian; its yearly value about £62. The present incumbent is the Rev. John Owen. Population in 1821, 43, and in 1831, 35. This small parish consists only of two houses, one of them anciently the mansion of the Wynne family, and has no parochial officers. In levying the rates, it is with the parish of Gwaredog considered as a fourth division to the three contained in the parish of Amlwch. The living was endowed in 1722, with 121 acres of land, and a rent-charge of £2, by Dr. Wynne, Chancellor of Hereford, and subsequently with £800 Queen Anne's bounty, and in the patronage of Sir John Thomas Stanley, Bart. of Penrhos. The church, dedicated to St. Mary, is a small ancient edifice, containing some monuments to the Wynnes, proprietors of the parish, and a brass plate recording the munificence of Dr. Wynne, who lies entombed in the church. A parochial school has been founded, and is supported at the expence of Lady Stanley, for the education of female children of this and the adjoining parish.

BODTWROG, distance fourteen miles from Bangor, and three from Llangevni, and in the hundred of Llivon, so called from being the residence of Twrog, a son of Ithel Hael, who flourished in the close of the fifth century, and part of the sixth. He accompanied Cadvan into Wales. The living is a perpetual curacy, and in the patronage of the principal and fellows of Jesus College, Oxford, to whom the tithes of this advowson were appropriated by Dr. Wynne, Chancellor of Llandaff, in 1648, subject to the payment of £1 5s. 0d. per annum, to the poor of this parish. Besides this, there is a small bequest of £12 given by Mr. John Lloyd for their benefit. About £99 10s. 0d. is annually expended for their maintenance. The church, a small edifice, situated on a lonely eminence, is dedicated to St. Twrog; his day kept on the first of January. In the extent taken of this township at Coedanau, in 1352, the tenants, Llewelyn ab Davydd Vân, and Davydd ab Gryffydd Vân, had their lands free, "paying no yearly rent to the Lord Prince, except suit to the county and hundred courts, without any other services or customs". The population of this parish in 1821 was 332, and in 1831, 312. The rates amounted to, in 1803—£45 3s. 0d. at 2s. in the pound; in 1831 they were £99 10s. 0d. The Rev. Henry Griffith is the minister.

CERCHIOG, OR BETTWS Y GRÔG, is situated ten miles from Holyhead. It is not mentioned in the extent so often quoted; the name implies "abounding with oats". The church, a small neat edifice, is a chapel of ease to Llanbeulan, and dedicated to the Holy Rood. Saints day kept on the 14th of September. The duty is performed by the Rev. William Roberts of Llanbeulan. A rent-charge of £2 10s. 0d. was left by Serjeant Wynne, for the benefit of the poor of this parish. The resident population in 1821 was 191, and in 1831, 168; and the parish rates in 1803 were, at 10s. in the pound, £42 8s. 5d.— Increased to £74 6s. 0d. in 1831. Edward Lhwyd, in a letter dated "Oxford, 1693", remarks upon the frequency of the name of Bettws, given to churches in South, as well as North Wales, adding an interrogation: "But what may this word mean? A Montgomeryshire gentleman writes to me, that it is nothing else but Beatus, and that it was an attribute of St. Beuno", &c. Mr. Lloyd in his 4th vol. Caerwys MSS, has inserted the following opinion on the same word. "Bettws, a name very common in Wales, which signifies a middling place, between a vale and high mountain, in the opinion of some, who say "we came to Bettws", that is, Bod-gwŷs, a place of some shelter; and this is most probable, from the situation of churches, in many parts of Wales, that bear that name. Others say again, that all Bettws's belonged to some abbey, and that it is derived from the latin word Abbatis."

CERRIG CEINWEN, in the hundred of Malltraeth, and within three miles of Llangevni. It is a curacy not in charge, under the patronage of the Bishop of Bangor. The parish contains from 1,500 to 2,000 acres of land; 200 of this is common. The resident population in 1821 was 375, and in 1831, 374. The parish rates in 1805 were £62 2s. 0d. at 6s. in the pound.—Increased in 1831 to £161 9s. 0d. Dr. William Lewis, born in this parish, was a great benefactor to this his native place, leaving £12 annually, for the education of two poor boys, who should be born here; and also several sums of money, as exhibitions for a limited term, for such young men of this county who should go to either of the universities. He was a principal contributor to the funds for the support of widows of deceased clergymen. The church, a neat small edifice, and appropriately fitted-up, is dedicated to St. Ceinwen (i.e. "fairest of the fair"), daughter of Brychan. The day of celebration, denominated wakes, is on the 8th of October. There is in the 1st vol. Cambro-Briton, a copy of a remarkable inscription on a tomb-stone, in this church, recording an act of heroism, worthy the most exalted era of chivalry. Morris Llwyd, a partizan of Charles I resided at Lledwigan, a well-known farm, near Llangevni. A troop of parliament soldiers, consisting of thirty, arrived at his house, and demanded from Morris (who was then thrashing in his barn) a certain sum of money, or his life; he bravely answered that he would not part with one, without the other; and having thereupon partially closed the door, he, with his flail attacked those who attempted to enter. Eight or ten fell in this contest before he was killed. Mr. John Williams, a tenant at Lledwigan Llan, restored the monument, which had been shamefully pulled down, when a flag-stone was wanted to repair some part of the church.

In the extent of Malltraeth, taken 26th of Edward III Lledwigan is styled Llŷs Lledwigan, and together with the hamlet of Berwyn, was at that time found in the possession of Einion ab Gwalchmai's heirs. Llan Lledwigan was a free township, and Howel ab Madog the sole heir. "His mill of Carreg Lwyd, was fallen down and useless, &c. only suit owing at the first comot court held in michaelmas."

COED-ANNA—COEDANEU—COEDANE. This parish is in the hundred or comot of Twrce-lyn, and partly in that of Talybolion, fifteen miles from Beaumaris, and seven from Llanelian, to the rectory of which it is a chapel of ease. The church, a small ancient structure, is supposed to have been built in 630, and dedicated to St. Ane, son of Caw Cawllog. Saints day kept on January 13. Divine service performed every alternate Sunday. This parish contains 1,500 acres of arable land, partly meadow, and all enclosed; containing 305 inhabitants in 1821, and 262 in 1831. Parish rates in 1803, at 8s. in the pound, amounted to £51 1s. 0d.—increased to £102 1s. 0d. in 1831.

In the extent of the comot of Twrcelyn, taken at Coedaneu, 26th of Edward III it is there ranked as a hamlet, and with the township of Trevadog, consisted of three free domiciles, &c. In one domicile, belonging to the heirs of Cyhelyn ab Cadrod, were "two oxgangs of escheat land, forfeited by Iorwerth Ddû ab Madog, which was wont to yield an annual rent of 6s. 8d.—this lies waste on the lord's hands", &c. "Y vlwyddyn 1190; y bu vrwydyr Coedaneu; y drydydd vlwyddyn y bu varw Rodri ab Owen Gwynedd; er pan lâs Owain ab Madawg, hyd hav y Gwyddyl, saith mlynedd,—1197."[195] William Thomas, in 1772, bequeathed £10, and Margaret Owen, in 1784, gave by deed £20 towards the endowment of a school, for the education of poor children.

EGLWYS-AEL, OR LLANGADWALADR. About two miles north-west of Rhosvair (Newborough) and eight from Llangevni, is Llangadwaladr church, remarkable for having over the south door, as a sort of lintel, and partly hid in the wall, a stone, with an ancient inscription, in memory of Cadvan, who governed the Principality of North Wales, about the end of the sixth century. He was at the battle of Bangor. "Cadvan, Brenin Gwynedd, Bletrwys, Tywysoc Cernyw, Brochwel Yscythroc, Tywysoc Powys, ac emladd", &c.[196] Eglwys-ell, or Ael, i.e. the church district, ranked as a free township, when the extent of Malltraeth was taken at Rhosvair, 26th of Edward III containing "two domiciles belonging to Ithel ab Trahaiarn, and Sanfraid ab Trahaiarn", owing neither yearly rent, nor suit to the comot, "nor do they pay relief; and it is said they have free mills in their own houses, but that they are bound to appear the two great tourns of the prince annually, as well as at all other services. The domicile of Sanffraid contains two oxgangs of forfeit lands, which belonged to Ievan ab Philip ab Davydd, and is now holden by the township in common, which pays for it, beyond the extent, the annual rent of 4s." &c. This parish is within seven miles of Caernarvon, containing a population of 404 in 1821,—increased to 573, in 1831. Parish rates were in 1803, £105 at 6s. in the pound,—increased to £177 17s. 0d. in 1831. The living is a rectory, with the chapel of Tal y llyn annexed, in the gift of the Lord Chancellor, and valued temp. Henry VIII at £16 7s. 10d. The present incumbent is the Rev. John Hughes. The church is dedicated to the founder, Cadwaladr, the last King of the Britains, who died at Rome; and having been canonized by Pope Sergius, in 688, he was surnamed "The Blessed".[197] He was grandson to the Cadvan above named, who was buried here. Edward Llwyd describes the stone commemorating this circumstance, "as rude, and placed above the church door", &c. adding, "I communicated a

195 Extract from the Red Book of Hergest.
196 Hengwrt MS.
197 Day of celebration is on the 22nd of April. "The three golden-banded ones of the Isle of Britain. Rhiwalon Wallt Benadlen, Rhûn ap Maelgwyn, and Cadwaladr the Blessed."

copy of the monument of Prince Cadvan, to Mr. Hicks of Trevithick, which he shewing, with some others, to Dr. Musgrave of Exeter, the doctor sent them to Dr. Sloan, who has printed them in the Philosophical transactions. I did not, I think, mention in my last, that it was dated 607, and that Cadvan was one of the British commanders at the Battle of Bangor Iscoed, which happened in that year. It is so plain and barbarous; that it contains nothing at all but "CATAMANUS REX SAPIENTISSIMUS OPINATISSIMUS OMNIUM REGUM." The stone is perhaps but a piece of what it was at first."

In Cathrall, p.35, may be seen a copy of an epitaph to the memory of Owen Wood of Rhosmor (the active opponent of Sir Richard Bulkeley), who was buried in this church in 1602, aged 76. This family, bearing the same name, possessed lands in Mona, so early as the 5th of Edward III but Rhosmawr (now called Rhosmor) at that time, when the extent of Tindaethwy was taken, "together with the hamlet of Trev-Iddon, was found in the possession of Llowarch ab Iddon Ddû". About three quarters of a mile from the church, are the ruins of the ancient chapel of Llanveirian, which appears to have been originally a parish church; having been suffered to fall into decay, about the year 1775. Mr. Hughes, the present rector, has caused the cemetery to be enclosed with a stone wall, and some yew trees planted within the area, marking the site of the old church. The present church is an elegant structure, consisting of a nave and chancel, with a north and south transept, called respectively the Bodorgan and Bodowen Chapels, forming a cross, with the body of the edifice; the one belonging to the Bodorgan family forming the north transcept, was originally built in 1640, by Richard Meyric, and rebuilt in 1801, in a style of inferior beauty, which forms a striking contrast to that of Bodowen. This latter chapel was built by Hugh Owen, son and heir of William Owen of Bodowen, alias Bodeon, who married Ann, inheritrix of Llysdulas, and daughter of Richard Williams. This chapel was finished in 1661, two years after Hugh Owen's death. It is divided from the chancel of Eglwys-ael church, by an arch that extends the full length of the chapel running parallel with the south side of the church, and is curiously built of free-stone. The windows are finely painted glass. Besides the family quarterings, there is in the east one a picture of King Charles I. In the north window is a representation of Meuric ab Llewellyn, who died in 1530, and was the first of the family that settled at Bodeon. He had (besides the Bishop of Bangor, whose life is given among the eminent men of Mona) a son called Owen, from whom this mansion took the name of Bodowen. His son, was Hugh ab Owen, who married Gwen Morris; their son Owen ab Hugh married Isabel, daughter to Sir William Griffith of Penrhyn; their son was Sir Hugh Owen, who married Elizabeth Wiriot of Orielton, in Pembrokeshire, and their second son William Owen had Bodowen (the eldest son succeeding to Orielton, in Pembrokeshire). William married Jane, daughter of Sir William Williams, knight, of Vaynol. Hugh, their eldest son married Ann Williams, daughter and heiress of Llysdulas. They had no children; but Henry Owen, William's second son, married Elizabeth, daughter and heiress of Hugh Gwyn of Mosoglen; and their only daughter and sole heiress, Ann, by marrying her cousin Sir Hugh Owen, bart. of Orielton, caused the Mona estates to be once more in the possession of the elder branch.

Bod-Gwrgan (the habitation of Gwrgan), as it is called in the extent of Malltraeth, made in 1352, has been the domicile of this distinguished race of warriors, since the time when Enion Sais, ab Davydd, married Eva, granddaughter to Llowarch ab Brân, sole heiress of Bodorgan. The Meyric family are derived from Cydavael Ynad, judge of the court of Powys, in the time of Llewellyn the Great, and his contemporary King John, who on an invasion of the English, seized a fire-brand, and flew from mountain to mountain, in the district of Cydewein; giving thereby such timely notice, as to enable his countrymen successfully to repel the invaders. For this service, Prince Llewelyn granted to him a coat of arms, i.e. on a field sable, three ragged staves or. This coat, at a much later period, was augmented by a fleur de lis, gules, inter two ravens on a chevron, argent, and a crest added indicative of the place where the court of Powys was held (Castell Dinas Brân), being a castle surmounted by a mound or dinas, on which stood a raven holding a fleur de lis. The loss of his lands in Cydewein, induced one of his descendants to retire to Mona, where Enion Sais, son or grandson of the emigrant (who had signalized himself at the battle of Agincourt) married Eva, the heiress of Bodorgan. "This Eignion" says Lewis Dwn, "was usher of the palace of Sheen, in the early part of the reign of Henry VI and this required his absence from his native country for such a length of time, that he acquired the name of Sais". Llewelyn his grandson, fought on the field of Bosworth; and his two-handed sword, saltseller, &c. are still preserved at Bodorgan, as also was his salade, until a few years back. Meuric ab Llewelyn, whose effigy is in the window of Bodowen chapel, was the first of that name in the family. He was standard-bearer of the yeomen of the guard to Henry VII and 'squire of the body to Henry VIII. His eldest son Richard continued at Bodorgan, where his descendants are to the present day, being represented by Mr. Fuller Meyrick. From the account in p.77, we find that Lord Essex resided, for many years, at Bodorgan. In Bishop Meurick's life there is an account of his branch from this family settling at Gwrych (Bush) county of Pembroke, and Goodrich Court, county of Herefordshire.

HEN-EGLWYS, i.e. "Ancient Church", is a parish in the hundred of Malltraeth, three miles from Llangevni. The church is an ancient edifice, distinguished by no architectural feature worthy of notice, and dedicated to Y Newdion. Day of celebration kept on November 22. A rectory under the Bishop of Bangor's patronage; hath under it one chapel. Trev Gwalchmai, valued temp. Henry VIII at £9 3s. 4d. Incumbent, the Rev. Thomas Evans. This parish consists of about 1,726 acres of enclosed land, and about 196 common. The population in 1821 was 385,—diminished in 1831 to 335; and the rates amounted in 1803 to £100, at the rate of 2s. in the pound,—increased in 1831 to £185 16s. 0d. Hen-eglwys is situated about half-way between Bangor and Holyhead, on the new line of road, which has rendered it a place of some traffic; and the "Mona Inn", a spacious hotel and posting house, has been erected here, for the accommodation of travellers; but the situation is bleak and uninviting. The Rev. Hugh Hughes bequeathed land for apprenticing a poor boy of this parish, and for other uses; and William Bold, in 1688, gave land for the poor. There are also some smaller charitable donations, the produce of which is distributed among the poor.

"In the extent of Malltraeth, so often referred to, ranked as a township, containing three hereditary domiciles, 'free, owing no yearly rent to the prince, except suit at the prince's court, no relief, nor marriage fine, nor are the tenants of Heneglwys to accompany him in his wars: they, holding the said domiciles from St. Francis and Bacellinus'. The heirs of the domicile of Iddon ab Idgwen, are Davydd ab Madog, and Methevel, daughter of Nest", &c.

HOLYHEAD, the Caer-Gybi of the ancient Britons (by which name *only* it is still known among the natives), is situated on the extremity of an island, of unequal breadth, and greatly indented. This is joined to the north-west part of Mona, by a bridge, called "Ponty Rhydbont", and lies, according to an extent of Talybolion (taken at Coedana, 26th of Edward III), within that comot; but Cathrall, in p.36, says that it is in the hundred of Llivon, having a resident population in 1821 of 4,071, and in 1831 of 4,282.

The land in this parish is in general rocky, especially towards the mountain, which is the highest in Mona: out of 3,000 acres, about one half is uncultivated; but there are many fertile spots, which produce plentiful crops of corn. It is computed that they export yearly from this harbour 40,000 bushels of grain.

At the time the extent alluded to was taken (1352), Caer-gybi ranked as a Hamlet, within the Township of Trev Llowarch ab Brân. "The Church was then rebuilding." Excepting "Melin Caer-gybi" (which belonged to Tudor ab Iorwerth) the whole of this Township was the inheritance of Llowarch ab Brân, head of the second of our fifteen tribes, and a contemporary with Owen Gwynedd. (They two, married sisters.) This property was divided between his three sons, and the parcel allotted to each still bears the name of him to whom it originally belonged, i.e. "Gwely Iorwerth ab Llowarch, Gwely Cadwgan ab Llowarch, and Gwely Madoc ab Llowarch", as in the the extent is manifest; being then found in the possession of these three nobleman "owing suit and service", &c. making the walls and roof of the hall, chamber and chapel of the manor-house of Cemmaes". "In Cadwgan ab Llowarch's domicile are two oxgangs of escheat land, that belonged to Mredydd ab Llewelyn, which now lie waste on the lord's hands for want of tenants; and they say that the same Mredydd has a share in the election of two prebendaries in Corgybi, which were lately belonging to Cadwgan ab Llowarch ab Brân." Like the celebrated college at Bangor Iscoed, this church was originally an establishment resembling Oxford and Cambridge, to educate the clergy, and was succeeded in the twelfth century by a college of presbyters, founded most probably by this Llowarch ab Brân. In the improvements that have taken place between Holyhead and London, since the time Mr. Pennant and Mr. Lloyd traversed it together, a more direct line of road has been struck out, crossing Lasinwen sands, over an excellent embankment, about a mile to the northward of the four mile bridge. This embankment, which cost £60,000 is about three quarters of a mile long, having an archway, nineteen feet wide, for water to pass through. This has been the means of shortening the road at least two miles between Holyhead and Bangor.

In August, 1776, Mr. Lloyd visited this celebrated "Cor of Gybi", in company with Mr. Pennant, and Mr. Hugh Davies, the eminent botanist, "recently" (Mr. Lloyd observes) "returned from the Snowdon hills, with a curious assortment of plants. He shewed me a MS copy of Nennius, with some part, if I mistake not, of Giraldus, which he had happily rescued from the flames. He supposed it to have belonged formerly to Chancellor Wynn". Mr. Lloyd left Plâs Gwyn early on the 19th, and passed by Pentraeth, Llanddyfnan, and many other churches, Presaddved, &c. "On our right hand" (he says) "to the bridge which joins Ynys Cybi to the continent or main-land of Mona, pass by Capel St. Ffraid, situated upon an artificial tommen, in Tywyn y Capel, and arrive at Holyhead, visited the church, which we found situated in an old square stone fortress, with a small half-moon tower, somewhat angular within. Three sides are tolerably entire; the fourth seems never to have had a wall, that being supplied by a pretty steep rock, washed by the tide at high water. The thickness of the main wall, six feet; of the half-moon tower on the outside, three feet; the breadth of the gateway, twelve feet; the height of the wall in some places, about eighteen feet. It had once a parapet, or battlement round it, like the walls surrounding Chester. The mortar, exceeding hard, mixed with a great quantity of very coarse gravel, and some marine shells, taken undoubtedly from the adjoining small bason or bay. "Besides Eglwys y Beddi, or Eglwys y Gwyddel", which I will describe in Mr. Lloyd's own words, "there are three other chapels: Capel y Llochwyd, in Caer-gybi, Capel y Gorlas, near which there is a famous spring called Ffynnon y Gorlas, also Capel St. Ffraid, above-named, built on an artificial mount, or tommen, by the sea-side, on a sandy beach, called Tywyn y Capel, about two miles from Holyhead. The Popish Legends say, that St. Ffraid, a virgin of great sanctity, sailed from Ireland to this place, upon a green sod, which on her landing, became a firm hillock, and thereon was built a chapel, &c.[198]—John Lloyd."

> " Da y noviast hyd yn Nyvi,
> " Dull Dow, ar dy vantell di "

sang the bard of Cardiganshire to the same lady, who is said to have landed on that coast, and not at Caer-gybi; and the fourth chapel is "Capel Gwrgeneu".[199]

Many are the superstitions concerning the origin of the name of Holyhead; some thinking it was so called from the number of chapels, or places of worship that might have been attached to the original monastery. "That it is not a very ancient name, is evident", says Mr. Lewis Morris, in his account of Holyhead, published in the 3rd vol. Cambrian Register, "for in an old deed upon parchment, temp. Edward IV, the whole Island, containing the parishes of St. Gwenvaen and Caer-gybi is styled "Insulae de St. Ceby". Mr. Edward Llwyd, in a letter, dated 1693, written to "Mr. John Lloyd, the master of Ruthyn school", thanking him for his account of the "Caereu, which was very welcome", thus explains the word Caer:—"Caer, we know, signifies properly, and strictly, no other than a wall or fence: we say every where, 'Caereu'r Drev', for the walls of it; and in Caermarddinshire they say, 'Caereu'r Fynwent'. I have seen several such Caerau as you describe. Cor-Cybi again, originates in côr, a circle or choir;— ban, high or superior;—Banchor, Côr Beuno, Clynog Vawr, a college founded by Beuno, in 616, in that place. Cor-Cybi generally, but erroneously called Caer-gybi, i.e. "Cebii Castrum', from a monastery or college, founded by him. But its most ancient name was 'Llan y Gwyddyl', signifying the Irishman's Beach or Shore. Our histories make frequent mention of the Irish revers landing here, and of their incursions into Mona, and also raising here some rude fortifications to protect their shipping", &c. "Eglwys y Beddi, or Capel Llan y Gwyddel", continues Mr. Lloyd, " is now erected into a public

---

198 Caerwys MS.

199 The stone that was formerly at the highway, near Brondeg, was erected by one Gwrgeneu, who had an estate about Mosoglen, and Miallt was heiress thereof.—*Ruthin MS.*

school,[200] by the munificence of Dr. Wynn". At the east end, and detached from it, there is an arch, under which there is a seat for people to sit on. Before the conversion of this chapel into a schoolhouse, a similar arch stood opposite to it. Tradition says, that the Irish and British Generals being both killed in the same engagement, were buried under these arches, hence it was called "Eglwys y Beddi". In removing the ruins of this chapel some years ago, a stone coffin, containing human bones of a prodigious size, was found in the north side of the chapel, where stood the shrine of Serigi, who was slain by Caswallon Llaw-hîr, in 640. He was afterwards canonized. I was assured by several masons, and others, that in digging the foundations of houses, now building to the south of the church, they found many graves, containing skeletons of enormous size. The sides were walled, the bottoms paved, and so closely covered with flags, that no soil could get in. Some of these graves measured eight, some nine feet, and one in particular, measured eleven feet in length. The skeletons of a correspondent size, were all entire, until handled and exposed to the air, when they fell into dust, except the teeth, which they all agreed were so hard, as to require some pains to be broken with their hammers. In these graves were found several hand-mill grinding stones, or what the Scots call and use at this day, querm (querns). These, it seems, were common to both Britons and Romans. In the fortress surrounding the church, we observed holes perforating the wall, similar to those in the old Segontium by Caernarvon. Here are two rows; the higher universally round, smoothly plastered within, and about four inches diameter, not equidistant, but nearly, if not entirely parallel to the lower tier, which runs not high above the present visible foundation. These lower ones are not generally round, but many of them square, and are about six feet distant from the other. This, with the same kind of zigzag masonry discernable here, like that at Segontium, induced me to conclude, that this, like that, was of Roman origin. At Conwy Castle, we observed a mixture of round and square holes running obliquely in the walls, and were evidently the marks of scaffolding, as these walls, especially in some places, bear distinctly proofs of their being built in that oblique manner. But here, I know not of what use they could be in scaffolding, as the lower row is so near the foundation; the same remark may serve for that of Segontium. The inscription in the north aisle, Mr. Thomas read "Sancte Kebie ora pro nobis", but here I observed the letter *y* after *k* in the second word, so that the true reading, perhaps is "Sancte Cybie, &c". There is no trace of Roderic ab Owen Gwynedd's grave, in the church; but we were informed that the antique monument, under an arch in the cross aisle on the south side of the church, was his, and the same which was discovered at the reparation of the choir in 1713, and on his coffin was a brass bell, curiously wrought through with net work. On the south aisle, amidst a variety of strange sculptures, is another inscription, defaced by time; and in the porch, on each side of the door, I observed two coats of arms, one belonging to Llowarch ab Brân, the founder of two canonries here. The other was too much defaced to be made out. These arms might belong to Tudor ab Gronw ab Ednyfed, who is said in vol.5, Sebright Collec-

---

200 Edward Wynne of Bodewryd, LL.D. gave by bond, November 25, 1748, the sum of £120, for the endowment of this school, "for teaching six poor boys of the town, to read and write. The interest to be paid annually on the 24th of November". Dr. Wynn appointed one John Edwards, a native of Bangor, to be the first master, who resigning in the year 1761, it was given to Lewis Owen, the surveyor of this port. The author has been informed that the national school is incorporated with this.

tion, to have founded the "Priordû Bangor, and the Cloister of Holyhead". By the same volume I find that he did his homage to Edward I at Chester, in 1301. Over one of these shields, amongst other fantastic ornaments of the gothic age, is that of the "ancient of days", with a crucifix. The masons were busily demolishing the remainder of the rock, at the east end of the church, where stood the mark of St. Cybi's foot, in order to get stone to repair the wall between the churchyard and the sea. The Romans or those that built the above-mentioned fortress, thought walls unnecessary. In the evening, we passed by the ruin of Capel and Ffynnon y Gorlles, and another dedicated to Gwyngeneu, son of Bawl Hên, &c. On our ascent to Holyhead mountain, alias "Mynydd y Twr", at the bottom we observed several tumuli, some newly demolished, and upright stones by them. Probably they were originally surrounded by such. We ascended to the fortress, which does not encircle the apex of the hill, as mentioned by my old friend Mr. John Thomas; that indeed would be needless, as one side of the hill is a perfect precipice; it is in the style of Penmaen Mawr, Caer Madryn, Tre'r Caereu, and "Castell Craig y Ddinas", by Cors y Gedol, &c. It is not near so considerable as either of the three former; nor did we observe any foundations of buildings, either inside or outside of it. The main wall itself is of considerable height and thickness. On the summit of the hill stands the foundation of a tower, *lately* much demolished, by some vulgar, curious persons, in search of *imaginary* treasures. This tower, which was originally round, had no reference to the old fortress, though it appears, as if it were in the middle of it. This was worked with hewn stones, and strong mortar, like the fortress surrounding the church, and was probably an exploratory tower, belonging to it; whereas this fortress, like the rest of its kind, consists of rude unhewn stones, without any cement. However it seems to borrow its name from this tower, for it is called Caer y Twr. We descended on the south-west of the hill, under two caves, said to have been once the residence of an outlaw or a robber. There is a communication between the two. As we descended, we saw the ruins of Capel y Llochwyd, standing on a hill; the name implies the situation,—a desolate place. It is above the sea, with a road down to it; and on a hill, near this chapel (one of several scattered about this holy place) we saw a huge heap of stones, like that on Caer Guwch, called "Arffedoged y Gawres". At Trevignedd, alias "Treseiriol", within a mile of Holyhead, and near the road to Beaumaris, is a monument of large rude stones, about twenty in number, some measuring four and five feet high, and those at the north side, six feet;—the upper stones are fallen off their supporters. These stones are called by the natives, "Llecheu Trevignedd", and the field this cromlech is in, is called "Caer Llecheu". They were never taken notice of till Mr. Aubrey accidentally saw them; whose papers Mr. Edward Llwyd sent to the editors of Camden, in their additions to Mona. There was another druidical altar, within half a mile of Caer-gybi, called "Coeten Arthur", i.e. "Arthur's Coit". The upper stone is now removed to a hedge, near. And not far from Holyhead, at a place called Borthwen, on the sea shore, the poor people dig at low water, a kind of earth; which they dry and burn instead of turf: it is often found full of nuts, branches of trees, and seeds of plants, preserved entire, though several yards under the Surface, and washed by the sea. The town of Holyhead, is one large long street, chiefly consisting of public houses, for the accommodation of passengers, to and from Ireland.—*J. Lloyd*".[201]

201 Caerwys MS.

In p.275, Mr. Pennant writes "Maelgwyn Gwynedd, in 580, is said to have founded a college here". There is every reason to suppose this to be true, for the Black Book of Basingwerk Abbey has these words:—"Maelgwyn adeiladodd Glaswrdû Côr Gybi, Glaswrdû Penmon, a Glaswrdû Bangor." The head of this college was called Penclas, or Pencolas. The Rev. Evan Evans considers it to have been Pencais, i.e. chief judge in ecclesiastical matters. He was one of the three spiritual lords of Mona. The archdeacon of the Isle was one, and the abbot of Penmon the other. His latin title was Rector, as appears by the ancient seal, inscribed "Sigillum Rectoris et capituli Ecclesiae de Caergybi". In a subsequent period he was styled Provost. The number of prebendaries is not known, but they must have been twelve at least;—that number being found on the pension-list in 1553, at £1 each. Before the dissolution, the rector or provost had thirty-nine marks; one chaplain had eleven, and the other two the same between them. The whole value in the 26th of Henry VIII was £24. Edward III bestowed what was called, "the provostship[202] of his free chapel of Caer-gybi", on his chaplain, Thomas de London, for which the king, in 1351, dispensed with his services to himself. It has been mentioned that Llowarch ab Brân, "Lord of Menai", founded two prebends, endowed by tithe lands from Trev Llowarch. Mr. Lewis Morris remembered having read in an extent of North Wales, taken in the time of Henry III that there were two prebends or canonries annexed to Trev Gov, in the said parish. Their revenues consisted of the tithes of the several parishes of Caer-gybi, Bodedern, Llandrygarn and Bodwrog, and it became the property of Rhys Gwyn of Bodewryd, soon after its dissolution in 1536, from whom by inheritance it came to Dr. Edward Gwynn, who about 1648, bestowed it on Jesus College, Oxon, for the maintenance of two fellows, and two scholars; which college has ever since presented to Holyhead, Bodedern, Llandrygan and Bodwrog. The Rev. John Jones has now this perpetual curacy, which was augmented in 1820, with an additional stipend of £20 per annum, by the principal and fellows of Jesus College, and endowed with £300 parliamentary grant. The annual expenditure for the maintenance of the poor amounts to £910 2s. 0d. Holyhead was made by the late act, one of the contributory boroughs with Amlwch, Llangevni and Beaumaris. The market is on Saturday. In the works belonging to the post-office establishment alone, more than four hundred men are generally employed, under the superintendance of a resident engineer. The church, a spacious cruciform structure, handsomely embattled, stands above the harbour, surrounded by its ancient fortification, and is dedicated[203] to St. Cybi, "who founded a monastery here in 380";[204] and Bishop Usher[205] says, that "one Kebius, son of Solomon, Duke of Cornwall, was consecrated Bishop of Anglesey, by Hilary of Poictiers, and had his seat here about 364".

In a MS book of genealogies, at Hengwrt, there is an account of St. Cybi, who is said to have lived in the sixth century (and not as Cressy and Bishop Usher say, in the fourth). He was the son of Selgi, by Fronwen, verch Cyngar. What goes far to corroborate this, is a tradition retained among the Mon-

---

202 Extent temp. Edward III 26th of his reign.

203 The reader is referred for an account of the celebration of this "joyous festival", which takes place on the 25th of July, to Cathrall, p.39.

204 Cressy's Church History, p.39.

205 Lewis Morris, in a short account of Holyhead Church, in the Isle of Anglesey, drawn up by this antiquary, in a letter to Browne Willis, p.312, 3rd vol. Cambrian Register.

enses, that Cybi and Seiriol used to meet weekly, at Clorach,[206] near Llannerchymedd, where are to be seen two wells, bearing their respective names, and within a few yards of each other. Seiriol was the son of Owain Danwyn ab Eignion Yrth, who lived, according to our chronicles, in the seventh century. Again there are in some very old MSS copies of a poem said to have been composed by Teilio, who died about the year 600, wherein there is evidence given that the Irish then inhabited Caer-gybi; and because of the complaints of the virgins of Britain, a certain hero would burn the top of Ireland, and be the occasion of lamentable cries at Caer-gybi", &c.

I have transcribed largely, and from different authors; but shall leave to others more competent in such matters, to elucidate the difficulties connected in the two accounts; but of one fact we are certain, that Cybi resided upon this promontory, and that among "Bonedd y Saint" he ranks as one of the "seven cousin saints", with Dewi, Beuno, Dingad, Cynvarch, Daniel, and Seiriol, "Gwynvvdde bob amser",

" A vûn y maen graen grunder,
" Ar saith a weles y sêr."

These were the seven church patrons, or saints, who were entitled to hold lands in capite, in this Island of Anglesey; and Cybi had his nawddva or sanctuary established here.[207] The town of Holyhead is twenty-four miles from Beaumaris, and two hundred and sixty from London. On the 7th day of August, 1821, this place had the honour of a visit from the late King, George IV, who landed here on his passage to Ireland, "an event" (Mr. Cathrall properly observes) "which forms an epoch in the history of the Principality"; and the reader is referred to a long and correct description given of the rejoicing triumphal arch, in p.42 of his work.

It is to the classic pen of Mr. Stanley, rector of Alderley, and brother to "Sir John Stanley, who received the king on the pier head", that we owe the admirable and amusing account given in Blackwood's Magazine, of the Southstack Light-house, built on the mountain above Caer-gybi. The first stone was laid in the month of August, 1808, and the light was first exhibited on the night of the 9th of February, 1809. The speck by night, the white tower by day, with its hammock and fancy bridge, comprises what is called "the south stack", and taken altogether, it forms a prominent feature in the bold and romantic scenery of this iron-bound coast. In this mountain, is a great variety of spar, and in the

---

206 "Seiriol Wyn",* said to have been the first to cultivate black cherry trees (called from him Seiriol) and Cybi Velyn, used to meet weekly, at a place called Clorach, near Llannerchymedd, to confer upon and settle abstruse points in religion." Clorach was the ancient name of Llannerchymedd. It is so called in the Black Book of Basingwerk; and there is a place in Ireland, bearing the same name in that old MS. In p.181, 1st vol. Archiology, is:—
　　"Ymddiddan y Saint Cybi,
　　"Wrth vyned i Ynys Enlli,
　　"Yno i govynent i Gybi ", &c.
　　* *The tradition that these two saints were called, one 'Wyn', the other 'Velyn', because the former, in his journey to meet his brother saint at Clorach, had the sun at his back, and so also in returning, from which circumstance his complexion was preserved fair; while Cybi, on the contrary, had to face the morning sun in going, and the evening sun in returning; consequently he became so tanned, as to acquire the cognomen 'Velyn' or yellow.*

207 Lewis Morris, p.217, 3rd vol. Cambrian Registers, who in p.216, says that "at a place called Treiorwerth, in this parish, there is a cromlech composed after a very artificial manner, and seems to be three monuments erected over the graves of some great men". Query.—If this be not the same that Mr. Lloyd describes as the one at Trevignedd.

neighbourhood, is a large vein of fullers' earth, both yellow and white; besides some profitable veins of the Mona marble, called "verd antique" which have been worked to some extent.

LLANEUGRAD, OR LLANEIGRAD, a parish in the hundred of Twrcelyn, five miles from Llannerchymedd, was anciently much more extensive than at present; and not far from the church, upon the site of a farm, called Park, are distinct traces of a town or large village. In 873 a memorable battle (see page 32) was fought at Bryngoleu, within its limits, in which the Danes were defeated with great slaughter, by Roderic the Great; and near the old town are the remains of an extensive and wellfortified camp, in which the king is supposed to have stationed his forces in this conflict with the Danes.

This parish contains 2,420 acres of fertile land, enclosed and cultivated. An extensive quarry of black and grey marble affords employment to a considerable number of the labouring poor. The living is a discharged rectory, with the perpetual curacy of Llanallgo annexed, in the gift of the Bishop of Bangor, valued in the time of Henry VIII at £9 11s. 10d. The Rev. R. Davies is rector. The church, supposed to have been erected in 605, is dedicated to St. Eigrad ab Caw. Wakes kept the 8th of June. It is a small but stately edifice, of lofty proportions and venerable appearance. The resident population was in 1821, 325, and in 1831, 323. Poor rates in 1803 amounted to £50, at 8s. 3d. in the pound,—increased to £97 2s. 0d. in 1831. The poor are entitled to one third of the rent of a farm, in the parish of Llanvair-mathavarn-eithav, now let for £75 per annum. In this parish, there is a spring, which was formerly held in great estimation, and on a farm called Llugwy, are the ruins of an old chapel belonging to the church of Llaneigrad, still known by the name of "Capel Llugwy". Davydd Ddû Eryri, in his list of ruins of religious houses (p.286, 1st vol. Cambrian Register), places this in Llanvihangel Penrhos parish. There is among the cattle in this district, a complaint or distemper, called "damp", which affects the joints, occasioning lameness, attributed by the natives to the waters rising and running among limestone, which the animals drink.

LLANALLGO, OR LLANALLGOV, joins the above parish, and is in the same hundred, containing about four hundred and fifty acres of cultivated land, situated on the Irish coast, seven miles from Llannerchymedd. Though of small extent, it is rich in mineral treasures. Having a resident population of 392 persons in 1821, and 417 in 1831. The rates in 1803 were £20 12s. 8d. at 3s. in the pound,—increased to £91 17s. 0d. in 1831. The living is a perpetual curacy, annexed to the rectory of Llaneugrad. The church, dedicated to Gallgov, the son of Caw of Prydain, is said to have been built about the year 605. The festival called wakes, is kept in honour of this saint, on the first sunday in May. The church is a small but handsome structure, containing in the east window of the chancel some fragments of ancient stained glass. It was thoroughly repaired in 1831. Near it is "Ffynon Gallgov", St. Gallgov's well. Its waters, which are strongly impregnated with sulphate of lime, were formerly held in high veneration for the miraculous cures ascribed to them, and are still regarded as highly beneficial in some chronic diseases. Adjoining the west front of the church is "Capel Ffynon", i.e. the Chapel of the Well, a small neat edifice, formerly appropriated to the use of the votaries of the patron saint, to whose influence, in popish times, the miraculous efficacy of the waters was attributed. There is in this neighbourhood a cromlech. In this parish are some quarries of black and grey marble of good quality, which afforded materials for the construction of the pier, and the erection of the light-house at Holyhead.

LLANBABO, a parish in the hundred of Talybolion, contained in 1821, 161 inhabitants, and in 1831, 174. The poor-rates in 1803, at 4s. in the pound, amounted to £29 6s. 7d.—increased to £47 19s. 0d. in 1831. This small but well-cultivated parish, is situated six miles from Llannerchymedd, and nearly the whole of it belongs to Sir Richard Bulkeley. The living is a perpetual curacy annexed to the rectory of Llanddeusant, in the patronage of the bishop.

The church, a small plain edifice, was dedicated in 460, to the founder, "Pabo, Post Prydain", the son of Arthwys, said to be the oldest saint in Mona. The day of celebration is on the 9th of November. Our early poems redound with his praises as a pillar of his country. He was a chief of the North Britons; and about the year 500, headed an army of them against the Gwyddil Ficti, or Picts. He was afterwards compelled to seek an asylum in Wales and had lands given him in Mona, where he led a holy life, and was eventually canonized. The grave of Pabo, under a stone, bearing an inscription round his effigy, is still to be seen at Llanbabo. But we owe to the persevering spirit and ingenuity of Mr. Lewis Morris, the identifying of this monument. In his letter to Mr. Carte, the historian, he brings this ancient inscription of the seventh century, in proof of our having an alphabet, and of the Saxons borrowing it. His words are "there was an ancient tradition in the parish of Llanbabo, that Pabo, with his son and daughter, were buried in that church-yard, opposite to certain faces carved on the wall, and which are to be seen at this day. About Charles II's time there was found a stone, by the sexton, in digging for a grave, about six feet deep. He picked some of the letter and broke the corner of it, before he knew that it was a tomb-stone. The characters are cut in bass-relievowise, in a soft stone of the nature of slate not of the produce of Anglesea; on the other side, is a true copy of the figure, and inscription, which I took with my own hand, and as far as I could find, I was the first (about 1730) who discovered whose tomb-stone it was. It would have been inestimable as an antique, if the letters had not been nearly demolished." This is transcribed from a MS letter, in the Caerwys Collection; and in a curious diary, containing memorandums, heads of chapters, notes of observations, &c. belonging to the late Mr. Lloyd, is one containing the following entry. "A pillar at Llanbabo, with an inscription, called Maen Llanol, broken; and at Bod Deiniol are two cromlechau. The letters on Pabo's tomb-stone are quite legible at this day, and may be read—

HIC JACET PABO POST PRYDAIN IN TELURE IMA

Dynawd Vyr, the son of Pabo, is mentioned in Brut y Brenhinoedd to have been one of the noblemen that attended King Arthur at his great feast, at Caerlleon. He with Gwallawg ab Llenawg, and Cynvelyn Drwysgl, formed a triad of "The three pillars of battle of Britain".

LLANBADRIG, is near Ynys Padrig, and in the hundred of Talybolion. The living is a discharged vicarage, valued temp. Henry VIII at £7 8s. 11d; endowed with £400 Queen Anne's bounty, and in the patronage of the crown. The Rev. Evan Owen Hughes is the present incumbent. The lands are generally enclosed, and in a good state of cultivation; the soil being very productive. The church (dedicated to St. Patrick, and wakes kept as in Ireland, on the 17th of March) is built most inconveniently upon a cliff washed by the Irish sea, and within the township of Cemaes, and so near the sea, that during the prevalence of northerly or north-westerly winds, the waves break over it with such violence, as to interrupt, and, frequently to prevent the performance of divine service, and even the funeral service has been unavoidably deferred several days, during the continuance of those winds, at which time the church is altogether inaccessible. By the Myvyrian Archiology, published in 1801, I find that "Llanbadrig in Môn, belonged to the Brython of Ystrad Clwyd", in the north, and that about 440, Padrig, the son of Allvryd ab Goronwy, was sent by Pope Celestine, to convert the Irish, and being come to Môn, chose this remote situation for his church, which is situated seven miles from Amlwch, northwest. The resident population, including the townships of Cemaes and Clegyrog, is 1,364. The parish rates in 1803, at 5s. in the pound, amounted to £42 17s. 8d.,—increased in 1831 to £364 17s. 0d. In the year 1723 Mr. R. Gwynn of this parish gave a tenement in Amlwch, called Nantglyn, to endow a freeschool for the poor of this parish, and Mr. William Davies, in 1751, bequeathed £60 to the poor, the interest of which, together with some other small donations, is annually distributed among them, and the poor children of Llanbadrig are eligible to the school founded at Llanvechell, by Mr. Wynne. The whole of this parish, which is seven miles in length, is cultivated. A quantity of yellow ochre, a fine, white clay of the cimolia kind, umber, manganese and some copper ore are dug up in this parish. At Cemaes is found blueveined and whiteveined grey marble; also the hard primitive rock, called serpentine. The small creek of Cemaes affords facility for landing coal and other commodities, and is highly advantageous for the shipping of marble and the other mineral produce of the adjoining parish of Llanvechell.

LLANBEDR-GOCH. Mr. Cathrall says that this parish is in the hundred of Tindaethwy; but according to the extent taken in 1352, of Twrcelyn, it is in that comot, and called there Llanbedrmathavarnwyan, the names it goes by in old MSS and deeds, to this day. But the "Hospital Gwion", is in the Comot of Tindaethwy, and ranked as a township, belonging to the heirs of Goronw ab Gwion, consisting of "five domiciles". This parish is situated within seven miles and a half north-west of Beaumaris, and contains about 1,200 acres of arable land, and about fifty acres appropriated to mining purposes. The resident population in 1821 was 391, and 1831, 439. The poor rates in 1803, at 5s. in the pound, amounted to £61 13s. 4d.—increased to £154 6s. 0d. in 1831. The living is a perpetual curacy annexed to the rectory of Llanddyvnan. The church, dedicated to St. Peter (whose day is celebrated on the 19th of June) is a small beautiful cruciform structure, with a handsome east window, situated on a rocky eminence, in a distant and exposed part of the parish. A national school has been erected, which is supported by subscription.

This parish abounds with lime-stone rock, which is considered of the best quality, of which quarries are worked upon a large scale, affording employment to more than 200 men. Many thousand tons are exported annually to different parts of the kingdom, from Red Wharf Bay, which is near. The sand in this bay, is said to be the best manure of any hitherto found in the Island; and the quarries of mill-stones in this neighbourhood, mentioned in the extent (26th of Edward III) as "royal property", supply nearly all Mona, and Caernarvonshire, with these necessary articles, which for their durability, are accounted preferable to any dug from the mines of Penmon. In my account of Traeth Coch Bay, is given the description of a block of marble which had been thrown out of its bed in the rock.

LLANBEULAN is situated partly in the hundred of Malltraeth, and partly in that of Llivon, six miles from Llangevni, and thirteen from Holyhead. The resident population in 1821 was 428,—reduced to 375 in 1831: and the parish rates in 1803, at 6s in the pound, amounted to £89 6s. 6d.—increased to £197 13s. 0d. in 1831. The living is a rectory in the Bishop of Bangor's gift, valued in the temp. Henry VIII at £23 6s. 8d. having annexed the perpetual curacies of Llechylched, Ceirchiog, Llannerchymedd, Llanvaelog, and Tal-y-llyn. The Rev. William Roberts incumbent. The rectory house is in the chapelry of Llanvaelog. The original church, dedicated to St. Peulan, the son of Pawl Hen of Manaw (whose wakes are celebrated on March 17th) was built about the year 630. The present edifice is a small cruciform structure, situated in a little barren valley, near the new line of road to Holyhead and the south transcept bears evidence of very great antiquity. It has some windows in the later English style, of good design, especially the east window of the chancel, which is a very superior composition. David Jones, in 1726, bequeathed £10, the interest of which, to be given annually to two of the oldest paupers belonging to the parish, who should be considered as deserving objects of charity.

LLANDDEINIOL VAB is a chapel (not in charge) annexed to the vicarage of Llanidan. Patron, Lord Boston, who is lay rector. The officiating minister having *only* a third of the great tithes. This parish, which is seven miles from Bangor, and situated on the great Holyhead road, comprises a large tract of land, 1,800 acres in all, and in a good state of cultivation. The church, dedicated to St. Daniel Vab (whose day is celebrated on September 11th) is a very ancient and dilapidated structure, originally erected in the year 616, and exhibiting some good specimens of the architecture of a very remote period. The resident population in 1821 was 384, and 372 in 1831. The parish rates in 1803, at 5s. in the pound, amounted to £70 4s. 11d—increased to £205 12s. 0d. in 1831. The interest of various charitable bequests amounting in the aggregate to £130 is annually distributed among the poor of the parish.

The progress of cultivation has nearly obliterated many of the vestiges of antiquity, which existed in this, as well as several other parishes in Mona. At Bryn Celli, are some traces of large carneddau, where two upright stones are still remaining, with some few others scattered around them, and in several of the adjacent fields are some upright stones, of large dimensions, apparently the remains of cromlechau and near Bodlew in this parish, is a deeply excavated and irregularly elliptical area, forty-three yards in length and twenty-seven in depth, across the centre, with an entrance at the smaller end. Near the middle of this enclosure, are the remains of an ancient small building, called Capel Cadwaladr, supposed to have been originally erected by Cadwaladr, the last king of the Britons. This is by some writers called "Yr Hên Vonwent", and thought to be the oldest if not the first place of christian worship established in the Island. Mr. Humphrey Thomas, brother of Davydd Ddû, the bard of Snowdon, was schoolmaster in the village of Llanddeiniol. By his letter written in 1801, to Mr. P. Bailey Williams, and published in the 2nd vol. Cambro Quarterly, he appears to have been very conversant with our bardic hoards of unpublished MSS.

LLANDDONA, in old MSS styled "Dena y Cravgoet y Môn", is situated in the hundred of Tindaethwy, about three miles and a half north-west of Beaumaris. It is a perpetual curacy, not in charge, but occasionally endowed with £1,000 from Queen Anne's bounty. Lord Boston is patron and impropriator of the tithes. This parish contains from 1,400 to 1,500 acres of arable land, and 100 of common, which being very rocky, is of little value to the poor people. The church, a very ancient structure was built in the year 610, and is dedicated to "Dona ab Selyv ab Cynon ab Garwyn ab Brochwell Yscythroc", who built a cell on the sea-shore. Day of celebration, i.e. wakes, kept on November 1st. The present incumbent is the Rev. William Lewis, and the resident population in 1821 was 382, and in 1831, 442. Parish rates in 1803 were at 6s. in the pound, £54 18s. 11d., and in 1832, £172 17s. 0d. Above Llanddona is a high hill, with a large plat of table land upon the top, called "Bwrdd Arthur". There is a cromlech at Cremlyn. A profitable herring fishery in the season gives employment to a considerable number of people, and the numerous farm houses scattered over the parish, give it an air of cheerfulness not generally found in this part of Wales.

LLANDDWYNWEN, is situated three miles south-west from Rhosvair. This spot, most interesting to the antiquary, is in the hundred of Menai, and as Mr. Pennant remarks, the parish extends below into the sea, terminating in a narrow peninsula. One small tenement is all that remains of this large tract of land, the whole being laid waste by sand hills. "Richard Cyffin, Dean of Bangor, who died in 1502, was rector of Llanddwynwen, where the ruins of his house are still to be seen. All the parish excepting that, the walls of the church, and the warrener's house, are swallowed by the sea." Thus writes Mr. Lloyd, in 1776, adding that it once formed part of the possessions of the magnificent monastery of Dwynwen, and afterwards endowed one of the richest prebends in the diocese of Bangor. William Vaughan was the first prebendary, appointed in 1404. He is mentioned as such in the document alluded to by Mr. Pennant, and which has been printed in p.151, 2nd vol. Cambro-Briton. This commission was issued by Gryffydd Yong, Owen Glyndwr's spirited chancellor, prohibiting Iorwerth Vaughan, Rector of Llanddoget, to appropriate to himself, the splendid offerings made at the shrine of Dwynwen, commemorated by Davydd ab Gwylym, in a poem addressed to Morvydd.—

"The charmer of sweet Mona's Isle,
"With death attendant on her smile,
" Intent on pilgrimage divine, &c.
" Speeds to St. Dwynwen's holy shrine."

"Here were constant wax lights kept at the tomb of this virgin saint, which brought no small gains to the monks, from the pious and superstitious people, who visited it from all parts of the kingdom, in those times of popery; for the whole machinery of that delusive church, and the juggling arts of mercenary priests were in this remote corner collected together and made use of to impose upon an ignorant and misguided populace. Mr. Hazlitt conceives that the literary brilliancy of the Elisabethean age, was owing to the unlocking of the bible, the great storehouse of the sublime and beautiful." That queen, like the Jewish king, found the ark of God without a shelter, and "she built for it" says Southey, "the noblest temple in the world! She consecrated her country into its temple, and every man's heart a separate one". In the memory of England, her name and her golden reign are alike immortal.

Surrounded by rocks, and near the shore, on a peninsula, which is about half a mile in length, are the ruins of the church, which was dedicated to St. Dwynwen, the daughter of Brychan Urth, one of the holy colidei, or primitive christians of Britain, who lived in the fifth century; and from what remains, we may judge that this church must have been a fine building. Its present ruinous and desolate appearance, contrasted with the former busy scene around it (owing to the crowded votaries), must forcibly impress the mind of every person, who may be induced to visit this retired spot, with the uncertainty of worldly grandeur. Soon after the reformation, it was despoiled of all the timber and lead, which the neighbouring families converted to domestic uses. The view from hence, is one of peculiar beauty and grandeur, and it is well worth a visit from every admirer of antiquities and fine scenery. It must not be forgot that Richard Cyffin, "y Deon Dû of Bangor", when rector of Llanddwynwen, resided here, in the time of Richard III and being a strenuous supporter of the House of Lancaster, in concert with Sir R. Herbert, contrived by means of fishing boats, and other small vessels, to carry on a correspondence with the Duke of Richmond, then in Brittany; his friend Bishop Morton being with Henry: Sir Rhys ab Thomas was an active agent in this affair. Dean Cyffin died in 1502, and founded a chantry in the cathedral of Bangor (where he was buried), endowing it with the tithes of Llaniestyn and Llanvihangel-tyn-sylw, in this Island, besides a farm, called Bronhaelog. At the time of the reformation, William ab Owen, a younger son of Bodowen, enjoyed this Llanddwyn, which is now become, by purchase, the property of Lord Dinorben, who has built upon the spot formerly occupied by the Culdees, cottages for pilots, to conduct vessels over the dangerous bar of Caernarvon. The trustees of that harbour, have also erected here a pier, as a shelter for small vessels waiting for the tide. From the narrow sandy coves between the rocks, affording shelter to smugglers, this was the favourite haunt of these illicit traders; but the commercial regulations adopted by government, have in a great measure, put a stop to them. Here are abundance of fish, and lobsters, crabs, &c. taken off this coast.

LLANDDYVNAN is five miles from Beaumaris, situated on the turnpike road to Llannerchymedd, and ranked as a township in the hundred of Tindaethwy, in the extent taken at Beaumaris, 26th of Edward III having then two domiciles; the tenants paying a yearly rent of £2, owing suit at the county and hundred courts. It is a rectory, having under it the chapelries of Pentraeth, Llanbedr-gôch and Llanvair-mathavarn-eithav, valued temp. Henry VIII at £38 6s. 8d. The Bishop of Bangor presents, and he has the tithes. The curacy, together with surplice fees, value about £63. The church is supposed to be built about the year 590, and dedicated to St. Dyvnan, son of Brychan, who lies buried here. He came from Rome, by the invitation of Lleirwg (Lucius), a Prince of the Silures, to assist in converting the Britons. This prince was the first who formed a design of diffusing the christian faith generally over his dominion. The resident population in 1821 was 810,—dwindled to 678 in 1831, and the parish rates were in 1803, £152 6s. 0d. at 8s. in the pound,—increased to £306 3s. 0d. in 1831. This parish contains about 2,000 acres of land, of which 200 are unenclosed.

LLANDRYGARN is in the hundred of Llivon, a perpetual curacy, and together with that of Holyhead, is under Botwrog Rectory, in the patronage of Jesus College, Oxford. Annual value about £66, endowed with £400 Queen Anne's bounty, and £600 parliamentary grant. This parish, with the chapelry of Gwyndy contains 449 inhabitants. Distance from Bangor, fourteen miles and a half, and from Llannerchymedd three miles. The church, dedicated to St. Trygarn, is a small and very ancient structure. Dr. Wynn, chancellor of Llandaff, gave a portion of the tithes to the principal and fellows of Jesus College, Oxford, in trust for the poor of this parish. The rates for their support amount to £197 1s. 0d. In the chapelry of Gwyndy, large hammers, rudely formed of trap rock; and hand-mills of various sizes, made of chert, marble and free-stone, of which the smaller were rudely and the larger well formed, have at various times been found. This parish is chiefly distinguished as having been the residence of Rhys ab Hwlcyn, who for his services at the battle of Bosworth, was appointed sheriff of Mona, for life, a place of great trust in those days. He assumed the surname of Bodychan, from his ancient family mansion. Of one of the towers, there are still some remains: this was formerly used as the county prison. The other parts of Bodychan, have been converted into a barn and farm offices.

LLANDDYVRYDOG is in the hundred of Twrcelyn, not far from Llanelian, two miles east from Llannerchymedd, and about three from the bay of Dulas. This place is noted for an extraordinary incident which happened in the church, and which Giraldus thus relates. "There is in this Island the church of St. Tevredacus, into which Hugh, Earl of Salop (who with Hugh, the Earl of Chester had forcibly entered Mona), on a certain night, put some dogs, which on the following morning were found mad, and he himself died within a month after." Tyvrydog, to whom the church is dedicated, was one of the sons of Arwystl Glôff, by Tegwared, verch Amlawn Wledig. This church, supposed to have been built about the year 450, is a spacious, lofty and venerable structure, in excellent repair, having a remarkable large chancel: it is sixty feet in length, and twenty-five in breadth, The day of celebration of wakes in honour of the saint is kept on January 1st. The living is a discharged rectory (having the perpetual curacy of Llanvihangel-tre'r-beirdd annexed), valued temp. Henry VIII at £314 9s. 7d. and in the patronage of the Bishop of Bangor. The present incumbent is Robert Williams, D.D. The resident population in 1821 was 695,—increased in 1831 to 853; and the parish rates were in 1803, £139 8s. 8d. at 10s. in the pound; and £242 16s. 0d. in 1831. In this parish are stone pillars, which the natives call "Maeni Gwyr". Some are deeply fixed in the ground, and others are fallen. It is conjectured by antiquaries that they had been set up for land marks, or to limit the extent of the jurisdiction of certain chiefs of the Druids. Among these is one to be seen of a particular form, in some degree representing the human shape: it is situated on a farm called Clorach, in a field that borders upon the public road, leading from Llannerchymedd to Beaumaris. The inhabitants call this monument "Lleidr Llandyvrydog"; from a tradition common among them, that a man who had sacrilegiously stolen a bible from the church, was on his way homewards transformed into this stone. "Nigh are also two wells on this farm", observes Mr. Cathrall, in p.54, "where, according to tradition, St. Cybi and St. Seiriol used to meet to consult about the religious affairs of this part of the principality"; the wells are still held in high estimation, and called Ffynnon Cybi and Ffynnon Seiriol, as before related in a note to p.104. This parish contains about 2,000 acres of level and well-cultivated land; the soil is generally argillaceous. Peat earth is found in the marshy land upon the banks of a rivulet descending from the Parys Mountain, and from this earth, after burning it for that purpose, a considerable quantity of copper ore is obtained. There are places of worship for anabaptists and calvinistic methodists; to the former of these is attached a burial ground. A national school, in which fifty poor children of this parish, and the adjoining one of Llanvihangel-tre'r-beirdd, receive gratuitous instruction, was erected in 1816. Dr. Wynne bequeathed a house in the borough of Caernarvon, which lets for £12 per annum, £6 of which, together with other charitable donations and bequests, is annually distributed among the poor at Christmas.

LLANDISILIO is situated in the hundred of Tindaethwy, and is a perpetual curacy under the church of Llanvair-pwllgwyngyll, in the gift of the Bishop of Bangor, and within five miles of Beaumaris; contains 557 acres of land in cultivation, and about 150 common. The rates were, in 1803, £47 10s. 3d. at 3s. in the pound, and in 1831, £54 16s. 0d. Within this parish are four great fairs, held annually on the four following days:—August 26th, September 26th, October 26th, and November 14th. The population in 1821 was 493, and in 1831, 479. On a rocky peninsula, about half-a-mile above the ferry of Porthaethwy, stands the small church of Llandisilio, dedicated to Tisilio, son of Brochwel Ysgythrog, Prince of Powys, commander of the British forces in the memorable battle of Chester, A.D.603, when they were defeated by Aethelfrith. It is a small edifice, remarkable for the bleakness of its situation. "It is remarkable", observes Mr. Pennant, "that most of the seventy-four parishes, which this Island is divided into, have their churches not remote from the shore". On a farm called Tan-yr-allt, are extensive remains of an encampment, said to have been Roman.[208] Some vestiges of the camp constructed by Hugh Lupus, at Cadnant, are still visible, and near them are the remains of a small circular building. Within the last few years, a very large hammer, rudely formed of hard stone, and of very ancient appearance, was found in the immediate neighbourhood, which has been preserved by Mr. Price at Cadnant; and in the course of subsequent researches, an immense rock of similar stone, equally hard and compact, has been discovered, extending across the parish; of which, it is thought, the ancient hammers were made. Cadnant was one of the oldest ferries across this part of the Menai, and having become a source of considerable revenue, was granted by Edward I to Anian, Bishop of Bangor, who had performed the ceremony of baptism on the young prince, Edward.

In this parish, and not far from the shore, are two eminences, commemorative of a visit made to this Island by Baldwyn and Giraldus, in 1188, to beg contribution in men and money, ostensibly to carry on a holy war against the infidels; but in reality, their crusade was against our primitive christian church (and its respectable married clergy)—a church, which we believe, was founded by the apostles,

---

208 Mr. Pennant queries if this is not the one at Cadnant.

and which continued pure till 1146, "when the firste abbey, or friars house, thatt we reade of in Wales (sith the noble House of Bangor, which savoured not of Romish dregges) was the "Tŷ Gwyn", built in the yeare 1146; and after, they swarmed like bees, throughe all the country, ffor soone the clergye forgot the lesson that they had received from the noble clerke Ambrose Telesinas; who, writinge in the yeare 540, when the righte christian faithe (which Joseph of Arimathea taught at the Isle of Avalon), reigned in this lande, before the proud and bloodthirstie Awstyn infected it with his Romish doctrine, in a certaine ode hath these verses:—

> "Woe to hym who doth nott keepe
> " From Romish wolves hys fflocks of sheepe,
>   " And preach his charge amonge;
> "Thatt will nott watch his fold alwai,
> " As toe his office doth belonge.
> "Woe to hym that doth nott keepe
> " From Romish wolves his flocke of Sheepe,
>   "With staff and weapon strong."[209]

We have reason to suppose from tradition, that the public meeting convened on the occasion, mentioned in the preceding page (and from the memorials of this visitation, as by names still retained), was held in an open place, admitting of a convenient surface for that purpose, and commanding a full view of the assembled people. The spot on which "Rodri, the son of Owen Gwynedd stood, surrounded by many chosen youths of this family", is called "Maen Rodri", now the property of Mr. Williams of Craig y Don, and the other where the Archdeacon of Bangor preached from, "Carreg yr Archdiacon", corrupted (says the ingenious author of "Beaumaris Bay"), to "Carreg Iago", belonging to Lord Anglesey; and on a little eminence, a seat cut in the rock, with a rude arch over it, where the Bishop sat, should have been called "Cadair yr Archesgob", but his business being to beg the people's alms, they upon that account, called the place "Cil-beg-le". Giraldus ends his itinerary by lamenting that the persuasive eloquence of Baldwyn, and his coadjutor, Alexander the archdeacon, failed in making converts: "not one of the chosen youths that surrounded their prince, could be prevailed upon to take the cross". Probably they did not like to give up the faith of the bible, which the British Church possessed, from the first preaching of christianity in this Island.

Edward Llwyd, in one of his letters, says that the oldest MS he had heard of, was an imperfect copy of the Gospels, at Lichfield Cathedral Library, which came originally from South Wales. It had belonged to the Church of Llandaff, about nine hundred years ago; and in Ireland he found the Book of Genesis in MS which a popish priest at Sligo, presented to him, which was written very little later than the first planting of christianity in that Island. This MS was burnt in the Sebright conflagration. I shall take leave to introduce here the following very just observations, bearing upon this subject, transcribed out of a popular review of books, published in February, 1833.

"It has been very confidently asserted that the Welsh Church is one of the most ancient christian

209 Welsh Chronicles p.254

churches in existence; that the gos pel was preached in Britain, by St. Paul; that when the Ancient Britons were driven from other parts of the Island by the ferocity of successful invaders, they retired to the mountains and fastnesses of the principality, carrying with them their religion, their ancient language, their ardent and determined love of freedom; and that these honourable characteristics have been preserved with less violation and interruption amongst them, than amongst almost any other nation; and there is abundant proof that the Welsh have, in almost every age, been distinguished for zeal and piety, and determined attachment to the cause of civil and religious liberty. Nor are the Welsh of the present day unworthy of their great progenitors. They still evince the same exalted character—they still cherish and cultivate their ancient language—they still are feelingly alive to the interests of true religion; though the Church of England is less prosperous in comparison with dissenting and methodist congregations in some parts of the principality than in England in general. This may fairly be ascribed to the inconsiderate or mistaken policy of appointing Englishmen to the Welsh Sees, who for a long period of years, seemed entirely to forget that a very large portion of the ancient Britons knew nothing of the English language, and that however eminent and exemplary the individuals were, whom the stream of episcopal patronage placed in the Welsh parishes, they were still as barbarians to those whose language they neither understood, nor took any pains to acquire. To the present Bishop of Peterborough, then Bishop of Llandaff, we are informed, pertains the honour of first in modern times, requiring that those who applied to him for institution in parishes, where the Welsh prevailed, should be able to officiate in that tongue. Yet still under every disadvantage, true religion has prevailed, and we are happy to say does still prevail, in a very eminent degree, in the principality.

LLANEDWEN is situated on the western shore of the Menai, and within that hundred, five miles from Caernarvon, and with the adjoining parishes of Llanidan and Llanddeiniol, anciently formed a district which was the principal seat of the druids. Here are still considerable remains of those deeply shaded groves, so well adapted to the performance of their religious rites. The shores of the Menai are rocky and precipitous—the scenery is bold,—striking, and in some places beautifully picturesque. This parish contains 1,500 acres of land, in a state of cultivation. The soil is fertile. Limestone of excellent quality is found in great abundance, affording employment to a considerable number of the inhabitants. Through the park of Plasnewydd runs a bed of granite, in a state of decomposition. The living is a perpetual curacy, annexed to the vicarage of Llanidan. The churchyard is one of the most beautiful in North Wales. The church is a small but neat edifice, of great antiquity, originally built in 640, and dedicated to St. Edwen, sister or niece to Edwyn, King of England; her wakes kept on the 6th of November. In this church is buried the Rev. Henry Rowlands, the learned author of Mona Antiqua, a work held in high estimation by antiquaries and the literary world in general. The resident population in 1821 was 289, and 299 in 1831. The average annual expenditure for the support of the poor amounts to £903 18s. 0d. A parochial school, in which forty-five girls receive gratuitous education, was founded by the Marquess of Anglesey. Bishop Rowland, in 1616, bequeathed £6 per annum, charged on his estate at Plâs Gwyn. Lady Bailey bequeathed a small sum, derived from Plasnewydd. Mr. Bagnall bequeathed a small rent-charge on the same property; and Mrs. Rowland, in 1740, gave £100 in money.

The three former gifts, together with the interest of the latter are annually distributed among the poor during winter. The estate of Llysllew,[210] producing £200 per annum, was given by Bishop Rowland as an endowment to the free grammar school, which he founded at Bottwnog. In this parish is the Moel y Don ferry, so noted in history for the attempt made by Edward I in 1281, "soe fatal to many a gallante man"; and here also "Aelodd King of Dublin, built a strong fortress, with its tommen and foss", as detailed in p.72, out of Mr. Lloyd's MSS who in vol. 4th gives a curious history of King Arthur, who built a bridge at this place. The extract relative to that prince, may perhaps be of use to elucidate the origin of romances, &c.

"M.S.I.G.L. Experta ex Historia Britanica Johannis Jones, Gelli Lovdŷ, additis quibusdam notis margin, John Griffith, de Cae Cyniog, apud Denbighshire, &c. This, like the poems above mentioned is split into two parts in the binding; it seems to contain a good deal of the legendary parts of our history, with very sober remarks upon them. It is written in Welsh, and if the original is to be found, it is a valuable book." In the Life of King Arthur (which is not so fabulous as that published by Geoffrey of Monmouth) he says that after the hero had overcome his enemies in the North of England, he returned into North Wales and had several contests with the then King of Mona, who had at that time a bridge over the Menai, at Bon y Don, guarded by a number of armed men. The author refers for further particulars in this and many other things relative to Arthur to a book, entitled the "Sangreal". He mentions some of his heroic companions, &c. Caw o Vrydain had two sons, and lived in Edernion; the eldest was Gildas, the querulous historian, an excellent scholar; the second was Huail, whom Arthur beheaded upon a stone, which lay in the street of Ruthin, which was from that event denominated "Maen Huail", and which name it retains at this day (1788). About this time, Arthur erected a palace, at a place now called Nannerch. It bore the name of "Llys Arthur" in the author's time, and it was said that the church of Nannerch which was formerly called "Capel Gwiail", was a chapel belonging to it. In the time of Henry VIII, there was affixed to the shrine of Edward the Confessor, in red wax, an impression of King Arthur, which that king had so great a veneration for, that he ordered it to be fixed in this manner to his shrine. The words upon it were "PATRICIUS ARTURUS BRYTTANIE, GERMANIE, GALIE DACE, IMPERATOR". It was in the custody of the confessor, and supposed to have been appended originally to some grant of King Arthur's, either to the abbey, at Westminster or Glastonbury. The author, in order to obviate the objection that the wax could not have lasted so long as from the confessor's time to Henry the Eighth's time, and that there were no seals affixed to deeds till after the conquest, adduces the following proof:—"That he himself had shewen to Sir William Jones, Judge of the Common Pleas, and to Sir John Lea, Judge of the King's Bench, a deed, with a seal of wax attached to it, which was then 800 years old, and if properly kept, might last 600 years longer. The impression was a man on horseback, with a sword in his hand. It related to lands in a place called Thickheindown, which place Sir John Lea knew." And to obviate an objection, that as Westminster was not built till long after Arthur's time, this seal could have no reference to any charter belonging to it, &c. He relates "that

210 Palace of the lion.

he himself had seen Madoc ab Gryffith Maelor's chartar for building the abbey of Glyn Egwesty, directed to the monks of four different monasteries for erecting the same; and that the deed was made a considerable time before its erection, and that it was many years in building.—John Lloyd." [211] Respecting the Sangreal alluded to in Mr. Lloyd's MS it has been ingeniously conjectured by a learned Welsh antiquary, that from a comparison of circumstances and names of places, given in "the Romance of the Sangreal", that the borders of the Menai were the scenes of contest between Arthur and the druids. What the Sangreal was in itself, has been much doubted. In the romance it is described as a sort of cup. Mr. Peter Roberts, author of "Cambrian Popular Antiquities" and other works, has given in Collectanea Camb. vol.1, p.309, the following very clever conjectures concerning the Sangreal, which he always maintained (when arguing the subject with the writer and others) was the identical "Santo Catino", carried to Paris by Bonaparte from Florence, a celebrated cup of peculiar beauty, of a composition (probably glass) resembling an emerald. The word "Grael" is said by Mr. Lewis Morris, on the authority of the "Speculum Historicum" of Vincentius, to be derived from Gradale, an old French word, signifying a little dish; and this seems to be the true signification. "Was it originally a divining cup of the druids?" asks Mr. Roberts, who adds "that divining cups were of the remotest antiquity, we know from the History of Joseph; and a vestige of that kind of divination is yet observable in the practice of divining by the coffee, or tea-cup. If the Sangreal were such a cup, it would have been considered, when obtained by conquest, as the noblest trophy of the victory of christians over the druids; and therefore might have been represented as the object of the war itself. Of course the vessel would be deposited in the place of the greatest security; and whether this conjecture concerning its original history be, or be not, well founded, that the Santo Catino was at St. David's, and stolen and carried off from thence to Glastonbury, with other valuables cannot now, I think, be doubted. I am not without some suspicion, that during the establishment of the druids at Glastonbury, the Catino or Sangreal, had been preserved there, and that it was from the celebrity of this vessel, the place took the name of 'Ynys Wydryn', or 'the Isle, or District of the Little Glass', and that Merlin, when he was at Bardsey, sailed not indeed in it, but with it, that is carried it with him thither; and that it was recovered by Arthur, and consecrated to the use of the church by St. David."

In this parish is situated "Llwyn y Moel", better known as "Plasnewydd", the mansion-house of the Marquess of Anglesey, lying close upon the water, protected by fine woods. It was originally built by Gwenllian, the widow of Ievan ab Howel, who enjoyed this estate as her dower, in 1352; it having formed part of the forfeited possessions belonging to Llewelyn ab Davydd, escheated in 1285. He was a strenuous adherent to the cause of Madoc ab Llewelyn, whose insurrection is related towards the conclusion of the "Chronicles of the Princes". This property, besides great possessions in Ireland, was acquired by the marriage of Dr. Bailey, Bishop of Bangor, with Ann, daughter and heiress of Sir Nicolas Bagnall, Knight, Marshal of Queen Elizabeth's army, in Ireland, who added this to his Irish estates, by marrying Ellen, daughter and heiress of Edward Griffith, descended from the Griffiths of Penrhyn.

211 Caerwys MS.

When the Bishop[212] re-edified this ancient mansion of the Griffiths, he changed the original name to the one it now bears, which does not well harmonize with its ancient cromlech and surrounding scenery.[213] This house will become still more celebrated in history from having been the temporary residence of their Royal Highnesses the Duchess of Kent and the Princess Victoria; in the summer of 1832. The magnificent acts and condescending manners of these illustrious ladies have left an impression of gratitude and admiration on the minds of the Cambro-Britons, that can never be effaced.

In the skirts of the woods is an artificial mount, called "Bryn yr Hên Bobl", supposed by Davydd Ddû, the bard of Snowdon, to have been a druidical sepulchre, that is, a tumulus; and Mr. Lloyd in his MS says, that "In the woods of Llwyn y Moel, now called Plâsnewydd, and behind the house are some remarkable druidical antiquities, the most magnificent we have seen, and the highest from the ground. The large cromlech measures 12ft. 7in. long, 10ft. 11in. broad, and 4ft. deep; stands nearly north and south. The north end is highest, supported by four stones, or perhaps three; the middle apparently split in two at the top, about thirteen inches asunder; the south end supported by two pillars; a large stone seemingly fallen down at the west entrance;—on the opposite entrance another large stone, the lesser about 5ft. 6in. each way, about 2ft. 3in. thick, supported by four stones, and a fifth, apparently placed at the south end of the great one, appears to have slid a little from the middle stone next the great cromlech,—the distance between the two scarcely a foot. South from hence and at some distance, stands the great carnedd mentioned by Rowlands, with a large breach on the east side in which appears a cistvaen, or cromlech; the bottom of it level with the natural surface; the entrance very low, over a stone laid edgeways; two semicircular segments cut out of it, similar to those in common stocks; the length from east to west about 7ft. the breadth, where narrowest, about 3ft. This is also supported by five large stones; the intermediate space filled up by the carnedd, except the entrance.—*J. Lloyd*".[214]

In Munimenta Antiqua is given the following description of the same cromlech. "The upper or high part consists of a large stone, 12ft. 7in. long, 12 broad and 4 thick, supported apparently some years ago, by five tall stones, near the upper end, but now only by three; one five, the other three, and the third three and three and a half feet high, which were most probably its original supports, the rest being here, as in other instances, merely appendant ornaments, and therefore easily thrown down.[215] The lower part of this double cromlech consists of another great stone, barely separated from the first, which is nearly a square, of about 52ft. or almost 6ft. and it is supported in like manner by three stones: one that for some time formed the appearance of a fourth, being thrown down.

Mr. Pennant, on his mention of this curious remain, adopts Dr. Borlase's idea of cromlechau being cist-vaens, or mere cells for interment. But it is very remarkable, that (as it were in full confuta-

212 "He was born at Caermarthen, and was Chaplain to Henry, Prince of Wales; held this see from 1616 to 1631, when he died in October.—*Browne Willis.*"

213 Cathrall, in p.55, describes the house, pictures, grounds, &c. And the distinguished head of this mansion is Lord Anglesea, "Llew Môn, Erryr Arvon". For an account of this hero's brilliant career in the last continental wars, the reader is again referred to Mr. Cathrall's History, which is embellished with an excellent likeness of the noble warrior.

214 Caerwys MS.

215 Mon. Ant. p.99

tion of his own and Borlase's conclusion) he immediately proceeds to describe an exceedingly large carnedd (which indeed was manifestly a sepulchre, or burying place) just by the spot, which he most unaccountably conceives to have been a prison for confining prisoners for sacrifice, and most strangely mistakes a deep buried sepulchre for a prison, for living condemned captives. Rowlands says the carnedd near this cromlech is one of the largest carneddau in the Isle of Mona, in his time hardly to be discerned and distinguished from a mount of earth, the stones being overgrown with earth and moss, and great trees growing thick upon it; and that it stands in a dry bottom, and without any pillars now standing by it. Since Rowlands's time, on its being opened, there has been found underneath a cell about seven feet long and three wide, covered with two flat stones and lined with others, and much more truly resembling a cist-vaen than the cavity under the cromlech could, and indeed much fitter for a tomb than for a prison; and truly that carneddau, or great and high heaps of stones so called, did really cover tombs, we have a strong proof from what appeared on opening another large one in Mona, not far from this very spot; for here was found a passage,[216] three feet wide, four and a half high, and about nineteen and a half feet long, which led into a room of an irregular hexagonal form, having the sides composed of six rude slabs, one of which measured diagonally eight feet nine inches. And this little room was covered by one stone, near ten feet in diameter, which was also supported by a rude stone pillar in the middle, four feet eight inches in circumference; whilst all round the sides of the room was a stone bench, on which were found human bones that fell to dust almost at a touch.[217]

For the more perfect explanation of the nature of the double cromlech at Plasnewydd, I have obtained more exact dimensions of all the parts, than could be had before. It is twelve feet nine long, and thirteen feet two inches broad, in the broadest part, whilst its greatest depth or thickness is five feet. Its contents therefore in cubic feet and decimal parts, cannot be less than 392—878—125. And as the specific gravity of one cubic inch of this stone, is as 1—6 in avoirdupois ounces, it follows that the weight of this mass must be no less than thirty tons, seven hundreds and four pounds. The dimensions of the four stones that support the north end are as follows:—

No. 1		FEET	INCHES
Length	. . . .	5	0
Breadth	. . . .	4	8
Thickness	. . . . . .	1	8

No. 2.		FEET	INCHES
Length	. . . .	5	6
Breadth	. . . .	5	6
Thickness	. . . .	1	6

No. 3			
Length	. . . .	4	5
Breadth	. . . .	5	0
Thickness v.	. . . . . .	1	6

No. 4.			
Length	. . . .	5	6
Breadth	. . . .	2	0
Thickness	. . . .	2	0

Outlines of the supporters of the south end one, of which No. 6, at present, lies lengthways on the ground.

216 Gough's Camden, vol.2, p.570.   Pennant's Tour in Wales, vol.2, p.262.
217 Munimenta Antiqua, p.233.

No. 5		FEET	INCHES
Length		4	10
Breadth		3	9
Thickness		2	0

No. 6		FEET	INCHES
Length		5	0
Breadth		2	6
Thickness		2	0

And it is very remarkable, that both this top stone and its supporters are of one and the same kind of stone, and must have been carried or rolled more than a mile, as there is no stone of that sort to be found near the spot. The dimensions of the top stone of the smaller or lower part of the cromlech, are in length six feet; in breadth five feet seven inches. It has at present only three supporters, but there are three other large stones of the same kind, lying underneath, which seem to have been intended for supporters, or at least to have had the appearance of supporters in ancient time, and are what occasion the apparent confusion and disagreement in the drawings and descriptions of this cromlech. The three supporters of the lesser stone which are now standing as such, are in length four feet four inches, and in breadth about three feet. Another double cromlech, not less extraordinary, is near a house called Trefor, about two miles and a half from Beaumaris, in the road to Plâs Gwyn. The only material difference between this cromlech and the former, is that the second or inferior altar is placed a little further off from its lower end, and that its top is somewhat gibbous. This latter circumstance however, is a peculiarity of some of the cromlechau, which may be suspected to have been rather of the later ages, and is so conspicuous in one called the "Giant's Coit" in Cornwall, as to render it exceeding difficult for any one to stand upon it at all; on which account Mr. Maton who describes it, was led to adopt Dr. Borlase's idea of all cromlechau being merely sepulchres. In the same island also we have another very remarkable double cromlech, which seems to have escaped the notice of the curious Rowlands. It is in the parish of Bodedern, in the second field, opposite the ninth mile stone from Holyhead, on the old road. The larger stone is about ten feet by eight, and two feet and half thick, apparently resting on four stones; the highest whereof is five feet; the smaller stone which formed the second or lower part of the cromlech, stood on three stones, and was about nine feet square, but is now thrown down. There are also remains of a double cromlech on the hill overlooking Holyhead.

LLANELIAN is on the north side of the Island, and seated on the rocks near the sea is the handsomely built church of St. Elian, with its tower surmounted by a spire, and consequently forming a considerable feature among the churches in this Island, they being destitute of this ornament, having only an arched belfry at the west end, a style of architectural simplicity much in character with the small building annexed. The entire edifice of St. Elian, which is embattled, is partly in the early and partly in the decorated style of English architecture, and built substantially of grit stone, with quoins and cornices of free stone; it comprises a nave and chancel, the roofs of which are internally of ancient carved oak; that of the latter resting upon finely sculptured corbels of angels playing on musical instruments. A splendid screen of richly carved oak, ornamented with a portrait of St. Elian, but much defaced with paint, separates the chancel from the nave, in the former of which are four stalls of tabernacle work, with the date 1533, and an altar piece of carved oak, of inferior execution. The east window of three lights, enriched with tracery, and surmounted by an elegant ogee canopy, contains some portion of ancient stained glass.

When the extent of Twrcelyn was taken at Bettws Geraint, the 26th of Edward III, St. Elian was ranked as a township, containing four domiciles, i.e. the domicile of Penrhyn, Bairach, Bodrugan and the domicile of Bodgynddelw, "owing no suit nor service to the Lord Prince, because they are held of St. Elian's, except that certain villains of the same are to present themselves before the sheriff for the time being, twice a year, at his two great tourns, without any other services to the Lord Prince, except that if any of them should appear before the sheriff, at his county or hundred court, in a suit, that the said sheriff should have an interest as may be then necessary, on the parts of the complainants; and if there be any amercement, it shall go to the Lord Prince. And there is in the aforesaid domicile of Penrhyn, a certain rent of sixpence three farthings per annum, payable at Easter and Michaelmas, to the Lord Prince, and which formerly belonged to Gryffydd ab Cyndal, one of the abbots of this township, who forfeited it", &c. This parish is a discharged rectory, and with the chapels of Coedane, Rhosbeirio, and Bodewryd is valued in the king's books, at £14 1s. 8d. The Rev. Morris Lewis is the present rector. The resident population in 1821 was 1,184, and in 1831 increased to 1,406, and rates at 9s. in the pound, were in 1803, £119 0s. 6d.—increased to £237 in 1831. The parish is situated within fifteen miles of Beaumaris, and contains 1,720 acres of land, in cultivation. The church, said to be built in 460 (and richly endowed) by Caswallon Llaw Hîr. It was a sanctuary, and dedicated to the most noted saint in Wales, Elian, surnamed Ganiad, or Bright. (Not to be confounded with Hilary, Bishop of Poictiers, although called in latin, Hilarius.)—

> " Yma y sant o lin brenhinoedd,
> " Ei vam—a thâd—ei dâd oedd. "

This Briton was one of the seven patron saints of Mona, commemorated in the englyn of the "Saith Cevnder", in p.212. This Elian was remarkable for his sanctity, employing his whole time in devotion, and acts of charity", and his miracles were so cried up by the Romish priests, that his shrine at St. Elian's in this county, is still resorted to, as well as St. Elian's[218] in Denbighshire. He was thought to perform surprising cures by the devotees, who after bathing in a well (sacred to him) deposited their offerings in what is called "Cyff Elian", which is in the church, and described in p.56 of Cathrall's, as being in the form of a trunk, studded with nails, and having an aperture at the top; to put in alms, &c. which amounted to so large a sum, that the parishioners purchased with it three tenements, for the aggrandizement of the benefice. Adjoining the church, by a passage from the chancel, is a small chapel. It appears to have been built as a cloister to St. Elian; it is called the "Myvr", or a place of meditation. In this "Myvr" there exists an old relic of superstition, which is an oaken box fixed to the wall. The church is built of grit stone; the corners, red free stone; "its inside adorned with paintings of the twelve

---

218 The writer of this Essay, even so late as last September, was in the habit of visiting a poor bedridden woman, who was suffering both in body and mind, under the delusion of being the victim of a revengeful neighbour, who had made her an offering of imprecation to the St. Elian's Well, by Abergeleu; but who speedily recovered her spirits and energies on her husband's return from what is termed "taking her name out of the well", at the expence of 2s. 6d. The wakes in honour of this popular saint, begin on the 13th of January. They used formerly to last three weeks. They are now continued the usual time, i.e. three days.

apostles, somewhat injured by time". "The neighbours have a tradition amongst them, that they were found in the wreck of a ship lost on this coast, and were originally intended for a church in Ireland. In the chancel is a half-length picture of St. Elian, in an attitude very expressive of devotion; and another of St. Paul shaking the viper off his hand.—*J. Lloyd*",[219] who further observes, "This parish is the most destitute of wood of any in the Island, scarcely a shrub growing in it. It is said that Caswallon Llaw Hîr had a llŷs (palace), near 'Maen y Driw'; it is now only the name of a house". In digging a grave in the church-yard, about thirty years ago, a deep trench was discovered, which extended about twenty yards, in a transverse direction. It was found to contain a great quantity of human bones, and is supposed to have been the place of interment of a number of sailors, who perished in a storm, that drove them on this coast.

LLANENGHEL, called Llanynghenedl, in the extent of Llivon, is a perpetual curacy, annexed to the rectory of Llanvachreth. The church, said to be built about 620, is dedicated to Enghenel, daughter to Brochwel Yscythroc, Prince of Powys (the day of celebration is Quinquagesima Sunday) is a lofty but small edifice, situated on a rock close to the old road leading from Llangevni to Holyhead. Several parts of the present structure, display marks of very great antiquity. The surrounding scenery, though not distinguished by any peculiarity of feature, is generally pleasing, and the adjacent country finely varied. The resident population in 1821 was 367,—increased to 411 in 1831, and the rates at 1s. 6d. in the pound amounted to £29 12s. 0d. in 1803, and to £164 10s. 0d. in 1831. This parish is situated within seven miles of Holyhead; and contains 1,700 acres of cultivated land.

LLANVAELOG is a chapel (not in charge) to the rectory of Llanbeulan. The resident population in 1821 was 538, and in 1831, 615; and the parish rates in 1803 were £87 2s. 1d. at 6s. 6d. in the pound,—increased to £167 11s. 0d. in 1831. This place is ten miles south-east of Holyhead, six from Llangevni, and situated on the bay of Caernarvon, in which abundance of soles, turbots, &c. are caught in summer. This coast is considered rocky and dangerous. The soil is generally good and in a state of cultivation. The church (supposed to have been built in 605 or thereabout) is dedicated to St. Maelog, son of Caw of Prydain. The day of celebration is kept on June 30th.

"At Neuadd Llanvaelog resided Gryffydd ab Iorwerth Gôch (descended from Hwva ab Cyndelw) and his wife, Gwenllian, granddaughter of Ririd Flaidd, to whose fostering care Edward I confided Edward of Caernarvon. 'Mamaeth Edward yr ail, oedd Wenllian, ac ar vroneu Sir Howel y Pedolau y macwyd ev. S. P. 495. Sic Per E. E. 40.' And on a farm called 'Tŷ Newydd' is a cromlech; the upper stone measures twelve feet long, quite bedded in the carnedd or heap of stones.—*J. Lloyd*".[220] A modern tourist describes it thus,—"Not far from the church, on an elevated spot of ground, is a large cromlech, consisting of five upright stones, supporting a large stone, nearly in an horizontal position, about twelve feet long, beneath which is a small cell or cavity."

219 Caerwys MS.
220 Caerwys MS.

LLANVAETHLU.—The church of Maethle, or nursing place, ranks as a township in the 26th of Edward III situated in the hundred of Talybolion, six miles from Holyhead and five from Bodedern. This parish is pleasantly situated on a tract of rising ground, containing 2,220 acres of arable land. It is supposed to have been known, at a very early period, to the Romans, who are thought to have had a smelting place here, for the ore of the Pary's mountain. This supposition is confirmed in some degree by the discovery of a cake of copper ore, weighing fifty-four pounds, about the year 1757, and by the quantity of charcoal and scoria of copper, which are frequently turned up by the plough. Fullers' earth of very superior quality abounds in this parish. The resident population in 1821 was 412, and in 1831, 433. The parish rates in 1803 amounted to £97 19s. 11d.—increased to £212 9s. 0d. in 1831. The living is a rectory, with the perpetual curacy of Llanvwrog annexed. The church is situated on a lofty eminence overlooking the Irish sea. It is a spacious structure of modern erection, and the interior, which is one of the neatest in the Island, is ornamented with a good east window, of three ogee-headed lights, embellished with modern stained glass. St. Maethlu,[221] to whom it is dedicated, was son to Caradoc Vraichvras; his mother was Tegeuvron. He lived in the sixth century, and was buried at "Carneddawr yn Mon".[222] Day of celebration is on the 26th of December. A handsome and commodious rectory-house has lately been built by the present rector, the Rev. William Lloyd. Near Plas-ucha, in this parish, there was another chapel dedicated to this saint. Near the church is a signal station, communicating with Holyhead on the west, and Llanelian on the east, and forming a link in the chain of posts between Holyhead and Liverpool. A charitable bequest of £38 was left to the poor, by an unknown benefactor; besides this, there are several smaller donations. Dr. Sion Davydd Rhys, a sketch of whose life is given at the end of this history, was born here.

Carreg Lwyd, belonging to a younger branch of the ancient family of Penrhyn, is in this parish, and still occupied by a descendant of the "potent Sir William Griffith, Chamberlain of North Wales". His son Edmund Griffith, Constable of Caernarvon Castle, had for his gavel (or portion) Tal-y-bont, whose son William was rector in 1544 of Llanvaethlu, and he purchased Carreg Lwyd for £700. Edmund his second son became rector of Rhosvair; and John, the eldest, resided at Carreg Lwyd, who was father to Dr. William Griffith, Chancellor of St. Asaph. This Dr. Griffith married Ann, daughter of John Owen, bishop of that see.[223] In the Salisbury Pedigree,[224] p.66, I find that Sir William Vychan Griffith, living in 1440, "a gavas dir ei dad oll, a thir Parys nevyd, drwy waith ei vam; ag yn 18 o Harri VI, y cavas ef ei wneuthyr yn ddinestydd, dan amod na priode un Gymraes; ynte a briodes merch Dalton, o Apthorpe. Mab o ordderch i William Vychan Griffith hwn, oedd Edmund Griffith, Cwnstable Caernarvon", &c. So late as 1632, I find in the annexed admirable letter written by the young Baronet of Lleweny (then in his non-age) to his uncle, of how much consequence it was for the heads of familes to marry a native. Sir J. Maynard in his letter writes as follows:—

221 "Cadvarch Sant yn Aberech yn Llŷn–Tangwn yn Llangoed y Môn–a Maethlu yn Carnnedawr y Môn."–*Gelli Lovdu MS.*

222 "Bonedd Saint."—*Caerwys MS.*

223 Mostyn MS.

224 John Salusbury of Erbistoc's celebrated Book of Pedigrees, which appears to have been commenced by Thomas Salusbury of Erbistoc, about the year 1640, and to have been carried on with many additions, by his son, John Salusbury, down to the year 1671. A folio two inches deep.

GOOD COUSIN,

       I am hartilye sorry to hear of my brother Salusbury's sudden departure, yett wee must submit to God's will and pleasure. I shuld be glad to see you here, att Berth Lwyd, that wee may confer together, of what is best ffor your good. My mother and myself can have no ends upon you; therefore you may safely trust us. I hope, now you know your own strength noe bodye as yett can doe you anie wrong. You often complained of your want of meanes: that is now removed, and your estates is in your own hands; and you that hav felt the misery of want and bondage, I hope you wil kepe your self free. As for Lettis Moor, I cannot deny but that she is a fayre lady, and well borne; and you have reason to value your selfe, for you hav fortune, person, birth and wit enough; only I would have you consider, whether you would not improve your education, which in my opinion you may doe in a short tyme, eyther in followinge the court (which yf you like, I dare undertake to have you sworn the kinge's or queene's servante), or els by travaeling in too France, which is the farthest way about. Ffor in a short time in court you will construe and understand man, as well as your own books, and I now question if you will study the world,—the court is the best librarye.

       I believe my brother Timothy before thys tyme has your wardship, for it is hys by the order of the court; and I dare answer for him, that you shall be well dealt with. That which now you must want, is good counsel, and I hope you will do nothing without the advice of your grandmother, which you have found your best frend, and is most desirous to speak with you.

       You must take hede of Sir Thomas Midelton, for fear of angring hym: it may cost your Kilfin farme. Cast not yourselfe awaye wilfully, for then you will both loose yourselfe and your frends. Beauties are rare in Wales, but if you kepe cumpany att court, your eyes will bee surffeted, as beauty for coyness ther is ridiculous. If Lettis Moor love you, I shall nott bee agaynst it, but if you bee too much undervalued, I will undertake to helpe you too a greater portion, and a baron or earl's daughter, who will fortifye you with many powerfull freindes, which shall be more worth to you than your fortune. Thus hoping to see you with all convenient spede,

I reste your lovinge uncle,

John Maynard.

"To his much esteemed kinsman, Sir Thomas Salusbury, Bart.
       At his house, Lleweni."

ANSWER TO THE FOREGOING LETTER.

HONOR'D UNKELL,

       I hav ever found great reason to be confident of your and my dear grandmother's good meaning towards me, and therefore mighte well incur the just censure of all men, should I not, with a glad eare, hearken after your advice. Your last letter advertised mee too wayes for the improvement of my education, travell, or the court. For the first, though it bee a way my nature is more inclined, and the rather being a thing you likewise approve of, yet a seeminge danger therein, might cause many to tax me with rashness, and folly, should I nowe leve my country, being the only hope of the direct line of my house, having no more hope full successor than Robert Salusburie, one whose dissolute life hath made a scorn to hys country and moreover am of an opinion, that it were more requisite for mee to acquainte myselfe with myne owne countrey, whether it hath pleased God to chouse for mee, than anye other; and there to be knowne to my frends and kindred, and to study rather the nature of those people amongst whom I am to live; and though I confess the court is an honourable calling, and is as you terme it, the beste library of men's nature, yet Sir, I am persuaded to come thence hether, I should finde myselfe in a new world. The disposition of our countrymen being somewhat different from all others. They are a crafty kind of people, and this much I have already found in their natures, that they beare an internal hate to such as make themselves strangers unto them. For Lettis Moore, you have given her due commendation, and for myself, though by your meanes I might perchance come to the choyce of many rare, and it may be some as pleasing beautys; yet I believe I shuld scarce find any soe fitt ffor mee in divers respects, her being from her childhood brought up in this country, and the long expectation of a match betweene us, hath bred in our tenants and frends, more love towards her than the muniments of a stranger could ever attaine. Our nature and disposition are known to each other, and besides the reciprocal love that is hetweene us, it was a thing desired so much by my ffather, that it is mentioned in his last will. Shee is noe stranger to my estate, and shee is well versed in the language, which is a greate meenes to conforme our hearts, and love our country and dependants. For her portion, the Lorde Moor hath promised the payment of £3,000. A part thereof by the beginning of Michaeimas terme. To confirme which promise, he hath left order with the Lorde of Mount Norris, to pass suretie thereof, upon conference with my unkell, Syr Thomas, whom I shall nott faile, if I may (with my utmost) please, according to your good advice.

As touchinge my wardship, I am much bound to my unkell Timothy, for his cares, for his prevention of trouble; that if some others tooke it, I mighte be put unto improving myself no wards. But thus much I am assured of, I pay no respite of homage, nor was there ever any of our ancestors found wards, or any liverons, sware unto, upon the death of any of them. I shall, God willing, with all possible speede, wait upon you, at Berth Lwyd. In the meane tyme wishing you mirth and health,

I rest, your assured loving Nephew to command,

Thomas Salusburye.

" Lluennie, August the 14th 1632."

LLANVAIR-YN-MATHAVARN-EITHAV is ranked as a township in the extent of Tindaethwy, taken at Beaumaris the 26th of Edward III, "containing eight domiciles, all free. In one of them was two oxgangs of land, which had formed part of the forfeited property of Cynric ab Madoc, and was then lying waste on the lords hands for want of tenants, which used to pay quarterly the sum of three shillings and a halfpenny (being one fourth of the rent of this domicile); besides paying at Easter and Michaelmas the yearly rent of fourteen-pence. All the heirs of eight domiciles owe suit and service at the county and hundred courts, paying relief of gobr and amobr of ten shillings, as it becomes due."

This parish is situated on the shore of the Irish sea. Black, grey, and variegated marble are found within its limits; the last of which is of very superior quality, and from the variety and brilliancy of its colours and the high degree of polish of which it is susceptible, is in great estimation, and is sent in considerable quantities to various parts of Great Britain. The living is a perpetual curacy. The church is dedicated to St. Mary, and is annexed to the rectory of Llanddyvnan, distant from Beaumaris eight miles and a half. The resident population in 1821 was 712, and 739 in 1831; and the rates in 1803 were £86 16s. 11d. at 5s. 6d. in the pound,—increased to £169 4s. 0d. in 1831. This parish contains 1,500 acres of cultivated land, and about 150 common. There is a cromlech at Marian-pantysaer (part of Rhôs Vawr) and formerly there used to be one at Llech-tal-y-Môn; but that is now destroyed. Mr. Cathrall, in p.59, describes a modern carnedd, in the British and Jewish customs, erected by Mr.

Wynn as a sepulchre for his family. In a small cottage in this parish, the celebrated bard Goronwy Owen was born on the first of January, 1722. A sketch of his life is given among the eminent men of Mona.

LLANVAIR-PWLL-GWYN-GYLL, situated in the hundred of Tindaethwy, is a rectory with the chapel of Llandisilio annexed, valued temp. Henry VIII at £6 15s. 0d. The present rector is the Rev. Richard Pritchard. The church, a small dark edifice, is in a greatly dilapidated condition, and dedicated to St. Mary. Day of celebration on the 2nd of February. It is built on a rocky part of the Menai, six miles from Beaumaris, and four from Bangor. Mr. Rowlands of Plâs Gwyn bequeathed £21, the interest of which, together with a small rent charge, is annually distributed among the poor of this parish, which contains 620 acres of cultivated land and ninety-five waste. The resident population in 1821 was 479, and in 1831, 497. Rates in 1803, at 10s. in the pound, were £60 11s. 10d,—increased to £126 5s. 0d. in 1831. Near the shore is the site of an old British fortification, called Craig y Ddinas, "where" (writes Mr. Pennant) "I was irresistibly delayed, by feasting my eyes with the fine view of the noble curvature of the Menai,—rode on towards the shore to admire the furious current of the Swelly, or 'Pwll Ceris', &c. a part where, by opposition rocks and narrow channels, are great waterfalls, causing whirlpools, &c. At low water, the channel for a considerable space appears pointed with rocks, black and horrible. The fury of the tides amongst them at times, is inconceivable, unless by the navigator. Rapid evolutions between rock and rock amidst the boiling waves and mill race currents. At high water all is still." This is a great obstacle to the navigation of large vessels, which must consult the critical season, aided by a good pilot. The rest of the strait is secure. Its whole length is fourteen miles; ten from Bay Glâs near Beaumaris to Caernarvon, and four from thence to its entrance at Abermenai.

On the commanding rock of Craig y Ddinas, a beautiful doric column, one hundred and thirty feet high (of Anglesey marble) designed by Mr. Harrison of Chester, was erected in 1815, by subscription, to commemorate the gallant services of the Marquess of Anglesey. The site is most happily chosen, being a large rock, nearly perpendicular, about one hundred feet above the great Irish road, and in full view of the noble hero's mansion. In a field near Tŷ Mawr, are the remains of a large cromlech, partly thrown down; the table stone of which now lies upon stones which formerly supported it.

LLANVAIR-YN-NEUBWLL is in the hundred of Menai, a chapel dedicated also to St. Mary, under the rectory of Rhôs Colyn (patron, the Bishop of Bangor), four miles distant from Holyhead, and contains about 900 acres of enclosed lands. The resident population was 310 in 1821, and 319 in 1831; and the rates in 1803, at 7s. in the pound, were £57 15s. 9d.—increased to £116 11s. 0d. in 1831. The church, a small irregular building, contains some excellent architectural details, which appear to have originally belonged to some ancient building, the remains of which have been probably incorporated with the present structure. It stands on the western brow of an eminence overlooking a small creek of the Irish sea. The surrounding country is richly diversified, and in some parts, highly picturesque; the views extending over the town and bay of Holyhead.

LLANVAIR-Y'NGHORNWY, i.e. "St. Mary in the Angle of the Waters", is in the hundred of Talybolion, a perpetual curacy annexed to the rectory of Llandeusant. The church, dedicated to St. Mary, is a spacious ancient structure, partly in the Norman style, with a lofty square tower, of rude architecture, at the west end. It consists of a nave and double chancel; the latter divided by a series of massive circular pillars and arches. The south chancel belongs exclusively to the proprietor of the Monachdŷ estate in this parish; and the north belonging to Caerau, is the sepulchral chapel of the family of Williams of Friars, and contains many monuments to the members of that and the Bulkeley family. Upon one of the pillars which separate the chancels, is a very ancient inscription in rude Saxon characters. The parsonage house is in this pariah, and has been lately rebuilt by the liberal incumbent, Mr. James Williams, in a style of gothic architecture, of peculiar good taste. It is distant from Amlwch, eight miles, and twelve from Holyhead. The resident population in 1821 was 324, and 310 in 1831. The rates in 1803, at 5s. in the pound, amounted to £47 17s. 10d.—in 1831, to £107 11s. 0d. This parish contains 2,044 acres of land. On a farm called Monachdy, there is the stratum of marble containing veins of the asbestos, described in my chapter on minerals. And on this turbulent coast, is situated the Isle of Skerries, i.e. "the Isle of Seals"—"Ynys y Moelrhoniad", with its "beneficial light-house". It once belonged to the see of Bangor, for we find that in 1498 a spirited Bishop Denys (or dean) contending, and successfully, a right to the fisheries, with the powerful Chamberlain of North Wales, Sir William Gryffydd, "who sente hys sonne and heire, with divers men in harnes, whiche ryetowsly in the seid countie of Anglesey, within the said bishopp's diocese, took the said fishes, from the said servants of the said bishop, who caused them to make restitution". Another diocesan, not so tenacious, nor so conscientious, alienated this Island, together with Monachdŷ (which had been part of the possessions of Conwy Abbey), to his son. This bishop was Dr. Nicolas Robinson, a native of Conwy, who was consecrated Bishop of Bangor, in 1566, and died in 1584. Further on there is some account given of this family. The last heir male of Monachdŷ, and Gwersyllt, in the county of Denbigh, leased this Island of Skerries to Mr. Morgan Jones of Cilwendeg; and in the year 1729–30, when a light-house was erecting there by Mr. Jones, he (Mr. William Robinson) with twelve other young gentlemen of fortune in North Wales, were drowned one stormy day, on their return from this dreary spot. It was an after-dinner frolic. The heir of Carreg Lwyd escaped the same fate, by hiding himself under a manger, to avoid accompanying the party. Mr. Robinson was not more than twenty-three when he perished in this unfortunate manner, leaving his immense estates, much involved, which were afterwards sold, by act of parliament, in 1737, "for the benefit of his creditors". Mr. Lytton Bulwer,[225] of Knebworth, Herts (originally from Lytton, in Derbyshire), a well-known name in English literature,—Mr. Humberston of Chester, and his brother, Mr. Floyer, are representatives of the Robinson family, in the female line. To the latter gentleman, the heirs of the lessee, Mr. Jones, continue to pay a yearly acknowledgment for Skerries. In 1804, the light was changed, from the uncertain flame of coal to beautiful oil lamps, with

225 Two sons of this ancient and distinguished house are at this time members of the British senate;—one for Coventry, and the other for Lincoln.

silver reflectors. "Although of the utmost service to navigation", observes Mr. James Williams, the intelligent Rector of Llanddausant, "there are still frequent wrecks on the coast. The emolument arising from the tonnage duty is variously estimated from £8,000 to £15,000 per annum:—every British vessel paying one penny per ton, and every foreign one, two-pence. The light from this beacon may be seen eight or ten leagues distant. Prior to its erection, scarce a winter passed here without shipwreck." This benevolent gentleman, aided by his lady, ever alert in the cause of humanity, are generally among the first on the shore, in case of accident, well supplied with restoratives, and other necessaries, to comfort and protect the suffering mariners.

About a mile from the church of Llanvair-y'nghornwy, is one of the ancient monuments, called "Meini Hirion". It is a large equilateral triangle, formed of three huge stones, placed upright, at a distance of 500 yards from each other. Two circular encampments, with a fosse and vallum, denominated "Castell Crwn", are in the vicinity of this monument; besides places called Pen-yr-orsedd, Castell Brynllawenydd, Bod-hedd, Caerau rhyd-y-bodiau, &c., indicative of this place having been the scene of great events.

LLANVAIR-YN-Y-CWMMWD is situated in the hundred and on the banks of the Menai, four miles north-east of Caernarvon, annexed to the vicarage of Llanidan, dedicated to St. Mary; has about seventy inhabitants. This small parish contains 150 acres of cultivated land. The church has been for years in a state of such dilapidation as to preclude the performance of divine service, but is at present being rebuilt.

LLANVECHELL is in the hundred of Talybolion, and in the extent taken of that comot, at Co-edane, the 26th of Edward III ranks as a township, belonging to the heirs of Iddon ab Caradoc and Mredydd ab Iorwerth Vôn, "held under St. Mechell", "they pay no annual rent for it to the prince, nor suit at the county and hundred courts, unless they chuse to come there, when they shall have a complaint against any one, or any one against them; and if they should be amerced there, the Lord Prince shall have their amercement, &c. and they must attend the two great tourns", &c. This living is a discharged rectory, valued in the king's books at £11 11s. 3d. The church, supposed to be built in 630, is dedicated to Mechell, verch Brychan, and the wife of Gynyr Varvdrwch, i.e. thick bearded. Her wakes celebrated on November 15. The rector is the Rev. John Lewis. The church was rebuilt about 1533, and is a spacious and venerable structure, in the English style of architecture, with a tower, surmounted by a low spire. It consists of a nave, chancel, and south transept, and is ornamented with an east window, done in good taste, embellished with ancient stained glass of brilliant colour, and contains several excellent monuments. To the west of the church, and about a mile distant from it, are three upright stones, ten feet in height, disposed in form of a triangle, twelve feet distant from each other, the remains of a cromlech, which must from the elevation of the stones, have been one of the loftiest monuments of that kind in the Island.—The table stone has disappeared. The farm on which the upright stones are found, still retains the name of "Cromlech". This parish distant from Amlwch six miles, and from Beaumaris twenty-six miles, consists of two townships, Caer Degog, and Llawr y Llan. It is three miles in length, and two in breadth. The population in 1821 was 1,035, and in 1831, 976. The poor rates in 1803 were £197 3s. 0d. at 8s. in the pound,—increased to £433 13s. 0d. in 1831. Fairs are annually held on February 23, August 3, September 21, and November 5 and 26. A parochial school was founded in 1723 by Mr. Richard Wynne, who endowed it with a farm called Nantglyn, in the parish of Amlwch (lets for about £23) for the gratuitous instruction of children of this and the adjoining parish of Llanbadrig. There were in 1831, only four boys in the school. Mr. Owen Williams, in 1657, bequeathed £2 14s. 0d. per annum, payable out of the tithes of Llanbadrig parish; and William Davies in 1752, bequeathed £60, to be distributed in bread and coarse woollen cloth to the poor. David Lloyd, in 1689, gave a cottage and garden in this parish, for the support of an aged and indigent man. John Bulkeley, in 1734, bequeathed a portion of land to the poor, and Catherine Bulkeley, in 1764, bequeathed £100 for the relief of poor distressed widows. There are also some other smaller bequests to the poor. Besides a mineral spring, near Cevn Côch and the fallen cromlech, there is in this parish, a quarry of curious and beautiful green marble, called the verd antique, intersected with asbestos. Some few years ago, £1,000 was given for the lease of a small quarry, by Mr. Bullock of London, who brought the Mona marble into celebrity. Cathrall, in p.62, describes this parish more minutely. French chalk is found here in profusion.

LLANFFINAN is in the hundred of Menai, a perpetual curacy annexed to that of Llanvihangel-ysceiviog. The church, a small neat edifice, said to be built about 620, is dedicated to Finan, a disciple of Eidan, Bishop of Llandisvern, who succeeded him in that bishopric. Rowlands in p.153, says that he, Finan, might have built this church, to follow the good works of his pious master, who erected that of Llandisvern. The day of celebration is kept on September 14. This parish is within seven miles of Beaumaris, and contains a population of 163 inhabitants. The rates in 1803 were £16 16s. 7d. at 2s. 6d. in the pound; and in 1831, £71 9s. 0d. Hirdevraig, a mansion belonging to a branch of the House of Gwydir, is now become the property of Mr. Lloyd Edwards of Nanhoron; whose mother was the heiress of the late Mr. Lloyd of Vronhaelog. Mallt, the wife of Siôn ab Ievan of Hîrdevraig, was commemorated for her bounties in this englyn,—

> " Gorau bara—garwa gwellt,
> " Gorau gîg, (medd meddig), mollt,
> " Gorau helva—garw gwyllt,
> " Gorau i mi—gwrw Mallt."

Six poor children of this parish are taught gratuitously in the parochial school of Llanvighangel-ysceiviog, under an endowment of Dr. John Jones, Dean of Bangor, who was for some years curate of this parish.

LLANVLEWYN, situated in the hundred of Talybolion, and within fourteen miles of Holyhead, is a chapel of ease to the church of Llanrhyddlad, dedicated to St. Vlewyn. Wakes kept November 12. This saint, with his brother Gredivel, first presided in the college founded about 480, by Pawl, on the river Tav, in Caermarthenshire, afterwards called "Tŷ Gwyn", or Whitland Abbey. This church of Llanvlewyn, is supposed to have been built so early as 630. The parish contains about 1,200 acres of land:— 400 of this is uncultivated. The church, a small plain edifice, is beautifully situated near a little lake, and surrounded with scenery of pleasing and rural appearance. A small parochial school, in which the poor children are taught, is supported by subscription. The resident population in 1821 was 122, and in 1831, 133. The rates in 1803 were £34 12s. 8d. at 5s. in the pound,—increased to £44 11s. 0d. in 1831. "Let me record" (says Mr. Pennant in 1776) "that a few years ago, were found on a farm called "Ynys y Gwyddel", in the parish of Llanvlewyn, four miles east of Carreg Lwyd, "three golden bracelets, and a golden bulla, in high preservation. Two of the former, I purchased and preserved as curious memorials of the residence of the Romans in ancient Mona". The bulla, or amulet, called "Ithyphallus", was in form of a heart, with a figure on it. These bullae were suspended from the necks of children, and originally designed to preserve them from "the effects of envy, and afterwards from all kinds of evil".[226]

LLANVIHANGEL-TRE'R-BEIRDD is in the hundred of Twrcelyn, four miles from Llannerchymedd, and a perpetual curacy, annexed to the rectory of Llanddvrydog. The church, a small plain edifice (containing some good monuments to the family of Lewis) is dedicated to St. Michael, whose day is celebrated on the 29th of September. William Jones, father of Sir William Jones, was a native of this parish, and Lewis Morris resided here some years. The resident population in 1821 was 296, and in 1831, 360; and the rates at 9s. in the pound amounted to £71 10s. 10d. in 1803, and in 1831, to £155 13s. 0d. There are several druidical monuments in this parish still remaining, confirmatory of its name, implying it to have been a distinguished station of the druids and bards. Near the church is a large pillar, called "Maen Addwyn", standing erect, and supposed to be one of those Meini Gwŷr, mentioned by Rowlands, and the cromlech on Bodavon mountain, which Davydd Thomas describes as three in number. The table stone of this "Maen Llwyd" measures ten feet in length and eight in breadth. Not far distant, at Banas, is a smaller one in ruins; and between these was another, now demolished, called "Carreg y Vran", which (when complete) was a double one, and must have been very similar to the one at Plasnewydd, described by Mr. Lloyd as being "the most magnificent which he had seen in the Island". In Sir John Wynne's Memoirs of the House of Gwydir, are several curious historical incidents. One relating to Caernarvon Castle, I will insert here.—"When that castle was besieged in 1404, by Owen Glyndwr, it was gallantly defended by Ievan ab Mredydd, and Hwlcyn Llwyd. Ievan died during the siege, and his body was smuggled out of the castle, and buried in the parish of Llanvihangel-tre'r-beirdd, in Môn, about twelve or fourteen miles distant."

LLANVIHANGEL-TY'N-SYLWY, a parish in the hundred of Tindaethwy, is five miles from Beaumaris. The living is annexed with that of Llangoed to the rectory of Llaniestyn, endowed together with £300 Queen Ann's bounty, and £900 parliamentary grant. The church, dedicated to St. Michael, is a small ancient edifice, in a dilapidated state. The pulpit, which is of very great antiquity, is rudely but curiously carved. The resident population in 1821 was 78, and in 1831, 62; and the parish rates, at 1s. in the pound, were in 1803, £4 8s. 2d.—increased to £14 16s. 0d. in 1831. There are some very extensive quarries of limestone and marble, which are worked upon a large scale, affording employment to

226 Roman History.

a considerable portion of the poorer inhabitants. The church, dedicated to St. Michael, which stands beneath a high precipitous hill, near Llanddona, takes its name probably from the remains of an old British fortification, called "Bwrdd Arthur", anciently denominated "Dinas Sulwy". This great British post is surrounded by a double row of rude stones, with their sharp points uppermost; and in some parts, the ramparts are formed of small stones. In the area are vestiges of oval buildings. The largest is formed with two rows of flat stones, set on end. These evidently had been the habitations of the early possessors. It was a place of great strength, for besides this artificial defence, the hill slopes steeply on all sides, and the brink next the rampart, is almost perpendicular. The prospect from hence is savagely grand, owing to an inter-mixture of sea, rocks, and mountains. This post, from the extensive view which it commands over the surrounding country, being admirably adapted for an exploratory station, was, after their conquest of the Island, occupied by the Romans. Numerous fibulae, coins and other Roman relies, have been frequently discovered here; and in the summer of 1831, a great number of silver and copper coins were found in this place, among which were some of Nero, Vespasian, Constantius, and Constantine, together with rings, keys, buckles, and clasps of copper, and other relies of Roman antiquity.

LLANVIHANGEL-YN-NHYWYN, sometimes called Llanvihangel-yn-y-traeth, situated in the hundred of Menai (not in charge), is attached to the rectory of Rhôs Colyn. The church is dedicated to St. Michael, whose feast is celebrated here on the 10th of October, at which time the farmers hire their servants. The resident population in 1821 was 205, and 153 in 1831; the rates in 1803, at 3s. 6d. in the pound, were £21 13s. 4d.—increased to £71 13s. 0d. in 1831. This parish is within eight miles south-east of Holyhead, and contains 900 acres of land. On the common are vestiges of such primaeval habitations as those noticed by Rowlands in his Mona Antiqua; and near Towyn-trewyn is a cromlech. The church is an ancient and venerable structure, built upon a lofty eminence, and forming a conspicuous and interesting object for many miles round. A national school was erected in 1826, and is supported by subscription. There are about ninety poor children belonging to this and the neighbouring parishes, educated gratuitously in it. This parish contains a considerable portion of fertile land, besides a large tract of common land, near the sea, bounded on the south by Cymmyran bay, and on the west by the narrow strait which separates it from Holyhead.

LLANVIHANGEL-YSCEIVIOG, a small village, is also in the hundred of Menai, eight miles from Bangor, and within nine of Beaumaris, containing a post-office dependant on that of Bangor. The soil is various in different parts. "Mountain coal", of a very soft quality, is found in this parish. The colliery is upon a limited scale, affording employment to about thirty men. The living is a perpetual curacy with Llanffinan annexed, endowed with £10 per annum, private benefaction, £800 Queen Anne's bounty, and £400 parliamentary grant, in the patronage of the Dean of Bangor, to whom the great tithes belong. In 1809, this cure was valued at £56 yearly. The church, dedicated to St. Michael, is a spacious and ancient structure, consisting of a nave, south aisle and chancel; and having on the north side a small building, called "Capel Berw". The east side is embellished with some portions of ancient stained glass, of brilliant colours. The Rev. Dr. John Jones, Dean of Bangor, in 1719, bequeathed £100 in trust, towards educating twelve poor children. A parochial school was built in 1828, by subscription, and is supported by the same means, aided by the interest of the above £100. About seventy children, including six from Llanffinan, are educated gratuitously. There are several small charitable donations and bequests left to the poor. The resident population in 1831 was 660.

LLANVUGAIL, i.e. the Shepherd's Parish, is situated in the hundred of Talybolion, and in an extent made of that comot, at Coedane, the 26th of Edward III is then ranked as a "township containing two domiciles, belonging to the heirs of Gryffydd ab Davydd, and Madoc Ddû ab Davydd, paying for each 6s. 6d. at the two terms of Easter and Michaelmas, owing suit and service, &c. at the county and hundred courts." "They are to make part of the manor-house of Cemmaes, and to pay *cylch stalon*", &c. In this township "there is also two ploughland of escheat, besides the sixth share of a mill, at Llanvugel, which belonged to Llewelyn ab Meredydd, now lying on the lord's hands, as waste, for want of tenants", &c. This chapel is now in ruins. It stands a mile and a half from the mother church of Llanvachreth, and within nine miles of Holyhead. The parish contains four hundred and fifty acres, and the population was 141 in 1821, and 146 in 1831. The rates at 2s. in the pound amounted to £15 4s. 3d. in 1803, and to £63 1s. 0d. in 1831. This small but fertile parish is situated on the banks of the "Avon Alaw".

LLANVACHRETH, a parish in the hundred of Talybolion, distant from Holyhead about seven miles, and three from Bodedyrn, containing in 1821, 246 inhabitants,—increased to 424 in 1831. This parish is situated in a fertile district, near the eastern shore of Holyhead bay, and is bounded on the south by the little river Alaw. It contains a considerable portion of enclosed and well-cultivated land, and formerly derived advantage from its proximity to the old Holyhead road, which, since the construction of the new line of road, has been materially lessened. The living is a discharged rectory, with the perpetual curacy of Llanenghenedl and Llanfigael, valued in the king's books at £14 2s. 1d. and in the patronage of the bishop. The Rev. John Jones is the incumbent. The church, dedicated to St. Machraeth, is an ancient structure, in the early style of English architecture, of which it exhibits some good details, and is ornamented with a handsome east window, of excellent design. Numerous charitable bequests have been made to the poor of this parish, but many, and the most important, have long been lost. The annual average expenditure for the support of the poor, is £110.

LLANVWROG is also in the hundred of Talybolion, a chapel under the rectory of Llanvaethlu, within five miles of Holyhead. This parish contains 1,600 acres of land, almost entirely under a state of cultivation. The resident population in 1821 was 296, and in 1831, 266. The parish rates in 1803, at 3s. in the pound, amounted to £83 13s. 0d.—increased to £191 7s. 0d. in 1831. The produce of some small charitable bequests and donations is distributed annually among the poor of the parish. The church dedicated to St. Mwrog, is a small ancient edifice, in a very dilapidated condition, containing some curious remains of old oak carving. Over the north entrance is a mutilated inscription, of which only a few of the letters rudely formed, are remaining. There is a curious legend belonging to the Romish Church, and here is a tradition that there was formerly a chapel, at a place called "Monwent Mwrog", on the farm of "Cefn Glas", about a mile from the church, but scarcely any vestige remains. In the list alluded to in vol.2, Cambro Register, p.286, it is entitled "Capel Nett".

LLANGAFFO is in the hundred of Menai, and a chapel (not in charge) to the rectory of Llangeinwen, under the patronage of the Earl of Pembroke. It is situated fourteen miles from Beaumaris, and five from Caernarvon. The resident population in 1821 was 154, and 137 in 1831. Rates, at 5s. in the pound, amounted to £53 5s. 0d. This parish contains 875 acres of land, in cultivation, besides 350 in pasture, not enclosed. The church is dedicated to Caffo, son of "Caw of Brydain, the Lord of Cwm Cawlyd". There is a well in this parish, called "Ffynon Gaffo", at which were young cocks offered, to prevent the crying of children, and were well accepted by the priests.

The 14th vol, of Caerwys MSS contains a copy taken from a llêch, by Lewis Morrris, and found by him upon the farm of Vrondêg, in this parish, which I take leave to transcribe verbatim, together with his clever comment upon the British alphabet. "The following inscription I copied in the year 1728, at a place called Frondeg, in the parish of Llangaffo. It was probably a trophy of victory, and seems by the letters to be very ancient.

VT	VГI
SNIJ<	WIH
FILINS	NH SU
CUURIS	UUURьB
GNI	IC HV I
EBE	ERC
XIT	INVICY
HUNC	HUNCь
LAPI	CVXPH
DEM	IOEUIY

The s, the e and t, being here used, and the two u's for the sound o o in the name GWRISCIN, the w being not then come to use. The alphabet of this stone ACSEFOHILIN PRSTVUU UX. It may be read perhaps TVISNIUS FILIUS GWRISCINI EREXIT HUNC LAPIDEM.—This seems to be a British inscription, soon after the Roman conquest, when the ancient British letters were not totally laid aside.—*L. Morris.*"

Several small charitable donations, have been made at various times, of which the greater part have been lost. The interest of the remainder is distributed annually among the poor. Two gold coins of Constantine's, in good preservation, were found near the church in the year 1829, and several copper and silver coins of that emperor and others, have been found in the parish.

LLANGEVNI is situated in the hundred of Twrcelyn, according to the extent (so often quoted) taken of this comot, at Bettws Geraint, the 26th of Edward III. But Mr. Cathrall places it in Menai hundred, which is correct. This parish contains 1,883 acres of cultivated land, besides the common of Rhôs y Meirch, lately enclosed, which is about 260 acres. This town is beautifully situated in a rich and fertile vale, distant from Holyhead fifteen miles, and from Beaumaris thirteen. It rose to its present comfortable and flourishing state, under the fostering care of the late Lord Bulkeley, when the new line of road was made to pass through Llangevni. The town is well built and of prepossessing appearance, consisting of several regular and wellformed streets, with a neat markethouse. On the river Cevni is a small factory for carding and spinning wool, bleaching, and weaving woollen cloth, which is manufactured here on a limited scale. The market is on Thursday. Fairs are annually held on March 14, April 17, June 10, August 17, September 15, and October 23. A post-office under that of Bangor, has been established in the town. Resident population in 1821 was 1,737, and in 1831, 1,753; and the parish rates at 6s. in the pound amounted to £109 15s. 0d. in 1803, and to £462 2s. 0d. in 1831. The living is a discharged rectory, and with the chapel of Tregaian annexed, valued temp. Henry VIIIth at £9 13s. 4d. The Bishop of Bangor is patron, and the Rev. Evan Williams is the rector. Here was an old church, supposed to have been built so early as 620 by Cyngar, to whom it was dedicated. This saint was the son of Arthog, and the grandson of Cynedda Wledig.—He lies buried in the church. The present edifice is a modern building, erected about the year 1825, partly by the parish rates, but principally by subscription, aided by a grant from government of £250, to which that most munificent friend of the church, the late Lord Bulkeley, added a handsome tower and a ring of bells. The rectory house is modern, and built by the present rector, about the year 1820, and in its situation and arrangement, does infinite credit to his judgement and liberality. Both its comforts, and beauty, have been greatly enhanced by a fine plantation, made also by Lord Bulkeley, with that view alone. By the late act, Llangevni is now one of the contributory boroughs. In taking down the old church, in 1824, a large stone was discovered with a curious inscription in Roman characters. The following part only is legible, "CVLIDON JACIT SECUND". It is now placed upright in the churchyard, upon the spot where it was found. In 1829, in removing a small fence at Glanhwva, near the town, forty human skeletons were found, and from the position in which they lay, appeared to have been hastily interred; and in the adjoining field, great number of human bones are scattered in every direction. These are supposed to be the remains of the men who fell at the siege of Ynys Gevni.

About a mile from Llangevni, are considerable remains of a paved road, which may be traced for a distance of two miles, in some parts in a very perfect state, being paved in many places with large masses of jasper, which is found in a quarry at no great distance, intermixed with the grit stone. It is thought by some antiquaries to be part of a Roman road, which anciently led from the Moel y Don ferry, across the Menai, to the station at Holyhead. Not far from the road is a valuable spring of water, impregnated with oxide of iron, which is strongly recommended by medical men, for its efficacy in rheumatic and other complaints. But what most distinguishes this parish, as Mr. Cathrall justly remarks in p.161, is Tre-garnedd,[227] one of the five palaces (enumerated in the Sebright Collection) " that fell hereditarily to the lot of Risiart ab Rowel ab Ievan[228] of Mostyn, whiche had belonged to Morvydd,

---

227 This ancient residence of Tregarnedd, was sold in 1750, by the late Sir Roger Mostyn, to the present Mr. Williams of Craig y Don's great-grandfather, Owen Williams, Esq. of Treffos.

228 Howel ab Ievan married Margaret, the sole heiress of Gloddaeth. In p.332, 1st vol. Cambrian Quarterly, may be seen an elegy written upon the death of Margaret's brothers and sisters, consisting of seven, who all died of the plague, in 1348.

the wiffe of Madoc Gloddaeth, who was the daughter of Sir Gryffyth Llwyd,[229] an honourable gentleman, whoe was knighted by King Edward I on bringing hym the newes of the birth of his son, Edward of Caernarvon". But however in 1322, he was disgusted with this king's oppressive conduct, for he had adhered to the English, "till he found their yoke intolerable, and rose in arms, overran North and South Wales, and seized the castle of Mold, in that year", &c.[230] I find by the Sebright Papers, that he fortified his house[231] at Tregarnedd,[232] with a very strong fosse and rampart, and made another stronghold in the morass of Malltraeth, called "Ynys Cevenni", which he insulated with water from the river Cevni. Both are still remaining. The fosse is four yards deep, eight wide, and nearly perfect. Sir Gruffydd Llwyd[233] was soon overpowered, and together with "the keepers of Mold and Chirke Castells was carried from Shrewsburie to London".[234] Mr. Pennant conjectures that he doubtlessly underwent the common fate of our gallant countrymen; but from a deed extant in vol.4, Sebright Papers, we have room to think and to hope that a recollection of former acts of kindness, might have induced Edward to forgive this patriotic chieftain, whose grandson Gruffydd residing at Gloddaeth, lost seven out of eight children, by the great plague of 1348, which also proved so fatal to the Laura of Petrarch in 1346. I shall take leave to insert here, my translation of a pathetic elegy, written on that lamentable occasion, by Robin Ddû, the black bard of Englefield.

> There was weeping and lamentation heard in Creuddyn,
>> A great tree has lost its branches,
>> And that tree is Gruffydd ab Rhys,
> Who has plenty of venison and metheglyn in his white palas.[235]
> Alas ! that the scion of his house should have fallen, and not fallen alone:
>> Except one poor little branch all are gone;
> God grant that this branch may bear good fruit, and ever flourish in pure verdure;
> The whole country feared that the last bud of Gloddaeth was sinking beneath its sod.
>> There was weeping and lamentation heard in Creuddyn,
>> Alas ! that Creuddyn should be the scene of such misery.
> The valley groaned when the sod covered so many lovely descendants of Sir Gruffydd Llwyd;
> Creuddyn, the once happy Creuddyn, is lonely and deserted;
> Gruffydd is become as the naked body of a tall tree robbed of its branches,
> Gruffydd is melancholy, and walks alone by the side of his mountain,
> And he seems like the tall spear of Gronw ab Tegerin despoiled of its head;
> Even the men of Oswallt[236] shed many a tear when they heard of thy misfortune.

229 Welsh Chronicles, p.383.

230 Caerwys MSS.

231 The present mansion-house is situated 300 yards to the north-east of the old fortified house.

232 In the extent of the comot of Menai, taken at Rhosvair, 26th of Edward III, Tregarnedd is said to be in that comot, and was a domicile township, consisting of three domiciles; one called the Domicile of Moel was in the lord's hands, through default of heirs, yielding by quarterly payment an annual rent of 21s. 8d. Another domicile was held by the heirs of Hywel Moel, and Davydd Dew. The third was held by the heirs of Llowarch ab Llowarch, and Iorwerth ab Llowarch; all owing suit and service at the mill of Rhosvair, doing the work of the Lord Prince at the manor-house of Rhosvair, paying for relief 10s. &c.

233 In the 1st vol. Myvyrian Archiology, p.409, is an ode written by Gwylym Ddû of Arvon, "I Sir Gryffydd Llwyd, pan oedd ev y'ngharchar y'nghastell Rhyddlan."

234 Welsh Chronicles, p.383.

235 The Cambro-British word *palas, plas*, is the original of *palace*.

236 Oswestry, between whose inhabitants and Gruffydd there had been a feud.

Thou root of an honourable branch,
Much as thou lamentest, there is one who feels thy sorrow doubly,
It is Jenet, thy companion, thy friend, the chosen among women,
Who was proud to be called the mother of men;
That would hunt the wild deer on the rocky mountains of their father,
And seek the timid doe 'mid the gloomy glens of Gloddaeth;
The bosom that nourished them is now beat by the agonizing hand,
And she who was so meek before dares murmur at the will of her God.
And the voice utters, "why are my lovely ones gone,
I had seven who called me mother,
And proud was I of the name; but no one speaks it now;
I will teach it my babe, who shall be to me as the seven which I have lost.
There was Davydd, the promising heir of Gloddaeth,
Full was the feast that celebrated his birth,
A light beams,—he saw heaven, and wished to be there;
And the same night Gwilym followed him;
Rhys, thou dear one ! tarry awhile with thy mother,
Or leave Llewelyn to soothe thy father for the loss of his sons;
Ievan, thou day-beam of hope to Gloddaeth,
Sad was the night that saw thee expire, thou fifth and last heir;
Oh ! hide Catrin, white as the winter snow and brilliant as the autumn moon,
Although the eldest, few were the months she saw.
Annes, thou fair one, and could not thy beauty save thee from being
a seventh in this mournful procession."
One mother bore them, one father owned them,
One week saw them laid in one grave,
One heaven contains them;
One tree produced these seven flowers, which are now seven blossoms blooming in Paradise.

Robin Ddû

LLANGEINWEN is in the hundred of Menai, a rectory formerly in the gift of the Earl of Pembroke, with the chapel of Llangaffo annexed, valued in the king's books at £19 1s. 2d. The rector is the Rev. William Wynne Williams, the present patron. The resident population in 1821 was 688, and 776 in 1831. The parish rates in 1803 were £202 18s. 8d. at 8s. in the pound,—increased to £280 5s. 0d. in 1831. The church, supposed to have been built about the year 590 (rebuilt in 1812) is dedicated to Ceinwen (Blanch Fair) and her day of celebration is kept on the second Sunday after Michaelmas. This parish is situated on the strait of the Menai, within one mile of Rhosvair, and opposite Caernarvon. Here is the ferry of Tal y Voel, which is a mile and half across, and has been celebrated in a poem by Gwalchmai, the son of Meilir, who wrote on the battle of Tal y Voel, as related in p. 14. Maes y Porth bestowed on the gateway of Conwy Abbey, by Llewelyn the Great, is also in this parish, and became at the dissolution of this religions house, the property of Lewis ab Even Llwyd, descended from Cilmin y Troed Dû. Margaret, the daughter and sole heir of Davydd Llwyd of Maes y Porth, married Rhys Hughes, whose son Davydd took the surname of Llwyd, which the family have continued to bear ever since. This parish abounds with limestone of excellent quality, of which extensive quarries are worked at Guirt, Gelleiniog Wen, Rhydgar and Penrhyn Bâch, affording employment to a considerable number of men. At Guirt are the remains of a chapel, for many years used as a stable, and now converted into a dairy. Over the east window are still preserved allegorical figures of Time and Death. Near the boundary of this parish, is a rude upright stone, with the inscription "FILIVS VLRICI, EREXIT HVNG LAPIDEM", supposed to be a monumental stone, erected to the memory of some chieftain, buried beneath it. In the quarries at Gelleiniog Wen, great numbers of human bones are frequently found; and on a farm within this parish, there was, a few years ago, a pillar of stone, which was probably one of those denominated by Mr. Rowlands, "Meini Gwyr". This one, when upright, measured twelve feet, and was sacreligiously broken up, when the present farm house was built, to make lintels, steps, &c. for it. The name is still continued, by calling the farm "Y Maen Hîr".

LLANGRISTIOLUS is in the hundred of Malltraeth, a perpetual curacy, in the Bishop of Bangor's gift. The church is said to have been built about 610, and dedicated to St. Cristiolus. Day of celebration is November 3. He was the son of Howel Vân ab Howel ab Emyr of Llydaw (Armorica). The yearly value of this perpetual curacy, from small tithes, easter-dues, with Dr. William Lewis's[237] stipend of £25, amounts in all to about £80 annually, to which, as well as to all his own curates, the present Bishop of Bangor, Dr. Bethell has made a most liberal addition of £40. The resident population in 1831 was 836, and in 1831, 873. The rates in 1803, at 9s. 6d. in the pound, were £236 4s. 2d.—increased to £472 2s. 0d. in 1821. A parochial school, in which a few boys are taught gratuitously, is supported by subscription, added to a small endowment. The Rev. Hugh Jones bequeathed £100; the Rev. Dr. Lewis, £50; John Griffith Lewis, £10; Owen Davydd ab Owen, £10, and various other benefactors, smaller sums of money; the interest of which amounting to £17 10s. 0d. is annually distributed among the poor of the parish, at Christmas. The church is a spacious structure, exhibiting some excellent architectural details, and decorated with an east window, of good design, enriched with tracery. It is situated within one mile of Llangevni. The parish contains 1,500 acres of enclosed land, and from fifty to sixty acres of common. Here was born Dr. Henry Maurice, one of the eminent men of Mona. At Henblas, in this parish, resided Dr. Robert Morgan, when he was ejected out of all his preferments, during the rebellion, in which he was a great sufferer. The name of this place describes its antiquity, and it happens to have been the seat of learned and good men. Davydd Llwyd lineally descended from Roderic the Great (who was King of Wales and Man in 873), married in the sixteenth century, Catherine Owen of Penmynydd (of which house Owen Tudor, great-grandfather of King Henry VII was a younger son) and by her he had nine children. He died in 1619, and was succeeded at Henblas, by his son William, Rector of Llanelian, whose daughter and heiress married Dr. Robert Morgan, Bishop of Bangor, by whom she had nine children, one of them William, Chancellor of Bangor, married Dulcibella, daughter of Henry Jones, Esq. of Plâs Llangoed, near Beaumaris, from whom descended the present possessor of Hênblas, Charles Henry Evans, Sheriff for Mona, in 1833. The Evans's of Kingsland,—Eyton, in Herefordshire, and the Rev. Henry Rowlands of Plâs Gwyn, in the maternal line. Another daughter of the Bishop of Bangor, married Edward Wynne, A. M. of Bodewryd, lineal ancestor of the present

237 Chaplain to Bishop Meyrick in 1561.

Sir J. T. Stanley of Penrhos. Another daughter, Ann, married Thomas Lloyd of Cevn Meriadog, county of Denbigh, Esq. and a fourth daughter married Dr. Humphreys, Bishop of Hereford, who died in 1712. Davydd Llwyd is said to have been a bard, and patron of bards, understanding well six different languages, besides the ancient British. From such a stock, descended in the person of his grandson, a man of universal learning and piety, Bishop William Lloyd, whose life is given among the eminent men of Mona. Bishop Robert Morgan, who married the heiress of Henblas, was descended from Gwathvoed, Lord of Cardigan, and bore for his arms, or, a lion rampant, regardant, with those of his wife, in an escutcheon of pretence, argent, three choughs, sable with ermine spots in the beak, chevron sable. I will transcribe the account of him, written by that learned genealogist, Bishop Humphreys, who married one of his daughters, in a note to Wood's Athanae Oxonienses, which is as follows:—

"He was born 1608, at Bronfraith, in the parish of Llandyssil, in Montgomeryshire, and was the third son of Richard Morgan of Bronfraith (who sometimes served in parliament for the borough of Montgomery) and of Margaret, daughter of Thomas Lloyd of Gwernbuarth, gent., his wife. He was bred at school, near that place, under one Mr. Lloyd, father of Simon Lloyd, Archdeacon of Merionith, and Edward Lloyd, mercer, at the Bear Inn, in Oxon. He was first admitted of Jesus College, in Cambridge, and continued there till after he was A.M. and upon Bishop Dolben's advancement to the bishoprick of Bangor, he became his chaplain, and was by him promoted first to the vicarage of Llanwnoe, in Montgomeryshire, September 16, 1632; then to the rectory of Llangynhaval, in Dyffryn Clwyd. Upon Bishop Dolben's death, he returned to Cambridge, and settled at St. John's College, with his great friend Dr. Beale; there he commenced B.D. Upon Bishop Robert's advancement, he returned again to Wales, as his chaplain, and was by him made vicar of Llanvair, Dyffryn Clwyd. He resigned Llangynhaval, and was instituted to Trevdraeth, in Anglesey, July 16, 1641, being then B.D. Then he resigned Llanvair, and was instituted of Llandyffnan, November 19, 1642. This Llandyffnan was then worth but 38 lib. per annum. The tithes being leased before the statute of limitation, for ninety-nine years, to the Bulkeleys of Baron Hill. But Mr. Morgan bought out that term, which was about fifteen or sixteen years unexpired; and when he was ousted of his other preferments, he kept this in the times of usurpation, by virtue of the assignment of that lease. He never renewed the lease, but left it free to the church (though it cost him above 300 lib.) and is now worth 200 lib. per annum, and the best living in the diocese.

After the king's restoration, he was restored to his preferments, and made archdeacon of Merioneth, and likewise D.D. 1660, and then made comportioner of Llanddinam, July 23, 1660. Upon Dr. Robert Price's death, he was elected to the bishoprick, and was consecrated July 1, 1666. Upon Archdeacon Mostyn's death, he took the archdeaconry of Bangor into his commendam, and took care to have it secured for his successor, who likewise enjoyed it, and had it annexed to the bishoprick, by act of parliament. He died September 1, 1673, and was buried the 6th of the same month, at Bangor, in the grave of Bishop Robinson, on the south side of the altar, where on a brass there is this inscription:—

ROBERTI MORGAN, S. T. P. EPISCOPI
BANGORIENSIS, QUOD MORTALE
FUIT HIC DEPOSITOM EST, IN

SPEM BEATOE RESURRECTIONIS ET
IMMORTALITATIS MDCLXXIII. ANNO
CONSECRATIONIS EJUS VIII°.
AETATIS AUTEM LXV°.

"He married Anne, the daughter and heir of William Lloyd, Rector of Llanelian, of the family of Henblas, brother to Richard Lloyd B. D., father of the present Bishop of St. Asaph, and had by her four sonns and four daughters, as (1) Richard his eldest, who dyed young; (2) Owen, who was first commoner, then scholar of Jesus College, Oxon, and after that a member of Gray's Inn, where (after he had for some time also attended Sir Leoline Jenkins, at the treaty of Nieumegen) he dyed April 11, 1679, greatly lamented, not only by his relations, but by all that knew him, as being a young gentleman of extraordinary hopes; (3) William, LL.B. of Jesus College, Oxon, and at this time Chancellor of the Diocese of Bangor; (4) Robert, now student of Christ Church. His eldest daughter was marry'd to Edward Wyn, cler. A. M. son and heir of John Wyn of Bodewrid, in Anglesey, Esq. The second was marry'd to Thomas Lloyd of Kefn, Register of St. Asaph. The third to Hum. Humphreys of Kyssail-gy-farch, com. Caernarvon, D.D. and Dean of Bangor. The 4th dyed unmarried.

"Bishop Morgan left behind him severall things fitt for the press, but because, as he say'd, they were ill transcribed, he forbid them to be published. He ordered the inside of the choir to be new done with good waynscoat seats for the deans, prebends, &c. and with the assistance of a legacy, left by Bishop Roberts, and the charity of several of the gentry, furnished the church with an excellent organ, and repaired the church, which then had not one farthing revenue to support its fabrick. He was a man of great prudence in business, good learning and eloquence in preaching, both in the English and his native tongue, and he perfectly spent and wore himself away by his constant preaching." (Humphreys)

"Near Henblas there is a cromlech, and at Cerrig y Gwydyl, in this parish, is a heap of stones, cast on the grave of a person supposed to be buried there."[238]

LLANGWYNLLO, LLANGWENLLWYVO, or LLANVAIR-LLWYVO, as it is sometimes called, is in the hundred of Twrcelyn, a chapel annexed to the perpetual curacy of Amlwch, dedicated to Gwen Llwyvo, a saint, whose pedigree is not known. Her Holyday is kept on November 30th. The great tithes belong to the Bishop of Bangor, excepting half of "Rhos y Manach", the Monk's Marsh or Common, which is attached to the living of Llanelian. In the extent of the comet of Twrcelyn, taken at Bettws Geraint, the 26th of Edward III, Rhôs y Manach was then ranked as a township, in the possession of Cynric ab Davydd, Davydd ab Adda, and others; they paying for it, to the Lord Prince, the yearly rent of £2 10s. 0d. "owing suit, &c. at the prince's mills, called Melin Dulas, Melin Bryn Gwydd, and Melin Adda". A moiety of this township fell into the lord's hands, by the forfeiture of Iorwerth Gôch. The prince granted two oxgangs of it to Gryffydd, the son of Iorwerth Gôch. "All these tenants make the roof, carry grind-stones, &c. to the said mills, and make part of the Lord Prince's manor-house, with the other free tenants", &c. This parish is five miles distant from Amlwch, and situated on

238 Caerwys MSS.

the sea-coast. The resident population in 1821 was 498, and 534, in 1831. Rates at 12s. in the pound, £91 8s. 11d.—increased to £176 11s. 0d. in 1831. In this parish is Llysdulas, the mansion of a branch of the Lewis's of Llechylched, descended from Hwva ab Cynddelw, "un o Dri Tylwyth Môn". This, together with part of Pary's Mountain, is now the property of Mrs. Hughes, sole heiress to the late William Lewis, Esq. She married the Rev. Edward Hughes, and their son, William Lewis Hughes, was ennobled in 1832, by the title of Baron Dinorben. Within the grounds of Llysdulas is situated, in a retired and sequestered spot, the church of Llangwynllo, a small neat edifice, appropriately fitted up for the performance of divine service; and there are some trifling benefactions for distribution among the poor. The service is performed by the Rev. William Johnson of Amlwch, this being a chapel of ease belonging to that church.

LLANGWYLLOG, a parish partly in the hundred of Llivon, partly in that of Malltraeth, and partly in that of Menai, three miles from Llangevni, and within five of Llannerchymedd. The land is in a good state of cultivation, and all enclosed, containing 267 inhabitants. The living is a perpetual curacy, endowed with £400 private benefaction; £600 Queen Anne's bounty, and £800 parliamentary grant, and in the patronage of Sir R. Bulkeley. The church is small, but remarkably well built, and has an ancient and curious chapel at the west end of the nave. The interest arising from some charitable bequests and donations is annually distributed among the poor of this parish. A sanguinary battle is said to have taken place on "Maes Rhôs Rhyvel", in 1143, between the forces of Owen Gwynedd, and the united armies of the Erse, Manks and Norwegians, in which the Welsh prince was victorious. At a short distance from this "field of battle", is a place called "Castell", the origin and history of which is unknown. Coins of Vespasian, Nero, and Constantine, have been found here at various times, in a state of good preservation, and in 1829, a gold coin of Vespasian's was dug up, the impression of which was quite perfect. The church is supposed to have been built about the year 605, and dedicated to Cwyllog, sister to the learned Gildas ab Caw, and the wife of Medrod, one of Arthur's knights of the round table. "She embraced a religious life after her husband's death." The resident population in 1821 was 277, and 267 in 1831; and the parish rates £78 16s. 10d.

LLANGOED, OR LLAN-COWRDA, is situated in the eastern extremity of Mona, in the hundred of Tindaethwy, and within three miles from Beaumaris. The church is dedicated to Cowrda, one of the ancient Colidei, who was buried here. The resident population in 1821 was 552, and 562 in 1831. Parish rates at 4s. in the pound, £61 15s. 0d. in 1803—increased to £162 13s. 0d. in 1831. This parish is a curacy (not in charge) and together with that of Llanvihangel-ty'n-Sylwy, is annexed to the rectory of Llaneistyn, endowed with £400 private benefaction; £600 Queen Anne's bounty; £900 parliamentary grant, and in the patronage of the Rev. Robert J. Hughes of Llangoed, a branch of the Hugheses of Plâs Côch, in Llanedwen parish, represented by Sir William Bulkeley Hughes. Their common ancestor Hugh Hughes, descended from Llowarch ab Bran,[239] sued a bard for reflecting upon his rapacity as a lawyer. He was Attorney General in the reign of Queen Elizabeth, and built Plâs Côch, which

239 Page 440, 2nd vol. Cambrian Register.

is a noble specimen of the architecture of that age, being a fine antique mansion, having over the entrance, the arms of the family, argent a chevron between three ravens, with ermine in their bills, and the date 1569.

The church of Llangoed is of very ancient foundation. The present structure was erected in 1613, at the expence of Henry Johnes, to whom James I granted the tithes of this parish; it is a spacious edifice, in the latter style of English architecture, consisting of a nave, chancel, north and south transept, and containing some good monuments to the memory of the deceased members of the families of Johnes and Hughes. William Wynn, by deed in 1670, gave a tenement called Tyddyn-llwyn, in the parish of Beddgelert, the rent of which is appropriated towards apprenticing poor boys of this parish, or that of Penmon, also for the purchase of six coats, to be given to six poor men annually at Christmas, and of six penny leaves to be distributed every Sunday. This tenement is now worth £200 a year. Plas newydd, a very extensive farm in this parish, was left by the foundress of Llandwrog alms houses, in Caernarvonshire, towards their support, and is now become very valuable property.

Mr. Gwylym Wynn of Llangoed, was a noted collector of old MSS. Some of them have been purchased by Mr. Justice Bosanquet, a gentleman, who has by application, become perfect master of the ancient British language. The trouble of acquiring this knowledge, he says, has been amply repaid by our beautiful Barddoniaeth. This distinguished and erudite scholar reads the productions of Aneurin, Taliesin, and Llowarch Hen, bards of the sixth century, with as much facility and understanding as he does the works of our later poets. Mr. William Davies, curate of Llangoed, transcribed several of Mr. Griffith Wynn's MSS and has written inside some of the covers, "Y llyvr hwn a scrivenodd William Davies, curat y plwy hwn, sev Llangoed, o oedran Crist, 1642."

LLANGWYVAN is in the hundred of Malltraeth, and a perpetual curacy annexed to the rectory of Trevdraeth, and situated within ten miles of Holyhead. This parish is about a mile in length, and has a resident population of 218 persons. Rates at 10s. in the pound amounted to £83 5s. 10d. in 1803, and to £149 6s. 0d. in 1831. The church is situated on the bay of Caernarvon, and like that of Llandisilio, is often surrounded by the sea, which rages violently, and the service, which is only performed once in a fortnight, is then performed in a room consecrated for the purpose, at the farm house, called "Plâs Gwyvan", the name of the saint to whom the church is dedicated. He lived in the seventh century, and was the son of Brwyno Hên; his mother was Canell of Bod Angharad, in Coleion. There is in this parish a quarry of white marble, which is said to be fit for statuary purposes.

LLANIDAN.—This parish, rich in druidical remains, is in the hundred of Menai, distant from Caernarvon five miles, and contains about 3,000 acres of land, generally enclosed, and in a state of cultivation. The resident population 800. The rates in 1803 were £226 9s. 2d. at 7s. in the pound,—increased to £452 18s. 0d. in 1831. This living is a vicarage, valued in the king's books at £10, and with the chapelries of Llanedwen, Llanddeiniol-Vab, and Llanvair-yn-y-Cymmwd, is in the gift of the lay rector, Lord Boston. The vicar, the Rev. Henry Rowland, having only a third of the tithes. The church, a spacious structure, containing several good monuments, is said to have been built about the year 616, and dedicated to St. Eidan, grandson to Urien Reged. Day of celebration is on September 30. Henry

Rowland, D.D. Bishop of Bangor, in 1616, bequeathed a rent charge £1 10s. 0d. on his estate of Plâs Gwyn, to be distributed among the poor; the estate of Llyslew he also left for the support of the free grammar-school, at Bottwnog, which is one of the best farms in this parish. The spacious grove and temple of Tre'r Driw, are now scarcely distinguishable, and only a few of the stones which formed the sacraria, are now remaining to mark out the site. Tre'r Beirdd has almost been demolished. Bodowyr contains a cromlech, supported by four upright stones, but the circle has been entirely removed. Trevry has only three upright stones remaining, at a great distance from each other; the foundations have been removed, and the site was levelled by the plough, in 1827. Tan-ben-y-Cevn remains in an entire state, though concealed from observation by the brambles with which it is overspread. Two upright stones only are left at Llyslew. "Caer Lêb", or the "moated entrenchment", supposed by Mr. Rowlands to have been the residence of the Archdruid, is in good preservation; it forms a quadrangular area, defended by a double rampart, with a broad intervening ditch, and surrounded on the outside by a ditch of smaller dimensions; within the area are the foundations of square and circular buildings. "In the church[240] is a relique, made neither of gold, silver, nor yet ornamented with precious stones, but of very ordinary material—a grit, with a roof-like cover. It might have contained a portion of the saint. Durham possessed his cross, three of his teeth, and his head", &c. Mr. Lloyd, when transcribing a MS written by Edward Llwyd, in the Sebright Collection, observes, "Near the latter end of this volume are inserted Mr. Henry Rowlands's answers to Mr. Llwyd of the Museum's queries, which take in the several parishes of Llanidan, Llanedwen, Llanvair-pwll-gwyngyll, and Llandisilio, in Mona. They contain very little that is remarkable, besides what is to be found in his Mona Antiqua, or in Mr. Llwyd's notes upon Camden, an account of a strange shower of hail fallen in Môn, on Monday, the 3rd of May, 1697, which Mr. Rowlands communicated to the editors of the Philosophical Transactions, &c. The small osteotheca, in Llanidan church, was found in his time; he conjectures it to be a "Creirgist", or a chest that held relics. It was found about two feet in the ground under the altar, and contained some pieces of bones. He supposes that it belonged to that church, Clunnog, or Llanddwyn, which had their "reliques", and was secretly deposited here during the demolishing proclamations of Edward VI. No corpse could have been buried there before. Mr. Rowlands mentions a fine gold medal of Constantine, or Constantius, near the size of a crown piece, found at Trev-Arthur, in Mona, and that it was then in the possession of Sir R. Mostyn, Bart. He quotes towards the last page, the following curious enigmatical epitaph:—

> Here lyes the world's Mother,
> By nature my Aunt,—Sister to my Mother,
> My Grand-mother,—Mother to my Mother,
> My Great-grandmother, Mother to my Grand-mother,
> My Grand-mother's Daughter,
> And her Mother:
> And all this may be without breach of consanguinity.—"*J. Lloyd.*"

240 Pennant, p.229.

This epitaph was occasioned by the following singular marriages:

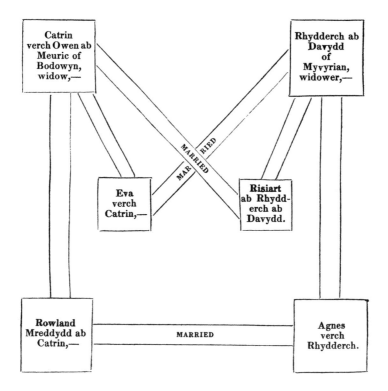

"There is a stone here" says the credulous Giraldus, "resembling a human thigh, which possesses this innate virtue, that to whatever distance it be carried, it returns of its own accord, the following night, as has often been experienced by the inhabitants. Hugh Lupus, Earl of Chester, tried the experiment, by throwing it into the sea, &c. but next morning it was found in its usual position". (Pennant, p.229) In a note from a MS of Mr. Rowlands, this stone is said to have been stolen, within his memory. There is a tradition that when a wish was made before it, if it was to come to pass, the person so wishing could lift up the stone with ease, but if not, then it became so heavy, that his utmost strength could not raise it. Thus "Maen Morddwyd" (concerning which there have been so many marvellous stories related) "is now well secured in the wall of the church", at Porthamel, not far from Llanidan, famed for being the place where Suetonius landed, in 61. His infantry passed over in flatbottomed boats, at the spot called Pont y Scraphie, or the Bridge of Skiffs. His horse crossed partly by fording, and partly by swimming (see p.26). "Near Llanidan is a hill, called 'Gwydryn', with two summits; on one of these there is an ancient fort, in ruins; and on the other, a pit, nine feet in diameter, sunk in the rock, full of pure sand; and in this neighbourhood are Tre'r Driw, and Tre'r Beirdd. On the confines of these places, there is a square fortification, supposed to be the first the Romans made after their landing. About a quarter of a mile off this, westward, there is a circular encampment, said to be that of the Britons; and westward of this, is a place called 'Cerrig y Bryngwyn' (no doubt where the Druids stood). Here are twelve stones, pitched on end (three very considerable); one of these twelve feet high, and eight feet broad. Bodowyr, north of the round camp, is a most remarkable cromlech, described in Mona Antiqua, p.250, wrought and cut into several angles, &c.—*J. Lloyd*". This slight notice, together with what is said of the Druids in the early part of this history, and the previous page, must content the reader, who is referred to the works of the learned authors, Dr. Borlase and Mr. Rowlands.

Lord Boston resides in a mansion, finely situated on an arm of the sea, which, with the church, belonged in former times to the convent of Beddgelert, and shared the fate of that house, in 1535. Queen Elizabeth granted this property to Edmund Downman, and Peter Ashton, who sold it in 1605, to Richard ab Rydderch (the subject of the preceding enigma) of Myvyrian, whose daughter and heir married Mr. Lloyd of Llugwy. On the extinction of that family, early in the last century, all their estates were bought by the then Lord Uxbridge, who left them to his nephew, Sir William Irby, created Lord Boston, in 1761. Pierce Lloyd of Gwaredog and Llannerchymedd, who purchased Llanidan, was sheriff in 1803, and his landed property was said to be the most extensive in the Island, valued at £1,000 per annum. Pierce his son, resided at Llugwy, and was sheriff for Mona (then a situation of great trust) in 1612, 1638, and 1651; and his son, Pierce Lloyd, lived at Llanidan, and served the same office, in 1699. Concerning an unfortunate marriage contracted by the son of this Pierce Lloyd, who squandered his inheritance, Mrs. Coytmor of Coytmor, wrote an admirable gossiping letter, to Lady Bulkeley, in 1725. After lamenting that she had "noe country newes to send, beinge most on end at home", she proceeds to say,—

> I know nott how to omitt to tell you one piece of newes we have in the daily, being the common teatable talk every where, that Mr. Lloyd of Llanidan is to be married (some fancies is married) to Mrs. Dolly Wynn of Gorddinog. I know not how to spend my judgement in it, because some are positive there is something in it,—ninety-five out of others not. But merriment and freedom having been most on end together, and the two younge Misses of Llanwnda, since a fortnight before Christmas, is between Caernarvon, Llanidan, and last at Gorddinog, where they have been this fortnight, which made his aunt Wynn very uneasie, that she sent the parson of her parish to fetch him to Llanidan, to meet her, and sent another messenger to Bodsallon, to fetch Mr. Wynn alsoe, to disswade him from it, if there was anything in it. He went with the messenger, and stay'd two or three nights with his aunt, and soe returned to Gorddinog, where he has been till last Saturday, and then they went, all in a body, to dine with Jack Roberts; and what is become of them since I know nott. I desire your ladyshipp would conceale the author of this newes, from Mr. Attkison, who I know, is great in the family. Another good newes I hear, which I am mightily rejoiced at, that we shall have your ladyshipp at Dinas, before May, and there to settle, which will be a great comfort and happiness to me and mine, and many more. I think it's time now to conclude, having made soe long an epistle, with my husband's and my most humble service to your good ladyshipp and Madam Cartar, presuming Mr. Cartar is at London, who am good Madam,
>
> Your Ladyshipp most ever obliged humble Servant,
> Margarett Coytmore.
>
> My daughter Peggy and Nelly is your Ladyshipp and Madam Cartar's most humble servants. Both our neighbours are gone to London, last week, to bear a rehearsing about the king's head, as their animosities and feuds is greater than ever.

LLANIESTYN, a parish in the hundred of Tindaethwy, and partly within the liberties of the borough of Beaumaris, from which town it is distant three miles and a half, contains 313 inhabitants, of which number 125 are in the former, and 178 in the latter portion. It is situated nearly in the centre of the promontory which separates Beaumaris roads from the Irish sea, and comprises a small tract of land, the greater part of which is enclosed and cultivated. The surrounding scenery is distinguished by features rather of a bold, than pleasing character. The living is a vicarage (not in charge) with the perpetual curacies of Llangoed and Llanvihangel-ty'n-Sylwy annexed, in the patronage of Mr. Hughes of Llangoed. The church, originally founded by Eistyn ab Geraint ab Erbyn, at the close of the sixth century, was granted by Prince Llewelyn ab Iorwerth, in 1243, to the priory which he had founded at Llanvaes, to which establishment it belonged at the dissolution of the ancient church. There are no other remains than the old tomb, erroneously supposed by some to be that of the founder, Iestyn, which has been deposited in the present church, a neat edifice, dedicated to St. Catherine. On the glass in the east window, is beautifully painted, a woman richly robed, and a crown like that of Pabo Post Prydain, on her head, and at her feet, an inscription, "ST. CATHERINE". The poor-rates, in 1803, at 4s. in the pound, amounted to £42,—increased to £72, in 1831. The income arising from some land, producing a trifling rental, is annually divided among the poor. "I descended", Mr. Pennant says, "to the church of Llaniestyn, remarkable for the tomb of its titular saint", &c. Upon the subject of this *really* being the monument of Iestyn, Mr. Lewis Morris comments [referring to pp.155/156 of the 1766 edition of Henry Rowlands's *Mona Antiqua Restaurata*] in these words:—"The following inscription of Jestinus is mere forgery; neither the letters of the copper-plate, opposite to p.156, nor the words, as read in p.155, being to be found on the stone at Llaniestyn; though it is plain, by the words 'Gryffydd ap Gwylym', and 'animarum' the same stone is meant. What a shame is this, that such trash should be foisted on the world. The truth of the matter is this:—The tomb-stone at Llaniestyn, in the chancel, is a curious monument, elegantly done, and serving like that of Pabo, at Llanbabo, for a bench to sit on. The effigy of a man in a sacerdotal habit, with the drapery, inscription, and ornaments are done by a masterly hand, and seem to me to be the tomb of some abbot, and have not the least connection with Jestinus. On the edge of the stone, above the head of the effigy, in large characters, is 'HIC JACET CRYRRIT A. P. GWILYM AMNIM MRVM. S'. Then on a circular label, on the left hand of the head, 'SALUTE NEM. P. SMNLTH': on another label, 'SCB . . . . IFIVM.'—Lewis Morris."

LLANLLIBIO, in the hundred of Llivon, and in the extent so often referred to, is ranked a "township of the nature of "Trev Gywr", and then in the possession of Thomas Hereley, a soldier, for the term of his life, under a grant from the present king (Edward III 1352) and the heirs and tenants thereof, are Bleddyn Gloff, Ieuan ab Adda, and others, they pay for it, in quarterly payments, £7 10s. od. and owing suit at the lord's mill. They make the roof, ditch, and watercourse of the said mill. The prince found the timber, and grinding stones; "and they shall carry them within the county of Anglesey and are to make the roof of the manor-house of Llanllibio, and nothing more." This parish is situated near the old road from London to Holyhead, and consists of a few farms, the produce of which is chiefly oats. The inhabitants, at present attend divine service in the church of Bodedern; but all ecclesiastical rites are performed at the mother church of Llantrisaint, for the chapel belonging to this parish, dedicated to St. Llibio, is entirely demolished; but the wakes are still kept in honour of the saint, on February 28. The rector, Mr. Wynne Jones, has in contemplation to rebuild the church. Llanllibio is one mile and a half from Bodedern, and eight miles from Holyhead, and contains about eighty-eight persons. Rates, at 3*s*. 3*d*. in the pound, £19 in 1803,—increased to £38 12*s*. 0*d*. in 1831.

LLANRHWYDRYS is in the hundred of Talybolion. I will here take leave to explain this name, as surmised by Mr. Rowlands, in Mona Antiqua, and corroborated by Dr. Owen Pugh. "Talebolion is said to be so called from the Roman General Suetonius Paulinus, or else a corruption of Talymoglion." In one of the Mabinogion, called "Hanes Brân", it is said to signify "the payment of colts"; an incident is related there to account for it. Llanrhwydrys is a chapel of ease to Llanrhyddlad, and the church, supposed to have been built about the year 570, dedicated to Rhwydrys ab Rhwydryn, King of Connaught; and the day of celebration is on the first Sunday in November. The church is a small ancient edifice, situated nearly in the centre of the headland projecting into the sea, near the small Island called the West Mouse, eight miles north-west from Llannerchymedd; and fifteen from Holyhead, and on the Irish sea, containing 1,200 acres of arable land. The resident population in 1821 was 171, and 178 in 1831. The parish rates at 6*s*. in the pound, amounted in 1803 to £78 15*s*. 3*d*.,—*increased* to £143 18*s*. 0*d*. in 1831. John Hughes, in 1778, bequeathed £50 to the poor of this parish, and a small parochial school, in which a few poor children are taught gratuitously, is supported by subscription. "About four miles from the shore, is Ynys y Moelrhoniad, alias Skerries (described in p.127 of Llanfair-y'ng-hornwy); and at Cae y Maes, in this parish, are three large stone pillars; one measures eleven feet six inches high, and four feet broad. Near one of them was discovered, by digging, an odd kind of a helmet;—*J. Lloyd*". [241]

LLANRHYDDLAD is also in the hundred of Talybolion, eight miles from Llannerchymedd, and twelve miles from Holyhead, a rectory, having the chapels of Llanvlewyn and Llanrhwydrys attached, valued temp. Henry VIII at £14 11*s*. 8*d*. The Bishop of Bangor presents, and the Rev. Stuart Majendie the present incumbent. The tithes of the ancient parish of Llandogvael are received alternately by the rectors of this parish and Llanvechell. The church, supposed to be built about the year 570, dedicated to St. Rhyddlad, is a small edifice, not distinguished by any architectural features of importance. This parish, which is of small extent, is situated on the shore of the Irish sea, containing 1,800 acres of land, about one-third uncultivated. Resident population in 1821 was 622, and 628 in 1831. The rates, at 7*s*. 6*d*. in the pound, amounted in 1803 to £102 3*s*. 6*d*., and in 1831 increased to £208 11*s*. 0*d*. The village lies at the foot of Moel Rhyddlad, one of the highest mountains in the Island, and for that reason selected by Colonel Mudge as one of the principal stations in making the trigonometrical survey of North Wales. Considerable quantities of manganese, and some copper ore have been found upon this mountain. The interest of some small charitable donations and bequests, two of which (portions of land) are annually divided among the poor, at Christmas.

241 Caerwys MS.

LLANSADWRN, a rectory in the hundred of Tindaethwy, and in the Bishop of Bangor's gift, valued in the king's books at £9 6s. 8d. The Rev. William Thomas is the present incumbent. The church, dedicated to the heathen god, Saturn, a popish saint (whose day is celebrated on November 29), is a small, but neat edifice, consisting of a nave, chancel, and north transept, and was thoroughly repaired, at a considerable expence, in 1829; outside the edifice is a head of a bear, with a muzzle and chain, curiously carved in stone; and there is "an uncouth head, projecting from the wall of the church, on the inside, said to be intended for the head of St. Sadwrn". The fragment of a stone, with an inscription, found in the time of Mr. Lewis Morris, is now placed under that head, which is close by a window, and described by him as follows:—"On a gritty broken stone, in the church of Llansadwrn, in Mona, taken out of a grave, by digging, and which I copied there, in 1742, is the following inscription (the stone is three spans long, and half a span broad): "HIC BEATISS SATVRNINVS SANC JACIT ET SVA SANCTA CONIVX PA CVIS". The sexton, who dug up this fragment, knows the place, and may possibly yet get the pieces, if any body went to the expence.—Lewis Morris." The late Rev. John Williams of Treffos, a remarkably learned and intelligent antiquary and botanist, never rested till he had discovered the remaining part of the grave of Saturninus, and *his wife*. "A very curious circumstance", observes his son, in a letter to the author, "proving that our Welsh clergy were married, and consequently not papist priests. The inscription is as legible as any one cut ten years ago, and alludes to 'Sanctus Saturninus et sua Conjux' ", &c. "On a tenement,[242] called Trevawr, in this parish, there are two cromlechau; one is a large stone, mounted high upon four pillars, its inclination westward; in length it is nine feet, and eight feet in breadth. Near it, and upon the same carnedd, is another, supported only by two stones, with great inclination northward.[243]—*J. Lloyd*".

There are some remains of an ancient fortress, near an old family mansion, called "Castellior", which, from several relics of antiquity, discovered in the immediate vicinity, is supposed to be of Roman origin. In the marsh, near Llwdiart mountain, fossil oak trees, acorns, and nuts, are found, several feet below the surface. This parish, which is situated in the eastern part of the county, within four miles of the Menai bridge, and three miles and a half from Beaumaris, contains from 1,500 to 2,000 acres of cultivated land. The resident population in 1821 was 335, and 391 in 1831. Their houses are scattered over the parish, in detached situations, not forming any village; and the surrounding scenery is pleasingly rural. The poor are maintained by an average annual expenditure, amounting to £137 10s. 0d. The farms of Bryn Eryr, and Rhôsowen, left by Dr. Rowlands for the support of his almshouses at Bangor, are in this parish. Rowland Jones, in 1715, left a tenement, called Gorslâs, the rent of which he appropriated, in equal shares, to the poor of Llansadwrn, and Pentraeth; and Mrs. Roberts, in 1736, bequeathed £150, the interest of which sum, she directed to be given, in equal shares, to three of the poorest and most deserving in this parish. About three miles off, is Porthaethwy; and in Llansadwrn is Treffos, once a considerable place, it having been the residence of the Bishops of Bangor; it is said to be the capital of the barony, by which the bishop claims a seat in parliament, and became the property

242 Caerwys MS.
243 This cromlech fell down in 1825.

of that see while Einian filled it. Edward I in token of remembrance for the office this prelate did in christening his son, Edward of Caernarvon, in 1284, bestowed upon him and his successors for ever, the ferries of Borthwen and Cadnant; the manors of Bangor, Castellmai, and Garthgogo, in Caernarvonshire; the rocks by Abergeleu, to get up limestone, with the manors of Cantred and Treffos, in Mona.

LLANTRISAINT, a parish partly in the hundred of Menai, but chiefly in that of Llivon, four miles from Llannerchymedd, having in 1821 a resident population of 589, and 537 in 1831. The average annual expenditure for the relief of the poor, is £223 13s. 0d. This parish, which is situated in the western part of Mona, and is intersected by the small river Alaw, comprehends a tract of about 4,400 acres of arable and pasture land, of which the greater portion is enclosed. Copper ore has been found upon Meinir farm, but not of considerable quantities to form a mine. The living is a rectory, with the perpetual curacies of Gwaredog, Llanllibio, Llechcynvarwy, and Rhôswyddgeidio annexed, valued in the king's books at £26, and in the patronage of the bishop. The present incumbent is the Rev. Hugh Wynne Jones, of Tre Iorwerth. The church, dedicated to Avran, Ievan, and Sanan, from which circumstance the parish derives its name, signifying the church of three saints, was originally founded in 570. The present is a good modern edifice, of comparatively recent erection, having no claim to architectural beauty. The Rev. Hugh Williams, D.D. of Nanthanog, was instituted rector of this parish in the year 1633; he died in 1670, aged 74. In the church is a handsome monument erected to his memory, describing him as "being descended from Cadrod Hardd, a British chieftain, and a native of Mona". His son, Sir William Williams, Bart. was a distinguished character in the reigns of Charles II and James II and founder of the renowned and distinguished families of Wynnstay, and Bodlewyddan. Sir William became a scholar of Jesus College, Oxford, in the year 1652, but removed two years after, to Gray's Inn, and having been called to the bar, was made Recorder of Chester, represented that city in parliament, and was elected speaker of the House of Commons. He married Mary, daughter and sole heiress of Watkin Cyffin of Glascoed, by whom he had two sons and a daughter; he died at his chambers, in Gray's Inn, July 11, 1700. A small sketch of his life is given among the eminent men of Mona; and the epitaph on his father's tomb, at Llantrisaint church, is copied in p.70 of Cathrall's History. A small parochial school, having an endowment of £8 per annum, was founded in the year 1822, for which ten children are taught reading and writing gratuitously; the instruction of others is paid for by subscription. Three poor men from this parish, are eligible to the almshouses at Beaumaris, under the will of the founder, David Hughes, who endowed them with a farm, called Meinir, here situated, and with various other lands, for the support of the inmates. Among the eminent men of Mona a small sketch is given of this benevolent man.

LLANDDAUSAINT, a parish in the hundred of Talybolion, six miles from Llannerchymedd, is of considerable extent, and near the river Alaw. The village is small, but pleasantly situated. Resident population in 1821 was 375, and 407 in 1831. The living is a discharged rectory, in the Bishop of Bangor's patronage, having the perpetual curacies of Llanbabo and Llanvair-y'nghornwy annexed, valued in the king's books at £20 11s. 2d. The church, dedicated to St. Marcellus and Marcellinus (their wakes kept on September 25), is a small but venerable edifice, in the early style of English architecture, with a good lancet chapel window, of three lights, at the east end, of which the gable is externally surmounted with an antique cross. The present rector is the Rev. James Williams, who resides in an excellent and commodious parsonage-house, built by himself, at Llanvair-y'nghornwy. Two poor men of this parish are eligible, by the will of David Hughes, to apartments in the hospital, or alms-houses, founded by him, at Beaumaris; and the produce of several small charitable bequests and donations in land, and money, is annually divided among the poor, in conformity with the will of the benefactors. The average annual expenditure for their support, is £163 2s. 0d.

LLECH-GYNVARWY, i.e. the Cliff of Cynvarwy, is situated in the hundred of Llivon, and is a chapel under the rectory of Llantrisaint. The church, said to have been founded about the year 630, is dedicated to St. Cynvarwy, the son of Hwy ab Lleinog of Cerniw. The day of celebration is kept on November 7. This parish is distant from Holyhead ten miles. The resident population in 1821 was 412, and 442 in 1831. The poor rates average annually £185 5s. 0d. This parish comprehends a large tract, of which the greater portion is enclosed and cultivated. It is situated in the western part of the Island, on the old line of road leading from Llannerchymedd to Holyhead. The church, within three miles of Llannerchymedd, is a spacious and handsome cruciform edifice, consisting of a nave, chancel, and north and south transepts. Within the limits of this parish, on a field adjoining, is an upright stone, called "Maen Llêchgwenvarwydd", which is more than nine feet high, and appears to be of great antiquity. Mr. Wynne Jones of Tre Iorwerth, the rector of Llantrisaint, in 1826 built a handsome parsonage house, which, with fifteen acres of land, he has given to the living for ever. The poor children of this parish, receive gratuitous education at the national school, at Llannerchymedd. Mrs. Margaret Wynne bequeathed a small portion of land, for the support of one poor aged woman, and Mrs. Catherine Roberts bequeathed £50 in money, for the support of two indigent housekeepers; there are also some smaller charitable donations, left for the benefit of the poor.

LLECHYLCHED is also in the hundred of Llivon, seven miles from Holyhead, and "with the hamlets of Bodedeyrn, Deubwll, Crigell, Tregadrod, Bodvarthon, Trev Griffri-yr-arw, Uchtred, and Llechgyvarwy, is in the extent beforementioned, ranked as a hamlet in the township of Conisiog, having five domiciles belonging to the heirs of Mathusalem ab Hwva, Cyvnerth ab Hwva, Iorwerth ab Hwva, and Bletheryd ab Hwva, all owing to the prince suit and service. The heirs of Iorwerth ab Hwva, Davydd Llwyd ab Cynric, Madoc Llwyd ab Llewelyn and others, pay every quarter, 13s. 3d. They have a mill of their own, called "Melin Cymynod"; they pay *cylch stalon*, and are to sustain the roof of the lord prince's hall and chamber, at Aberffraw, besides other services; and there are in the same domicile four oxgangs of escheat land, which belonged to Tegai Rwth, which are now held by Bleddyn ab Tegai, and Madoc ab Gryffydd Vân, and they pay for their brewhouse (Bracina), or malthouse, as above. They have a share in Melin y Twr, and make part of the lord prince's hall, at Aberffraw, owing suit at county and hundred courts to the prince's mill, at Dindryval", &c. Llechylched is a parish of very moderate extent, and lies in the south-western part of the Island. The road from London to Holyhead passes through the village. The church is situated far from any house, in a marshy valley, watered by a stream which falls into the bay of Caernarvon. The living is a perpetual curacy under the rectory of Llanbeulan; and the church, a small edifice, is dedicated to St. Ulched. The saint's day kept on January 6. The resident population was 267 in 1821, and 405 in 1851. The poor are maintained by an average annual expenditure, amounting to £196 7s. 0d. A national school for the instruction of poor children, belonging to this and the neighbouring parishes, was established in 1829, and is supported by subscription. The present number of children is seventy-five.

RHOSIR, RHOSVAIR, OR NEWBOROUGH.[244]—This parish is a discharged rectory, in the Prince of Wales' gift, and valued temp. Henry VIII at £10 13s. 10d. The present incumbent is the Rev. Henry Rowland. The church, dedicated to St. Peter (day of celebration on the 29th of June), is a small edifice, possessing no claims to architectural description. It stands on an eminence, in a bleak and exposed situation. Rhosvair, or Newborough, is situated near the southern extremity of Mona, bordering on the extensive sea marshes of Malltraeth, and near the mouth of the small river Braint, distant from Beaumaris sixteen miles, and from Caernarvon four miles. This parish, including the small remains of that of Llanddwyn, contains 1,000 acres of land, one third of which is common. The resident population in 1821 was 756, and 804 in 1831. The average annual expenditure for the maintenance of the poor, amounts to £182 19s. 0d. The market, which was formerly held weekly, has been discontinued for many years. Fairs are held annually on March 11, June 29, August 16, September 25, and November 11. By virtue of its first charter, Newborough was governed by a mayor, two bailiffs, and a recorder, &c. who kept regular courts here; but the glory of this once celebrated royal spot, with its "golden bells" and its "Lord Llewelyn", have "passed away like Tyre and Sidon", it has dwindled into an insignificant obscure village, "a place for the fisherman to spread his net upon". The few inhabitants that are left, support themselves by the manufacturing of matting, nets, ropes, cordage, &c. composed of a species of sea-reed grass, called Bent Môrhesc, a plant which Queen Elizabeth, in tenderness to such of her subjects who lived on sandy shores, prohibited extirpating, in order to prevent the misfortune, which has since happened, of having half the parish buried in sands. This was a royal manor of great note, under the Welsh princes, and the seat of justice for the comot of Menai. In the time of Edward I it was made a corporate town, &c. and these privileges were confirmed by Edward III in whose reign it was first called Newborough; and when the extent of Menai was taken, the twenty-sixth of his reign, at Rhôsvair, it possessed at that time "a palace, and royal chapel, which all the tenants of the comot were bound to keep in repair, but in the township (continues the extent) of Rhôsvair, "there are pure tenaunts, or natives, called 'Maer Drevwyr',[245] and other natives, who call themselves free, who hold twelve gavels and a half in the township; they pay the annual rent to the lord prince for them, in quarterly payments of £6 16s. 5d. and they do the work of the manor-house, like other bond servants of the same comot, owing suit, and doing the work of the lord prince's mills, at Rhôsvair, and Melin Newydd, pay reliefs of ten shillings, and they are to carry the victuals for the lord and his household,

244 J. Lloyd.—Caerwys MS.
245 Synonymous with "Gwŷr y Vaerdrev", mentioned in the Laws of Howel Dda.

taking one penny and a halfpenny per day, for a man and horse. One of the gavels is called Porthwae-
sion; another Porthorion; another Meudwy; another Wastewy. William ab Meilir held lands that belonged to Gorddvor." The names of all the tenants are given, and as this is the last comot named in the
extent, it ends in these words: "Thus by the favour of God, the extent of the whole county of Anglesey,
was made by John Delves Broughton, the representative of Richard, Earl of Arundel, in the 26th of Edward III." "The tenants of Trev Vallwyn did part of the work of the lord prince's manor-house of
Rhosyr. The tenants of Dinam, with other native tenants, besides work at the hall, they did the work of
the fences round the manor-house, carrying stones and timber to the mills of Rhosyr and Melin
Newydd. The heirs of the Ysceiviog township, and Howel Voel Ddû of Gaerwen, besides other services, did work at the manor-house of Rhôsvair", &c. "The township of Hirdrevaig, if there be but one
tenant, he ought to be burthened with the whole rents and services, owing suit at the lord prince's mill;
fence about the manor-house of the lord prince; do his part of the chapel, in the same manor-house,
the stewards chamber, and the laundry, and the lord prince's stable there; he is also bound to carry the
timber, and grinding stones, for the mill, and other necessaries for the carpenters; which business the
lord prince shall do at his own proper expence", &c. The foundation of this palace, and the chapel at
Rhosvair, was to be seen in Mr. Rowlands's time, a little south of the church, which is supposed to have
been a domestic chapel attached to the palace when. Edward I granted a charter to Nevyn, it was the
same as that of Rhôsvair, or Newburgh. This one to Nevyn, and confirmed by Richard II being the
most legible, I have transcribed it, in preference to the other, which contains exactly the same privileges.

Pat. 6, R̃. II. pt. 3, M. 14. D. confirmãcoe ꝑ hoĩbus de Nevyn. R̃. omnibus ad quos, &c. salt̃m. Inspeximus ĩras patentes carissimi đni & patris ñri đni Edwardi illustris Regis Angł & Franciæ primo-
geniti nup̃ Princip⁹ Wałł, ducia Cornũb & comitis Cest̃r in hæ verba Edward⁹ illustrĩ Regis Angł &
France primogenitus Princeps Wałł dux Cornũb & comes Cest̃r Archĩepis Epĩs Abbibus prioribus
comitibus Baronibus Justic vice comitibus ꝑpositis, ministris & omnibus Ballivis & fidelibus suis ad
quos pr̃sentes hẽ pervenerint salt̃m sciatis quod nos voluntate & assensu dilic̃ & fidelis ñri Nigelli de
Lohareyn militis camerarii ñri cui nup̃ dedimus & concessimus villas de Nevyn & Purthely in North-
wałł cũ omnibus pertiñ suis ad terminu vite sue & ꝑ finem 36 librãr nob̃ ꝑ comt̃atem norãm pedicte
ville de Nevyn fĩm dedimus & concessimus ꝑ nobis & heredibus ñris hoibus dic̃ ville de Nevyn quod
diã villa de Nevyn de cetero liber Burgus sit & quod Hõies dim̃ Bur̃gũ inh̃atantes de cetero lib̃i sint
Burgenses et quod habeant Gildam mercatoria cũ Hansã & omnibus lib̃tatibus & lib̃is consuetudinibus
lib̃o Burgo qualitercumqꝫ pt̃in, tales scĩlt lib̃tates & consuetudenes quales Burgenses ñri villi de Newburgh in com̃ Anglẽs sient in Burgo suo ibiđ. Et quod dc̃i Burgenses et eõr successores impꝑm habeant
& teneant ad feodi firmã de dĩo Nigello ad terminu ville sue et post ipsius decessu de nobis & heredibus ñris dĩam villam cũ omnibus libtatibus pr̃dictis et aliis ꝑfituis & ꝑt̃in unveris salvis semp̃ dĩo
Nigello ad terminũ ville sue et post ipsius decessu de nobis & heredibus ñris post ipsius decessu molendinis ñris de geyr & gonu⁹ cũ exitibus & ꝑt̃en suis & 40 solidis anni redditiu debites loco & ñoie repaĩois
manerii ñri ibidem annuatim. Dedemus etiam & concessimus ꝑ nob̃ & heredibus ñris dc̃is Burgensi-
bus de Nevyn et successoribus suis impꝑm quod habeant & teneant in dc̃a villa duas nundinas ꝑ annu,

unã videlt in vigilia et festo pentecostes & aliam in vigilia et festo Assumptionis b͠c marie et heãnt mr-
catũ ibidem die sabͨbi qualt septimana impͬpͫm sicut ante hec tempora huerunt ad quod mercatũ concedimus quod gentes comoti nͬri de Dynthlayn venire teneantur et alii qui ante hec tempora venire
solebant ad mercat supradictũ reddendo dcͦo Nigello ad terminũ vite et nobis et heredibus nͬris ͬpost
ipsius decessũ 32 Libras annuatim ad festu Pasche et sͥti michͥiͣ equaliter ͬℲℲ feodi firma prdicta & ͬℲℲ
omnibus libtatibus et ͬpfituis predictis diis duobus molendinis & annuo redditu quadraguinta solidorũ
dio Nigello ad terminũ vite sue et nobͦ & heredibus nͬrispost ipsͥius decessũ ut pemittitur reservatis
quare volumus et firmiter ͬprcipimus & concedimus & nobis & heredibus nͬris quod dcͣa villa de Nevyn
de cetero liber Burgus sit et quod Hoͥies dͥm Burgũ inhatantes de cetero ͥibi sint Burgenses et quod
heant Gildam mercatoriã" &c. "The very same words repeated as before, dated at Caernarvon, the 1st
of February, in the 12th of his principality. Witnessed Johͤe de Delves locu tenͤent Justicͥ nͬri Northwaᴛᴛ
Robͦto de Pary's Camerario nͬro ibidem et aliis. Richard the Second's confirmation of this charter of his
father, the Black Prince, is dated at Westminster, the 20th of March. This seems to be the first royal
charter to Nevyn, as it does not quote any one preceding it.—*J. Lloyd.*"

P. 800. "Pat 33, E. III. pt. 3, M. 20, ͬp Nigello de Loryng, R̃. omnibͦ ad quos & saltͫm", &c. This recites a deed of his son, the Black Prince, giving to this Nigell de Loryng, the manors of Nevyn and Purthely, as hinted in the last charter, which makes the former a free burgh. This is dated at Caernarvon,
20th of July, in the fifteenth of his principality; that is, three years after the date of the charter of Nevyn,
and yet such a deed is hinted in that; so that either there must have been a deed of gift, prior to this, or
else there is a mistake in this date. This mentions Pwllhely being made a free burgh, as well as Nevyn,
by the consent and desire of this Nigell de Loryng, who it seems deserved well of the prince, for several good services, particularly "ͬp bono & laudabile servicio, quod ͬpefatus Nigellus nobis impendit
tam in ͬptibus vascͦn quã alibi & pecipne apud Bellũ de Poyters in quo circa corpus nr m̃extiterat q̃aliter
assignatus." He entitles him "serviciis quorum cumque tenentiũ tam lͥiborum quam nativͦr", by
which last word might be inferred that the natives were not allowed to be free burghers. He gives each
burgh the same privileges, "in Burgis suis ͬprdictis quales Burgenses de Rhosfeir tͤent et utuntur in Bur-
gosuo & "eidem Nigello annuatim reddenͩd videᶠt ͬp dͥio Burgo de Nevyn 32 libras per annum & ͬp dͥio
Burgo de Purthely 14 libras ͬp annuͫm", &c. He bestows upon him freely these two burghs, with all their
appurtenances, together with 4 librates of lands, towards the repairs of his mansions, &c. "Hͤend &
tenͤend de nobis et Heredibus nͬris eidem Nigello & heredibus de corpore suo ligitme ͬℲℲ creatis ͬℲℲ ser-
viciũ unius rose ͬℲℲ annũ ͬℲℲ omnibus serviciis", &c. By this clause, he was only to pay a single rose annually, in lieu of all services whatever. If he died without legitimate issue, the whole was to revert to the
prince, and his heirs, &c. Then follows a recital of a grant, in French, of the same prince, to this Nigell
le Loryng, of several lands, and in some parts of England; both confirmed by his father, Edward III
which confirmation is dated at Sandwich, September 9th. "Per v̄re de privato sig."—*J. Lloyd.* It appears also by the Sebright Papers, as well as by the extent, quoted in p.304-5, that the palace and chapel
existed in the time of Edward III.

Vol.5, a thick 4to. containing Escheats Patents, Inquisitions, &c. "Yn y Twͤr." Page 3, Anglesey, &c.
"Quod tenentes R̃. Comoti de Meney teneantur repare mañor Rͦs de Rosfeyr Escͪh Aͦ 11, E. iii. No.

108", &c. Page 4—"Inquĩs Capta apud novu Burgũ in Comoto Meney in Cõm Anglesey coram Willo de Shaldeford locũ tenente dñi Rici Cõm Arundel Justic dñi Reǧ in Northwaꝉ die px̃ post festũm aptõr petri et Pali anno Reǧn Reg E. 3tii post conquestum decimo virtute dñi Regᵍ Justic Northwaꝉ et ejus locũ tenenti dirĕct vidꝉt quos custus circa reparacoem̃ Camere et Capelle dc̃i Regis in manerio suo de Rosfeyr in ꝑ dco comoto durãtor et ꝑstxaꞃar et sustentacoem eãr ꝑ annum apponi operteret", &c.

The purport of these two last instruments is the same;—the first sets forth, that the king's "liberi tenentes et nativi" of the comot of Meney, were obliged by their tenures, to repair at their own costs, "omnes demos maner ñri de Rosfeyr in dc̃o comõt custibᵍ suis ꝑpris in quo quidem manerio quedam parva camera et quedem Capella dirula et ꝑstrata". The tenants further allege that if the palace and chapel in question were repaired, they would be of little or no advantage to the king; he therefore directs his justiciary, &c. to enquire into the truth of the affair, and whether it would not be better for him to take a sum of money annually, in lieu of the repairs of this palace, chapel, &c.

The second instrument sets forth, that such inquisition was made before twelve men of the comot of "Meney", and thirteen of the comet of "Lywan", all whose names are inserted; and that they all declared upon oath, that the repairs of the above chapel and palace, were worth annually xxiii s. iiii d. and that it would be to the king's advantage; to take the sum annually, instead of repairs. These upright men, being further interrogated, whether it would be to the king's advantage, or loss, &c. They say upon oath, that the king would be the loser, &c. As there is no royal palace, as much as hinted at in the extent of Aberffraw (p.87) and as I am informed, there are not at this time, the least traces of such a place, I am strongly of opinion, that the prince's palace was at Rhosvair (Hodie-Newburgh), which is in the neighbourhood of Aberffraw, where such ruins have been traced. The word "*Camera*", signifies a royal residence, and the two last instruments prove the existence of such a place at Rhosvair, and as a further proof, the following epigram, preserved by the annotator on Camden, and others, proves it to be the residence of Prince Llewelyn.

" Mae Llŷs yn Rhosvair—mae Llyn,
" Mae Eurglŷch—mae Arglwydd Llewelyn,
" A gwŷr tàl yn ei ganlyn,
" Mil myrdd, mewn gwyrdd a gwyn." [246]

"There is a Lake at Rhosvair—there is a Palace
" Containing golden bells, and a Lord Llewelyn;
"Tall men compose his princely train,
"Thousand and ten thousand dressed in green and white."

In page 57 is a description given of part of the regalia, belonging to the Princes of Wales, having been given up to Edward I and the remaining part was accidentally found by some men, who were cutting a road in the park, behind the Palace of Maesmynan, near Caerwys, the usual residence of Prince Llewelyn, in times of peace. The workmen discovered a casket, made of brass, and curiously wrought, which crumbled in to dust, when exposed to the air; it was buried three feet under ground, and near a

246 Caerwys MS.

large stone. It contained seven armlets of twisted, or wreathed gold, fastened by hooks, in the manner of a torques[247]; a large piece of solid gold, heart shaped, with a rind adhering to the broadest end of it; four torques, one of these being much heavier than the others; a large chain, composed of beads, about the size of pigeons eggs, having a ring between each to connect it together. The treasure altogether, weighed twelve pounds, for which the men (seven in all) received from Mr. Richard Richardson (father to Mr. Richardson of Greenfield Hall, by Holywell), then a silversmith in Chester, more than £27 each. Ten years afterwards, the wife of one of the men, found in a drawer, where these ornaments had been deposited, a brooch, consisting of a large discoloured pearl, surmounted by small precious stones in the centre, which she sold to a watchmaker, at Holywell, for £10. Thomas Jones, one of the workmen, confirmed the above facts to the writer, and others, in 1831, when shewing the spot from whence the treasure was dug.

In the 5th vol. Sebright Collection, are the rules settled by Llewelyn ab Iorwerth the Great, and his council, for the management and regulation of his household. He had his several officers, stewards to his household, ushers of hall, butlers, bakers, gentlemen of his horse, cooks, almoners, chaplains, chamberlains, doorkeepers of his hall, chambers, &c. grooms of the horse, porters, and overlookers, with their assistants, &c. The order relative to every officer and servant in the palace, is laid down separately, and are very fully and particularly given in page 43 of this history. When the prince rode out he was attended by all his officers, and about a dozen 'squires. 'Villa de Llỳs Dunwallon' is mentioned: know not whether this refers to Llys, in Melidan parish, belonging to the Bishop of St. Asaph. 'Compositio Paris inter Principem Davydd filium ejus.' This is dated at Aber, in the presence of the Bishops of St. Asaph and Bangor."[248] It appears by p.292, ibid, that the men of Cardigan used to pay to the last Prince Llewelyn, and his progenitors, 100 de potura servientium et canum. By this record we may learn that this county, though in South Wales, was in possession of the Princes of North Wales, to the last. "This word, potura (observes Mr. Lloyd) occurs again in a record belonging to the abbot and convent of Basingwerk, who in consideration of their territories in Penllyn, were obliged to make some compensation to our princes, i.e. in the time of Llewelyn ab Iorwerth, and his son Davydd, when princes; they found patura for themselves and 300 men, when they went to Llanvawr to hunt, once a year; but the year in which they did not go, they exacted nothing from them, in lieu of it. The last Prince Llewelyn, claimed it as a right, and compelled them to find the same for himself, and 500 men, when he went there to hunt; and if he omitted going, he obliged them to pay the value of it in money, but to what amount, the jury in this inquisition (taken at Llanvair, 13th of Edward I) were ignorant; though it seems to me that £6 and 40s. mentioned in a survey made by Richard de Abindon, was the sum. When I found the word *patura*, spelt "potura", as it is once in this record, and in several other places, in these volumes, I concluded that it meant "potable liquids". But here, I find, it means another species of provision, i.e. bread, butter, fish, and cheese. "Et duos Pullos ad valencium 40 solid, cum duobus

247 In p.164, Cambrian Quarterly, is an account given of a torques, picked up on a mountain above Dolgelleu; and Mr. Pennant, in his History of Wales, describes the one at Mostyn.

248 J. Lloyd.—Caerwys MS.

pullis S͞r an͞atis". I cannot tell what to make of "S͞r", in this last place, but by the word "*anatis*" we would conclude that these *pulli* were ducklings, but how came two of them to be valued at forty shillings, at a time when two oxen were scarcely worth twenty shillings, is beyond my comprehension. We find here also something of the mode of living and diversions of our princes, and of the great retinue that attended them upon those occasions, &c.[249]

This Sebright volume contains much that is interesting concerning the Island of Mona, on which account I am tempted to quote largely. If it should be thought that too many extracts out of the Sebright Papers, have been blended with this history, it is hoped, the intimate and almost inseparable connection with the subject, will be accepted as an apology.

"Page 107, Escat de A° 12mo. E. I, No. 68, Inquisicio capta f͞ca apud Kaernv͞ar coram J. de Havring Justic Snaudon sub d͞no oton de Grandisono ꝑ sae͞rns Ade fil Leuelin", &c. The above inquisition, and the following page 108, taken the same year, at Llanbadarn Vawr, relates to the "Prior et fratres Hospit͞al sci Johnan͞es Jorl͞m in Anglesey", &c. By both which it appears that they had great privileges in all parts of Wales, "a temꝑe quo non extat memoria solebant n͞re chaciam ad o͞ms feras salvis cervis & Bissis, et quod solebant placitare in cu͞r suis omni placita de hoibus propriis salve Judic͞o vite & membr͞or. Et expedores sui signo hospit͞al signati solebant esse quieti de exercitu Principu͞ Cariagiis & ull allis opi͞bus. Et quod h͞is expedores non possunt singno signati ab sq₃ voluntate dn͞orsusun s͞c fuerint villani. Et quod sic licenciati possunt exire terras dn͞orcum su͞or salvis i͞m servicuis dnorum suorum x terris suis. Et quod Expedores sui possunt singnare fit suos sine licencia dn͞or su͞or. Et de filiabus expedor͞ su͞or forinsecor͞ habebunt p₃dicti Prior & fr͞es midietatem amobragii cum acciderit et de ꝑpriis hoi͞bus totu͞ &c. &c. et de qualibet domo in Wallio ꝑ annu͞ unu͞ den͞ si possessor ejus hea͞t volorem decem den͞ & eos ad hoc compellere, &c". Their privileges in Wales seems little short of royal. Their revenue must also be very considerable, for exclusive of their landed property, they were entitled to a penny every year, from every householder, that was worth ten shillings. Their "*Expedores*" (who it seems had a hospital mark set upon them) had likewise their privileges. What their office was, I cannot tell;—the word seems to come from "*expedio*", and probably they were some kind of light troops.

Another in p.828, is concerning Nantmawr, in the hundred of Twrcelyn. "Fines 2 E. III. M. 11. P. Willo de Shaldeford. R̃ omnibus ad quos, &c. salt͞m sciatis quod concessimus dit͞co nobis Willo de Shaldeford villam n͞ram de Nantmawr[250] in com de Angleseye in Wall hend ad tot͞a vit͞a su͞a Reddendo inde nobis ꝑ annu ad s͞ocium n͞rin de Caernavon centu͞ solidos ad terminos s͞ci mich͞is et Pasche ꝑ equalis pos͞coes salvis nobis serviciis de eundo ad excercitu͞ n͞im ꝑ un͞a Dietam samptibus ꝑprus et

---

249 J. Lloyd.—Caerwys MS.

250 In the extent of the commot of Twrcelyn, taken 26th of Edward III Nantmawr is there mentioned as a township, in the holding of different persons. "Edmund de Daunage, Knight, holds two parts, for the term of his life, under a grant from the Lord Prince that *now* is; and Thomas de Bodenham, and Alice his wife, hold the third part, as the dowry of the said Alice." Howel ab Llewelyn's part was free, &c. "The heir of the domicile of Davydd ab Ewryd was Einion ab Adda (who was a prisoner in the castle of Pontefract) all paying rent or acknowledgement to Edmund and Thomas and Alice; but the tenants owing suit and service at the Lord Prince's mill, called Melin Bryn y Gwydd, grinding there, &c. owing suit at the two great tourns of the prince's lieutenant", &c.

sectã ad cũr ñiam ville p3dicte faciend de tribus septimanis in trẽs septimanas pũt hactenus fieri con-
suerit. Ita quod post mortem ejesdem Willi villa pr̃dicta cũ ptm ad nos & heredes nr̃os integre rever-
tatur. In cujus, &c. T. R̃. apud Northampton quarto die Martii. ⱳ ñie de private Sigillo.

"This volume of the Sebright Collection has many records relating to Gryffydd, the last lord of
the unfortunate Dinas Brân family, which Mr. Llwyd has transcribed into one of his own valuable
books; and commenting upon their curious deeds, grants, &c. "containing many particulars very little
known at present,—it is evident however, he says, that the children of Griffith, Arglwydd Maelor, were
not in a state of infancy at the time of their father's decease; though every historian that mentions
them, asserts it; and what is still more improbable, they represent the two eldest as mere infants, when
they were disinherited and destroyed by their guardians, many years after; whereas we find here, that
all the four were witnesses to the settlements their father made on their mother; and in the latter end
of the year 1270, the year in which Gryffydd died, we find the four joining in the renewal and confirmation of their father's settlement, and in making considerable additions to it, which could not be the
acts of infants.—*J. Lloyd*". The above document is signed by Mr. Lloyd, a name that gives authority
and weight to his opinion on any subject connected with "Cymru and Cymraeg.

Edward I by erecting Rhosvair "into a gild mercatory", &c. evinced a regard for departed
grandeur; and a respect for a royal palace and court was still maintained by the kings of England, his
successors, who continued it a seat of judicature, for the hundred of Menai. The crown had its steward
for this district, with a salary of £10 annually, paid by the Governor of Caernarvon Castle,[251] and
Henry VII (thereby proving himself worthy a Tudor name) granted to this seat of fallen majesty, the
honour of sending a member to the British parliament, and Richard ab Rhydderch (the subject of the
riddle in p.288-89) was the first who represented this place, in the 3rd of Henry VIII. Towards the latter end of that reign, Newborough consisted of ninety-three houses, thirteen gardens, one orchard,
twelve crofts, and sixty small pieces of ground, called Erwau, enclosed for the use of the houses. "[252]

PENMON, OR GLANACH.—On the eastern part of Mona, and in the hundred of Tindaethwy,
is situated Penmôn, memorable for having been a priory of Black Canons of the order of St. Augustine.
This parish, together with Llanvaes, is a perpetual curacy, under the patronage of Sir Richard Bulkeley, Bart. The Rev. John Williams is the incumbent. The living has been endowed with £400 private
benefaction, £800 Queen Anne's bounty, and £600 parliamentary grant. Penmôn, as its name implies,
is at the extremity of Mona, distant from Beaumaris four miles, on a promontory boldly projecting into
the Irish sea. This parish is not of very great extent, but comprises nearly equal portions of arable and
pasture land, in a tolerable state of cultivation. The houses do not form any village, but are widely scattered over the parish. The resident population in 1821 was 290, and 240 in 1831. The average annual
expenditure for the support of the poor, amounts to £92 12s. 0d. The church is dedicated to St.
Seiriol, and called from him, "Capel Seiriol". He was son to Owen Danwyn. The day of celebration,

---

251 Sebright Papers.
252 Ibid.

called the wakes, is on February 15. This was formerly the conventual church, belonging to the ancient priory, founded here in 540, and was originally a spacious cruciform structure, in the Norman style of architecture, with a square tower in the centre; but the nave and choir are all that remain of the ancient building: the former is in a state of great dilapidation; and the latter, which is appropriately fitted up, for the performance of divine service, is embellished with some of the richest details of the Norman style. Within is a small monument to the memory of Sir Thomas Wilford of Kent, whose daughter married Sir Richard Bulkeley;—he died in 1645. The principal remains of this ancient establishment, besides the church, the refectory, and part of the prior's house, is the dove cote, with its cupola, shingle-roof, massive pillars, semicircular arches, with zig-zag mouldings, and is unique as a fine specimen of the architecture of those days, being in a high state of preservation. This, together with Seiriol's well, close by, are objects worthy the antiquary's attention. On the northern side, is a valuable quarry of millstones, of the grit kind, and also a ridge of limestone, of an excellent quality, which is carried in great quantities to all the adjacent counties; and the parish abounds with beautiful grey coloured marble, susceptible of a high polish. The quarries, which are very extensive, have been worked for a considerable period, with great success. On the estate of Trôs yr Avon, there is a copious spring, the waters of which hold in solution a sulphate of lime, and contain a considerable portion of fixed air. It is much resorted to, and held in high estimation for its efficacy in chronic diseases. In the Chronicles of the Abbey of Basingwerk, recording the deaths of princes and noblemen, there is the annexed entry:—"Maelgwyn, Brenin y Bryttanied, sydd yn gorwedd yn Ynys Seiriol, a wnaeth priordû in Penmôn, a chlaswrdû Caer Gybi." The priory, he built on the shore, about the year 540, and dedicated it to St. Mary, which afterwards was so liberally endowed by Llewelyn the Great, that he was supposed by Tanner to have been the founder. About a mile from the shore is Ynys Lenach, now known among the English as Priestholme, and among the Cambro-Britons as "Ynys Seiriol", from one Sirolius, as Leland says, a hermit, who lived here, in the sixth century. It is also mentioned in the Sebright Papers, under the appellation of "Insula Glanaugh", and the priory goes under both names. Perhaps this insulated spot, might have been the principal residence of the religious, and probably part of the community might reside on the main land, to look after their property, while the others were engaged in acts of devotion. The only remains of their residence, are a square tower, serving as a land-mark; the foundation of several similar buildings destroyed by the violence of the northern gales, to which the Island is particularly exposed, and a hut, inhabited by a man who attends a signal staff, erected here, in 1826, in connexion with Llandudno, on the east, and Llanelian, on the west, and forming a link in the telegraphic communication between Liverpool and Holyhead. The abundance of bones found every where in the ground, are strong proofs of the reputed sanctity of Ynys Seiriol, and that persons were brought here to be buried. The first recluses of the Island, according to Giraldus, were hermits, of whom he tells a superstitious tale. "Whenever they disagreed, they were plagued with swarms of mice, which quitted them as soon as they laid aside their animosity." Mr. Lloyd in his MSS has given a recital of the grants made to their successors, the black monks of this priory, by Prince Llewelyn and his brother Davydd, as well as the confirmation of them by Edward I by which it appears that "Côr Penmôn", alias "Côr Seiriol", with its appurtenances, was granted and confirmed to the prior and canons of this Island, by Edward I in the 17th of his reign.

Sebright Collection, vol.4, a thick 4to. bound in calf, containing Grants, Charters, Inspeximus;—all in latin. In the beginning are some Grants, &c. concerning Scotland.—*J. Lloyd.*

"Page 215, Cart 23 E. I, No. 17. P. Canonicis de Insula Glannauch. R̃. Archiepis sp salm̃. Inspeximus cartam quam L. quondam Princeps North Waħ fecit Canonicis de Insula Glannauch in hec verba Universis Xti fidelibus, &c. L. Princeps North Waħ saltm̃ in dnõ vestre duximus notificare univẽrsitati nos, &c. contulisse totam Villam de Bagiñg libere &c. quiete &c. diħiis fratribus nr̃is canicis de Insula de Glannach, &c.—His Testibus Patre Abraham de Aberchond mag̃ro Ada de sca trinitate mag̃ro instructo mag̃ro Ric̃o widone canonico de Enli Ada clico filio Oweyn, Ennio fil Walchmai Ennio Bichane Grono filio kenõr et multis alliis actum ap̃d Kaerinarvan anno Gr̃e 1221 idis Octobris. Inspeximus etiam cartam confirmationis quam David filius þedicti principis fecit priori et canonicis de predicta Insula in hec verba Uniṽsis Xti fidelib⁹ saltm̃ in Dn̄o novit univrsitas vr̃a nos. Donacoem L. þris nr̃i sup tota villa de Bag̃, &c. Priori et canonicis de Insula Glannauc concessisse et þsenti carta nra confirmasse, &c. His testibus Mared fil Richard Ririd fil Kadugaun L. filio Griffed Karuet filio Tudor, Lewelino filio Richardi Lewelino filio Mered, David filio Gwranu Ennio notario nostro et multis alliis actum apud Insulam Glanauc anno Gr̃e 1299 in die Cathedre sc̃i petri valeat universitas vra sẽp in dnõ. Omnibus S̃te matris Ecc̃ie filiis has littras visuris vel andituris Lewelinus Princeps de Aberfrau dñs Snaudon salt̃em in dnõ novet univ̄sitas vr̃a nos, &c. Confirmasse Priori et Canonicis de Insula Glanauc deo et b̃e Marie ibidem servientibus totam Abbadaeth de Penmôn cum omnibus þt̃in suis, &c. Usq ad Villam que vocatur Trefakastell, &c. Dat apud Rosver 4to. Idus April ano Gr̃e 1237, &c. Ibidem. Inspeximus etiam Cartam Confirmat̃ois quam Lewelinus fil Griffini fecit þrdictis Priori et Canonicis in hec verba Univr̃sis X̃t fidelibus, &c. saltm̃ in dnõ. Novet univr̃sit⁹ vr̃a nos divine pietiatis intuitu donatiem̃ et confirmatim̃ dnõr̃u L. Principis et David antecessorum nrõru sup̃ totam Abbadaeth de Penmôn cum omnibus þt̃in suis et tota Villa de Cremlin, &c. Priori et Canonicis de Insula Glanauc dedisse et þsenti carta confirmasse, &c. His testibus David fil Griffini, Tudor fil Madauc Joret iii Grugnnan senescaħ ñris Gruffudo fil Gugaun ſre Adda Lippa Madauc fil Bledin Madoco clico ñro David Coch assistentibus fratribus minoribus Gervasio Mared et David actum apud Lammaes anno Gr̃e 1247 die Eph̃ie His testibus edm̃o fr̃e ñro Johanno de Warrena com̃ Surr Heñr de Lacy comite line, &c. Dat per manu nrm̃ apud Lammays 4to die Maii anno Regni ni. 23.

It appears from the above transcript, that these charters are very much abbreviated. They belong to Priestholme Isle. The first of them is of Prince Llewelyn ab Iorwerth, dated at Kaernarvon, in 1221, which contradicts the common erroneous opinion, that Edward I imposed that name upon the town. Insula Glanauch, is Priestholme.—*J. Lloyd.*" p.472, ib. Pat 18, E. III. p.1, M. 9. "Priore et Conventu de Angleseye." "This probably refers also to Penmon Priory, in Anglesea. It recites that the king empowered them to hold 20 librates of land, besides what they held of the king in capite "Tam de feodo sue þ prio qm̃ alieno exceptis terris & redditibus que nõb tenentur in capite adquirere possint heñd & teneñd sibi & successoribus", &c. He further gives licence "Willo de Arderne Capellan & Semiano capellano quod ep̃i tria messuagia unam loftum quinquaginta acras cum libertate unius falde & decem solidatas redditus cum þt̃in in Bodesham Stowe Queye ffulburne & parva Wilburham que de *nobis* non *tenen-*

tur", &c. These parcels seem to constitute "20 librates" above-mentioned, and exclusive of the "decem solidatas" above cited; they were valued at twenty four shillings, &c. By an inquisition, taken by "Warinum de Basingbourne escatorem nr̄m in Com̄ Can̄tebr. So I guess that these lands lay in Cambridgeshire."

P. 885, ib. P. 3, H, 6. Pro John Tiptoffte. "This patent appoints the above John Tiptoffte, to be governor and chief seneschall of all the castles, manours, dominions, and possessions in the principality, and marches of Wales, which belonged to Edmund Mortimer, Earl of March, lately deceased, to hold the same during the minority of Richard, Duke of York, heir to the said earl." Mr. Lloyd again remarks upon the grants preceding this one to Tiptoffte, that he could not tell "where the lands are". But it may be observed that a librate here differs in quantity, and the acre in value, from what is mentioned in p. 88 of this book. He supposed "that a librate of land was a pounds worth of land, let the quantity be what it would;—the word indeed imports as much. This ample grant shews that this priory was a place of note and great dignity." Among[253] the Plâs Gwyn MSS is preserved the grant of a free pardon to Robert ab John, with a fragment of the seal of the priory, bearing the upper part of the virgin and child, with the legend "PENMONA ✠ SIG". The prior was one of the three spiritual lords of Mona. At the dissolution, the revenues were valued at £47 15*s*. 3*d*. The site, with the park of Penmôn, and other appurtenances, was granted by Queen Elizabeth to John More. The fretum, which separates the Island from the mainland, is about half a mile across. The Island itself is about a mile long, lofty, and bounded by precipices, except on the side opposite Penmôn, and even there the ascent is very steep. Besides the man at the station, it is now inhabited only by a few sheep and rabbits, sea fowls, &c. and in summer the whole place swarms with birds of passage; puffins resort thither in April, in great flocks, leaving it in August, or the beginning of September. Query—If Glanauch did not take its name from Glanaugh, the father of Helig. This Helig had three sons, who were "holy men; Pado and Gwyn lye in the churche of Dwygyvylcheu, i.e. in the little chapel at the West end of it, and another son who did serve God, lieth in Llanvrothen church. Seiriol, brother of Helig, was termed the "holy priest", and was the head of the religious house in Priestholme, which house was called "Priestholme", &c. From Seiriol, it is called Ynys Seiriol. "This Seiriol had also a hermitage on Penmaenmawr, and he had a chapel there, where he did bestowe much of his time in prayer; the place being then an uncouth desert, steep rocks, and inaccessible owing to their steepness, and the woods so thick, that if a man entered therein, he could see neither sky, nor firmament. From Priestholme to Penmaenmawr, did Seiriol cause a pavement to be made, whereupon he might walk dry from his church at Priestholme to hys chapel at Penmaenmawr, which pavement may at this day be discerned, when the sea is clear, if a man liste to go in a boate to see it; sythence thys great and lamentable inundation of Cantrev Gwaelod; the way and passage being stopt in this strait, in regard the sea was come in and did beat upon the rocks of Penmaenmawr, this holy man Seiriol, like a good hermit, did cause a way to be broken and cut through the main rock, which is the only passage that is to pass that strait. This way leadeth from Dwygyvylchau to Llanvair

---

253 Caerwys MS.

Vechen, and is the king's highway from Conway to Beaumaris, Bangor, and Caernarvon, and the only passage that the king's post hath to ride to and from Ireland."[254]

Penmôn Park originally belonged to the priory, but is now part of the Barren Hill property; it was surrounded by a wall, and stocked with deer, by the late Lord Bulkeley's father. From Cathrall not mentioning a carved pillar, which stood in this park when Mr. Lloyd visited Ynys Seiriol and Penmôn, I fear that it has been demolished. "It stood (he writes), twelve feet high, two feet and two inches broad at the bottom, and ten inches thick; the base is let into another stone; the top is round, encircled in raised work, in the form of a Greek cross; beneath, about the middle of the shaft, is another in the form of St. Andrews; on the middle and side of the column, are represented some animals; the rest is covered with beautiful fretwork, like what may be seen on another pillar, called 'Maen y Cwynvan', in the parish of Whitford, Flintshire".[255] Situated on the coast, about a mile from Penmôn, towards Llanvaes, is "Castell Aberllienawg", a small square fort, with a little round tower, at each corner; in the middle stood a square one a fosse surrounds the whole. A hollow way is carried quite to the shore; at the extremity is a large mound of earth, designed to cover the landing, &c.[256] This castle was founded by Hugh Gôch de Montgomery (the Red Earl of Salop) and Hugh Vrâs, the Earl of Chester, "whoe came to the Isle of Môn,[257] with a huge armye, in 1099, and there dyd build a castell of Aberllenawg, when Gryffydd and Cadwgan dyd go to Môn, thinking to defend the Isle, and sente for succour to Ireland, but they received verie small; then the treason appeared, for Owen ab Edwyn, whoe was the Prince Gryffydd ab Conan's chieffe councellor, and his father-in-law, was the chieffe caller of these strangers into Wales, whoe openlie wente with all hys power to meet and to lead them to Anglesey, whiche thinge, when the princes perceived, they sailed to Irelande, mistrustinge the treason of theire own people, and at the verie same tyme, Magnus, the sonne of Harold, came with a greate navie of shippes towards Englande, mindinge to laie faster holde upon that kingdome, than hys father had done; and beinge driven by chance to Anglesey, would have landed there, but the Erles kept hym from the land, and there Magnus with an arrow, stroke the Erle of Salop in the face, and hee dyed thereof, and sodenlye either parte forsooke the Isle (p. 90) and the Englishmen returned to Englande, and lefte Owen ab Edwyn Tegengl, prince in the Island, who had allured them thither." This fort was garrisoned so lately as the time of Charles I when it was kept for the parliament, by Sir Thomas Cheadle, and in 1645, Colonel John Robinson of Monachdy, took it from him. The Robinsons of this Island, and of Gwersyllt Park, in Denbighshire, were always a very loyal race. John Robinson, who inherited Gwersyllt and Monachdy, was eldest son to Nicolas Robinson, Bishop of Bangor, and was Sheriff for Mona, in 1632 (having served for Denbighshire the year previous). His estates in 1660, were worth annually £800. This gentleman was an active partisan on the side of the unfortunate Charles I and commanded a company in the battle of Rowton Heath, near Chester. After the commonwealth's army gained the vic-

254 "Hanes Helig ab Glanawg".—*Caerwys MSS*. The whole of this curious history, is now published in the Cambrian Quarterly.

255 J. Lloyd.—Caerwys MS.

256 Pennant p.248.

257 Welsh Chronicles p.156.

tory, he retreated to his own home. A party of soldiers was dispatched to take him; when they arrived at Gwersyllt, Colonel Robinson having no means of escaping (the place being surrounded by his enemies), disguised himself as one of the labourers who were then working in front of the house; they were strictly questioned, but true to their master, did not betray him. On the party retiring, they were heard to express their disappointment, declaring if he had been found, they would have hanged him on the old oak, before his own door, which tree is still in a state of vegetation, and a very picturesque object. Colonel Robinson escaped to the continent, and did not return till after the restoration. He died in 1680, aged 65, and is buried in Gresford church, where there is a handsome monument erected to his memory, having the royal oak medal upon it. Gwersyllt being seized by the parliament, was bestowed upon one of Oliver's officers, who rebuilt the house and afterwards gave it up to Colonel Robinson, on his paying a compensation. In 1737, it was sold by act of parliament for the benefit of Mr. William Robinson's creditors (who was accidentally drowned, as related in p.127). In 1761, Mr. Gwion Lloyd of Hendwr, purchased it from Mr. Barton, and left it to his sisters, Mary and Catherine, who disposed of it in 1775, to Mr. Humberstone Cawley of Upper Gwersyllt, a descendant of the Robinsons. Both places, are since, become by purchase, the property of Mr. Williams (second son to the patriotic Mr. Williams of Tregarnedd, in Mona) by whose liberality and correct taste, Gwersyllt forms a distinguished feature in the Gresford neighbourhood.

PENMYNYDD is in the hundred of Tindaethwy, and a prebend in the cathedral church of Bangor, in the Bishop's gift, valued at £8 13s. 4d. The prebendary is the Rev. Henry Majendie,[258] who presents to the perpetual curacy of Penmynydd, which was endowed with £400 Queen Anne's bounty, and the Rev. D. Hughes is the curate. The church, a very ancient structure, situated an an eminence, is said to be built about the year 630, and dedicated to Gredival ab Ithel Hael (or the generous) of Armorica, a saint who lived at the close of the fifth century, and first presided over the College of Tŷ Gwyn (p.262) His day is celebrated on the 30th of November. This parish is distant from Beaumaris, six miles and contains 3,840 acres of arable and pasture land, which, with the exception only of a very small portion, is enclosed and cultivated. There is a fair on Easter Monday, principally for hiring servants. The resident population in 1821 was 337, and 377 in 1831. Six alms-houses, which had been previously founded in this parish, were endowed in 1623 by Lewis Owen (one of the Penmynydd Owens, residing at Twickenham) with the tithes of the parish of Eglwys Rhos, for the better support of the ten poor alms people. These tithes have long been held by the family of Mostyn, who have paid an annual sum for the support of the almshouses, amounting to £60 per annum; there are also other bequests of land and money, for the poor. The average annual expenditure for their support, is about £208 13s. 0d. In the church is a very superb altar tomb, without arms or inscription, supporting the effigies of two recumbent figures, one, a warrior, in complete armour, with a helmet of a conical form; and the other a female, in flowing robes, and a square hood; the heads rest upon angels, and the feet upon lions. This

---

258 This gentleman reads and comprehends the mountain Greek better than any Anglo-Cymro known to the writer of this history, yet he conscientiously resigned a valuable living, because he was deficient in the idiom of the country, and therefore justly considered himself incompetent to administer consolation to a dying man.

was removed hither from Llanvaes priory, and said to have been erected to the memory of some of the Tudor family, as that was the place of their interment,—

" De'wn i Benmynydd uvydd ovwy,
" Dinas dan solas, a Din Sylwy."

This is, to the Cambro-Briton, a sort of hallowed ground. Plas Penmynydd, the ancient residence of the Tudors, in this parish,—the remains—a gateway, and the chimneypiece in the hall, having on it their arms and initials, engraven, will be always regarded by the antiquary as sacred, while a fragment remains, and also by the protestant, and the freeborn sons of Great Britain, be their creed what it may, for—

"Till heaven in blissful healing hour,
" Our sires restor'd to London throne, &c."

the History of England is only a recital of civil wars, reciprocal inroads, and injuries by rival kings, and turbulent barons; the sword being the chief arbitrator of rights, in those dreadful days of anarchy, and confusion. Besides these causes of natural decay, there was a total inattention to their naval power, owing to the want of finances; the wealth having gradually centred among a set of lazy, disreputable monks, who were the worms feeding at the root of the constitution, destroying the vital power of the state. It was a descendant of this house that Bacon eulogised as "England's best son, and greatest of sovereigns", from whose wise policy may be traced the elements of those enlightened institutions that have made England the freest of nations, and the bulwark of the world's freedom,

" I Harry[259] lân hir lawenydd,
"Yr hwn, a rhoes ninnau yn rhydd."

claiming the crown under the ancient banner of his country,[260] wearing its cognizance, and calling his eldest born, "Arthur", as an honourable testimony of respect to his great predecessor (who governed these realms, in the sixth century), that did credit to Henry's feelings as a king, and a Briton.[261] It is to a princess of the Tudor race, England owes her commerce, her dominion of the seas, Elizabeth "shivered the sword of Spain, and paralized the power of Roman idolatry". This distinguished race claim descent from Llewelyn's chief councellor, and leader of his armies, "whoe gained to hymself a notable coat armour, commemorating a victory obtained by hym, when Ranulph, Earl of Chester, invaded the marches of Wales, he killing with his own hand, three of his chief captains, whose heads the prince bade hym wear in his armes. Hys posteritie have ever since continued "to be greate men in Wales".[262]

---

259 So sang the bard to Henry VII and in vol.4, Cambrian Quarterly, p.157, may be seen a curious prophecy concerning Henry VII which throws some light upon Walpole's historic doubts. This was written by a contemporary bard of Henry's time, and it has been faithfully translated by Mr. Justice Bosanquet.

260 The liveries of this House were green and white, and Henry VII bore in the battle of Bosworth, the cognizance of uther, and his son Arthur, upon those colours, i.e. the red dragon, still identified in the rouge dragon of the College of Arms.

261 The nurses to Henry the Seventh's children, were Welshwomen. This I learnt from the Salusbury Pedigree, and Hengwrt MSS confirmed by Ellis's Letters, in one of which allusion is made to Henry VIII allowing an annuity of £20 a year, to "Philip ab Howel and Jane his wiffe, sometyme our norrice". p.171

262 Wynnstay MS.

Sir Tudor ab Ednyved and his grandson, Gronw ab Heylyn, were chief commissioners, appointed by the last Prince Llewelyn, to settle the peace between him and Edward I in 1281. This Grono was one of the most aggrieved of any of Llewelyn's subjects, and he drew up his complaints in five items, enumerating unheard of acts of oppression, concluding in these pithy and comprehensive words after saying he could get no justice, "but labour and expences of fifty-four marks, and more; and for thatt he durst nott in hys own person go to court, he sente letters,—one to the kinge, another to hys brother, Llewelyn (then being at court), to signifie to the kinge, that he shoulde loose all the favour of the countrie, if he kepte noe promise with them, and soe itt came to pass, because the men of Rhôs and Englefield, could get no justice, the kinge neglecting those, lost the whole countrie."[263] Princes may be thus taught a lesson, not to irritate the feelings of a subdued people, by forcing upon them new laws and customs. It was this attempt, that caused Mredydd, son of Grono, to kill William de Sutton, as related in my account of Penrhôs.

Vol. 5, p.127, Sebright Collection, contains an inquisition, taken at Caernarvon, in behalf of another branch of this potent family. "Escheaƭ capta apud Kaerñ com̃ dño W. de Grandisino & R. de Standone die lune ₶xĩa post festũ sti Barnabe Apƚi año regni Regis Edwardi 17mo. ₶ br̃e dñi Regis inter Pryorem de Bedkellard petentem & Tuderũ Vachan & Griffinũ frem̃ ejus tenentes de quibusdam Terris & Tenementis in Peñant Gwernogon per hos subscriptos Griffinũ Vachan", &c. The jury consisted of nineteen persons, and the cause was between Philip, Prior of Beddgelert, and the two brothers, Tudor and Gryffydd Vân, concerning these lands, that were given to the prior and convent, by Davydd ab Llewelyn, formerly Prince of Wales, to which these brothers laid claim, after the death of their father, Tudur ab Madoc. The jury admitted their claim, and gave their verdict against the prior and convent. It may be surmised, that this prince, upon some pretence or another, had wrongfully dispossessed their father of these lands, and bestowed them on the convent, by way of atonement.[264] When the extent of the comot of Tindaethwy was taken, at Beaumaris, the 26th of Edward III a moiety of Penmynydd was found in the hands of the celebrated self-knighted Sir Tudor ab Grono, "who renders nothing thereout annually, to the Lord Prince, excepting suit at the county court only. He has a moiety of the mill of Trevraint, and is to accompany the Lord Prince, in his wars, as appears above, in the township of "Trev Castell", and his bond servants shall present themselves before the sheriff, at his two great tourns, annually; and the other moiety of Penmynydd, is in the possession of the Abbot of Conwy, and of convents in that place, who neither pay any rent, nor do any service to the Lord Prince." In the Hengwrt pedigree, he is called, "Sir Tudyr a laddodd y drygae, ag a vu benniaeth holl Wynedd". He was very popular among his countrymen, being extremely wealthy, having married "un o'r dair aires"; he was much given to hospitality, and on account of the above feat, killing the drygae, he assumed to himself, says Powel (confirmed by the Salusbury Pedigree), the honour of knighthood, which Edward I allowed. Sir Tudor died in 1367. I find by the Welsh Chronicles and Mostyn MSS that his sons sided with Owen Glyndwr. Rhŷs, the third son, "a ddihenyddwyd (beheaded) y'Nghaerllëon

263 Welsh Chronicles p.137.
264 J. Lloyd.—Caerwys MS.

am sevyll gyda Owain Glyndwr", and at the same time part of their immense possessions, became for-feited; for by the law of Gavel Kind, every one had a holding. Gryffydd, the second son, was exempted by Henry IV in his pardon published for "paste offences";[265] and Meredydd the eldest son of Sir Tudor, by his second wife (Arglwyddes Mowddwy, the Lady of Mowddwy) was reduced to shelter himself as a scutiger to the Bishop of Bangor (this place being a sort of sanctuary), whence he was roused to avenge a tyrannous act, committed by William de Sutton, whom he murdered, as will be hereafter related. In this deed originated the old proverb, "haws dadleu evo Sais yn varw, na Sais yn vyw". Meredydd fled; his son, Sir Owen Tudor,[266] "the most accomplished knight of the court" (who married the Queen Dowager of England), must have recovered some part of his paternal property, for when Sir Rowland Velville alias Brittain, married Agnes, the daughter of Sir William Griffith of Pen-rhyn, this moiety of Penmynydd, consisting of 486 acres, was bestowed by his father Henry VII upon him, besides lands in Pentraeth and Beaumaris.

Vol.5, Sebright Collection, contained a grant to Sir Owen Tudor, from his stepson, Henry VI. "Page II, Prims pars, Pat. de Aº H.VI. 38 M. 6, Pro Oweno Tudyr. This, I believe, is in the 2nd tom̃ of the Foedera, p.439, constituting Owen Tudor, ranger of the parks of Moylewoke, Caresnodoke, Kyl-ford, Bghm̃, and Posciy, in dnio nr̃o de Dynby in North Watt."[267] And in the Hengwrt MS recording the names of Sir Owen Tudor's children, by Queen Catherine, is the following curious observation: "Edmund mynach yn St. Edmundsbury, a hwn a gynhedlwyd cyn priodas ei dad, Sir Owen, ai vam, y Vrenhines Catrin."[268] The estate of Penmynydd was annexed to Berain, by the marriage of Tudor ab Robert, in 1532, with Sian Bryttain, the eldest daughter and heiress of Sir Rowland Velville, alias Bryt-tain. Their only child, Catrin y Berain (of marrying celebrity) added it to the great possessions of Lleweny, by her union with John Salusbury, after whose death, she bestowed her hand on Sir Richard Clough, a merchant, and partner to the wealthy Sir Thomas Gresham of London. Tradition says, that when Catrin was following her husband's remains to the grave, according to the fashion of the times, she was supported by Sir Richard Clough, and in returning from church, by Morris Wynne (brother to Sir John Wynne of Gwydyr) who took the earliest opportunity (as he thought) of whispering to her his wish of being her second, she refused him with great civility, informing him that she had accepted the proposals of Sir Richard Clough, in her way to church, but assured him (and she kept her promise) that in case she performed the same sad duty (which she was then about) to the knight, he might de-pend upon being her third. Mr. Thellwall of Plâs-y-ward, became her fourth husband, Sir R. Clough, was her favourite; he dying at Antwerp, of the plague, his body was burnt, and part of the ashes pre-served, in a gold box, suspended to a chain, worn by Catrin y Berain to the day of her death, which happened on the first of September, 1591. The deeds belonging to this property, containing names of places and tenants, together with the marriage settlements and wills, are now in the possession of Lord

265 Caerwys MS.

266 The reader will see a very correct account of this brave but unfortunate man, in Pennant, p.257, and Cathrall, p.73.

267 J. Lloyd.—Caerwys MS.

268 Edmund, a monk of St. Edmundsbury, and this son, was born before the marriage of his father, Sir Owen, and his mother, Queen Catherine.

Combermere, the descendant of the last Sir Harry Salusbury, Part. of Lleweney. When a survey was made of these estates, in 1686, they let for £204 annually. A branch of the Tudors assumed the name of Owen, from Owen ab Tudor Vychan of Penmynydd, "yr hwn Tudor Vychan[269] oedd wirion, ni chavodd ev ddim o dir ei dad, ond tir ei mam, etiveddes Grono Vychan ab Tudor y gadd." The parents of this unfortunate imbecile, were cousins,—their fathers being brothers. Richard Owen, a lawyer of Gray's Inn, was Sheriff for Mona, in 1657; his daughter and heiress, Margaret, married Coningsby Williams of Glân-y-gors, in this Island, who possessed the ancient residence of the Tudors, during his life; it was afterwards sold to Lord Bulkeley, and it is now the property of Sir Richard Williams Bulkeley, the tenth baronet of the name of Williams of Caerau, Nant, and Friars. In p.65 of this history, and in the notes to that page there is a further account given of Sir Rowland Velville, who was portioned by King Henry VII with what remained of his share of the Penmynydd estate; and I here take leave to transcribe out of the Velville Papers, the following extracts from the marriage settlements of Robert Vychan of Berain, and Jane, eldest daughter and heir of Sir Rowland Velville, alias "Bryttayne", partly latin and partly English. It was "drawne on the 6th of June, 23rd of Henry VIII. Sir Rowland Velvelle, Knight, Constable of Beaumaris Castel, on the one part, and Robert Vychan ab Tudor ab Ievan, gentilhomm, on tother part. "Sir Rowland Velvell, Constable of the Castell of Beaumaris, whoe by the Grace of God, gives and consents, that hee Robert Vychan, &c. shall have and take to wyff, Jane Velvell, daughter to the said Sir Roland, by the ffeste of Trinitye; he settling halfe hys lands within the County of Denbigh, upon the saide Jane; and Sir Roland settled all "hys, and the lands of Agnes, hys wiffe", &c. on the heirs of this marriage. In p.194, will be seen the great estates which Catrin y Berain, carried with her to the Lleweny family, she being the only child of these, Robert and Jane.

DAME AGNES VELVELL'S WILL.

" In the name of God, Amen, the 16th day of December, the year of our Lord, 1542. I Agnes Velivel, widowe, hoole of my mynde and of perfect memory, make thys my laste wyll and testament, in fforme following;—Fyrste I bequeathe my soule to Almighte God, and my bodye to be buried in the Chappell of the Blessed Virgine Mary of Beaumares, where my husbande was buryed. Item, I bequeathe to the repariacyon and buyldynge of the saide chappelle iiiil. sterlinge. Item, I bequeathe to a preste of good conversations, to sings ffor the helthe of my husbande's soul and myne, ffor one woole yere, iiiil. Item, to Alice Gryffydd, daughter to Edmund Gryffydd, xxiii kyne, ffourty shepe, one bedde, wherin the said Alice slepeth, with all that belongethe thereto: alsoe to the said Alice, my greateste ring of golde, one onely of golde, one cappe of velvet, one saltseller of sylver, one cuppe of sylver, a gowne of iii yardes of cloth, the price of every yarde, vs. fyve platters, syxe poringers, vi saucers of pewter, one pott of brasse, and a pan, one horse and a mare, one table cloth, and a carpet for a table, one napkyn, and iiii small napkyns, one cofer wheryn myn apparell dothe lye, syx sylver spones, and a pare of bedes of jet, I bequeathe to the said Alice, one close, called Cay Hyde, sterwyne "Cae beth Seiriol ucha", durynge the terme of her lyfe, and affter the terme of or desese of Alice, the said close to returne to my executors; alsoe I bequeathe to her a tenement, called Cevn Côch, in the whyche

269 Salusbury Pedigree, p.62. Hengwrt MS, p.600.

Richard Gôch ap Thomas dwelleth durynge my takinge, in the saide tenement, as dothe appere in writynge. Item, I bequeathe to John Lee, the house whereyn hee dwelleth, duringe the time of hys natural lyfe, frelye and without any payment. I ordeyne and mak my two daughters, thatt ys to saye, Gras Velivell and Jane Velivell, true and lawfull executors, to the wyche two, my daughters, I give and bequeathe all my landes and tenement, as well withyn the libertyes of the towne of Bewmarys as with-outte the libertyes, within the Countie of Anglesey, and elswher. I alsoe bequeathe to them all my goodes, moveableand unmoveable, whersoever they may be found, they my seyde doughters to give for the helthe of my sowle, as to theym shall be thoutt expediente, and to the pleasure of God. Item, I ordene, make, and constitute Sir Richarde Bulkeley, Knight, Rowlande Griffith, Esquer, and Thomas Grono Preste, super—, and overseere of my sayde executores. Item, I will and bequeathe, ordayne and make and constitute Sir Richard Bulkeley, Rowland Griffith, and Thomas Grono Preste, true and lawful tutors of my daughter Grace Velwell, the one of my executrixes, and iff the saide Grace do nothinge in disposynge the landes, tenements or goodes afforesayde to her bequestis, with-out the councill, advysement and ayde of the saide tutors, and thys I knowledge and declare to be my laste will and testament, before and in the plesure of John Lee, Thomas Grono Prest, Alice Griffth.

Proved at Bangor, 15th December, 1543. "

PENRHOS LLUGWY is situated on the Irish sea, five miles eastward, from Llannerchymedd, and in the extent taken of Twrcelyn, 26th of Edward III, it ranked as a township within that comot, containing "fifteen gaval, owing suit at the Lord Prince's mill of Melin Gwydded, and pay relief of 5s. if they have wherewith so to do, and an amober of 2s. and do the work of the barns and stables belong-ing to the manor-house of Penrhôs, i.e. the walls and the roofs of the same; and are to carry timber, within the County of Anglesey, for the same; and they do the work of the lord's mill of Dulas, like the "Gwyr Gwaith" of Cemmaes; and they are to provide carriages, for the Lord of Penrhôs, as far as Cemmaes, and Llanvaes, with man and horse, to be taken by the day, for 5d. and no more. And all these tenants, as well free as natives of this comot, pay for every ale brewery, 6d. and six flaggons of ale to the Rhaglaw (or the lord) of the comot for the time being, and all the free tenants of this comot shall pay annually for the repairs of the aforesaid manor house." "This township is of a three-fold nature, i.e. there are therein, certain persons, called 'Gwyr Mael', 'Gwyr Gwaith', and 'Gwyr-tîr-y-Borth', and which township of Penrhôs, John de Kennesholne holds for the term of his life, from the king, by a grant from the present lord, King Edward III. The tenants of the gavel of Einion ab Adda, are Einion Gôch, and Ievan ab Adda, and they pay for it, by quarterly payments, an annual rent of 15s. 5d." &c. This Einion ab Adda, when a prisoner in Pontefract Castle, had the celebrated old copy of the Laws of Howel Ddâ, given to him by the governor or constable, which MS is now in the Hengwrt Collection.

Page 415 of Sebright Collection, contains a "Pat. Pro Villanis manerii R. de Penrhôs". This is di-rected to John Grey, Justiciary of North Wales, ordering him to enquire into the truth of the petition of the inhabitants of Penrhôs, in Mona (cum) "invenissit quod omnes terre et Tẽr que Villani, nr̃i tenent in Penros in cõm p̃rdicto tempore dñi E. quondam Regis Añgl p̃ris nr̃i post conquest suum terr̃e Waᵗᵗ extendebatur ad quadraginta et octo l̃ibr̃ novem solidor unum Deñar unum obolum & unum quad-rantem & quod error fuit tuuc in eadem extenta usque ad sum̃am 21 libr̃ 7 solidõr et 1 oboli p̃ut ᶣ ex-aminacõem vice comitum Ballioru͠m & aliorum ministrorum nrorum p̃ciam illarum et ᶣ examinãcoem memorandorum Willi de Sutton dudum justic þc̃ium pr̃dictorum in Cameraria þrdicta inventorum", &c. It further appears that this overcharge was never paid, and to prevent its being demanded in future, this King Edward II absolves them entirely from it. It is dated at Westminster, 5th July."—No year specified. This William de Sutton, quondam justiciary, was murdered by the contrivance of Meredydd ab Grono of Penmynydd; hence this proverb, "Haws dadleu a Sais yn varw, na Sais yn vyw."—"It is easier disputing with a dead Saxon, than a living one." Transcribed out of a MS in the Gloddaeth Library, No. 53, p.265.[270] Thus did this man draw upon himself the just vengeance of the most powerful family in the Isle of Mona,—a family destined to sway the British empire, and always in consequence of their position, objects of jealousy to the reigning dynasty, for the Salusbury Pedigree records the marriage of William Vychan ab Gwylym (a cousin of Owen Tudor), to Alice, daughter and heir of Sir Richard Dalton of Abthorpe, Northamptonshire, and of his being; previously made "Free Denison of England", the 18th of Henry VI "soe that he married noe Welshwoman". Party feeling must have run high against the demiroyal claimants of the crown, in those days; it is evident that they did not sleep upon beds of roses, although they were allowed to wear them as badges. This parish is of considerable extent, and is principally distinguished for the fine quarries of Mona marble, with which it abounds, giving employment to its inhabitants. A small creek running up from Dulas bay, affords every facility for conveying their produce to the shipping place there, from which great quantities are sent to Liverpool and London. At a short distance from the bay, is the small Island of Ynys Gadarn, a lofty rock of marble, on which is placed an occasional light, to direct mariners in the navigation of these dangerous coasts. The living is a perpetual curacy, endowed with £200 private benefaction, £800 royal bounty, £500 parliamentary grant, and in the patronage of Lord Boston. The Rev. Gethin Williams is the present incumbent. The church, a neat modern edifice, is dedicated to Michael, whose wakes are kept on September 29. In the churchyard, are two very ancient sepulchral stones, with inscriptions in rude antique characters, of which one is mentioned by Mr. Rowlands, as covering the grave of Mechell, Bishop of St. Maloes, and founder of the church of Llanvechell, who was massacred in "Twyll y Cyllill Hirion", at Stonehenge, in the time of Vortigern. A farm, letting for £70 per annum, in the parish of Bangor Iscoed, was bequeathed by Owen Llwyd (a son of Llugwy), a citizen of London, towards apprenticing poor boys of this parish, to some trade in London; he also left £400, to be laid out in the purchase of land, for the endowment of two exhibitions in the University of Oxford, for two boys, one a native of this parish, and one a native of any other part of Mona; both are appointed by Mr. Meyrick of Bodorgan. A woollen manufactory, for spinning and carding wool, gives employment to a few of the inhabitants. There are some small charitable donations bequeathed to the poor, the average annual expenditure for their support amounts to £61 4s. 0d. In this parish was born Lewis Morris, an abridged sketch of whose life is given at the end of this volume. Proceeding along the shore on the left, are the remains of the woods of Llugwy, which were, in the last century, considered the most extensive in the Island, and were attached to the venerable mansion of the Lloyds, mentioned in p.291. On this estate are the ruins of an ancient chapel, situated on an eminence overlooking the bay of Dulas; the architecture, which is of the rudest kind, bears testimony to its great antiquity. It is supposed to have been a private chapel to Llugwy. On digging out a fox which had taken shelter in the ruins of this building, a large square vault was discovered, containing several human skeletons, which crumbled into dust, when exposed to the air; and on searching further into the interior of the building, the ground which it enclosed was found to consist of a large mass of human bones, several feet in depth, and covered only by a covering of plaster, forming the floor of the chapel, which was most probably erected over them. "About a quarter of a mile to the south of these ruins, and not far from the road, in the lands of Llugwy, is a most stupendous cromlech, of a rhomboid form, the greatest diagonal is seventeen feet six inches; the lesser, fifteen feet; the thickness, three feet nine inches; its height from the ground is only two feet, and is supported by five low upright stones, having one end resting upon a rock; the natives call this relic of antiquity, 'Arthur's Quoit'. In the woods are some druidical circles, and at Parciau, near Vedw Isav, in this parish, is another druidical altar."[271] This Arthur's Quoit, has been noticed in a previous page.

PENTRAETH, in the extent so often quoted, is ranked as a township in the comot of Tindaethwy, consisting of "three domiciles, belonging to the heirs of Geraint ab Tegwared, Madog ab Meilir, and Morau ab Aerau, descending from one stock, owing suit at the county and hundred courts, paying reliefs of amobyr, 10s. The lands of Madog ab Ithwal, and Heilyn Twrch, were forfeited, and lying waste on the lord's hands, for want of tenants", &c. This parish is pleasantly situated upon Traeth Côch, five miles from Beaumaris. The resident population in 1821 was 829, and 938 in 1831. Here are three fairs held annually; namely on May 5, June 24, and September 20. The church, a small neat edifice, is dedicated to St. Mary, and with those of Llanvair-mathavarn-eithav and Llanbedr, is dependant on the rectory of Llanddyvnan. It was put in complete repair in 1821, and contains some good monuments to the memory of deceased members of the families of Plâs Gwyn, and Tŷ-frŷ; this is one of the only two churches in the Island, noticed by Grose, who describes Pentraeth, as being more remarkable for its "simplicity and the rural beauties of the surrounding scenery, than for its antiquity"; a number of paper garlands used to decorate its roof, commemorating the death of unmarried women. The village, which is very neat, and of prepossessing appearance, is situated in a narrow sheltered vale, on the turnpike road from Beaumaris to Llannerchymedd. Richard Jones, in 1715, bequeathed a tenement called Gors Las, in this parish, the rental of which he directed to be divided, in equal portions, among the poor of Pentraeth and Llansadwrn; and Dr. John Jones of Plâs Gwyn, Dean of Bangor, in 1719, gave £100 to the rector, in trust, for teaching ten poor children to read the scriptures in their native language. Mrs. Ann Williams charged the estate of Plâs Gwyn, with the payment of £50, the interest of which, together with the rental of a tenement in Holyhead, an annual payment in money, from Tân y Lôn, and £28 per annum, arising from a mortgage on a tenement, called Pen y Lôn, have, it is said, from some unknown cause, been withheld or diverted from their proper object. There are also various other charitable donations left to the poor of this parish; the average annual expenditure for

271 J. Lloyd.—Caerwys MS.

their support amounts to £261 8s. 0d. About half-a-mile from the church, is situated Plâs Gwyn, a handsome and spacious mansion, belonging to Mr. Jones Panton, inherited from his mother, who was daughter and heir of Mr. Jones (descended from Einion ab Geraint). John Jones, D.D. the second son of this house, was in 1683 Dean of Bangor and Rector of Llandegvan. The father of Mr. Jones Panton, was a great encourager of Welsh literature; he had a well-selected library, enriched by valuable collections of Welsh MSS consisting of ninety-one volumes, bequeathed to him by the Rev. Evan Evans, "Y Prydydd Hîr", for the small pension of ten pounds, which, with from five to ten pounds more, was all that he had to subsist on; for notwithstanding Mr. Evans's well-known celebrity as a scholar and a bard, he had no preferment, not even a curacy, to the time of his death. David Thomas, better known to his countrymen by the bardic appellation of Davydd Ddû, Erryri, or the black bard of Snowdon; was of great use in arranging this choice collection; he being, by the kindness of Mr. Panton (and under his patronage), settled as a village preceptor, in the early part of his life, at Pentraeth. This celebrated son of genius, when in his sixty-second year, was accidentally drowned, on March 30, 1822, by crossing a mountain-torrent, called Aber Cegin, during a tempestuous day. A sketch of his life (well drawn up) is given in p.430, of vol.3, Cambro-Briton. A little below Plâs Gwyn, is Abernodwydd, immortalized by Einion ab Gwalchmai, who gained

> " Angharad wych Einion ei rhiw,
> " Rhodd Ednyved Vychan."

by succeeding in performing the feat of "Naid Abernodwydd", which is a narrow dingle, and in it there is to be seen three stones, pitched on end, commemorative of this extraordinary leap of forty-two feet, which was also performed by Howel ab Owen Gwynedd; "am yr hyn enillodd ev briod iddaw, ferch Einion ab Geriaint cyph genedl y Plâs Gwyn, a Thân yr Allt."

> " Naid vawr er vwyn gwawr i'w gwydd,
> " A'r naid yn Abernodwydd.
> " Dwy droedvedd hoyw wledd hylwydd—a deugain,
>   " A digon o wrantrwydd,
>   "Yr hyn a wêl pawb yn rhwydd,
>   " Ar nodau'n Abernodwydd."
>   *Englynion i Naid Howel ab Owen Gwynedd, Y'mhentraeth, y'Mon.*[272]

RHOSBEIRIO is situated in the hundred of Twrcelyn, three miles from Amlwch, containing thirty-two inhabitants. This parish, which is situated on the shore of the Irish sea, is of very limited extent, and comprises only a small portion of arable and pasture land. The living is a perpetual curacy, annexed to the rectory of Llanelian, in the archdeaconry of Anglesea, and diocese of Bangor. The church, dedicated to St. Peirio (from whom the parish derives the name), is a small ancient structure, said to have been built about the year 605, and is situated in the centre of a level field, at some distance from the village. Divine service is performed in it only every third Sunday.

272 Mostyn MS.

RHODWYDD-GEIDIO, a parish in the hundred of Menai, intersected throughout by the small river Alaw, is of inconsiderable extent, containing only a small portion of enclosed and cultivated land; the surface is undulating, rising, in some parts, into eminences, affording good prospects of the adjacent country,—the surrounding scenery being pleasingly varied. The living is a perpetual curacy, annexed to the rectory of Llantrisaint. Five poor men from this parish, are entitled to participate in the benefits of the alms-houses, founded by David Hughes, at Beaumaris. The church, a small edifice, supposed to be built about 630, is situated in a dreary spot, on the river Alaw, and dedicated to St. Ceidio, son of Caw Cawllwg. This parish is distant from Llannerchymedd, one mile, and had a resident population of 301 in 1821,—increased to 316 in 1831. There are some trifling bequests to be distributed among the poor. The average annual expenditure for their support, amounts to £82 19s. 0d.

RHOSCOLYN, is said in the extent of Menai, taken at Rhôsvair, 26th of Edward III to be in that comot, "a free township, containing four domiciles; the first enjoyed by the heirs of Ednyved ab Iorwerth, Griffith ab Einion, and others. The domicile of Davydd ab Ievan, and Einion ab Iorwerth, has the twentieth part escheated, which was forfeited by Ievan Vychan, and which land, they the above-named Davydd ab Ievan, and Einion ab Iorwerth hold, paying an annual rent, by quarterly payment", &c. Rhôs Colyn, including the two hamlets, called Bryngwallen, and Sybylltir, is a discharged rectory, having the chapels of Llanvair-yn-neubwll, and Llanvihangel-y'nhowyn attached, valued in the king's books, £10. The bishop presents, and the Rev. Evan Williams is the present incumbent. This parish is situated on the Irish channel, forming the southern half of Holy Island, being connected with that of Holyhead, which forms the other half; distant from that town five miles, south south-east, containing 1,300 acres of land,—about 200 are common. The resident population in 1821 was 509, and 495 in 1831. Some small charitable donations and bequests, have been left for apprenticing children, and for distribution among the poor. The average annual expenditure for their support, amounts to £205 17s. 0d. The rocks, called "Creigiau Crigyll", where so many shipwrecks have happened, are in this parish. Rhôs Colyn, takes its name from an ancient column or stone pillar erected on the Rhôs (i.e. common) by the Romans, commemorative of a victory, and to mark the extent of their conquests. The church, a small edifice, supposed originally to have been erected about the year 630, is dedicated to Gwenvain (fair and fine-formed) daughter to Pawl Hên of Manaw, and sister to Peulan, who had her cloister here; the church, built on the site, was called anciently from that circumstance, "Llanwenvaen". The burying ground of the original establishment, is still distinguishable by the number of bones found, whenever the spade or plough are used in that spot. Near Bodior, an ancient mansion in this parish, is the finest quarry of the beautiful variegated marble, called verd antique, in the Island. The specimens obtained here, in diversity and brilliancy of colour, surpass every other; it is curiously intersected with asbestos of soft and silky texture, of very superior quality. Bonaparte had a table of this celebrated quarry, executed by Bullock, and sent to him at St. Helena. Bodior is supposed, by Camden, to have been so called, from having been the residence of a commander, or prefect (praefecti mansio). It continued for two or three centuries, to be the paternal residence of the Owens, descended from Llewelyn Aurdorchog. John, the last of the name, died in 1709, leaving one daughter and sole heiress, Margaret, who married Mr. Roberts of Caerau; he was sheriff for Mona, in 1713.

TREV-DRAETH, i.e. SANDY TOWNSHIP, in the hundred of Malltraeth, ranked as a township 26th of Edward III consisting then of "six free domiciles, the heirs thereof owing suit and paying rent to the prince's mill of Dindryval, but shall grind their wheat, rye, and malt, to the thirty-sixth part; but when the mill is at work they are at liberty to grind what they chuse; and they make part of the court of Aberffraw with other tenants", &c. "And in the domicile of Hywel ab Tudyr is a moiety of land, forfeited by one Ievan Fwlbert, now lying waste on the prince's hands", &c. "The heirs of the domicile of Meilyrion ab Gwalchmai, are Madog Chwith, and Ievan ab Einion; besides suits, service, &c. they make part of the prince's court at Aberffraw. And there is in this township, one free native domicile, belonging to the heirs of Bleddyn Goeg, who owe suit at the prince's mill of Dindryval, and are to provide for the carriage of the lord prince, pay cylch stalon, cylch raglon, cylch hebogyddion, and cylch dorgon; and they shall repair part of whatever mansion the prince pleases in the manor of Aberffraw." The Welsh princes, and other lords of particular territories, were the proprietors in *capite* of all lands, and were sovereign lords of all their subjects; to these, the princes or the lords, distributed townships, or particular tenures, called Weles Seats or dwelling, by way of martial distribution, on such conditions as those lords and princes thought proper to impose. The lands so granted, were either freeholds or villainage, and the persons to whom they were given, were called freeholders and vassals; the tenants of these freeholds, were called Uchelwyr, from their having the privilege of sitting higher than the other tenants, in their Gorseddau, and of assisting and passing judicial decrees. The prince excepted, there was an equality among all the nobility. The rents of some tenures, were paid in money, those of others, in goods and cattle. The tenants in common, were obliged to array and follow the prince to war, whenever summoned for that purpose. This was a general obligation, equally imposed on the nobility and on the people at large. There were five other duties of a civil nature, incident to particular tenures; the courts of the Welsh princes were moving from manor to manor, their houses being insufficient to hold their numerous retinue. A suitable provision was everywhere made for their reception and maintenance. The tenants of that manor in which the prince came to reside for a certain time, were obliged to receive and to support so many of the prince's officers and servants, as each of them was under the obligation of doing. The duty called "cylch stalon", was that of entertaining the prince's grooms, and finding provisions for so many of his horses, for such a time, &c. by such tenants of the manor, as were specified in the tenures of each; "cylch raglon", was entertaining the prince's steward, by such of the tenants as were by their tenures, bound to do so; "cylch hebogyddion" was the obligation of entertaining and providing for the prince's falconers and his hawks; "cylch dorgon", i.e. "dorgwn", was the obligation on tenants, by turns, to receive and provide for the huntsman and his dogs.

Trev-draeth, the Town on the Marsh or Moor, with the chapel of Llangwyvan annexed, is a rectory in the Bishop of Bangor's patronage, and valued in the king's books, at £14 8s. 10d. Robert Williams, D.D. is the rector. The church, said to be built about 616, and dedicated to St. Beuno, is a small neat edifice, situated at the extreme border of the perish, and has an east window of modern date and of good design. The parish register, which is quite legible from 1550, is the oldest in North Wales,

with the exception of that of Gwaenyscor. The rectory house, called "Siamber Wen" (White Chamber), and situated about two miles from the church, on the margin of Llyngoron, was erected in 1819.
It is a spacious and handsome building, surrounded with pleasant grounds, and overlooking the most
beautiful and picturesque portion of the parish. The resident population in 1821 was 601,—increased
to 835 in 1831. A national school was founded here, in 1828, for the education of 70 children, of both
sexes, belonging to this parish, and that of Llangadwaladr. A small farm, in the parish of Rhôsvair, was
bequeathed, many years ago, to the poor of this parish, which, owing to the encroachment of sea, and
drifting sand, produces but a small income, which is applied to the diminution of the poor rates. John
Pugh Gwilym, in 1633, bequeathed to the poor, £46 3s. 4d., Ellen Griffith, a small portion of land, and
Owen Williams left some land, the rent of which is appropriated to apprenticing of children; there are
some other small donations for charitable purposes. The average annual expenditure for the maintenance of the poor amounts to £300 17s. 0d. Two fairs are held here annually, on the first of May, and
first of November, on one of which the wakes are celebrated, and the farmers hire their servants.
"Henry Parry, a Flintshire man, was rector of Trevdraeth, in 1606; and died in 1617,—he was a great
help to poor scholars, he also contributed very much to keep up the pure style of his native tongue, by
publishing William Salusbury's Rhetoric", &c. The present worthy and learned incumbent seems, by
his partiality and admiration of the aboriginal language of Britain, to have received the mantle of his
patriotic predecessor. This place, distant from Llangevni, eight miles, is situated between the Malltraeth Marsh, by which it is bounded on the south-east, and St. George's Channel on the south-west;
it comprises a tract of enclosed and cultivated land, according to Mr. Cathrall's statement, in p.79,
"three miles long, and two and a half in breadth, besides two miles long, and one broad, of marsh land,
adding that the waste land, called 'Malltraeth', or Sandy Marsh, is supposed to be six miles in length,
belonging to different parishes adjoining." About 1,000 acres of land has been recovered from the sea,
since the enclosure of the marsh in 1818. A colliery of inferior coal has been opened here, which has
been highly advantageous to the inhabitants of this part of the Island. The enclosing of the marsh, and
the working of this colliery, has caused the increase of population: many new buildings have been
erected, and its situation on the road from Holyhead to Moel y Don Ferry, affords facility of conveyance for the produce of the colliery, and of intercourse with the neighbouring districts.

TREV-GWALCHMAI is ranked as a hamlet in the extent of Malltraeth, taken at Rhôsvair, 26th
of Edward III.—Part of the parish is now stated as being in the hundred of Llivon. It is situated on the
new line of road from London to Holyhead, distant from Llangevni, five miles, and comprises a moderate extent of arable and pasture land, enclosed, in all 1,425 acres; a small common of 120 acres, affords good pasturage for sheep. The village has increased considerably, is neatly built, though small,
and makes a pleasing appearance, from being situated on an eminence. The church (a chapel of ease,
annexed to the rectory of Hên Eglwys), dedicated to St. Mordeyrn, is a small ancient edifice, consisting of a nave, with a north aisle, or chapel, extending the whole length of the building, having an east
window of good design. William Bold, in 1688, the Rev. Hugh Hughes, and an unknown benefactor,
severally bequeathed portions of land for the benefit of the poor of this parish; the average annual ex-

penditure for their support, amounts to £165 19s. 0d. The resident population was 670 in 1821, and 719 in 1831. There is a tradition, that Einion ab Gwalchmai, who lived at Treveilir in this parish, left his wife and family in discontent, and lived abroad for twenty years; but returning home, it is said that he came to the door of his house, the very day on which his wife was married to another man; and as he played on his harp, and sang at the door, being disguised in the habit of a minstrel,—his wife coming thither, asked who art thou?

> " Einion, I am, of Meilir's noble race,
>   "The son of Gwalchmai, hero of renown !
> " In foreign climes I staid so long a space,
>   "That now, my friends no longer will me own.
> " Look not, Angharad, on my silver hair,
>   "Which once shone bright of golden lovely hue,
>
> "   *   *   *   *   *   *   "

To gain this lady, who was Angharad, a celebrated beauty and daughter to Ednyved Vychan, he performed that extraordinary feat, "Naid Abernodwydd". This Einion ab Gwalchmai, was an eminent bard, who flourished from 1170 to 1200; some of his compositions are printed in the Welsh Archaiology. He was sole proprietor of Trev-Gwalchmai, which was enjoyed by his grandchildren in 1352, he having (according to the Law of Gavel Kind), divided it between his three sons. By an extent taken at that time, I find that "they had a mill, owing suit and service at comot and hundred courts, all doing work at the prince's palace of Aberffraw; and they had a third part of Melin Gwnau, on which account they owed no suit at the prince's mill, pay relief amober and gober, ten shillings each, besides annually seven shillings, and nine-pence, in quarterly payments;—they have a share in Melin Gwalchmai. There is in this hamlet, a moiety of one gavel, called "Gavel Lleweiyn Gam", and the heir of it is Lucci Gôch, for which she pays annually, three shillings and eight-pence, besides suits, and ten shillings for relief from services,—she has a share in Melin Gwalchmai. There is also in this hamlet, one oxgang of escheat land, which belonged to Howel Ddû ab Goronw ab Einion, which is now on the lord's hands, a frith; it used to pay the yearly rent of 6s. 8d. and also ten shillings annually, by equal payments at Easter and Michaelmas", &c. The mansion of Treveilir is situated at a short distance from the bay of Malltraeth, on the western side of the Island, and so called from Meilir, the grandfather of Einion ab Gwalchmai ab Meilir, its first known founder and resident. The descendants of this Meilir, were for many generations, noted in our MSS for their opulence and talents; but the estate, by repeated divisions among all the children, was much diminished; and Trevilir itself above a century back, passed by sale to William Evans, Esq. great-grandfather to the present proprietor, Charles Henry Evans, Esq. now residing at Henblâs, which was left by Evan ab Llewelyn of Treveilir, about the reign of Henry VII, to his fifth son, Robert ab Evan, as his share of the then extensive estates.

TRE-GAYAN, OR TREV-GAIAN, is a parish, partly in the hundred of Menai, partly in that of Tindaethwy; the village is within three miles of Llangevni, and pleasantly situated on the great turnpike road from Beaumaris to Holyhead, and nearly in the centre of the Island. This parish comprises a con-

siderable tract of land, in all about 1,870 acres, which is, with the exception of a small portion, enclosed, and in a good state of cultivation; the surface is boldly undulated, rising in some parts into
abrupt eminences, and has a greater proportion of woodland than is generally found in this part of the
principality. The living is annexed to the rectory of Llangevni. The church is a small but neat edifice,
having a south door and a handsome east window. The population in 1821 was 178, and 179 in 1831;
the average annual expenditure for the support of the poor is £73 11s. 0d. Tregayan Hall, the seat of
Admiral Robert Lloyd, is a handsome mansion, surrounded by some flourishing plantations, and
forming a prominent object in the scenery; he inherits this place from his grandmother. I learn by the
Caerwys MS that the last heir male, John Edmunds, was accidentally drowned near Harlech, and that
his sister Margaret, who married Robert Lloyd of Gwynis, succeeded to his estate. The same volume
contains, in p.123, "Coffadwriaeth am ŵr a fu gynt y'mhlwy Tregayan, yr hwn a vu varw 12ed dydd o
vis Mawrth, 1581; a'i henw oedd William ab Davydd ab Howel ab Iorwerth, yr bwn a briododd dair
gwraig;—y gyntav oedd Catrin, verch William, o hon y bu iddaw 22 o blant;—yr ail elwyd Catrin ach
Risiart, o hon bu iddaw ddeg o blant;—a'r drydedd oedd Elin ach William, o hon bu iddaw bedwar o
blant." This noted old man is called by Mr. Pennant, "the Great Patriarch of Tregayan, who died 12th
of March, 1581, aged 105; three hundred of his descendants being alive at the time his eldest son in that
year was eighty-four."

BIOGRAPHICAL SKETCHES

OF

EMINENT MEN BORN IN THE ISLAND OF MONA

———

ARTHUR BULKELEY was cousin of Sir Richard Bulkeley of Baron Hill, "but whether he was of Mona, or Cheshire, I know not", says Anthony Wood, "my firm belief is that he was the son of Arthur Bulkeley, ab Sir Richard Bulkeley, who married Jane, daughter and heiress of Rhys ab William of Bryn-ddû, in Mona; he was educated at New Inn. His first preferment was Llanddeusant, to which he was instituted, August 18, 1525, and about the same time made Canon of St. Asaph, and LL.D. On July 15, 1531, he was admitted Rector of St. James's, London, at the presentation of the Abbot of Westminster, which he resigned in 1544. In 1537 he had Clynogvawr given him, but was ousted out of it by Thomas Cromwell, Earl of Essex, who had it given him by Bishop John Capon) for his nephew, Gregory Williamson, a boy, aged eight years. This caused much oppression from the Earl of Essex, who was opposed by Sir Richard Bulkeley, in behalf of his cousin, Dr. Bulkeley, who afterwards, on the fall of Cromwell, enjoyed it quietly. He was confirmed Bishop of Bangor, in 1541. "It is very true" (observes Wood of him) "that he ruined his bishoprick, but it is as true that some of his predecessors shewed him the way. He lived hospitably, and lived upon his see, which caused him to grant long leases, dispose of several things belonging to the church, such as mitres, bells, &c. As none of his predecessors had resided here before his time, for at least a hundred years, he was induced to keep a good table, and he did no worse than they did, who were Englishmen, and residing at some abbey, farming the revenue of Bangor, &c. executing jurisdiction by vicars, and so letting all go to ruin; but Bishop Bulkeley was very careful of the rights of his see, and kept good discipline." He died March 15, 1552, and was buried in his own cathedral. For his curious will, and many instructing anecdotes, see Browne Willis's Bangor.

LANCELOT BULKELEY was the eleventh son of Sir Richard Bulkeley of Baron Hill, by his second wife, Agnes Nedham; he was ordained deacon, by Bishop Bellot, in the private oratory in the bishop's palace, at Bangor, on the 13th of November, 1593, and instituted the same day, to the rectory of Llandyfnan; on the 4th of March following, to the rectory of Llandegfan, or Beaumaris, and on the 25th of March, 1594, he was ordained priest, in the cathedral church of Bangor, by the same bishop. He entered a commoner at Brazenose College, at eighteen years of age, in the beginning of the year 1587, and when A.B. he placed himself at St. Edmond's Hall, and as a member of that community, took the degree of A.M. in 1593, the year in which he was ordained; soon after this, he went to Dublin, and became archdeacon there, taking the degree of D.D. at that university, and at length became archbishop of that city, in 1619. When James I appointed him a privy councellor of that kingdom, he lived to be a spectator of the miseries that befell that realm, occasioned by the rebellion that began in 1641, at which time he was in great danger, but happily escaped out of the city of Dublin, and lived in a retired situation for several years, at Tanlaughta, dying there at the age of eighty-two, on September 8th 1650, and he was buried at St. Patrick's, Dublin. Archbishop Bulkeley married Alice, daughter to his cousin, Rowland Bulkeley of Caernarvon, by whom he had one son and two daughters. His son, the Archdeacon of Dublin, was educated at Christ College, Oxon; he wrote a very ingenious pamphlet, and much to the purpose, entitled "Proposals for sending back the Nobility and Gentry of Ireland". Sir Richard Bulkeley, the archdeacon's son, was fellow of Trinity College, Dublin, in which university he was brought up. The eldest daughter to Archbishop Bulkeley was second wife to Dr. Aungier, father to the Earl of Longford; and Mary, the second daughter, married William Bulkeley of Porthamel, in Mona.

WILLIAM GLYNN, S.T.P. was born at Glynn, in the comot of Malltraeth, in the parish of Hên Eglwys; "he was a priest's son, as I have heard" (says Sir John Wynn of Gwydir). His father, John Glynn, was rector of Hên Eglwys, and his mother was Jonet, verch Mredydd ab Gwylym. This John Glynn, was the son of Sir Griffith ab Evan ab Tudor, a priest, descended from Einion ab Gwalchmai of Treveilir; he had several children besides William. John, the eldest, was Dean of Bangor, in 1508, and dying in 1534, was buried in the chancel of the cathedral; Jeffrey Glynn, LL.D. was of Doctor's Commons, died in 1557, leaving his brother, Bishop Glynn, his executor,—he was founder of the school at Bangor; David, Owen, M.D. Hugh Glynn, and two daughters. William Glynn, the subject of this memoir, was instituted on February 13, 1551, to Hên Eglwys, his father's preferment, then worth £40 per annum. Fox says, he was one of those clergy, who in 1554 disputed with Bishop Ridley, at Oxford, and obliged to ask pardon, for the strong language he had used on September 8, 1555. William Glynn was educated in Queen's College, Oxford: after Bishop Bulkeley's death, the see of Bangor was left vacant for three years, when this William Glynn was consecrated bishop and appointed to succeed him in this see. On Monday next after Trinity Sunday, in the year 1556, he held a synod,[273] wherein he ordered a solemn procession to be made, carrying the mass, &c. he preaching and enforcing the canons and decrees of Cardinal Pole to be promulgated, and exhorting his clergy to due submission, by obeying them; this mummery, being the last that was ever performed in the principality, closed with reading the pope's bull, together with a mandate from Bonner, to observe all these ceremonies. Bishop Glynn was a zealous papist, behaving with great cruelty to the married clergy, persecuting and depriving them of their livings. He died on May 21, 1558, and was buried in his own cathedral.

SION DAVYDD RHYS—JOHN DAVID RHYS, was born at Llanvaethlu, Mona, elected student of Christ's Church College, Oxon, December, 1555, at the age of twenty-one. He travelled beyond the seas before he took a degree in that university, became M.D. of Sienna, in Tuscany, and public moderator of the school at Pistoia, in that country, he understanding the Italian language as well as a native; afterwards he returned to England, where he practised medicine with admirable success, and was held

273 Browne Willis.

in high esteem by learned men, for his excellent knowledge in all kinds of literature, especially physic, poetry, the grammatical part of the Welsh tongue, and antiquities; yet by the generality he being not understood,—his rare acquirements and curious learning, were in a manner, buried where he lived. He hath written in the Italian language, "Rules for attaining of the Latin Tongue", printed at Venice; and in latin, the two following books,—"De Italicæ Linguœ Pronunciatone", printed at Padua (both were in their time, held in great repute by the Italians) and "Cambro-Britanicæ, Cymericœ, Linguae Institutiones et Rudimenta, ad intelligend, Biblia sacra nuper in Cambro-Britannicum Sermonem, eleganter versa."—London, 1592, fol. This last was much admired by strangers, who travelled in Italy; it was dedicated to Sir Edward Stradling of St. Donats Castle, in Glamorganshire, a great promoter of learning. To this said book is a preface, written by Humphrey Pritchard of Bangor, an Oxford scholar. In his Compendium of Aristotle's Metaphysics, a MS formerly in Jesus College Library, Dr. Rhys says, "that the British language is as copious in expressing congruous terms, as the Greek, or any language whatsoever". Henry Vaughan (Olar Isianus) told Anthony Wood that he had written other excellent works, which are lost; he died near Brecknock (where he mostly dwelt, practising as a physician) about 1609, aged seventy-five. By Stradling, the epigrammatist, he was much extolled for his learning, who styles him "Novum Antiquae Linguae Lumen", and by Camden, "Clariss and eruditissimus Linguae vir D. Johannes David". It was said that Dr. John David Rhys died a papist, but no one can believe it who reads the preface to his grammar, written by Humphrey Pritchard, wherein it is remarked, that the book was written purposely for the *promoting* and *better understanding* of that excellent translation of the bible into the British tongue, and that also principally for the sake of the ministers, and to make the scriptures more intelligible to them and the people, and it is moreover said that he was "sinceræ religionis propagandæ avidissimus", by which, no doubt, Mr. Pritchard (a clergyman himself) must mean the protestant religion. The reader is referred, for further particulars, to the Cambrian Register, and vol.4, Cambrian Quarterly. David Rizzio is said to have been the son of Dr. David Rhys, his real name being Davydd Rhys. Mr. Lloyd observes in one of his MSS, that "Italianizing of names, was much in fashion in the sixteenth century. Inigo Jones, after his visit to Italy, changed his name "Ynyr" into Inigo. Peter Phillips styled himself "Petro Philipi", &c. Mr. William Vaughan in his MS History of the Cors y Gedol Family (now in the library at Mostyn) mentions that William Vychan's monument in Llandwna church, erected in 1616, and the gate-house at Cors y Gedol were designed by his "countryman, Ynyr Shôn, alias Inigo Jones, the royal architect, with whom this William Vychan was very intimate".

HUMPHREY PRITCHARD before alluded to; of him Bishop Humphreys gives the following account:—He was, in his youth, instituted to the rectory of Llanbeulan, Anglesea, by the name of Humphrey Pritchard ab John, by Bishop Arthur Bulkeley: his institution bears date at Bangor, August 6, 1548. On the 6th of November, 1570, the 13th of Elizabeth, he appeared before Bishop Robinson, at Bangor, and subscribed to the thirty-nine articles. He continued Rector of Llanbeulan till 1586, for on September 28, that year, he appeared at a visitation as such; but then advantage being taken of his nonresidence, and the irregularity of his ordination, one Hugh Edwards was instituted into Llanbeulan,

"Jure legitime vacantem", the last of June, 1587; but Mr. Pritchard kept his possession against him till he was summoned to the bishop's court, and then upon a full hearing of Mr. Pritchard, and his allegations and proofs, it was finally adjudged by Dr. Henry Mostyn, then chancellor, that Mr. Pritchard was a mere layman, at the time of his appointment, and that by consequence, his institution and title to the said rectory, was null and void, and ordered Mr. Edwards to be reinstated. This was in a court held at Bangor, October 13, 1587. We have no further mention of Mr. Pritchard, though he lived some years after, as the prefatory epistle to John Davydd Rhys's Grammar, was written between 1590 and 1592.

DAVID ROWLAND was born in the Isle of Mona, and educated at St. Mary's Hall, Oxford, which he left without a degree being conferred upon him, and was appointed tutor to the Earl of Lenox,— travelled through France and Spain with his pupil, and thereby obtained some knowledge in the modern languages. After his return, he became a professed tutor of the Greek and Latin Tongues, and wrote for the use of his pupils, "A Comfortable Aid for Scholars, full of variety of sentences, gathered out of an Italian author"; printed in London, 1578; and he translated from the Spanish, "The Pleasant History of Lazarillo de Tormes, a Spaniard, wherein is contained his marvellous Deeds and Life". "David Rowland also wrote an Epitaphe on my Lorde of Pembroke."[274] This was licensed to Thomas Colwell, in 1569.

ROWLAND MEYRIC, was second son of Meyric ab Llewelyn of Bodorgan, in the parish of Llangadwaladr, Mona, by his wife Margaret, daughter of Rowland ab Howel of Caer Ceiliog, Mona, and was born at Bodorgan, in 1505; mostly educated in academical learning in St. Edmund's Hall (a noted place for civilians), became principal, while he was LL.B. of New Hall, Oxford, and when D.D. he was nominated to the chancellorship of St. Davids, and Canon Residentiary in the time of King Edward VI, he being then one of the persons that drew up articles against Robert Feriar, Bishop of that place. The 1st of Queen Elizabeth, he was commissioned with Dr. Richard Davies, Dr. Thomas Yong, and Richard Pates, to visit the four Welsh dioceses, together with Hereford and Worcester; and when the visitation was ended, he was consecrated Bishop of Bangor, December 21, 1559, and soon after he procured a renewal and confirmation of the ancient charter of all the rights, privileges, and royalties, &c. belonging to the Bishops of Bangor, which were first granted by Edward I to Einnian or Einion, Bishop of Bangor, at Rhuddlan, November 18th in the second year of his reign. Bishop Meyric married Catherine, daughter of Owen Barret, and had issue Sir Gelly Meyric, Harry, and John, besides two daughters, who died unmarried. He died January 24, 1565, and was buried at Bangor, on the south side of the altar, near the wall, where there was an effigy in brass, on a flat stone, over his grave,—but all is torn off. In the same vault lies Bishop Bayley. Sir Gelly Meyric lived at Hascard, in Pembrokeshire, was a great favourite with Robert, Earl of Essex, and suffered death at Tyburn, in consequence of being implicated in his treason. In p.77 is given an account alluding to this Earl of Essex, leading a retired and contented life for some years, with the Bodorgan family; Bishop Meyric was most

274 Bodl. Papers.

probably his tutor. From Sir Francis Meyric, the son of Sir Gelly, are descended the families at Goodrich Court, and Gwrŷch, County of Pembroke. Sir Samuel Rush Meyrick, K.H. is author of a celebrated and splendid work upon Armoury, and is in possession of the first collection of ancient armour in Europe, now deposited in Goodrich Court (County of Hereford) where there is a room, built purposely for it, by Blore, who planned the house and grounds.

LEWIS OWEN, was born at Bodowen, in the parish of Llangadwaladr, an ancient family, now represented by Sir John Owen of Orielton, his brother, Hugh Owen of Bodowen, having married Elizabeth, daughter and heiress of George Wiriott, Esq. of Orielton, County of Pembroke. Lewis Owen was educated in the school founded by Wykeham, in Winchester, elected Fellow of New College, Oxford, in 1553, took the degree LL.B. in 1558. His opinion as to religion, not suffering him to proceed in his academical progress, he left the university about 1561; his fellowship was not pronounced vacant till 1563. He went to Douay, where he was made Regius Professor of his faculty. In a pamphlet, entitled "The State of the English Fugitives under the King of Spain", &c., Dr. Lewis Owen is mentioned as having great quarrels and broils with Dr. William Allen (once a fellow of Oriel, and after his perversion to the popish faith, created a cardinal). Dr. Lewis Owen is there described as a man "very wise and learned, and by reason of his age, gravity, and long continuance in those parts, of great authority in the court of Rome". He was by Pope Gregory, created Bishop of Casano, in Naples; but in consequence of a bitter enmity which he bore towards the jesuits, he lost the cardinal's hat, which Sextus intended for him, which was, by the intrigues of the jesuits (who spared no travel or expence in the matter), bestowed upon their staunch friend, Dr. William Allen, also an Englishman. Lewis Owen was Bishop of Casano seven years, and died full of commendations and praise, on the 14th of October, 1594, and was buried in the chapel belonging to the English students at Rome; and soon after there was a marble monument placed over his grave, with this inscription:—

> " D.O.M. Audoeno Ludovico Cambro-Britanno, I.V.D. ac professori, Oxonii, in Anglia, ac regio Duaci, in Flandria, Archidid, Hannoviae & Can. in Metropol. Cameracensi, atque officiali generali, utriusque signaturae referandario, Caroli Cardinalis Borromae Archiepiscopi Mediolanensis Vicario Generali, Gregorii XIII & Sexto V in congregatione de consultationibus episcoporum & regularium a' secretis, episcopo Cassanensi, Gregorii XIV ad Helvetias nuncio, Clement VIII apistolicae visitationis in alma urbe adjutori, Anglos in Italia, Gallia & Belgio, omni ope semper juvit, sc ejus imprimis opera hujus collegi ac Duacensis Rhemensis fundamenta jecit. Vixit an. 61, menses 9, dies 19. Exul a' patria XXXVI. ob. 14 Oct. MDXCIV. Ludovicus de Torres archiepiscopus montis regalis amico possuit. "

DR. HENRY MAURICE was born in Llangristiolus, his father being then curate of the parish, and Henry, after receiving an excellent scholastic education at Beaumaris school, was, in 1664, when sixteen years of age, admitted Servitor of Jesus College, Oxford. His extraordinary genius was soon discovered by the celebrated principal, Sir Leoline Jenkins, a sagacious observer of men and manners, who elected him scholar, and on the next vacancy advanced him to a fellowship. On Sir Leoline being appointed ambassador to Cologne, in 1673, he took Mr. Maurice as an attaché, who continued with him during the time he was at Nimiguen, in 1675; and at different courts afterwards when with Lord

Berkeley and Sir William Temple. Mr. Maurice returned to England, where he distinguished himself in the profession he had chosen, i.e. the church, and was patronized by Dr. Lloyd successively Bishop of St. Asaph and Litchfield. In 1691, Dr. Maurice, then Rector of Newington, was elected Margaret Professor of Divinity at Oxford; and soon after taking possession of a prebendal stall in Worcester Cathedral, in the same year died, very suddenly, dropping from his chair in an apoplectic fit, when in the forty-fifth year of his age. It is somewhat remarkable, that when Dr. Maurice began to flourish, there were about the same time, a considerable number of eminent men of the Principality of Wales preferred to fill some of the greatest offices in church and state, most of them educated in Jesus College:— we had Dr. Dolben, Archbishop of Canterbury; Dr. Lloyd, Bishop of St. Asaph; Sir George Jefferies, Lord Chancellor of England; Sir William Williams, Speaker of the House of Commons; Sir John Trevor, Master of the Rolls; Sir Thomas Jones, Lord Chief Justice; Sir Leoline Jenkins, Secretary of State, and others.

NICOLAS BAYLEY AND HIS BROTHERS.—Dr. Lewis Bayley, Bishop of Bangor, was born in Caermarthen, consecrated Bishop of Bangor, in 1616;—died in October, 1631, leaving by his wife Ann, daughter and sole heiress of Sir Nicolas Bagnal, four sons, Nicolas, John, Theodore, and Thomas, all born at Llwyn y Moel,[275] in Llanedwen pariah. Nicolas, the eldest, was distinguished for his loyalty during the civil wars; and his son, Edward, was created a baronet, in 1730, whose son, Sir Nicolas Bayley, took the surname of Paget, upon his marriage with Caroline, daughter and heir of Thomas Lord Paget; from this stock is descended the noble and distinguished warrior, the Marquess of Anglesey, "Llew Môn—Eryr Arvon". John Bailey, second son of the bishop, was made Precentor of Bangor Cathedral, in 1617, and in August 1618 presented to the rectories of Llanddyvnan, and Llantrisant; he was a Fellow of Exeter College, and Warden of Ruthin, which he resigned in favour of Dr. David Lloyd, in the year 1631. He published some sermons. Thomas, the third son, was educated in Cambridge, and was ordained deacon in 1629, and priest, by his father, in May, 1630. In August, 1631, he was presented to the livings of Llaniestyn and Llanddyvryd. In 1638, he took the degree of D.D. and was made Subdean of Wells, by King Charles I and in 1646 he was, with the Marquess of Worcester, defending Ragland Castle, which surrendered the same year; he then went to France, and when he returned into England, published "A Conference, held between Charles I and Henry, Lord Worcester, concerning Religion, when they were in Ragland Castle, A.D.1646".—London edition, 1649. He also printed a work entitled, "A Royal Charter granted unto Kings from God"; which he had the temerity to re-print, in 1656, wherein he took an opportunity of railing against the commonwealth: he was, in consequence, committed to Newgate. He published other works; in one, a very slight production, he says, that he was a peer's son, and that his mother was a knight's daughter, and that he had "lost by the civil war, £1,000 per annum, besides much blood and liberty, for the late king's sake", &c. He, very soon after publishing this book, declared himself a papist, went into Italy, where he became an attaché to the notorious Cardinal Ottoboni, and died at the hospital in Ferrara, very poor, leaving one son to the care

275 Plas Newydd.

of Prince Cajegan, who seems to have deserted him, for he was seen by some English travellers at Bononia, serving in the pope's army as a common soldier. Theodore Bayley, the bishop's youngest son, died in 1689, a major in the army. Bishop Bayley was the author of the "Practice of Piety".

DR. JOHN JONES; Dean of Bangor, was the second son of Rowland Jones of Plâs Gwyn, in Pentraeth parish, where he was born on June 2, 1650; instituted Prebendary of St. Asaph, September 4, 1689, he being at the time Rector of Llanllechyd and Arllechwedd; and when Humphrey Humphreys, S.T.P. was elevated from the deanery of Bangor to the bishoprick, on December 16, 1689, Dr. John Jones succeeded him. "He is" (observes Browne Willis, in 1700) "the present worthy dean, a native of Wales, as have been all his predecessors, by birth or descent, for upwards of 200 years last past"—(p.130.)

EDWARD WYNN, D D. Rector of Llangeinwen, in Mona, and Llanllechyd, County of Caernarvon, was the eldest son of Edward Wynn of Bodewryd, by Margaret, daughter of Bishop Morgan, consecrated to the see of Bangor in 1666. Dr. Wynn wrote a small Manual of Prayers in his native tongue, for the use of his parishioners, which he afterwards thought fit to publish, for the common benefit of those who understood the Mountain Greek. He bequeathed and founded a public school, at Holyhead, and died in 1669, and was buried at Llangaffo. Dr. Wynn being the last male heir of Bodewryd, and having no children by his wife, the daughter and heir of Mr. Lloyd of Plas Eignion, his only sister Ann, who married Robert Owen of Penrhos, became sole heiress of Bodewryd, and her grand-daughter, Margaret, conveyed this property into the Stanley family, by her marriage with Sir John Stanley, Bart. of Alderley Park, Cheshire, father to the present Sir John Thomas Stanley of Penrhos and Alderley.

BISHOP LLOYD.—William Lloyd, D.D. was son to Richard, fifth son of Davydd Llwyd of Henblas, in Llangristiolus. He has been described by contemporaries, as well as subsequent biographers, as a person rarely equalled. He was one of the seven bishops sent to the tower, by James II for their inflexible integrity in the maintenance of the protestant religion. It would occupy too much space to record one half of what has been written of him, but the opinion of such a man as Bishop Burnet, no less flattering than true, justifies the transcript of it in these pages. "Lloyd was a great critic in the Greek and Latin authors, but chiefly in the scriptures, of the words and phrases of which he carried the most perfect concordance in his memory, and had it the readiest about him of all the men I ever knew. He was an expert historian, and the most punctual in chronology, of all our divines; he had read the most books, and with the best judgment, and had made the most copious extracts out of them, of any in this age, so that Wilkins used to say, he had the most learning, in ready cash of any he ever knew. He was so exact in every thing he set about, that he never gave over any part of study, till he had quite matured it; when that was done, he went to another subject, and did not lay out his learning with the diligence with which he laid it in. He had many volumes of materials upon all subjects, laid together in so distinct a method, that he could, with very little labour, write on any of them. He had more life in his imagination, and a truer judgment, than may seem consistent with such a laborious course of study; yet as much as he was set on learning, he had never neglected his pastoral care. For several years he had the greatest cure in England, St. Martins, which he took care of with an application and diligence beyond any about him, to whom he was an example, or rather a reproach, so few following his example. He was a holy, humble, and patient man, ever ready to do good, when he saw a proper opportunity,—even his love of study did not prevent him from that."[276] He was first preferred to the see of St. Asaph,— thence to Litchfield,—subsequently to Worcester, where he died in 1717, in the ninety-first year of his age; his remains being deposited in the church of Fledbury, in that county, of which his son was rector, as well as Chancellor of the Diocese. His son survived him only two years, leaving a family, now worthily and most respectably represented by T. Lloyd Baker, Esq. of Hardwick Court, in the County of Gloucester.

The following inscription is translated from one in latin, on a monument erected to the memory of Bishop Lloyd.—

Sacred to the memory
of William Lloyd, s.t.p.
born at Tielhurst, in the County of Berks,
August 17, 1627;
his father, Richard, the son of David Lloyd
of Henblas, in the Isle of Anglesea, Esq.
being minister of that parish.
When yet a boy
he gave those specimens of the most fruitful genius;
he so laboured over the Greek and Roman writers;
he so applied his mind to the study of the Oriental languages,
that in his eleventh year
he proved himself no common ornament
of the University of Oxford.
In those unhappy times, when the established church
was beginning to fall to ruin,
he took upon himself the sacred order of deacon;
when it was entirely trampled on,
he dared to take that of priest.
At length upon the restoration of Charles,
who had constantly sided with the afflicted church,
being promoted to the dignities
of the now prosperous and flourishing establishment,
he held and adorned the different offices
of archdeacon, vicar, canon, dean;
at last exalted to the episcopacy.
He first presided over the see of St. Asaph,
and to the then daily encreasing superstition
of the Romanists,
he showed himself a strenuous and successful opponent;
always the most ready
to refute the adversaries of the reformed faith,
to call back those who strayed from it
and to confirm the wavering.
When James II raged against the rights
of the church and his subjects,
he with six other prelates,

276 Vide Burnet's History of his own Times. Sub. Anno 1661.

whose fame no age shall bury in silence,
being imprisoned in the Tower of London,
esteemed it the more preferable
to shew his attachment to the cause of religion
and liberty, now almost extinct,
than to betray either at court.
When William and Mary, princes of most blessed memory,
not without singular marks of Divine Providence,
ascended the throne;
and when affairs were again safely established,
he was appointed royal almoner;
he was shortly afterwards translated to the see of Litchfield,
and for many years he was
the most favoured chaplain of that most pious queen.
After that, having appointed to the guidance
of the diocese of Worcester,—
he watched over its interests
with the greatest prudence, for eighteen years.
At length, baring exceeded his ninetieth year,
his intellect even at the close of life by no means failing him,
he gave up his soul to God,
August 30th, 1717.
Behold ! reader, in this most illustrious prelate,
a surpassing example of virtue and learning !
Behold a man, for a genius—keen in devising;
for strength of memory;
for a quick and refined judgment; for eminent candour of mind;
for peace and spotless piety; for apostolical seriousness—
demanding admiration ! Look upon his fidelity and zeal for truth
As an historian;
his most accurate knowledge of dates
as a chronologist;
his altogether amazing acquaintance with holy writ
as a theologian !
How liberal, how beneficial he was,
let the tears of the prostrate whom he raised,
of the afflicted whom he comforted,
of the poor whom he assisted,
bear witness !
how solicitous and indefatigable he was
in discharging his episcopal office,
let as many of the clergy as were admitted
by him to holy orders, or appointed to the cure of churches,
and finally the well-established order
of the whole of this diocese,
shew proofs.
His wife, Ann,
the daughter of Walter Jones, S.T.P.
Prebendary of St. Peter's Church, Westminster,
and likewise Sub-Dean of the Chapel Royal,
wishing that her remains should be laid by those
of her dear husband,
erected this monument.

Bishop Lloyd distinguished himself as an author by his "Five Tracts against Popery", and other theological writings. In Browne Willis's History of St. Asaph, p.123, is a long account of this excellent man; and the second volume of the Sebright Collection, has several of his letters, shewing his great attachment to his native country. Edward Lhwyd bears high testimony to his talent as a Welsh antiquary. The following unpublished letter, written at that time, gives a strong picture of religious persecutions in Ireland, which called forth from Bishop Lloyd his admirable tracts against popery.

> To the Gentlemen lately come from the service in Ireland, commanded
> by Lieutenant Colonel Marrow.
>
> Gentlemen,
>
> We are heartily sorry that you have made such an unhappy exchange of enemies, to leave Irish to fall upon English, and papists to fall upon protestants. We had hoped the blood of that noble gentleman, Sir John Harcourt, and the many thousands of protestants, who have fallen by the fury of those bloody monsters of Ireland, could not so soon have been forgotten. What course the court of England runs, how destructive to the protestants, you cannot but know (with us) by sad experience; and therefore we desire (before you pass further) your thoughts may make a pause, lest you find that God of the protestants against you, whom you have hitherto found miraculously for you. We fear the loss of our religion, more than the loss of our dearest blood; do not therefore we beseech you, desire us to betray it, and ourselves. We hope your second thoughts may take off the edge of your former resolutions; however we are resolved to make good our trust, and put our lives into the hand of that God, who can, and we hope will, secure them more than our walls and weapons.[277]
>
> John Warren,
> Alexander Elliot.
>
> Hawarden Castle, November 21, 1643.

THE REV. HENRY ROWLANDS.—I cannot begin the life of this celebrated man more appropriately than in Mr. Pennant's words;—"I am sorry that it is not in my power to give a better account of this prodigy of learning", who was the son of William Rowland of Plâs Gwyn, in the parish of Llanedwen, by Mawd, the daughter of Edward Wynne of Penhescyn; this Williams's grandfather, Henry, son of Edward Rowland, was nephew to Henry Rowland, Bishop of Bangor, he married Martha, daughter of Dr. Williamson, Physician to Queen Elizabeth, by whom he had Henry Rowlands, married to Jane, daughter of Edmund Griffith, Bishop of Bangor; Henry, their grandson, the subject of this memoir, was instituted to the vicarage of Llanidan, in 1690; he married Elizabeth Nicolas of Plasnewydd, and by her had four sons and two daughters. It is said that he never travelled farther than Conwy. The world is indebted to this great man, as an historian and antiquary; his Mona Antiqua has rendered his name famous throughout Great Britain. He published a Treatise of Geology before it was a science; he also began a detached History of Mona, in latin, but finished only the hundred of Menai. This MS is now in the possession of Mr. Panton of Plâs Gwyn, being one of those in the collection of Evan Evans. Mr. Rowlands corresponded with Edward Lhwyd, and generally in his native tongue. In a letter written to Mr. Mostyn, Mr. Lhwyd says,—"I received a Welsh epistle, in my own orthography, from

277 Hawarden Papers.

Mr. Rowlands of Anglesey, where he maintains that we and the Irish came to Britain at once." In another addressed to Mr. Rowlands, he humorously describes his reception in Bretagne, being taken for a spy, &c. Mr. Rowlands died in 1723, aged sixty-eight, and was interred under a black slab of Mona marble, in the parish church of Llanedwen: the inscription on his tomb was of his own composing, and is as follows:

> " M.S. Depositum Henrici Rowlands, de Plâs Gwyn, Clerici, Hujus Eccleriæ Vicarii, qui hinc cum-hiscæ exuviis per spiritum Jesu, animam interea refocillantem, in ultimo die se fore resussitatum pia fide sperabat: ac inde Triumphante Misericordia in eternum cum Christo gandium fore susceptum quod maxime anhelabat; id est esse simper cum domino. Obiit 21 die Novembris, Ætatis suæ 68: spiritus ubi vult spirat. Laus tota triuni: omnia pro nihilo nisi quae tribuebat egenis, ista valent cum artes pereant & scripta fatiscant. "

The present worthy and respectable owner of Plâs Gwyn (who is also Vicar of Llanidan), is Mr. Henry Rowlands, lineally descended from John Rowlands, the fourth son to the above named distinguished Henry Rowlands.

DAVID HUGHES, the liberal founder of a grammar school, and alms-houses, in Beaumaris, was a native of Llantrisaint parish, and born in humble life, about the middle of the sixteenth century, having accumulated in England, by prudence and perseverence, a decent fortune, with which he returned to his native place, disposing of it in acts of charity, and forming benevolent institutions, for the benefit of his countrymen. He, by his will, dated December 30, 1609, after providing for the maintenance and support of the school, and alms-houses, at Beaumaris, directs that any surplus should be distributed among the poor of the parish of Llantrisaint; but although a considerable sum has been accumulated for many years, no distribution has yet been made. The affairs of the charity, are at present, under the investigation of the just, diligent, and humane Lord Chancellor Brougham, at whose suggestion, investigation into charitable institutions has been made, and it is expected that a very considerable distribution will eventually be made among the poor, according to the tenor of David Hughes's will. In my description of the parish of Llantrisaint, and p.70 of this history, there is more said about this excellent man and his bequests.

DR. LEWIS of Cerrig Ceinwen.—Robert Lewis of Cemlyn, descended from Hwfa ab Cynddelw, married Gaynor, daughter to William Roberts of Caerau, by whom he had five sons; William, the eldest, married Ann, daughter of William Bulkeley of Coedan, relict of the Rev. Richard Hughes, who died 1626, being the year in which he was presented to the living of Llanddeusaint. Samuel, the third son, of whom there is no account. Ambrose Lewis, the fourth son, lived at Wrexham, where he died. John Lewis, M.D. was the sixth son, and died unmarried, bequeathing £12, to be annually paid for the education of two poor boys, who should be natives of the parish of Cerrig Ceinwen.

SIR WILLIAM WILLIAMS, BART., one of the most eminent lawyers that Great Britain ever produced, was born at Nantanog, his father was Hugh Williams, D.D. Vicar of Llantrisaint, and married Emma, daughter and sole heiress of John Dolben of Cae Gwynion, by Denbigh. This branch of the

Williams have been settled in Mona ever since 1100 when their primegenitor Cadrodd Hardd, resided at that time at Trevadog, in the parish of Llanvaethlu. William Williams of Chwaen Isa, the father of Dr. H. Williams, was fourteenth in descent from that chieftain. Sir William Williams was brought up a barrister, became Recorder of Chester, and represented that city in three parliaments, in the latter of which he was chosen speaker. The Lord Chancellor Jeffries became his enemy, in consequence of receiving on his knees a reprimand from him, as Speaker of the House of Commons. At Jeffries's instigation he was prosecuted, and made to pay a fine of £8,000, tried for a libel 36th of Charles II for causing to be printed the information of John Dangerfield. He appears by the debates and state trials to have been the active and zealous advocate of the popular party, in those days. The following anecdote is related of this speaker, indicative of his great love of ancient lore,—a taste inherited by some of his descendants in an eminent degree. He having fainted, owing to excess of business, some one observed, "carry him into the fresh air", upon which a witty member called out, "put his nose in an old volume of parliamentary records, he will soon recover, for that is his native air". In April 14, 1864, he married Margaret, daughter and heiress of Watkin Cyffin of Glascoed, and in July 11, 1700; he died, and was; buried at Llansilin; his son, Sir William Williams, married another great heiress, Jane, daughter to Edward Thelmall of Plâs-y-ward and they were parents to the justly-termed "Great Sir Watkin Williams Wynn", who from his splendid possessions and love of his country, was generally styled "King of Wales"; among other public measures England is indebted to him for, is the "Act for the more effectual preventing Bribery and Corruption in the election of Members to serve in Parliament". The noble stand made, and the uncompromising spirit evinced by his patriotic descendants lately in defending and keeping inviolate the constitutional laws of these realms, show that they are not degenerated in their race. In the Baronetcy may be seen, a more detailed account of Sir Watkin Williams, the speaker, and his family.

LEWIS MORRIS.—This celebrated antiquary and eminent poet, was the son of a cooper; he was born on St. David's day, at Penrhos Llugwy, a true or a more faithful son of Britain, our patron, saint never had, nor ever will have. He it was who boldly wrote to one of the greatest linguists in Europe, that "the language of all Britain, including Armorica, Ireland, and Scotland, was the same as it is now in Wales, 1200 years ago". Alluding to the music of Wales, he says, "The Druidical Bards knew how to sing, before Rome had a name, so never" (he continues) "hereafter mention such moderns as Horace and Virgil, when you talk of British poetry; Llywarch Hên, Taliesin, Aneurin, those followers of the druids, are our men, and nature our rule", &c. This useful and scientific man, died at Penybryn, in the sixty-third year of his age, on the 11th of April, 1765. Lewis Morris published under the Lords of the Admiralty, Charts of the Coast, and Plans of the Harbours from Orme's Head to Milford Haven, from actual surveys made by himself, though he had no education, but what he acquired by his own genius and industry. These are by far the most correct charts of those coasts extant; he pointed out the very spot, subsequently chosen by Rennie for the pier, at Holyhead. Had the latter followed more closely the directions pointed out by this clear-headed native, the harbour would have been less liable to the dreadfully frequent catastrophe of shipwreck, owing to its too narrow entrance. William, his eldes brother, was a Welsh naturalist and botanist, and Richard, another of this clever family, was the founder of the Cymrodorion Society, in London, superintended the printing of two editions of the Welsh Bible, the one in 1746, and the other in 1752; and also supplied the Rev. Peter Williams, with maps for his valuable 4to. edition of the Welsh Bible, with notes, in 1775. The reader may see an excellent account of the three Morrises in the 2nd vol. of the Cambrian Register and Cathrall's History, p.75. The former volume is enriched by several of Mr. Lewis Morris's instructive and agreeable letters.

GORONWY OWEN, A.M.—The life of this unfortunate and expatriated son of genius, is so complicated, and so very painful in the detail, that I would willingly draw a veil over the pages that recite nothing but poverty and distresses, which he had to contend with from the first dawn of his youth, for Goronwy the acknowledged "chief bard among the modern poets of Cymru", went to school by stealth, his father beating him for it, unless his mother was by to prevent him. In 1745, he was ordained to a curacy, in Mona, i.e. Llanvair-yn-mathavarn, the parish in which he had been born; out of this he was soon ousted by the bishop's chaplain, who wanted "a title for his friend Mr. John Ellis". He was obliged to go and serve a church, near Oswestry; where he married in 1747, a person whose family were reputed affluent, "but says Mr. Owen, I have never been the better for them". This was written in a letter to Lewis Morris, his first patron, about the year 1750, in which he says, "Pray look out for a situation for me in Wales: I care not a rush in what part, for here I am serving the curacy of Uppington, and together with a school, is only £26 a year, and what is that to keep a wife and two boys, especially in England, where every thing is so dear." In 1755, he was curate of Northolt, in the same county of Salop. Worn out with unavailing expectations of obtaining some small preferment in his native country, he, in 1757, addressed a letter to the Cymrodorion Society, praying for some small allowance towards paying the passage of himself and family to America, "and thus" (observes his feeling biographer and brother bard, the amiable Dr. Owen Pugh), "was the fairest flower of British genius, transplanted to wither in the ungenial climes of America". In 1767, he sent over an elegy on the death of his earliest and true friend, who first found out his abilities, Lewis Morris; this was the last account which ever came from himself, and, when in 1793 some gentlemen who revered the memory of Goronwy Owen tried to obtain information respecting the time he died, and with a view of setting up a monument, "sent letters to his son, him they found perfectly Americanized". Before answering the queries, he wished to know "who would pay him for his trouble". Cambrian Biography, and the Cambrian Registers, Cambro-Briton, &c. contain notices of his life, and some of his very clever and amusing letters are inserted in those works. Goronwy Owen wrote Cywydd y Varn, which is considered one of the best poetical compositions in the Cambro-British language; he also translated several of the Odes of Horace, in all their native force and humour into Welsh, so pure and classical as to defy criticism, and (unlike some of our modern learned) so plain as to be "intelligible to the meanest capacity".

THE REV. HUGH DAVIES, Rector of Aber, was born at Beaumaris, and from a child was observant of plants; in this his favourite pursuit and study, he was greatly assisted by the late Mr. Williams of Treffos; and by publishing the result of his labours, he has conferred a lasting benefit on his country. Mr. Davies's "Botanology; or Welsh Botany", as he calls it, enriched by his judicious remarks, will be considered a standard work, while the language remains. The writer of this history laments that no answer was given to queries sent, concerning this clever naturalist, who was Fellow of the Royal Society, and who when visiting the metropolis, had the honour of being presented to the late Queen Charlotte, at her particular command.

WILLIAM JONES, father of the celebrated oriental and general scholar, Sir William Jones, was the son of Siôn Siôr, alias John George, and was born in the parish of Llanvihangel Tre'r Beirdd, in Mona; his father removed from thence to a small tenement, called Tyddyn Bâch, in the parish of Llanbabo, belonging to Lord Bulkeley, and the son was sent to a charity school, in the adjoining parish of Llanvechell, from whence he went about the year 1714, with Lord Bulkeley's family to London. An old woman now living, told Mr. James Williams of Llanvair-y'nghornwy that she recollects Mr. William Jones, "yn lâs lanc", setting out; and this patriotic gentleman contemplates setting up a monument, commemorating this event, and his subsequent fame, in hopes that other "lâs lanciau" may be stimulated to follow his example. I insert without apology, the following letter from Lewis Morris, as a memorial of an old custom.—

"To William Jones, Esq.

SIR,

It was a custom among the Ancient Britons (and still retained in Anglesey) for the most knowing among them in the descent of families, to send their friends of the same stock, or family, ar Ddydd Calan Ionawr, a calenig,[278] i.e. a present of their pedigrees, which was in order I presume, to keep a friendship among relations, which these people preserved surprisingly, and do to this day, among the meanest of them, to the sixth and seventh degree. Some writers take notice that the Gauls also were noted for their affection and regard for their own people, though ever so distantly related. These things to be sure are trifles, but all other things in the world are trifles too. I take men's bodies in the same sense as I take vegetables. Young trees propagated by seed or grafts, from a good old tree, certainly owe some regard to their primitive stock, provided trees could act and think; and as for my part, the very thought of these brave people, who struggled so long with a superior power for their liberty, inspires me with such an idea of them, that I almost adore their memories; therefore to keep up that old laudable custom, I herewith send you a calenig of the same kind as that abovementioned, which I desire you will accept of. I have reason to know it is founded on good authority, for both my father and mother were related to your mother, and came from the same stock, mentioned in the enclosed, which is the reason I am so well acquainted with your mother's descent. As you were young when you left the country, it cannot be supposed that you could know much of these things. If this give you any pleasure, I shall be glad of it; if not, commit it to the flames.

And believe me to be, with truth and sincerity,

Lewis Morris."

Mr. Jones received from his parents the best education which they were able to afford. From his earliest years he discovered a propensity to mathematical studies. The industrious exertion of vigorous intellectual powers, supplied the defects of inadequate instruction, and laid the foundation of his future fame and fortune. He began his career in life, by teaching mathematics on board a man of war;

278 On the calends of January, a New Year's Gift.

and in this situation, attracted the notice and obtained the friendship of Lord Anson. In his twenty-second year, Mr. Jones published a "Treatise on the Art of Navigation", which was received with great approbation. He was present at the Capture of Vigo, in 1702, and returned to England with the fleet, and immediately afterwards established himself as a teacher of mathematics, in London, where at the age of twenty-six, he published his "Synopsis Palmariorum Matheseos", a decisive proof of his early and consummate proficiency in his favourite science. The private character of Mr. Jones was respectable, his manners agreeable and inviting; these qualities not only contributed to enlarge the circle of his friends, whom his established reputation for science had attracted, but also to secure their attachment to him. Amongst others who honoured him with their esteem, were Lord Hardwick, Lord Parker (afterwards President of the Royal Society), Sir Isaac Newton, Bailey, Mead, &c. who may be classed among the intimate associates of Mr. Jones. By Sir Isaac Newton he was treated with particular regard and confidence, and prepared, with his assent, the very elegant edition of Small Tracts on the higher Mathematics, in a mode which obtained the approbation, and increased the esteem of that great man for him. Mr. Jones resided as a member of Lord Macclesfield's family, at Sherborne Castle, and instructed his lordship in the sciences: while in that situation he had the misfortune to lose the greatest part of his property, by the failure of a banker; to make up for this, Lord Macclesfield procured for him a sinecure place of considerable emolument. In this retreat he became acquainted with Miss Mary Nix, the youngest daughter of George Nix, a cabinet-maker, in London, who had raised himself to eminence in his trade, and from the honest frankness of his conversation, was admitted to the tables of the great, and to the intimacy of Lord Macclesfield. The acquaintance of Mr. Jones with Miss Nix terminated in marriage, by whom he had three children, the youngest, Sir William Jones, was born in London, on the Eve of St. Michael, in the year 1746; and the second child, Mary, who was born in 1736, married Mr. Rainsford, a merchant retired from business in opulent circumstances; this lady perished miserably, during the year 1802, in consequence of an accident from her clothes catching fire. George, the eldest boy, died in his infancy. Mr. Jones survived the birth of his son William, but three years; he was attacked with a disorder, which the sagacity of Dr. Mead, who attended him with the anxiety of an affectionate friend, immediately discovered to be a polypus in the heart, and wholly incurable. He died in July, 1749, leaving behind him a great reputation, and moderate property. The library of Mr. Jones, by a bequest in his will, became the property of Lord Macclesfield. The writer being informed that it contained many valuable MSS connected with British history, applied to the present possessor, for permission to have a catalogue made of them; this was refused on the plea that "they were not worth the trouble". It is asserted by the compilers of the Biographical Dictionary, in their account of Mr. Jones, that he had completed a work of the first importance, entitled "Introduction to the Mathematics", and had sent the first sheet of it to the press, when the indisposition that terminated so fatally, obliged him to discontinue the impression. A few days before his demise, he entrusted the MS to the care of Lord Macclesfield, who promised to publish it for the benefit of his family: this was never done, although the earl survived his friend many years, and after his death the MS was not to be found. Such of the mathematical works of Mr. Jones as have been published, are much admired for neatness, brevity and accuracy. The care of the education of his son William, now devolved upon his mother, who in many respects was eminently qualified for the task. Her character as delineated by her husband, with somewhat of mathematical precision, is this; "that she was virtuous, without blemish; generous, without extravagance; frugal, but not niggard; cheerful, but not giddy; close, but not sullen; ingenious but not conceited; of spirit, but not passionate; of her company, cautious; in her friendship, trusty; to her parents, dutiful; and to her husband, ever faithful, loving and obedient". She had by nature a strong understanding, which was improved by his conversation and instruction. Mrs. Jones, after the death of her husband, was urgently and repeatedly solicited by Lady Macclesfield, to remain at Sherborne Castle; but having formed a plan for the education of her son, she declined accepting the friendly invitation of that lady, who never ceased to retain the most affectionate regard for her; and such was Mrs. Jones's talent for instruction, and her pupil's facility for retaining it, that in his fourth year, he was able to read distinctly and rapidly, any English book. To his incessant importunities for information on casual topics of conversation, which she watchfully stimulated, she constantly replied, "read and you will know"; a maxim to the observance of which he always acknowledged himself indebted for his future attainments. If from the subsequent eminence of Sir William Jones, any general conclusion should be eagerly drawn in favour of early tuition, we must not forget to advert to the uncommon talents both of the pupil and the teacher. In his fifth year, as he was one morning turning over the leaves of a bible, in his mother's closet, his attention was forcibly arrested by the sublime description of the angel in the tenth chapter of the apocalypse, and the impression which his imagination received from it was never effaced. At a period of mature judgment, he considered the passage as equal in sublimity to any in the inspired writers, and far superior to any that could be produced from mere human composition. He was fond of retracing and mentioning the rapture which he felt when he first read it. 1783 was the period when Mr. Jones had the happiness to gain the accomplishment of his most anxious wishes; in March he was appointed a Judge of the Supreme Court in India, on which occasion he was knighted, and in April following married Anna Maria Shipley, the eldest daughter of the Bishop of St. Asaph. In his private memoranda was entered the number of languages he had acquired: "eight he understood critically,—eight less perfectly, but all intelligible with a dictionary;—twelve studied less perfectly, but all attainable." His native tongue, the British, is among the twenty-eight enumerated: perfecting himself in this seems to have been a favourite plan. In a letter written to Mr. R. Morris from Calcutta, in 1790, he says, "as one of the Cymrodorion, I am warmly interested in British antiquities and literature, but my honour is pledged for the completion of the new digest of Hindu laws, and I have not a moment to spare for any other study." This very able and learned man, whose attainment placed him upon the highest rank of intellectual eminence, after possessing himself of all that the sages and philosophers of all times have said and thought upon the works of nature, wrote the following note at the end of his bible:—"I have regularly and attentively read the holy scriptures, and am of opinion that this volume, independent of its divine origin, contains more beauty, more pure morality, more important history, and finer strains both of poetry and eloquence, than can be collected from all other books, in whatever age or language they may have been composed. The two parts of which the scriptures consist, are connected by a chain of compositions, which bear no resemblance in form or style to any that can be produced from the stores of Grecian, Persian, or even Arabian learning. The antiquity of these compositions, no man doubts; and the unrestrained application of them to events long subsequent to their publication, is a solid ground of belief that they are *genuine*, and consequently inspired." In the act of adoration to his Creator, on the 20th of April, 1794, and at the early age of forty-eight, Sir William Jones expired, universally regretted; his remains rest in the Cathedral Church of Calcutta.

The following extract from one of Lewis Morris's letters, shews by whom and in what manner the MSS left by Mr. Jones were collected. "Moses Williams, A.M. educated at Jesus College, Oxford, an able and indefatigable Welsh antiquary, assisted Dr. Wotton in his edition of "Leges Wallicæ", borrowed many MSS which he never returned, particularly from Hengwrt; as Mr. Vaughan informed me; some he bought, some he begged, and stole a great many; and they are all now in the hands of William Jones; London.—Lewis Morris, 1748."

THOMAS WILLIAMS, ESQ., M.P. for Marlow.—Few men have done more essential service to their fellow creatures, than the subject of this memoir did in his day. He was born on the 13th of May, 1737, and was the eldest son of Owen Williams of Tregarnedd; a descendant of Llowarch ab Brân, one of the Tri Tylwyth Môn, by Jane, daughter of Thomas Lloyd of Hendre, and her mother was Margaret, daughter of Pierse Lewis of Tre'r Bardd, in Mona, Registrar of. Bangor. After having had an excellent classic education, he was articled to Mr. Lloyd of Tre'r Beirdd, in Flintshire, a leading solicitor, then re-siding at Caerwys. To a naturally well-endowed mind and clear judgement, was added a high principle of integrity which gained him, from the many thousands he employed, the honourable appellation of "Twm Chwarae Teg", i.e. Tom Fair Play. With the ample means of befriending and relieving the dis-tressed, he possessed a generous heart, and a hand ever ready to do good and to distribute. Mr. Williams was eminently qualified for discovering the leading point of merit in the human character. To this faculty of quick discernment, and to the decision with which he executed his well-arranged plans, may be attributed, in some degree, the great success which attended all his schemes of aggrandizement and improvement. For many of the latter years of his life, the whole copper trade of the kingdom was under his guidance. Mr. Williams, with the assistance of expensive and scientific experiments of the first chemists in Europe, has been the means of considerably improving the art of ship-building, by in-troducing the use of copper bolts, of such a quality as would bear being driven into oak timber; a most valuable discovery, in the attainment of which he expended many thousands of pounds, as the iron bolts and copper sheathing formerly in use were found to be destructive of each other. To the activity, judgement and perseverance of this benevolent and liberal son of Mona, the noble families of Uxbridge and Dinorben are much indebted for the wealth they possess. It is well known that the pro-duce of the sale of copper at Pary's Mountain, in one year, amounted to the immense sum of £300,000. Mr. Williams died at Bath, November 19, 1802, leaving by his wife Catherine, the daughter of John Lloyd, Esq. of Tre'r Beirdd and Plâs-yn-Rhal, two sons and three daughters; his eldest son Owen, died in 1832, leaving by his wife Margaret, sister to Lord Dinorben, two sons, the eldest, Thomas Pierse Williams, succeeded him in his estates, and the representation of the Borough of Mar-low, in parliament.

LIST OF THE BARDS OF MONA.

A.D.

MEILIR BRYDYDD o Dre Feilis.—Some of his compositions are in the Welsh Archaiology.
He died about 1150

GWALCHMAI AB MEILIR, one of the most celebrated poets of the twelfth century.
Some of his compositions appear in the Welsh Archaiology. He died about 1180

EINION AB GWALCHMAI. Some of his works have been printed in the Welsh Archaiology.
He died about 1200

MEILIR AB GWALCHMAI. Some of his works are printed in the Welsh Archaiology.
He died about 1200

EDNYVED VYCHAN.—See a Sketch of his Life in Dr. O. Pugh's Cambrian Biography.
He died about 1230

GORONWY GYRROG. Several of his compositions are extant. He died about 1360

GORONWY DDU AB TUDUR AB HEILYN. He died about 1370

GRUFYDD GRYG of Aberffraw, who had several poetical contests with the celebrated
bard Dayydd ab Gwilym. Many of his compositions still remain. He died about 1370

ROBIN DDU o VON, or ROBIN DDU AB SIDNEY BLEDRYDD, an eminent poet.
He died about 1370

SIR DAVYDD TREVOR, Rector of Llanallgo and Llaneugrad. He died about 1500

LEWIS MON. Several of his compositions are still extant. He died about 1500

DAVYDD ALAW, who resided on the banks of the river Alaw. He died about 1540

SION BRWYNOG, or SION AB HYWAL AB LLWELYN AB ITHEL. Some of his
compositions are still extant. He was the proprietor of Brwynog, and died about 1540

ARTHUR BULKELEY, Bishop of Bangor. He was educated at New Inn Hall, Oxford,
and died about 1541

WILLIAM GLYNNE, Bishop of Bangor. He was born in the parish of Hên Eglwys, at
a place called Glynn. He was Master of Queen's College, Cambridge, and died about .. 1555

ROWLAND MEYRICK, Principal of New Inn Hall, Oxford. Born at Bodorgan, in the
County of Anglesey, Bishop of Bangor, and died 1561

HENRY PARRI, Rector of Rhôs y Colyn and Llanvachraeth, and author of Egluryn Ffraethineb,
or a Treatise on Rhetoric, was of the Maes Glâs family, in Flintshire. He died about ... 1590

Dr. JOHN DAVID RHYS, or REES, an eminent poet, grammarian and physician; elected
Fellow (Student) of Christ Church, Oxford, 1555, and afterwards went to Italy at the expence
of Sir Edward Stradling of Glanmorganshire, and studied physic at the University of Sienna.
He published his Linguæ Cymmraecœ Institutiones (in which there is a great deal of
Italian) in 1592. He was a native of the parish of Llanvaethlu, and died about 1600

HUGH HUGHES *or* BARDD COCH, an excellent poet. Some of his pieces are printed in
the Diddanwch Teuluaidd. He was son to Gryffydd Hughes, whose mother Elizabeth
ought to have been heiress of Tai Croesion; her youngest sister Mary, wife of Ellis Ellis,
had Tai Croesion, &c. He died about 1770

JOHN OWEN. He translated Dr. Valentine's Devotion into Welsh, and died about 1670

RICHARD LLOYD of Henblas, married Anne Vickers of Broadfield, Berkshire, by whom he had William
Lloyd, afterwards Bishop of Worcester, a man of great learning and considerable attainments, and
author of several works.

CONCLUSION.

To the mineralogist and lover of picturesque scenery, much remains to be investigated within the Island of Mona,—once the chief residence of the British princes and the strong-hold of their expiring armies.

It will always be viewed by the warrior and historian with peculiar interest, from the circumstance of its sovereignty having been so often and so sturdily contested for a period of upwards of four centuries, and particularly from the memorable circumstances of its being the scene on which the last decisive battle was fought between the Britons and English "at the action of the Menai", when Prince Llewelyn witnessed the total overthrow of his rival Edward, and the discomfiture of his whole army, with the loss of "manye a gallant knighte". Alas the the triumph was but a momentary sunshine that glimmered on his declining day, for on the tenth of February, a few weeks after this victory, Llewelyn himself, "the flower of knighthood", was betrayed into the hands of Adam de Francton, together with two thousand of his guards.

To the antiquary, this insulated spot must always be an object of veneration, from its containing so many valuable monuments of the highest antiquity, coeval with its ancient inhabitants,—the druids.

The numerous quotations signed *"J. Lloyd"* are all from the Caerwys MSS six quarto volumes, collated and written by the late Rev. John Lloyd, rector of that place, towards a history of his native country, who as a scholar and antiquary was eminently qualified for the undertaking; adding to his critical knowledge of the ancient British tongue the accomplishments of botany, mineralogy, and heraldry. They are written in a style of elegant simplicity, and with a force and reasoning which truth alone could dictate. It affords the compiler of this work much pleasure to have an opportunity of rendering this just tribute to the acknowledged historical accuracy of her highly gifted father, justly said by his friend and fellow traveller, Mr. Pennant, "to be equalled by few in his knowledge of the language and the history of the Ancient Britons, and few so liberal in his communication".

APPENDIX.

SHERIFFS OF ANGLESEY.

A.R.   A.D.

HENRY VIII.

— Rice ap Llewelyn ap Hwlkin,
    Bodychan, during life.   ——
32. Rowland Griffith, Esq. Plâsnewydd   1541
33. Sir Richard Bulkeley, Knight   1542
34. John ap Rees ap Llywelyn ap Hwlkin, Esq.   1543
35. William Bulkeley, Esq. Porthamel   1544
36. Rhydderch ap David, Esq. Myvyrian   1545
37. Richard Hampton, Esq. Hênllys   1546

EDWARD VI.

1. Sir Richard Bulkeley, Knight, Baron-Hill   1547
2. Rowland Griffith, Esq. Pâsnewydd   1548
3. William Lewis Esq. Presaddved   1549
4. David ap Rees ap David ap Gwilim,
    Llwydiart   1550
5. Hugh Peake, Esq. Caernarvon   1551
6. Sir Richard Bulkeley, Knight   1552
7. Rowland Griffith dying,
    Rees Thomas, Esq. succed.   1553

MARY.

1. Thomas Mostyn, Esq. Mostyn   1554
2. John ap Rees ap Llewelyn ap Hwlkin, Esq.
    Bodychan   1555
3. Thomas ap William, Esq. Vainol   1556
4. Robert Bulkeley, Esq. Gronant   1557
5. William Lewis, Esq. Presaddved   1558

ELIZABETH.

1. Lewis ap Owen ap Meurick, Esq. Vrondêg   1559
2. Sir Nicolas Bagnal, Knight, Ireland   1560
3. Sir Richard Bulkeley, Knight, Baron-Hill   1561
4. Maurice Griffith, Esq. Plâsnewydd   1562
5. Owen ap Hugh, Esq. Bodeon   1563
6. Rice Thomas, Esq. Aber   1564

7. Richard Owen, Esq. Penmynydd   1565
8. John Lewis, Esq. Presaddved   1566
9. David ap Rees ap Dayid ap Gwilim, Esq.   1567
10. Richard White, Esq. Monachlog   1568
11. Rowland Bulkeley, Esq. Porthamel   1569
12. Sir Richard Bulkeley, Knight, Baron-Hill   1570
13. Lewis Owen ap Meurick, Esq. Brondêg   1571
14. William Lewis, Esq. Presaddved   1572
15. Richard Owen, Penmynydd   1573
16. John Wynne ap Shenkin ap John, Esq.
    Hîrdrevaig   1574
17. Thomas Mostyn, Esq. Mostyn   1575
18. Edward Conway, Esq. Bodryddan   1576
19. Owen Wood, Esq. Rhosmore   1577
20. Dr. Ellis Price, Esq. Plâs-Iolyn   1578
21. William Thomas, Esq. Aber   1579
22. Owen ap Hugh, Esq. Bodeon   1580
23. Hugh Hughes, Esq. Plâs Côch   1581
24. John Griffith, Esq. Cichle   1582
25. Richard White, Esq. Monachlog   1583
26. Thomas Glynne, Esq. Glynllivon   1584
27. Maurice Kyffin, Esq. Mainen   1585
28. Dr. Ellis Price, Esq. Plâs-Iolyn   1586
29. John Griffith, Esq. Trevarthen   1587
30. Thomas Mostyn, Esq. Mostyn   1588
31. Richard White, Esq. Monachlog   1589
32. Roger Mostyn, Esq. Mostyn   1590
33. Owen Holland, Esq. Berw   1591
34. Hugh Hughes, Esq. Plâs Côch   1592
35. John Griffith, Esq. Cichle   1593
36. Richard White, Esq. Monachlog   1594
37. Pierce Lloyd, Esq. Goredog   1595
38. Arthur Bulkeley, Esq. Coeden   1596
39. William Glynne, Esq. Glynllivon   1597
40. Richard Bulkeley, Esq. Porthamel   1598
41. Owen Holland, Esq. Berw   1599
42. Hugh Hughes, Esq. Plâs Côch   1600
43. Thomas Glynne, Esq. Glynllivon   1601
44. Richard Bulkeley, Esq. Porthamel   1602

JAMES I.

1.	Pierce Lloyd, Senior, Esq. Llugwy	1603
2.	William Lewis, Esq. Chwaenwen	1604
3.	William Griffith, Esq. Trevarthen	1605
4.	John Lewis, Esq. Presaddved	1606
5.	Richard Glynne, Esq. Glynllivon	1607
6.	Sir Hugh Owen, Knight, Bodeon	1608
7.	Thomas Holland, Esq. Berw	1609
8.	William Owen, Esq. Bodeon	1610
9.	John Bodwell, Esq. Bodwell	1611
10.	Pierce Lloyd, Junior, Esq. Llugwy	1612
11.	John Wynne Edwards, Esq. Bodewryd	1613
12.	Owen Wood, Esq. Llanygwyvan	1614
13.	Richard Meurick, Esq. Bodorgan	1615
14.	Hugh Lewis ap Howel, Esq. Llachylched	1616
15.	Richard Williams, Esq. Llysdulas	1617
16.	John Lewis, Esq. Presaddved	1618
17.	Sir William Glynne, Knight, Glynllivon	1619
18.	Henry Lloyd, Esq. Bodwineu	1620
19.	Hugh Wynne, Esq. Maesoglan	1621
20.	Sir Thomas Holland, Berw	1622
21.	Richard Owen, Esq. Penmynydd	1623
22.	John Bodychen, Esq. Junior, Bodychen	1624
23.	William Thomas, Esq. Quirt	1625

CHARLES I.

1.	William Griffith, Esq. Trevarthen	1626
2.	Hugh Morgan Esq. Beaumaris	1627
3.	Edward Wynne, Esq. Bodewryd	1628
4.	Richard Wynne, Esq. Rhydgroes	1629
5.	Thomas Glynne, Esq. Glinllivon	1630
6.	William Robinson, Esq. Monachdy	1631
7.	Thomas Chedle, Esq. Lleiniog	1632
8.	William Owen, Esq. Brondeg	1633
9.	Hugh Owen, Esq. Bodeon	1634
10.	Edward Wynne, Esq. Bodewryd	1635
11.	Robert Wynne, Esq. Tre'r-go'	1636
12.	William Bulkeley, Esq. Coeden	1637
13.	Pierce Lloyd, Esq. Llugwy	1638
14.	Richard Bulkeley, Esq. Porthamel	1639
15.	Owen Wood, Esq. Rhosmor	1640
16.	Richard Meurick, Esq. Bodorgan	1641
17.	Thomas Bulkeley, Esq. Cleiviog	1642
18.	Thomas Chedle, Esq. Lleiniog	1643
19.	William Bold, Esq. Tre'r-ddôl	1644
20.	Robert Jones, Esq. Dreiniog	1645
21.	Robert Jones, Esq. Dreiniog	1646
22.	Richard Meurick, Esq. Bodorgan	1647
23.	Richard Meurick, Esq. Bodorgan	1648

CHARLES II.—*During the Usurpation.*

1.	William Bold, Esq. Tre'r-ddôl	1649
2.	Owen Wood, Esq. Rhosmor	1650
3.	Pierce Lloyd, Esq. Llugwy	1651
4.	Henry Owen, Esq. Maesoglan	1652
5.	Rowland Bulkeley, Esq. Porthamel	1653
6.	Hugh Owen, Esq. Bodeon	1654
7.	William Bold, Esq. Tre'r-ddôl	1655
8.	Richard Wood, Esq. Rhosmor	1656
9.	Richard Owen, Esq. Penmynydd	1657
10.	Robert Lord Viscount Bulkeley, Baron-Hill	1658
11.	Henry Lloyd, Esq. Bodwina	1659

After the Restoration.

12.	Henry Lloyd, Esq. Bodwina	1660
13.	Thomas Wood, Esq. Rhosmor	1661
14.	William Bulkeley, Esq. Coeden	1662
15.	John Lloyd, Esq. Llandegvan	1663
16.	Richard Wynne, Esq. Penheskin	1664
17.	John Owen, Esq. Maethlu	1665
18.	Rowland Bulkeley dying, Howel Lewis, Esq. succed.	1666
19.	John Owen, Esq. Penrhos	1667
20.	John Glynne, Esq. Glynllivon	1668
21.	Rowland White, Esq. Monachlog	1669
22.	Conningsby Williams, Esq. Penmynydd	1670
23.	Edward Price, Esq. Bodowyr	1671
24.	Richard Bulkeley, Esq. Porthamel	1672
25.	Owen Williams, Esq. Croesvechan	1673
26.	Hugh Williams, Esq. Waen	1674
27.	William Meurick, Esq. Bodorgan	1675
28.	Thomas Wynne, Esq. Rhydgroes	1676
29.	Thomas Michael, Esq. Maen y Driw	1677
30.	Hugh Wynne, Esq. Cromlech	1678
31.	David Lloyd, Esq. Llwydiarth	1679
32.	Thomas Wynne, Esq. Glagloed	1680
33.	Rowland Wynne, Esq. Porthamel	1681
34.	Robert Parry, Esq. Amlwch	1682
35.	Owen Hughes, Esq. Beaumaris	1683
36.	Owen Bold, Esq. Tre'r-ddôl	1684

JAMES II.

1.	Roger Hughes, Esq. Plâs Côch	1685
2.	Maurice Lewis, Esq. Trysglwyn	1686
3.	William Bulkeley, Esq. Coeden	1687
4.	Sir Hugh Owen, Knight and Baronet	1688
5.	Henry Sparrow, Beaumaris	1689

WILLIAM & MARY.

1. John Griffith, Esq. Carreglwyd	1690
2. Samuel Hanson, Esq. Bodvell	1691
3. David Williams, Esq. Glanalaw	1692
4. Owen Williams, Esq. Carrog	1693
5. William Jones, Esq. Pentraeth	1694
6. John Thomas, Esq. Aber	1695
7. Henry White, Esq. Friars	1696
8. Hugh Wynne, Esq. Tre-Iorwerth	1697
9. William Griffith, Esq. Carreglwyd	1698
10. Pierce Lloyd, Esq. Llanidan	1699
11. Francis Edwards, Esq. Penheskin	1700
12. John Williams, Esq. Waen-isa'	1701

ANNE.

1. John Wynne, Esq. Waen-wen	1702
2. Robert Owen, Esq. Penrhos	1703
3. William Owen, Esq. Cremlyn	1704
4. Hugh Wynne, Esq. Cromlech	1705
5. Owen Meurick, Esq. Bodorgan	1706
6. Owen Roberts, Esq. Beaumaris	1707
7. John Sparrow, Esq. Beaumaris	1708
8. John Griffiths, Esq. Llanddyvnan	1709
9. William Lewis, Esq. Trysglwyn	1710
10. John Morris, Esq. Celleiniog	1711
11. William Roberts, Esq. Caerau	1712
12. Thomas Roberts, Esq. Bodiar	1713
13. William Lewis, Esq. Llysdulas	1714

GEORGE I.

1. William Bulkeley, Esq. Brynddu	1715
2. Maurice William, Esq. Havodgaregog	1716
3. Edward Bayley, Esq. Plâsnewydd	1717
4. William Bodvell, Esq. Madrin	1718
5. Hugh Hughes, Esq. Plâs Côch	1719
6. Rice Thomas, Esq. Coedalen	1720
7. Thomas Lloyd, Esq. Llanidan	1721
8. Richard Hampton, Esq. Henllys	1722
9. William Owen, Esq. Penrhos	1723
10. John Griffith, Esq. Carreglwyd	1724
11. John Owen, Esq. Presaddved	1725
12. Thomas Rowlands, Esq. Caerau	1726
13. Henry Morgan, Esq. Henblâs	1727

GEORGE II.

1. John Morris, Esq. Celleiniog	1728
2. John Williams, Esq. Trearddur	1729
3. Henry Williams, Esq. Tros-y-muriau	1730
4. Henry Powel, Esq. Llangevni	1731
5. Robert Hampton, Esq. Henllys	1732
6. William Evans, Esq. Treveilir	1733
7. Robert Bulkeley, Esq. Gronant	1734
8. Richard Lloyd, Esq. Rhosbeirio	1735
9. Richard Roberts, Esq. Bodsyran	1736
10. Edmund Meurick, Esq. Trevriw	1737
11. William Roberts, Esq. Bodiar	1738
12. Robert Williams, Esq. Pwll-y-crochan	1739
13. Robert Owen, Esq. Pencraig	1740
14. Rice Williams, Esq. Quirt	1741
15. Hugh Jones, Esq. Cymynod	1742
16. Hugh Williams, Esq. Pentir,	1743
17. Richard Hughes, Esq. Bodrwyn	1744
18. John Nangle, Esq. Llwydiarth	1745
19. Henry Williams, Esq. Tros-y-muriau	1746
20. William Thomas, Esq. Coedalen	1747
21. William Lewis, Esq. Llanddyvnan	1748
22. Owen Wynne, Esq. Penheskin	1749
23. John Jones, Esq. Henllys	1750
24. John Lloyd, Esq. Hirdrevaig	1751
25. Charles Evans, Esq. Treveilir	1752
26. Bodychain Sparrow, Esq. Bodychain	1753
27. Richard Hughes, Esq. Bodrwyn	1754
28. Hugh Davies, Esq. Brynhirddin	1755
29. Charles Alanson, Esq. Erddreiniog	1756
30. John Rowlands, Esq. Heneglwys	1757
31. John Griffith, Esq. Carreglwyd	1758
32. Robert Owen, Esq. Penrhos	1759
33. Robert Lloyd, Esq. Tregauen	1760

GEORGE III.

1. Francis Lloyd, Esq. Monachdy	1761
2. Hugh Barlow, Esq. Penrhos	1762
3. Felix Feast, Esq. Bodlew	1763
4. John Lewis, Esq. Llanvihangel	1764
5. Herbert Jones, Esq. Llynon	1765
6. Hugh Williams, Esq. Tŷ-vrŷ	1766
7. Hugh Williams, Esq. Cromlech	1767
8. William Hughes, Esq. Plâs-Côch	1768
9. William Smith, Esq. Erddreiniog	1769
10. John Hampton Jones, Esq. Henllys	1770
11. Paul Panton Esq. Plâs Gwyn	1771
12. John Jones, Esq. Penrhos-brodwen	1772
13. Henry Sparrow, Esq. 'Rallt-gôch	1773
14. Owen Putland Meurick, Esq. Bodorgan	1774
15. William Lloyd, Esq. Llwydiarth	1775
16. Hugh Hughes, Esq. Bodrwyn	1776
17. Rice Thomas, Esq. Coedalan	1777
18. Owen Jones, Esq. Penrhos-brodwen	1778
19. William Peacoke, Esq. Llanedwen	1779

20. Holland Griffith, Esq. Carregwlyd   1780
21. John R. Sparrow, Esq. 'Rallt-gôch   1781
22. William Vickers, Esq. Llanvawr   1782
23. Morgan Jones, Esq. Skerries Lighthouse   1783
24. Thomas Asheton Smith, Esq. Trevarthen   1784
25. Richard Llwyd, Esq. Rhosbeirio   1785
26. William Pritchard, Esq. Trescawen   1786
27. John G. Lweis, Esq. Trysclwyd   1787
28. Henry Pritchard, Esq. Trescawen   1788
29. John Williams, Esq. Nantanog   1789
30. Thomas Williams, Esq. Tregarnedd   1790
31. Herbert Jones, Esq. Llynon   1791
32. Hugh Price, Esq. Wern   1792
33. Evan Lloyd, Esq. Maes y Porth   1793
34. Hugh Jones, Esq Carrog   1794
35. John Bulkeley, Esq. Presaddved (knighted) 1795
36. John Morris, Esq. Conway Gelliniog   1796
37. Richard Jones, Esq. Tros-y-marian   1797
38. William Evans, Esq. Glanalaw   1798
39. Hugh Wynne, Esq. Chwaenddu   1799
40. William Harvey, Esq. Parciau   1800
41. John Price, Esq. Wern   1801
42. Gwylim Lloyd Wardle, Esq. Cevn Côch   1802
43. William Bulkeley Hughes, Esq. Plâs Côch   1803
44. Charles Evans, Esq. Treveilir   1804
45. John Williams, Esq. Trelan   1805
46. Sir Hugh Owen, Bart. Bodeon   1806
47 Paul Panton, Esq. Plâsgwyn   1807
48. John Jones, Esq. Penrhôs-brodwen   1808
49. Sir John Thomas Stanley, Bart. Bodewryd   1809

50. Hugh Evans, Esq. Hênblas   1810
51. Henry Williams, Esq. Trearddyr   1811
52. Hugh Bulkeley Owen, Esq. Coedanna   1812
53. John Hampton Hampton, Esq. Henllys   1813
54. George Francis Barlow, Esq. Ty'nllwyn   1814
55. Robert Hughes, Esq. Plâs Llangoed   1815
56. John Price, Esq. Plâs Llanvadoc   1816
57. Rice Thomas, Esq. Cemmaes   1817
58. John Price, Esq. Plâs Cadnant   1818
59. William Pritchard Llwyd, Esq. Llwydiarth 1819

GEORGE IV.

1. Robert Lloyd, Esq. Tregauen   1820
2. James Webster, Esq. Derry   1821
3. William Wynne Sparrow, Esq. Redhill   1822
4. Jones Panton, Esq. Plâs Gwyn   1823
5. John Owen, Esq. Trehwva   1824
6. Thomas Meyrick, Esq. Cevn Côch   1825
7. Hugh Davies Griffith, Esq. Caerhun   1826
8. Owen John Augustus Fuller Meyrick, Esq.
   Bodorgan   1827
9. Jones Panton, Esq. Llanddyvnan   1828
10. Henry Prichard, Esq. Maen Dusui   1829

WILLIAM IV.

1. Thomas Williams Esq. Glan'ravon   1830
2. Owen Owen, Esq. Llanvugail   1831
3. Sir John Williams, Bart. Tŷ-vrŷ   1832
4. Charles Henry Evans, Esq. Hênblas   1833

A LIST OF MEMBERS

WHO HAVE

SERVED IN PARLIAMENT FOR THE COUNTY AND BOROUGHS OF ANGLESEY

A.R.	MONA COUNTY.	BEAUMARIS BOROUGH.

HENRY VIII.

| 33. | Torn out . . . . | Risiart ap Rhydderch, of Myvyrian. |

EDWARD VI.

| 6. | Lewis Owen ab Meuric, of Bodorgan . . . . | John ap Robt. Lloyd, Esq., and Mauris Griffith of Plasnewydd.—[These two are said to have been returned for Newborough.] |

MARY.

| 1. | William Lewis of Presaddved, ... and Sir Risiart Bulkeley, Knight. | Rowland Bulkeley, Esq. of Porthamel, Rowland Bulkeley, Esquire. |

PHILIP & MARY.

1. & 2.	Sir R. Bulkeley . . . . ★ ★ ★	Merchant
2. & 3.	The same . . . . ★ ★ ★	Ditto
2. & 3.	William Lewis, Esq. of Presaddved	Hugh Goodman, Merchant
4. & 5.	Rowland Meredith, Esq. of Bodowir	William Prees ap Hywel

ELIZABETH.

1.	Rowland Meredith, Esq. . . . . ★ ★ ★ ★	
5.	Richard Bulkeley, Esq.	William ap Rees, Gentleman
13.	Sir Richard Bulkeley, Knight	William Bulkeley, Gentleman
14.	Lewis Owen ap Meyrick, Esq.	Rowland Kenrick, Gentleman. [He was Town Clerk of Beaumaris.]
27.	Owen Holland, Esq. of Berw	Thomas Bulkeley, Gentleman
28.	Sir Henry Bagnal, Knight	Thomas Bulkeley, Junior, Esq.
31.	Thomas Bulkeley, Esq. of Llangevni	Thomas Bulkeley, Esq.
35.	William Glyn, Gentleman	The same
39.	Hugh Hughes, Esq. of Plâs Côch	William Jones, Esq. of Castellmarch
43.	Thomas Holland, Esq. of Berw	William Maurice, Esq. of Clenenney

JAMES I.

1.	Sir Richard Bulkeley, Knight	William Jones, Esq. of Castellmarch
12.	★ ★ ★ ★ ★ ★ ★ ★ ★ ★ ★	
18.	Richard Williams, Gent. of Llysdulas	Sampson Evans, Esq.
21.	John Mostyn, Esq. of Tregarnedd	Charles Jones, Esq. of Castellmarch

CHARLES I.

1.	Sir Sackvil Trevor, Knight	Charles Jones, Esq.
1.	Sir Richard Bulkeley, Knight	The same
3.	Richard Bulkeley, Esq	The same
15.	John Bodwel, Esq.	The same
16.	The same	John Griffith, Senior, Esq. of Cefnamlwch

COMMONWEALTH *

William Jones, Esq., Bushy Mansel, and five more.

1654 George Twisleton	1653 Wales.
William Foxwist, Esq.	Bushy Mansel
1656 George Twistleton, Esq.	James Philips
Griffith Bodwrda, Esq.	Hugh Courteney
1658 Col. G. Twistleton, Esq.	James Williams
Griffith Bodwrda, Esq.	Ris. Price, and Jo. Brown.

[* The above is an exact copy from notes in the Caerwys MS, but the writer is at a loss how to account for the unusual number of representatives mentioned, or to distinguish between the County and Borough members.]

CHARLES II.

12.	Rt. Honorable Robert Lord Bulkeley	Gryffyth Bodwrda, Esq.
13.	Nicholas Bagnal, Esq. of Plasnewyth	Colonel William Robinson, Manachty.
		—[Sir Heniage Finch quitting it.]
30.	Henry Bulkeley, Esq.	Richard Bulkeley, Esq.
31.	The same	The same
32.	Richard Bulkeley, Esq.	Henry Bulkeley, Esq.

JAMES II.

1.	Rt. Honorable Robert Lord Bulkeley	Henry Bulkeley, Esq.

WILLIAM & MARY

1.	Honorable Thomas Bulkeley, Esq.	Sir W. Williams, Knt. and Bart. Llanvorda
2.	Rt. Honorable Richard Lord Bulkeley	Honorable Thomas Bulkeley, Esq.
		[Sir W. Williams of Vaenol dying.]

WILLIAM III.

7.	Rt. Honorable Richard Lord Bulkeley	Sir W. Williams, Knt. and Bart. Llanvorda
10.	Rt. Honorable Richard Lord Bulkeley	Owen Hughes, Esq.
12.	The same	Conningsby Williams, Esq.
13.	The same	Honorable Robert Bulkeley, Esq.

ANNE.

1.	Rt. Honorable Richard Lord Bulkeley	Honorable Robt. Bulkeley, Esq. [He dying, Conningsby Williams, Esq. was returned.]
4.	Rt. Honorable Richard Lord Bulkeley . . . . [Returned on his father's death.]	Honorable Henry Bartie, Esq.
9.	Rt. Honorable Richard Lord Bulkeley	Honorable Henry Bartie, Esq.
12.	The same	The same

GEORGE I.

1. Owen Meyrick, Esq. of Bodorgan . . . . Honorable Henry Bartie, Esq.
8. Rt. Honorable Richard Lord Bulkeley . . . . the same

GEORGE II.

A.D.

1727.	Hugh Williams, Esq. Chester	Sir W. W. Wynne, Bart. Wynnstay
1734.	Sir Nicholas Bayley, Bart. Plâsnewydd . . .	Richard Viscount Bulkeley
1741.	John Owen, Esq. Presaddved	James Viscount Bulkeley
1748.	Sir Nicholas Bayley, Bart.	Richard Price, Esq. Vaenor

GEORGE III.

1761.	Owen Meyric, Esq. Bodorgan	Richard Price, Esq. Vaenor
1768.	Sir Nicholas Bayley—[Owen Meyric dying.]	Sir Hugh Williams, Bart.
1770.	Sir Nicholas Bayley, Bart.	Sir Hugh Williams, Bart.
1774.	James Viscount Bulkeley	The same
1780.	The same	Sir George Warren, K.B.
1786.	Nicholas Bayley, Esq.	Honorable Hugh Fortesque
1791.	William Paget, Esq.	Sir Hugh Williams, Bart.
1794.	Arthur Paget, Esq.	Sir W. W. Wynn, Bart.
1796.	Honorable Arthur Paget, Esq.	Rt. Honorable Lord Newborough
1802.	The same	The same
1806.	The same	The same
1807.	Honorable Bulkeley Paget	The same—who died soon after; and on the 10th of September, Sir E. P. Lloyd, (Lord Mostyn) was elected.
1810.	Honorable B. Paget was re-elected, 6th of July, being appointed one of the Commissioners of the Treasury.	
1812.	Honorable Bulkeley Paget, Esq.	Thomas Frankland Lewis, Esq.
1818.	The same	The same

GEORGE IV.

1820	Lord Uxbridge	Thomas Frankland Lewis, Esq.
1826.	The same	Sir Robert Williams, Bart.
1828.	The same—re-elected 3rd April, his seat being vacated on his appointment to be Steward of the Household to the Lord Lt. of Ireland (Marquess of Anglesey, his father).	

WILLIAM IV.

1830.	Lord Uxbridge	Sir Robert Williams, Bart, who died at Nice, 1st December, 1830.
1831.	. . . .	Sir R. B. Williams Bulkeley, Bart. son of Sir R. Williams (February 8th).
1831.	Lord Uxbridge (May 10th)	Sir R. B. Williams Bulkeley, Bart. (May 2nd.)
1833.	Sir R. B. Williams Bulkeley, Bart	Sir E Paget, for Beaumaris, Holyhead, Amlwch, &c. under the Reform Bill.

For the Lady Catherine, Queen of England, mother of our Lord the King,
    A.D.1422.   1 *Henry VI.*

Grant to the Queen of 40,000 scutes (two equal to the value of one Noble—English).

THE PORTION OF THIS MONEY THAT WAS PAID BY THE ISLAND OF ANGLESEY.—

Commote of Dynde, beyond £100, granted to William Halley, £34 2s. 9½d.

Commote of Talibolion, £66 8s. 7¾d.

Commote of Llivayn, £60 11s. 3½d.

Commote of Meney, together with the stewardship of Meney £100 1s. 4d.

Commote of Malltryth, £45 9s. 5½d.

Vill of Kemes and Neweburgh, £47.

Castle and Vill of Beaumarys, £39 12s. 3¼d.

Stone Quarry in Turkell Commote, £7.

Manor of Aberfraw with the Mill of Dynde, beyond £10 granted to Robert Orell, to the value of
    £28 12s. 8d.

Stewardship of Rossair, beyond £10 granted to Hugh Orell, of the value of £66 0s. 8d.

The office of escheator beyond ten marks for the fee of the said escheator, to the value of £8 2s. 1d.
    The commote of Turkell and the office of shrievally of the County of Anglesey beyond the fee of the
    sheriffs, and a certain annuity of £100 granted to William Karynton, chevalier, to the value of
    £61 7s. 11½d. in the Isle of Anglesea, in North Wales, which said commotes, vills, castles, manors,
    stewardships and offices, with the appurtenances, beyond the annuities and charges aforesaid, and £40
    for the fee of the constable of Beaumarys; and beyond £36 10s. for the wages of the six soldiers abiding
    in the said castle, to be received yearly of the Principality of Wales aforesaid, are worth £425 5s.

Taxatio Bonorum Spiritualium et Temporalium, in Dioc. Bangor. Anno 1291.

SPIRITUALIA.—IN ARCHIDIACONATU DE ANGLESEY.

Hoc est Taxatio Decanatus de Tindaethwy.

Beneficium Decani ejusdem loci vij*m*.

Rectoria Gervatii in Ecclesia de Llanvaes xij*m*. et dimid.

Portio Thome Pulesdon in eadem vj*m*. iij*s*. iv*d*.

Rectoria Ricei (vel Richardi) in Ecclesia de Llanddyfnan x*m*.
Summa xxiij*m*. xvj*s*. viij*d*.

Hoc est Taxatio Decanatus de Talebolion.

Rectoria and obventiones Decani vj*m*. et dimid.

Rectoria Magistri Clementis vj*m*. iij*s*. iv*d*.

Rectoria Hugonis in Ecclesia de Llanelian vj*m*. et dimid.

Portio Tegerini capellani in Ecclesia de Amlhwch x*m*.

Rectoria Laurentii ap Ishun in Ecclesia Beate Marie (Y'nghornwy likely) vj*m*. et dimid.

Ecclesia de Llanvechell x*m*.
Summa xxxj*l*. iij*s*. jv*d*.

Hoc est Taxatio Decanatus de Rhosur, i.e. Meney and Malltraeth.

Prepositura in Ecclesia de castro Kybii xxix*m*.

Portio Gervasii Capellani in eadem, xj*m*.

Portio Clementis Capellani in eadem, vj*m*.

Portio Philippi filii Bleddyn in eadem, xj*m*. et dimid.

Ecclesia de Llanvihangel y Towyn cum sua Capella, vj*m*. et dim.

Rectoria Ecclesie de Aberffraw, x*m*.

Beneficium Hugonis in Ecclesia Llanpeulan, xij*m*.

Ecclesia de Rhoscoloun, vj*m*. v*s*.

Ecclesia de Llangeveny, vj*m*. et dim
Summa lxix*l*. x*s*. viij*d*.

Summa Taxationis Archidiaconatus Anglesey, una cum Bonis Episcopi et Canonicorum Ecclesie Bangor, ccclvj*l*. ix*s*. vij*d*.★

★ Browne Willis's Survey of Bangor, p.*201*.

"John de Pulle, with fifteen men at arms, and a hundred and forty archers, kept Beaumaris, at the yearly expence of £988 10*s*. 10*d*." (This was in the time of Glyndwr.)

A BRIEF SKETCH

OF THE

ROYAL EISTEDDFOD,

HELD AT BEAUMARIS

ON TUESDAY 28th, WEDNESDAY 29th, THURSDAY 30th, AND FRIDAY 31st OF AUGUST, 1832 :

SELECTED FROM THE BANGOR AND CHESTER PAPERS.

THE beautiful town of Beaumaris, the capital of Anglesey, was converted into a theatre of gaiety during four days of the past week, by the celebration of the Royal Eisteddfod, patronized by their Royal Highnesses the Duchess of Kent, and her illustrious daughter the Princess Victoria. The weather was not so favourable as could have been desired; Monday, the day preceding the festivities, was cold, rainy, and comfortless; and the morning of Tuesday was not calculated to dispel our fears and doubts. However, about ten o'clock, the sky assumed a more cheerful aspect, and by eleven the sun gleamed occasionally through the heavy clouds by which it had been obscured. The town instantly became a scene of bustle and animation, which reminded us of those beautiful lines by one of the modern Welsh poets—

> Aflonydd dwrf olwynion
> A drystiant y'mhalmant Môn.

We had prepared an introductory article upon the Eisteddfodau, which we reluctantly withdraw to make room for the proceedings of the week; the details of which are so voluminous, that our prefatory remarks must be very brief indeed. We must, however, observe that in consequence of the number of subjects given for competition, and the rewards attached to them, exceeding those of any preceding Eisteddfod, the bards and minstrels on this occasion were proportionally numerous; and though a few straggling rhymers will always be found to attend meetings like these, we are happy to state that nearly all the candidates were persons of reputation and talent, who had been drawn to Beaumaris by no other motive than a lowly ambition to excel their fellow competitors in any contest in which they might be respectively engaged.

The Royal party quitted the Bulkeley Arms, on Saturday, with their suite, by which time all the beds in the town were engaged. The company was very numerous and highly respectable, comprising a large portion of the gentry, nobility, and clergy of North Wales, and the bordering English counties.—

We observed Lord Robert Grosvenor and Lady—Lord and Lady Mostyn—Lady Helena Cooke—Honorable E. M. Lloyd Mostyn and Lady—Lord and Lady Fingal—Archbishop of Tuam—Lord Bishop of Bangor—Lord Bishop Dromore—Lord Boston.—Sir W. W. Wynn, Bart. M.P.—Sir Edwyn Mostyn, Bart. and Lady—Sir S. R. Glynne, Bart. M.P.—Sir R. Vivian, Bart. M.P.—Sir John Jennings, Bart.—Sir John and Major Hilton.—J. Maddock, Esq. Glan-y-Wern—P. York, Esq. Erddig—O. Stanley, Esq. Penrhos—Pierce Mostyn, Esq. &c. &c.

On Tuesday morning, about twelve o'clock, a procession was formed at the Town Hall, which, headed by a band of music, escorted the president Sir R. B. W. Bulkeley to the castle, in the area of which was erected a spacious and commodious platform, surrounded by seats for the accommodation of the company. Sir Richard, on taking the chair, was most enthusiastically greeted.

The Heralds having advanced to the front of the platform, and sounded their trumpets three times, in order to command attention and silence, the Rev. J. Blackwell opened the proceedings by reading the following proclamation in Welsh:—

" Y GWIR YN ERBYN Y BYD."

"Yn y flwyddyn 1832, pan yw yr huan yn nesau at Alban Elfed, yn awr anterth, ar yr 28ain o fis Awst, gwedi cyhoeddiad teilwng, agorir yr orsedd hon yn Nghastell Beaumaris, yn Ngwynedd, i roddi gwys a gwahawdd i bawb a gyrchont, lle nad oes noeth arf yn eu herbyn, ac y cyhoeddir barn gorsedd ar bob awenydd a barddoni a roddir dan ystyriaeth, yn llygad haul, ac yn ngwyneb golweuni.—*Y gwir yn erbyn y byd.*"

Mr. Aneurin Owen then favoured the company by giving the following translation:—

" THE TRUTH AGAINST THE WORLD."

"In the year 1832, and the sun approaching the Autumnal Equinox, at the hour of noon, on the 28th day of August, after due proclamation, this *gorsedd* is opened in the Castle of Beaumaris, in Gwynedd, with an invitation to all who may come, where no weapon is naked against them, and judgement will be given upon all works of Cimbric genius submitted for adjudication, in the eye of the sun, and in the face of the light.—*The truth against the world.*"

The President, Sir Richard Bulkeley, Bart., M.P. for the borough, now stepped forward, and following the example of Presidents on former occasions, made the following brief observation which were delivered in a very graceful and animated manner, and received with loud applause:—

He feared he would incur the charge of presumption for having accepted the high and honourable office to which he had been called, as he felt himself sadly deficient in two very necessary qualifications. He was not so well acquainted as he ought to be with the history of his native country, and he was totally ignorant of the language that would be employed in a great part of the proceedings. It was nothing but the pleasure which he experienced in contributing, as far as he was able, to the advancement of Welsh literature, that could have brought him to place himself in that distinguished situation. In confessing his own incapacity, he would claim the indulgence of the meeting, and confidently depend on receiving from those around him any assistance of which he might stand in need. As some ladies and gentlemen might not be fully acquainted with the precise nature of an Eisteddfod, he would endeavour, in a few words, to explain its origin and its design. In days of yore Eisteddfodau were held every three years. The primary object of them was the cultivation of literature, the improvement of the morals of the people, and especially the encouragement of poetry and music. For these purposes Eisteddfodau were then held, and he could not say that at the present day these purposes were at all altered. The productions in the Welsh language that would be offered to the meeting, he was told by persons competent to form an opinion on the subject, had seldom been equalled and never excelled. He was obliged to be indebted to others for the pleasure of understanding this, so that the ignorance he had confessed carried with it its own punishment. To the bards of Cambria the assembly would owe the amusement which awaited them. He sincerely lamented that the condition of this most honourable class of men was different from that of the bards of former days. The situation, though not the character of the bards, was much changed. In the days to which he had referred they were the constant and familiar companions of the native princes, accompanying them to their wars, encouraging and animating them in the field of battle, and, in times of peace, cheering and solacing them in their halls and palaces. It was a subject of regret that the present race did not equal them in station, but they were in no respect inferior to them in talents. He sincerely rejoiced that although the meeting was not summoned, as had been the case in days that were past and gone, by royal authority, yet it was under royal patronage; and he was delighted to see, in the present literary contributions, which, as he had before said, had rarely been equalled, and had never been surpassed either in number or in excellence, that the Welsh *Awen* was in no wise extinct. The result of the Festival, he was confident, would be to inspire them all with loyalty and patriotism, and at the same time, with the sacred love of liberty and freedom. He had to thank the ladies and gentlemen present for the kind indulgence with which they had heard him; and having thus endeavoured, though imperfectly, to describe the nature and objects of the meeting, he would conclude with taking his leave.

At the conclusion of this very neat and appropriate address, the secretary, Mr. W. Jones, solicitor, of St. Asaph, invited such Bards as had Englynion to recite, or were prepared with any other compositions in honour of the meeting, to ascend the platform. Several persons immediately obeyed the summons, and the company were successively addressed by them in English and in Welsh. We trust the following selections will prove interesting to our readers:—

ADDRESS TO THE CHAIRMAN

Henffych o ddawnwych ddywenydd—Syr Risiard,
 Syw rasol Gadeirydd;
 I Awen fad iawn ef fydd,
 A chu lais yn achlesydd.

O'i dda rinwedd ddewr hynod—cu lwyddawl
 Coledda'r cyfarfod,
 Noddwr y gân glân ei glod,
 Wâs da addfwyn Eisteddfod.

Llawenydd ein Llyw union—eich gweled
    A'ch golwg mor foddlon,
    Ym mysg Beirdd, a miwsig bôn,
    Dewr addas y Derwyddon.

I noddi Awenyddiaeth—wych alwad,
    A choledd Dysgeidiaeth,
    Yn glau yn ddiau e ddaeth
    Athronwyr yn feithriniaeth.

Brythoneg bêr iaith union—law-forwyn
    Lefain tra gwendôn,
    Tra amser, tra ser, tra sôn,
    Tra mwyn naws ter Monwysion.

    Mor hyfryd eres, dymor Frodorion,
Clywed y bonedd clau eu dybenion
Ceuai'r Seneddwyr dros Awenyddion
A gwar Rïanod mor wiw gywreinion
Llên mâd yn lloni Môn—mor weddawl
A dala'n wrawl hên delynorion.

Richard Parry, Llannerchymedd.

ANNERCHIAD I EISTEDDFOD BEAUMARIS

Henffych well, *Gastell*, ein Gwestawr—mirian
    Beaumaris brydferthfawr,
    Eisteddfod, yn west hoeddfawr
    Daeth o lwydd, dïau i'th lawr.

Yn awr Môn wèn, crechwena—iawn achos
    Yn uchel banllefa;
    Caed Eisteddfod hynod, ha !
    Llòn wychawl, llawenycha.

Syw roesaw i *Syr Risiad*—ein dewrwych
    Gadeiriwr, mwyn penllad,
    Baron-hil, o bur iawn hâd,
    Mynweswn y *Monwysiad*.

Ac i'r Awen ein goreuwyr—ddaethant
    Yn ddoethaf Achleswyr;
    Sai'n haeddawl ein Seneddwyr,
    Cadw'n hiaith yw gwaith y gŵyr.

Heb *Iorwerth*—er ein cyfnerthu—wele
   Anwylion o'n deutu;
   Hil Tudor ein Cynor cu,
   Hyneif o Fôn yn hanu.

  Er alltudio hyd i orwyllt oedwig,
Goronwy o'r *Mawrion,* i gwr *Amerig,*
Daw i Fôn raddau, diau'n fawreddig,
Daw i'n Hawen fwyn addien foneddig,
Chwâl y braw uchel eu brig—a'i graddau,
Yn bur ei moesau, yn ber ei miwsig.

  Daw ail *Oronwy,* od eiliwr union
Etto rhyw *Feilir,* welir yn wiwlon,
A gwiw Feirdd enwog, fo o radd *Einion*
Ednyfed a *Gwalchmai,* garai ragorion
Cyfyd o'u mysg—cofiwyd Môn—a'n mamiaith
Ha ! Ha ! i'n eilwaith, a ddaw anwylion.

                THOMAS PARRY, *Llannerchymedd.*

———————

Breathes the soul of a Goronwy through Mona's fair Isle ?
   Wafted hence may the muse, borne along
On the wings of sweet zephyrs and grac'd with a smile,
   Preside at the feast of the song !

Dwells the spirit of Ionawr with mortals below ?
   Is the genius of Wallia his care ?
Or in heav'n, to the harp, do his joys ever flow,
   While he sings to the Trinity there?

Shall Kerry's blest Shepherd, retir'd to the shade,
   Neglected, sweet moralist, lie ?
My country forbid it ! Or virtue shall fade,
   And charity weep in the sky.

Strike the lyre ! May his praise, as the seasons roll on,
   Embellish the soul-thrilling strain !
While the walls of our Beaumaris Castle, anon,
   Respond the fair theme o'er again.

Unassuming, the muse, from Siluria remote,
   Greets the Congress of Cambria so fair;
While the bard and the minstrel its mirth shall promote,
   Will the hearts of Siluria be there ?

              H. JONES, Merthyr Tydvil.

Hail, Cambria, hail gladly this festival day;
    Entwin'd be thy muse with the brightest of flowers;
Illum'd be that genius, immortal the day,
    That the minstrel-bard chaunts in these grey hoary towers.
For the harp's swelling strains with emotion's more sweet
When the bards and their patrons thus happily meet.

The strains of our *Cynfeirdd*, inspired of yore,
    Awake, and repel the proud Borderer's tale;
His disdain shall not sully our minstrelsy more—
    Your fire is not quench'd—your accents reveal:
And the grateful thrill'd patriots will never refuse
A just meed of praise to Cambria's sweet muse.

Hail, hail, and thrice welcome, brave patriot band,
    And thrice welcome sons of the *Awen;*—to ye
The proud rocks of Arvon, to Mona's bright strand,
    Exulting, re-echo the songs of the free.
This Congress of Bardism and Royalty—Fame
To long unborn ages shall proudly proclaim.

Within these bold turrets, 'mid our ancestors' wail,
    Did the tyrant depose e'en that dear minstrel band.
Forbid the dark record, and deem it a tale
    By horror once vision'd of old in our land;
For allay'd were the wrath of that proud ruthless king
Had he heard but the minstrel of Cambria once sing.

The drear clang of war alarms *Cymru* no more,
    The bright sun of Freedom's gold radiance distils;
Let's forget now the dark gloomy ages of yore—
    The gory fiend's vanish'd that dyed our green hills:
To Freedom unbounded our sweet lays invoke—
The gyve now lies shatter'd, the tyrant-spear broke.

Sweet harp of old Cambria, this hour thou art tuned,
    Approving, fair Royalty listens to thee;
In the courts of the kingly thou'st often communed,
    Thy magic delighting the noble and free.
Now, benignantly smiling, princesses command
With joy the fond lays of our dear mountain land.

Immortal Goronwy's wreath'd lyre shall string
    To the fair race of Tudor, brave sire of Môn;
The hoar cromlech echoes, the Druid groves ring,
    Joy, joy to our nobles !—True Britons have shown,
And declare that each bosom with loyalty thrills,
And welcomes their visit to Cambria's green hills.

Again, let the Awen's sweet accents prepare
   To the much honour'd patriot—record we the fame
Of Baron Hill's *nenbren*—he graces the chair;
   While the minstrel and bard their fond raptures proclaim
In greeting the fam'd one, whose munificent hand
Revives the fond strain of his dear native land.

Hil telynorion, doed adnerth i'ch tannau;
   Boneddio'n gwladgarawl a dyrant yn nghyd
I noddi y beirddion, ac ennyn plethiadau
   Yr awen, fu bellach heb achles gyhyd.
Mawrion feithrinant wir ddawn awenyddion,
Blodeued yr awen tra saif Cymry dirion,
Mewn côf tra daiaren, boed iaith yr hen Frython,
   Ei beirddion yn enwog hyd ddiwedd y byd.

THOMAS LLOYD JONES, *Holywell.*

PREMIUMS AWARDED.

Mr. W. Jones, the Secretary, stated that the next business would be the adjudication of prizes to the successful authors of literary compositions. They came on in the following order:—

PRIZE I.—For the best Six Stanzas *(Chwe Englynion)* on Menai Bridge, a premium of £7 and a medal of the value of £2. For the second best on the same subject, a premium of £3 10s.

The Secretary called upon the judges to come forward and declare the successful candidates.

The Rev. Evan Evans, who was one of them, said that the subject had excited great interest among the sons of the *Awen*, for no less than 62 compositions had been sent in ! Upon a subject so confined, and allowing so little scope for the display of superior genius, they (the judges) had felt great difficulty in coming to a decision. There were eight poems of merit, seven of which were so much upon a par, that they would consider it an act of injustice to award the second prize to any one in particular, to the exclusion of the other competitors. They considered the paper signed "DEINIOL" the best, and recommended that the medal and £3 10s. should be given to him; and the £7 equally divided among the rest.

"Deiniol" was requested to declare himself, and immediately the Rev. David Williams, of Clynnog, answered as the representative of Ebenezer Thomas, of the same place. The Rev. Gentleman was invested with the medal by Lady Williams of Beaumaris. When the ceremony was concluded, Mr. Williams observed that the successful candidate was a very young man, of splendid talent, but that his modesty was so great that he could not be prevailed upon to appear in person on the occasion. The following are the stanzas:—

ENGLYNION AR BONT MENAI.

Pont Menai pa'nd dymunol—ei chadwyn
    A'i chydiad gorchestol;
    Di lerw Dîd, o lawer dôl,
    A phlethiad, asiad oesol.

Oesol adail seiliedig—ar waelod
    Yr heli chwydddedig,
    Niweidio 'i mûr unedig
    Nid all y dòn a'i dull dig.

Er dull dig rhuad hallt eigion—ni syfl
    Nes syflo *Eryron;*
    Ac o'i ffurfio caiff *Arwo n*
    Bont tra myg i ben tîr *Môn.*

Pen tîr Môn pa antur mwy—ei gyrhaedd
    Tros gerynt *Porthaethwy;*
    Nid bâd, y Bont safadwy,
    A ddaw a glàn yn ddi glwy.

Di glwy yw tramwy a gwneud tremiad—ar
    Yr oruwch adeilad:
    Uwch o ran ei chywreiniad
    At iawn lês na phont un wlâd.

Nid oes un wlad îs y Ne' lòn—fyth deifl
    Y fath Dîd dros afon;
    Na chynnygiwch, Enwogion,
    Heb wneud taith hyd y Bont hon.

The second prize was divided among the seven competitors, according to the recommendation of the judges.

PRIZE II.—The president's premium of £10, to the author of the best Elegy on Owain Myfyr. The secretary said he was sorry only two compositions had been received upon this subject; neither of which were considered by the judges of sufficient merit to claim the prize. The subject would therefore be left open to future competition.

PRIZE III.—A premium of £15, and a medal of the value £5, for the best Essay, in English, on the History of the Island of Anglesey, with Biographical Sketches of the eminent men it produced; and a premium of £7 10*s.* for the second-best Essay, in English, on the same subject.

The judges being called upon to declare the successful competitors, the Rev. J. H. Cotton said that he had been among others selected to pronounce a decision as to the comparative claims of the several Essays on the History of the Island of Anglesey. He felt himself in many views incompetent to the task;

in particular he was not a native Cambrian; and even if he had possessed all the requisite qualifications, he must lament that the time which he could bestow upon the subject had been much too limited. He had however no hesitation in declaring it to be his opinion that the Essay which assumed the fictitious name of "BRONWEN" had by far the greatest merit. The writer seemed to possess stores of information which had never previously been opened, and which, perhaps, would never have come to light had it not been for the industry of the author. Indeed the Essay was like the Island of Anglesey itself; it contained ore of inestimable price, ore which it was difficult to find, but which, when discovered, proved not only to be valuable, but most abundant. There was, as he already intimated, a distinctive character about the Essay; it was peculiarly national. A tone pervaded it which constituted its high recommendation to the meeting: the author, he felt persuaded, must be a *Cymro*—a Cymro not by name only, but *intus et in cute*. To none could the words of the immortal bard be more justly or more appropriately applied:

> Eu Nêr a folant,
> Eu hiaith a gadwant,
> Eu tir a gollant,
> Ond gwyllt Walia.

These lines he would take the liberty of translating for the benefit of some of the "country gentlemen": the translation would not present the characteristic alliteration of the original, but this he trusted would be forgiven:

> Their Lord they laud,
> Their language love,
> Their land they lose,
> Except wild Wales.

He was about to hazard a remark which might appear in a Saxon to be a stretch of the imagination, but he hoped that under such circumstances, even a Saxon might be allowed to catch a small portion of poetic fire. Who that examined the Essay which had called forth these observations, and saw its correct and beautiful representation of the Island of Anglesey, but must be excused if he indulged in a flight of fancy, and imagined the author to have soared to the heights of Snowdon itself, to have plucked a quill from one of its own eagles and to have described with it in language of incomparable accuracy and taste all the varying characteristics of the Island. The Essay to which he adverted was beyond question the most valuable that had been offered on that occasion. There was however another, the production of a writer who signed himself "Investigator", which contained a fund of good sense, and which was drawn up with much perspicuity, and in excellent taste. It was calculated to afford both information and delight to the general reader. It entered very circumstantially into the History of Beaumaris, its antiquities, and its later improvements. It told the world of that which it was impossible for those before whom he had the honour of speaking, ever to forget: it expatiated on the signal munificence which distinguished the former illustrious and benevolent possessor of Baron Hill; but in offering this deserved tribute on the altar of departed excellence, the writer had not exhausted his

subject. He had recorded many delightful instances of liberality on the part of the present justly respected proprietor, while he left much indeed for the future historian to hand down to posterity of the
patriotism and liberality of that truly exalted and noble house. The Rev. gentleman concluded, amidst
the loudest acclamations of the meeting, by applying the following stanza to the president:—

> Llwyddiant i'w deulu,
> Llwyddiant i'w dŷ,
> Llwyddiant i'w gariad,
> A dedwydd bo hi.

The secretary having called the person using the signature of "Bronwen" to come forward, and
no one answering, broke open the sealed leaf, and declared Miss Angharad Llwyd of Caerwys to be
the author. Miss Charlotte Williams was invested with the medal as the representative of the author,
Miss Llwyd, by the president.

To diversify the morning's amusement, the secretary said he would now introduce one round of
Pennillion Singing. Several harpers and singers, apparently peasants, in mean attire, were accordingly
stationed upon the stage, and commenced a kind of singing, or musical recitation, which we believe
no person but a Welshman can either comprehend or describe. It would be folly, therefore, in us to
make the attempt, but the performance excited the greatest amusement among the Welsh portion of
the audience, and drew from it continued peals of laughter and applause. We understand it is a national
custom confined exclusively to the Welsh, and they seem passionately fond of it. The Eisteddfod Committee were no doubt aware of its peculiarity, for in the programme of this day's proceedings is the following note, which we copy for the information of our English readers. "To sing Pennillion the singer
is obliged to follow the harper, who may change the tune whenever he pleases; also perform variations,
while the vocalist must keep time, and end precisely with the strain. Those are considered the best
singers who can adapt the stanzas of various metres to one melody, and who are acquainted with the
twenty-four measures, according to the bardic laws and rules of composition. The amateur will see that
the singer will not commence with the strain, but take it up at the second or third bar, as best suits the
metre of the pennill he intends to sing,—and this is constantly done by persons totally unacquainted
with music !"

Henry Davies. Esq. of Cheltenham, then came forward and recited the following ode with very
good effect:—

I.

Isle of the Druid and the Bard ! since thou
Wert chronicled in song, the ebb and flow
  Of times and tides have ceased not:—
    Centuries have rolled
With more to thee than centuries of woe;
  Yet hath dishonour left no blot
Upon the 'scutcheon of thine ancient fame,—
  And oh ! how blest thy lot !

Had history's muse still left untold
The tale of Mona, when the Roman came,
Buckler'd and helm'd, and panoplied in flame !
Nor traced one line of triumph to record
The course of Loigria's desolating sword;
When crimson conquest's sanguinary flood
Dash'd through the barriers that had long withstood
Its lurid deluge;—and the Awen light
Of Cambria that, undimm'd and bright,
 Had blazed for centuries, was quenched in blood !

I I .

Mother of Wales ! Nurse of the free and brave !
Dense was the gloom that gather'd round thee then;
And hoarser than the thunders of the wave.
 The cry of anguish and despair arose
  From mountain-cave and glen !
 Seem'd it not then, dark island, unto those
Who loved thee most, and served thee unto death,
That night eternal was about to close
Around the land, where erst alone
The light of Freedom and of Genius shown ?
The dauntless heart that never quail'd
In battle's onset, fainted now;—
Patriot alike and poet fail'd
 To mourn their country's overthrow !—
Torn were the harp-strings—hush'd the voice of song;
And echoless our father's halls, our father's hills among.

I I I .

Five hundred years went by, and still
 The lyre of Mona slept,
Nor was there one to wake the thrill
Of rapture, and of hope, until
 Her own Goronwy—bard beloved !
Its chords in triumph swept;
And to the Loigrian scoffer proved
That genius from Cynddelw's land
Should never pass away:
But long as Arvon's mountains stand
Should sound, through Time's remotest day,
"To high-born Howel's harp, and soft Llewelyn's lay."
  And lo ! again, again
  The bardic strain
Echoes along the bosom of the main
 That belts with billows Mona's sacred shore;

While, louder than the ocean's roar,
  The voice of fame
Gladdens the welkin, and with loud acclaim
Peals a new era to the Cambrian name !

IV.

The spirits of the mighty dead,
Hail the glad pæan, and, rejoicing, spread
Their viewless pinions to the eternal blaze
Of sunless glory that around them plays,
Commission'd earthward upon high behest.
    Breaking the gloom
    That mantles round the past, they come
From the green islands of the far off west,
Unseen of vulgar eye, but not the less
Present, the gifted and the good to bless;
To welcome those who, led by genius' light—
Inheritors of inspiration's might—
    Are destined soon
To share with them the high and holy noon
Of immortality;—and wear the wreath
That fades not, withers not, and owns not death !

V.

They came to hail a brighter morn
  Than ever yet to Mona's Isle,
In the fair orient of the past, was born,
  Or woke creation's smile.
Mother of Wales ! Around thy shore,
  Songless and harpless long,
Behold ! from North and South, once more,
  Thy gifted children throng !
Fired by the spirit that of yore
  Inspired the masters of the lofty tongue !
Nor seeks in vain the youthful bard,
  The minstrel aged, and the seer
Renown's fair guerdon and award,
  The smile of beauty, and the cheer
Of gratulation—proud reward,
  To every child of song and every minstrel dear.
And these to other times shall tell,
  Through other lands proclaim,
How Cymru's Awen broke the spell
  That manacled her fame.
When Wallia from her deepest dell,
  To Snowdon's sun-lit peak,

Echoes exulting to the swell
 Of joy and triumph, that bespeak
The smile to Cambria long unknown,
The presence of the princely heir to British Arthur's crown.

PRIZE IV.—The Gwyneddigion Society's medal, to the author of the best stanzas on Adam and Eve in Paradise.—The secretary stated that as the judges of Adam and Eve in Paradise were not present *(laughter)* the adjudication of the prize would be deferred until the following day.

PRIZE V.—A premium of £10, and a medal of the value of £3, for the best Elegy *(Rhyddolaeth)* in Welsh blank verse on *"Ifor Ceri"* (the late Rev. J. Jenkins, Kerry), and a premium of £5 for the second-best Elegy in Welsh blank verse, on the same subject.

The Rev. J. Blackwell read the following adjudication, signed by that learned critic Dr. Owen Pughe, and himself:—"Eight compositions have been received on the lamented death of one of the best of men and of Welshmen—one of the principal promoters of modern Eisteddfodau. We are glad to see in our bards a growing taste for a species of metre in which the sweetness of their national *cynghanedd* is not likely to lead them astray. Of these eight compositions, four are excellent: those are signed, 'Galarwr'—'Cynddelw'—'Ymddifad Hiraethog', and 'Cynddelw'. But we consider the two signed 'Cynddelw' the best; that commencing 'Tàn ywen hên' is evidently the production of a man of much poetic talent. His imagination is warm, his taste good, his language elegant, and he would, most probably, have gained the prize, had not the merits we have mentioned, united to other merits peculiarly his own, been possessed by his rival 'Cynddelw'. We conceive 'Cynddelw' commencing 'Pan y machludo huan araul nawn' to be eminently worthy of the prize."

The secretary called upon "Cynddelw" to declare himself, when Mr. Thomas Lloyd Jones of Holywell answered, and was invested with the medal by Miss Charlotte Williams.

The premium of £5 for the second-best Elegy on the same subject was adjudged to the Rev. John Jones *(Tegid)* of Christ Church, Oxford, a distinguished Welsh scholar.

PRIZE VI.—A medal for the best Ode, on the coming of age of Pyers Mostyn, Esq. eldest son of the worthy and much esteemed Sir Edward Mostyn, of Talacre, president of the late Denbighshire Eisteddfod.

The Judges in this case were the Rev. J. Blackwell, and the Secretary, Mr. Wm. Jones. The latter gentleman read the following adjudication to the meeting, signed with both of their names.

"We do not recollect having a severer task to perform than to determine the palm of victory between two competitors on this exhilarating subject—'Simwnt Vychan', and 'Simwnt yr oes yma'. Both are, in our opinion, deserving, and almost equally deserving of praise; but as the medal must be awarded to one competitor, we think, that the striking national peculiarity of 'Simwnt yr oes yma' entitles him to a very slight preference over his rival. When we venture to say that these poems are not utterly unworthy of their subject, we feel that we pay them the highest compliment in the estimation of all who are acquainted with the rising and manly virtues of the young chieftain of Talacre. We think so very highly of 'Simwnt Vychan' that we would wish him to declare himself, and if we dared, we would earnestly recommend him to the consideration of the committee."

The Secretary having called upon "Simwnt yr oes yma" to declare himself, Mr. William Edwards, of Ysceiviog, Flintshire, answered, and being introduced upon the platform, was invested with the medal by Mrs. Brice Pierce.

The person using the signature of "Simwnt Vychan" was called to declare himself.—Mr. William Edwards, Llanberis, answered.

PRIZE VII.—A premium of £20 and a medal of the value of £5 for the best *Awdl* (Ode) on the wreck of the Rothsay Castle *(Llong-ddrylliad y Rothsay Castle)*; and a premium of £10 for the sec-ond-best Ode on the same subject. On this subject 19 compositions were received, the judges of which were the Rev. Walter Davies and Mr. Wm. Jones. A long and critical letter was read to the meeting, from the former gentleman, by which it appeared that he considered the poem by *"Un a gâr fyw yn nglan y môr"* the best composition, although several of the others were of great merit. Mr. Wm. Jones, the other judge, stated that at the request of the Rev. Walter Davies he had read the two best poems, and cordially agreed with that gentleman in his decision, and he considered the composition above men-tioned, one of the finest bursts of poetic genius, and the most striking ebullition of the Welsh *Awen* which had ever fallen under his observation. In confirmation of that opinion he made several quota-tions and concluded by observing, that if the Eisteddfod had been got up for no other purpose than the production of this poem, its promoters and the principality would have been amply rewarded. The fol-lowing are some of the extracts read to the meeting:—

> Bawb un ddull, myn'd bob yn ddau,
> Hyd lenydd pysgodlynau;
> A sylwi ar risialwawr
> Gloywddwfr glân, a'i wiwlan wawr;
> Dw'r, o'i yfed, yr afiach
> Gwan ei wedd a ddwg yn iach;
> Lle mae'r pysg yn cymmysg wau
> Mor lòn mewn amryw luniau.

> A weled, gyda'u gilydd,—ugeiniau
> O agenawg greigydd;
> A'r rhaiadr ar raiadr rydd
> Dwrw gwyllt drwy y gelltydd.

> Bistyllia, ffrystia 'n dra ffrom;
> Chwyrna wrth edrych arnom.—
> Cael rhoi gwib hyd grib y graig,
> Iach ael-gref yr uchel-graig,
> Chwilio'i chau fwngloddau glân,
> A'i chelloedd yn wych allan;

*   *   *   *   *

Gwelir o'r cwr bwygilydd,—i lawer
 O luoedd o wledydd,
 A'r haul mâd ar doriad dydd
 Yn agoryd ei gaerydd.

 Ei dêr wynebpryd eirian,
 Aur liw, wrth ddringo i'r làn,
 A'i wrid yn ymlid y nôs
 O'i ddorau yn ddiaros

 ★ ★ ★ ★ ★

Crychferwai, ymrwygai y mawr eigion,
Ewynai'i aflonydd dònau'n flinion;
Unwedd a 'mwriawl fynyddau mawrion.
Och ! oedd ei grothawg fawr-chwydd hagr, weithion,
Ymluchiai, taflai bob tòn—hyd y sêr
Yn eu gorwyllter a'u dagrau heilltion.
E ddeiai eilwaith yn nerthol ddyli'
O entrych hoywnef, gan wyllt drochioni,
Nes rhwygo y safngerth, aelgerth weilgi
Anferthawl, a'i ddreigiawl gynddeiriogi;
Y llong, yn mherfedd y lli',—ymsiglodd,
A tharanodd pob peth ei thrueni !

 Duw, arwr gorddyfnderoedd,
 A'i enwog lais yn galw oedd;
 Ni welid pelydr haulwen,
 Y ne'n ddu, bygddu uwch ben;
 Twrf corwynt, drowynt, o draw,
 Yn yr awyr yn rhuaw.

Dan chwiban d'ai allan o'i 'stafellau,
A heriau fydoedd drwy 'i gynhyrfiadau;
A Duw a roddodd lacâd i raddau
I ffrwyn gadwynog y ffyrnig dònau,
Rhuthrodd, fe ddyrnodd yh ddau—'sglyfaethgar
Drwy'u bâr anwar nes duo'r wybrenau.

 A'r *Rothsay* hithau ar hynt,
 I dir angau'n myn'd rhyngynt.

  The successful bard, being called upon to declare himself, stood confessed before the meeting in the person of the Rev. W. Williams, of Caernarvon, and as it was the principal literary prize, the Rev. gentleman was installed in the bardic chair by the bards then present, namely, Rev. E. Evans, Robert Davies, of Nantglyn, and Wm. Jones, of Carmarthen. Lady Bulkeley then invested him with the medal amidst the approbation of the meeting.

The second prize was awarded to Mr. Griffith Williams, alias Gutyn Peris, of Landegai; and Mr. Blackwell observed that his poem was scarcely inferior to the other.

Pennillion singing was introduced again; after which the secretary announced that the subject fixed upon for the prize Englynion for the medal, given by their Royal Highnesses the Duchess of Kent and Princess Victoria, was "the Marriage of Sir R.B.W. Bulkeley, Bart".

The Eisteddfod was then adjourned to the next day.

THE CONCERT.

In the evening a very numerous and fashionable company assembled at the Town Hall, to witness a concert of vocal and instrumental music, under the superintendence of Mr. John Parry. We have neither time nor room to enter at length into a critique upon the performances. The vocal performers were Mr. and Mrs. Knyvett, Miss Cramar, Mr. Horncastle, Mr. Parry, sen. and Mr. Parry, jun. The instrumental performers were Mr. Cramar, leader; flute, Mr. Nicholson; trumpet, Mr. Harper; violoncello, Mr. Lindley and Mr. Jackson; principal violin, secondo, and viola, Messrs. Herrman; clarionets, Mr. Stubbs and Mr. Entwhistle; double-bass, Mr. Hill; patent symphonia, Mr. Parry; pedal harp, Mr. Parry , jun.; grand-piano-forte, Mrs. W. Knyvett.

WEDNESDAY.

The morning of this day was decidedly unfavourable; rain descended and the wind blew cold. The town, however, appeared all alive, in order to give their Royal Highnesses the Duchess of Kent and Princess Victoria, a cordial and loyal reception. The heralds perambulated the streets, and ever and anon sounded their trumpets by way of reminding the bards and other personages of the important business of the day. It is not possible to describe the feelings of a Welshman at a meeting of an Eisteddfod; his very soul seems absorbed in the proceedings; our readers may therefore form some idea of the anxiety and sad faces which were manifested, when it became evident that the clouds and rain were not disposed to clear away. Hope, says Sir Thomas More, is sometimes a good breakfast, but often a bad dinner; on this occasion it was a good supper but a bad breakfast, for every one in Beaumaris supped heartily upon hope the preceding evening, as the rain descended and the winds blew, but found nothing substantial for a morning's repast. Things however altered for the better before dinner, and we were not made acquainted with the unfortunate and heart-rending case of any individual who was starved to death. Good eating and drinking by the bye is an essential ingredient in a modern Welsh Eisteddfod; and we suspect it was the case many hundred years ago. As the weather continued unfavourable, it was intimated that the company would assemble in the Town Hall; every place was in consequence literally crammed.

At half-past twelve o'clock, Sir R. B. W. Bulkeley entered and stated he had received a letter from Sir John Conroy, which he would read. The letter was expressive of the regret of her Royal Highness that the state of the weather prevented her intended presence at the Eisteddfod, and announced her intention of being at Baron Hill in the evening at four o'clock, when the Princess and herself would invest the successful candidates with the medals. Sir Richard then proceeded to say that as the room would not hold one-third of the ladies and gentlemen who wished to be present, it was proposed to adjourn to the castle; and that he should be happy to see such of the company as wished to be witnesses of the investiture of the successful competitors with medals by their Royal Highnesses, at Baron Hill at four o'clock in the evening. These announcements were received with loud cheers, and the company began to move towards the castle.

A little before one o'clock the band announced the arrival of the president, by striking up a national air.

The President upon entering advanced to the front of the platform amid loud cheers, and repeated the information respecting the intentions of their Royal Highnesses which he had previously given in the Town Hall. Sir Richard concluded by inviting such of the company as might be desirous to be present at the ceremony of investing the successful candidates with the medals given by their Royal Highnesses, to Baron Hill, in the evening.

The Rev. Henry Parry, of Llanasa, opened the proceedings of the morning with the following address:—

"It may appear intrusive in me to address this splendid assembly, met to celebrate the bardic festival, as I am no bard myself; but I assume the liberty, as being present when this Eisteddfod was first thought of, being on its committee, and as being a hearty well-wisher to the order of bards. I shall endeavour to give a brief outline of the history of the institution, occupying as little as possible of your time; and on that account I shall omit all that bears upon the subject before the time of Edward the First. From the period of the conquest of Wales by that great monarch, till the accession of the House of Tudor to the throne of England, a dismal cloud hung over the bards and minstrels of the Principality. We have a tradition that Edward massacred the bards in this very place, where their successors this day hold their festival. But that is a point supported by such a slender testimony, that it is not credited at the present time, though it furnished an occasion for one of the sublimest odes in the English or any other language. The bards were inimical to the government of Edward, and as the press now, were powerful agents in forming and directing public opinion. With the insurrection of Owen Glyndwr—must I call it rebellion?—the bardic spirit seemed to rekindle a little, but it was soon suppressed by the vigilance and prompt measures of Henry IV. In the time of his grandson however, Henry VI, a very great Eisteddfod was held at Caermarthen, under the presidency of Gruffydd, grandfather to the great Sir Rice ab Thomas, so well known for assisting and placing Henry VII on the throne, and ancestor to the present Lord Dynevor. This Eisteddfod was attended by all the bards and minstrels of Wales and under the conduct of the well known Llawdden. Two silver badges were provided; a silver chair and a silver harp. Both these badges were triumphantly carried away by a bard from Flintshire and a minstrel from the same little county. The silver chair after being honourably borne by Tudor Alde, passed back into South Wales, and was lost. The silver harp never revisited our southern brethren, and is now in the possession of the Hon. Edward Ll. Mostyn, of Mostyn. Some half a century after this Eisteddfod, brighter days shone upon the bards and minstrels. A Prince of the House of Tudor was on the throne. Henry

VIII distinguished himself for his great literary attainments and love for music, for he was a composer in that noble science; he summoned in the 15th year of his reign, an Eisteddfod, which was accordingly held at Caerwys, in 1526. This was under the presidency of Richard ap Howel Vychan, Esq. of Mostyn. Of this meeting we know but little, for in those days there were no reporters to cook up an account of it. But his daughter, Queen Elizabeth, called, by a royal commission, now extant, a meeting to be held at the same town of Caerwys, which was accordingly held there in May, 1568. This commission is directed to Sir R. Bulkeley, Thomas Mostyn, and Peers Mostyn, Esquires; and it is singular that the representatives of those gentlemen are now here, possessing the same ardour for promoting Welsh literature as their ancestors in the reign of the virgin Queen. We are acquainted with every thing that was done at the Eistddfod; for a contemporary author, the learned Dr. J. David Rees, a native of Llanvaethlu, in this Island, had given us a full account of it. From this era to the latter part of the eighteenth century, the Eisteddfodau were entirely dropped. But they were partially revived by the exertions of the Cymmrodorion Society in London, in the end of the eighteenth century. Then the nobility and gentry of Wales caught the flame, and Eisteddfodau have been ever since held, every third or fourth year, in different provinces of the principality. As the encouragement increased, the productions of the bards and minstrels also improved. The Royal Eisteddfod held four years ago at Denbigh, under the presidency of Sir Edward Mostyn, left all others far behind it. But what shall we say of this, under the presidency of Sir R. Bulkeley, in ancient Mona, '*Môn Mam Cymru*'; the land that gave birth to Owen Tudor, the founder of the house of Tudor; that gave birth to Lewis Morris and Goronwy Owen; from which sprung Sir William Jones, and the brave warrior now holding the vice-regal sceptre on the other side of the water, and who derives his title from this beloved Island. The bards were always loyal, and they often suffered for their loyalty. For their attachment to their native princes, Edward I discouraged and repressed them; for their attachment to their legitimate sovereign, Richard II when he was deposed, Henry IV took severe measures, and enacted cruel laws against them; and, on account of their supporting the falling cause of monarchy in the time of the first Charles, Cromwell, when he obtained the supreme power, visited them with his severest vengeance. But now their prospects are splendid." There was much cheering during the time that the Rev. gentleman addressed the meeting.

We subjoin the following document alluded to by Mr. Parry.

" BY THE QUENE.—Elizabeth, by the grace of God, of England, Fraunce, and Ireland, Queene, defendor of the fayth, &c. to our trustie and ryght wel-beloved Sir Richard Bulkley, Knight, Sir Rees Gruffuth, Knight, Ellice Price, Esq. doctor in cyvill lawe, and one of our cousail in our marches of Wales, William Mostyn, Jevan Lloyd of Yale, John Salisbury of Ruge, Rees Thomas, Maurice Wynne, Willm. Lewis, Peers Mostyn, Owen John ap Holl. Vaughan, John Willm. Ap John, John Lewis Owen, Moris Gruffyth, Symound Thelwall, Ellice ap William Lloyd, Robert Puleston, Harry Aparry, William Glynne and Rees Hughes, Esqurs. and to every one of them greeting.—Wheras it is come to the knowledge of the lorde president, and other our said counsail, in our marches of Wales, that vagrant and idle persons, naming themselves *mynstrells, rithmors, and barthes*, are lately grown into such an intollerable multitude within the pricipalitee of North Wales, that not only gentlemen and others, by their shameles disorders, are oftentimes disquieted in their habitacons, but also thexpert mynstrells and mucisions in toune and contry therby much discouraged to travail in thexercise and practize of their knowledge, and also not a little hyndred in theire lyvings and preferments. The reformacon whereof and the putting of these people in order, the said lorde president and counsail have thought verey necessarye; and knowing you to be men both of wysdome and upright dealing, and also of experience and good knowledge in the scyence, have appointed and authorised you to be commissioners for that purpose. And forasmuch as our counsail of late travayling in some part of the said principalitee, had perfect understanding, or credible report, that thaccustomed place for the execution of the like commissyon hath bene heretofore at Caroyes, in our countie of Flynt, and that *William Mostyn, Esq.* and his ancestors have had the gyfte and bestowing of the *silver harpe* appertayning to the cheff of that facultie, and that a yeares warning at the least hath bene accustomed to be geaven of thassembly, and execucon of the like commissyon. Our said counsail have, therefore, apoynted thexecucon of this commissyon to be at the said town of Caroyes, the Monday next after the feast of the blessed Trynitee, which shall be in the yeare of our Lorde God 1568.

" And therefore we require and command you, by the authoritee of these presents, not only to cause open proclamacons to be made in all ffayors, marketts, townes, and other places of assembly within the counties of Angleze, Carnarvon, Mayryonneth, Denbigh, and Fflynt, that all and every person, and persons that entend to maynteingne theire lyvings by name or color of mynstrells, rithmores, or barthes, within the Talaith of Aberfiowe, comprehending the said fyve shires, shal be and appeare before you the said day and place, to shewe theire learnings accordingly: but also that you 20, 19, 18, 17, 16, 15, 14, 13, 12, 11, 10, 9, 8, 7, or 6 of you, whereof you, Sir Richard Bulkley, Sir Rees Gruffith, Ellice Price, and Wm. Mostyn, Esqrs. or 3 or 2 of you be of the number, to repayre to the said place the day aforesaid, and calling to you such expert men in the said faculties of the Welsh musick, as to you shall be thought convenient to proceade to the execucon of the premises, and to admyt such and so many as by your wisdomes and knowledges, you shall fynde worthy into and under the degrees heretofore in semblable sort, to use, exercise, and folowe the scyences and facultes of theire professyons, in such decent order as shall appertainge to eche of their degrees, and as your discrecons and wisdomes shall prescribe unto them, geaving straight monycons, and commandment, in our name and on our behalf, to therest not worthy, that they returne to some honest labour, and due exercise, such as they be most apte unto for mayntenaunce of theire lyvings, upon paine to be taken as sturdy and idle vagaboundes, and to be used according to the lawes and statutes provided in that behalf, letting you wyth our said counsail look for advertisement by due certificatt at your hands of your doing in the execucon of the said premises. For seeing in any wise that upon the said assembly the peas and good order be observed and kept accordingly, assertayning you that the said *Wm. Mostyn* hath promised to see furnyture and things necessary provided for that assembly, at the place aforesaid. Given under our signet, at our citie of Chester, the 23rd of October, the nynth yeare of our raigne.

Signed her Highnes counsaill in the marches of Wales."

The Rev. E. Evans, of Chester, stated that the prize for the best composition on "Adam and Eve in Paradise", which had not been awarded yesterday on account of the absence of the judges, was declared in favour of the writer using the appellation "Eryron Gwyllt Walia". The author, Robert Owen, not being present, Lady Bulkeley invested Mr. John Parry as his representative.

Prize I.—A medal to the author of the best six Welsh Englynion on "the honour conferred by the presence of their Royal Highnesses the Duchess of Kent and the Princess Victoria at our National Festival". The Secretary stated that on this subject eighteen compositions had been received, from which the judges selected two as the best. They could not satisfactorily determine to which of these two the palm of superior merit ought to be given, and had therefore called in a third friend, who had pronounced in favour of the composition signed "Owen Tudor".

Robert Davies, of Nantglyn, a chaired bard, on whom had been conferred many prizes at former Eisteddfodau, was introduced with "all blushing honours thick upon him", and was invested with the medal by Lady Harriet Mostyn, of Mostyn. After the ceremony the successful bard, at the particular request of the company, recited his Englynion. As it was received with great applause, and was highly praised by eminent Welsh scholars present, we have great pleasure in presenting a copy:

> I Dduges Caint, braint i'n bro,—bid mawl mawr,
>   Bid mîl a myrdd croeso,
>   A'i seren drylen deg dro,
>   Hoen ddiwrnod i'n haddurno.
>
> Teyrnwaed Tudurwaed, da dirion,—oreu
>   Aeres Prydain goron,
>   Derchafid yn dra chyfion
>   O blanwydd Penmynydd Môn.
>
> Màl cenedl, grym hawl cynhes,—i'n tirion
>   Victoria, D'wysoges,
>   Mae ynom o wraidd monwes
>   Galon yn wreichion o wres.
>
> Da deuodd, a Duw i'w dewis,—i Fôn,
>   Tros Fenai Bont fawrbris,
>   Urddasodd, graddodd bob gris,
>   A'i mawredd dre' Bewmaris.
>
> Os bu Iorwerth gerth, waith gau,—yn tòri
>   O'n tîr ein beirdd gorau;
>   Daeth hon i'n gwlad, clymiad clau,
>   Er nawdd i'r awenyddau.
>
> Casglwn, cofleidiwn flodau—tyner,
>   I'w taenu'n ei llwybrau,
>   Am ei rhwysg, i'w thra mawrhau,
>   Wrth adwaen tîr ei theidiau.

The premium for the second-best was given to Mr. William Ellis Jones, of Caermarthen.

Prize II.—An elegant silver gilt Medal, presented by their Royal Highnesses the Duchess of Kent, and the Princess Victoria, for the best four Welsh Englynion on the Marriage of Sir R.B.W.

Bulkeley. Ten excellent compositions had been sent in, and the award of the judges was declared in favour of the composition signed "Dewi". The author being desired to make himself known, the Rev. J. Blackwell stood forward, and was invested with the medal by Lady Robert Grosvenor. Mr. Blackwell then recited the Englynion and translation as follows:

> Eto unwyd mewn tynion—aur rwymau,
> > Rymus ddwy lîn Brython
> > Treiddia trwy wlad Derwyddon:
> > Gerddi mawl—nes gwardda Môn.
>
> Iforaidd yw myfyrion—Syr Risiart,
> > Rhoes roesaw i feirddion:
> > *Ystanley* fydd Nest hoenlon
> > Iddo—a merch newydd Môn.
>
> Golou haul, a gwawl hylon,—tirion wên
> > Datry'n ol gysgodion
> > Od oedd ddwl îs ddydd alon,
> > Nid tywell mwy mantell Môn,
>
> Dwy oes hîr, hyd i oes wyrion,—i'w rhan,
> > A gwir hedd yn goron;
> > A gadael tra Caergwydion,
> > Lu o'u meib i lywio Môn.
> > > DEWI.

TRANSLATION.

> Once more, in golden bands, the
> Two nations of the land of *Brython* are
> United. The Island smiles—a loud acclaim
> Re-echoes the home of the Druids.
> In the steps of the reverend Ivor [279] Sir Richard
> Treads—to the relics of ancient bardism he
> Extends patronage. *Stanley*, amiable as Ivor's
> Bride, is ranked among Mona's fairest daughters.
> In the days of border warfare, Cothi's bard
> Deemed the Island gloomy. [280] The sunbeams
> Of peace, the sweet smiles of happiness now dispel
> The shadows. Mona's mantle is no longer sable.
> Enwreathed with peace, may their days be long—even to the days of
> Their descendants. And while a star brightens
> The brow of *Caergwydion*, may their sons
> Be found among the chieftains of Mona.

---

279 The Welsh Mæcenas of Basaleg. 1380.
280 "Nos da i'r Ynys Gywyll."—L.'G. COTHI. 1400.

At the conclusion of the recitation, the Rev. J. Blackwell addressed the meeting in a very animated speech, in which he vindicated the Eisteddfodau from several misrepresentations, and contended that a country could not change its language in a day, and as the Welsh was still the vernacular language with more than half of the population, every effort ought to be made to convey instruction through it to those who understand no other tongue. It may be asked, said the reverend gentleman, why are extraordinary meetings of this kind held amongst us?

We conceive that the poverty of our land, which would check much literary enterprize, and the smallness in number and the scattered character of our population, render them necessary to arouse and keep up national talent and energies. And what has been the result of this attention to native literature and vernacular instruction? I remember well the interest excited when our eloquent friend, Mr. Price, of Crickhowel, whose absence to-day we deeply regret, at the Brecon Eisteddfod in 1826, threw down upon the platform specimens of six or eight Welsh monthly periodicals. The number of our periodicals is now increased to eighteen, and they still possess the same characteristics. Almost all are supported by the peasant, both as writers and readers. The Welsh press has produced lately a second edition of a large Welsh-English Lexicon, by our first of Celtic scholars, Dr. Pughe.—Paradise Lost has been translated by him also, who alone was able properly to accomplish the task; and as proof of the reading propensity, may be mentioned that of a Welsh work on the New Testament, now being published in monthly numbers at Mold, no less that 8,000 copies are sold. Next year we hope to commence a Welsh Cyclopædia. We trust, under the patronage of the London Society for the Diffusion of Useful Knowledge, which through the instrumentality of Mr. Ker, have lately evinced considerable interest in the welfare of the principality. As a proof that the Eisteddfodau have not been useless, it may be mentioned, that to the Wrexham Eisteddfod, in 1820, only 74 compositions in the whole were sent in for adjudication. At this Eisteddfod no fewer than 300 were received. Every cottage has its reader; every hamlet has its bard; every market-town has its press; and that press has been hitherto kept pure, unpolluted by any immorality, unsullied by any impiety. It has hitherto worked so well, that at the present moment our cottage library is pretty well furnished. But there are higher and nobler results arising from the cultivation of native literature, and these are found in the improvement of our national character. In days of sedition and threatened anarchy, the Principality has been always tranquil and happy as a Goshen. Our peasantry are loyal, quiet, and industrious; they are growing in intelligence, and are growing in moral worth. Our hearts, if they are not filled with plenty, are filled with contentment; our prisons are empty. Mark the genuine peasant of our hills; if we mistake not, there is an impress of moral dignity upon his brow. Though inferior in intelligence to none in the same rank, yet concerning things beyond his sphere he matters little. He knows little of political economy; he leaves things that he considers above him to wiser heads; he does not look much into the machinery of governments to see if every wheel is in its proper place. In saying this, we have no political bias, we only describe the character of our peasantry, who, however unlearned they may be in other sciences, are learned and exemplary in all the duties of their station: they fear their God; they honour their king.

But an ancient Briton feels that he condescends rather low in arguing this point respecting the cultivation of his native literature upon utilitarian principles merely. Every nation has some distinct peculiarities. We have ours; and as long as the cultivation of these does not make us worse subjects or worse men, there can be no harm in maintaining them. Is not nationality, and even national vanity, very frequently the root of patriotism: and if the maintenance of national peculiarity be allowed to any people, it must be allowed to ourselves. The mountaineers of every country are notoriously attached to the customs and even prejudices of their fathers. There throbs a heart and there beats a pulse in the mountains, far more warm and bounding than are to be found in the plains. This may be owing in some measure to physical situation: the light and shade, and mossy summit, the deep blue and clear sky, the curtain of white and trailing mist which evening draws around the couch of the mountain spirit, the dancing stream, the bounding waterfall; all these scenic sticheries must and do give a spring and elasticity to the soul not to be found in the lowlands. But this is not all: in these peculiarities, also, we find traditions which were fastened first and deepest upon our infant memories. In them we find proof of the antiquity and distinctness of our race. The origin of the Cimbric nation and of the Cimbric language, eludes the keenest glance of the antiquary. He cannot carry his researches beyond a time when these customs were established, when these traditions were tales of old. Other languages can be traced to their origin, other nations may have grown old, and her bards and minstrels were bald and blind with years, before history had ever commenced her chronicles of the Western World. And that which has not only its maturity, but its old age, beyond the perceptions of men and the recollections of time, must be immortal.

PRIZE III.—A silver Medal to the successful author for the best Essay on Agriculture.

The Rev. Mr. Metcalf (private chaplain to Sir Edward Mostyn, Bart.) stated that not only had numerous compositions been received on this important subject, but many of them were replete with talent and information. There were three of them which possessed extraordinary merit; and of these the judges had decided in favour of "Amaethon", of whose composition the reverend gentleman spoke in very high terms. Aneurin Owen, Esq. having declared himself the author, was invested with the medal by Lady Mostyn.—The second premium on this subject was adjudged to Mr. William Jones, of Pwllheli.

The Rev. Mr. Metcalf stated that there was another production on this subject (agriculture) which merited particular notice. He might say of it, that it was perhaps the most beautiful composition in any language; but as it did not immediately suit the farmers, for whose use the two first appeared to be better calculated, the judges had ranked it in the third place, but, impressed with a sense of its very great merits, they were anxious to recommend that it should be published in addition to the other two. The composition bore the signature of "Ralph Aricula Robinson", and he called upon the author, if present, to declare himself. The author not appearing the seal was broken, and the name of the Rev. Samuel Roberts, Llanbrynmair, appeared as the author.

PRIZE IV.-The medal of the Royal Cambrian Institution, for the best Essay on the Welsh Grammar. There were only two competitors for this prize, and as both Essays were considered of equal merit, the judges proposed that medals should be presented to each of them. The first of them was Mr. Hugh Jones of Chester, for whom Mr. Edward Parry of Bridge-street, in this city, was invested with the medal. To the Rev. J. H. Williams, Llangadwaladr, Anglesea, was awarded the other medal, and the

Rev. J. Jones, of Holyhead, was invested as his *locum tenens*.

PRIZE V.–An elegant Silver Medal, the gift of Sir Edward Mostyn, Bart. For the best Poem on David playing the harp before Saul. The Rev. Henry Parry said he had the honour of being one of the judges on this subject. No less that twenty-seven compositions had been sent in, six of which were excellent. The palm of superiority was after careful investigation awarded to "Hanesydd". Mr. Robert Davies, the bard of Nantglyn, presented himself amid loud tokens of approbation, and was invested with the medal by Lady Mostyn, of Talacre. The premium for the second-best composition, on the same subject, was awarded to Mr. W. E. Jones (Cawrdaf).

The president begged to state that the successful candidate for the best History of Anglesea was not present yesterday, he was most happy however to announce that the lady was among the company to-day. (*Cheers.*) He then took the opportunity of passing a very warm encomium upon the lady's industry and talents, and observed that the work would, when published, embellish the library of every gentleman throughout the Principality of Wales.

Lord Mostyn immdediately introduced Miss Angharad Llwyd, who was invested with the prize medal by Sir R. Bulkeley.

CONTEST FOR THE HARP.

The judges in the contest for the prize were Mr. John Parry, and Mr. Aneurin Owen. The candidates came forward in the following order:—

Miss E. Jones, of Corwen: tune, "Serch Hudol" (the Allurements of Love).

Griffith Jones, Capel Curig: tune, "Bro Gwalia" (Country of Wales).

William Jones, Beaumaris: tune, "Pen Rhaw" (Spade's Head).

Richard Pugh, of Corwen: tune, "Black Sir Harry".

John Williams, of Oswestry: tune the same. His performances elicited much applause.

Hugh Pugh, of Dolgellau: tune, "The King's Joy".

Rees Jones, of Llanrwst: tune, "Sweet Richard".

The contest was listened to throughout with great attention but the wind being high and the weather extremely cold, it did not excited so much pleasure as it otherwise would. The Silver Harp was awarded by the judges to Mr. John Williams, of Oswestry, formerly a pupil of the celebrated blind harper, Richard Roberts, of Caernarvon.

The Rev. Henry Parry addressed the meeting, and dilated at great length upon the merits and antiquity of the tune "Black Sir Harry". It was written, he said, by an Anglesea bard upon the deposition of Richard the Second; and had survived the Plantaganets and Tudors. It was now contemporaneous with the House of Brunswick; the Welsh called it *"Creigiau'r Eryri"*, or the Rocks of Snowdon; and they most ardently wished that the Brunswick family might be as firmly seated in the affections of the people, as the Snowdon hills were in the heart of their dominions. *(Cheers.)*

Pennillion singing followed, when the president stepped forward and stated the contest of Pennillion singers would take place at the Town Hall, in the evening. Mr. Parry sang a stanza of our inspiring national anthem, "God save the King". The whole meeting enthusiastically joined in the chorus. Sir Richard then called for three times three cheers for the King, which were given, as well as three times three for the president. The company then separated.

PENNILLION SINGING.

In the evening at eight o'clock, the Pennillion singers met at the Town Hall, and a very interesting contest was carried on for three hours. The medal was awarded to Joseph Williams, of Bagillt; and the premiums were equally divided between all the other competitors. The hall was crowded to excess, and the audience seemed to take the most intense interest in the proceedings. A literary gentleman has favoured us with the following article upon this subject:—

"We consider this ancient practice one of the most distinguishing and interesting features of our Eisteddfodau, and we are exceedingly pleased to find that prominence given it, which its antiquity and national character deserve. It was arranged that the candidates should occupy the platform erected for the English orchestra, and the following gentlemen were appointed judges on the occasion. A. O. Pughe, Esq., Rev. E. Evans, of Christleton, the Bard of Nantglyn, and Mr. John Parry, of London. At the hour appointed, the hall was crowded to excess by a very respectable assembly, anxious to witness this very interesting and, to many, novel scene. Twelve persons mounted the stage, and entered their names as candidates for the awarded premium, and the individual who had gained the silver harp in the morning, was appointed to play on the occasion. Every thing being now arranged, the contest was commenced by the harper striking up the sweet air of "Serch Hudol", and the Rev. E. Evans announced the names of the candidates, as they came, in succession. This tune went round, and every one of the candidates performed his part so well, that the judges found it impossible to decide in favour of any one in particular. They were tried by another air, but with the same success, and a third was called for, which, however, enabled the judges to reduce the competition to four, whom they considered pre-eminent. Here again commenced a second and more severe contest. Every one executed his part so well, as to draw from the judges the gratifying declaration that they never heard singing with the harp better performed. After a long and an arduous struggle, in which the company seemed particularly interested, the judges decided in favour of Mr. Joseph Williams, of Bagillt, who was accordingly invested with the medal.

Before we conclude this part of our subject, it may not prove altogether uninteresting briefly to explain the manner in which the Welsh mode of singing with the harp is performed. The poetry and language of Wales seem strikingly suited to each other, which may probably account for this practice being exclusively confined to that country. The singer is not allowed to select his own tune, but must hold himself in readiness to adapt his words to any air which the minstrel may happen to play. Neither is he permitted to commence with the strain, as in English, where the tune and the metre are adapted to each other, and of uniform and corresponding length. But the Welsh vocalist must take up the tune at any bar which may best suit the measure of the verse he intends to sing. He must, however, be particularly exact in ending precisely with the tune; to err a single note in this respect is considered a great fault, and is hardly ever committed by first-rate singers. However strange it may appear, still it is a well known fact, that there are some performers who are capable of adapting no less than twenty-four different metres to the same air !

PROCEEDINGS AT BARON HILL.

About the hour of four in the afternoon, a large concourse of spectators assembled at Baron Hill, the splendid seat of Sir R. Bulkeley, to witness the ceremony of investing the successful candidates with silver medals, by their Royal Highnesses the Duchess of Kent, and her interesting child.

Baron Hill is situated on eminence about one mile from Beaumaris, at the head of an extensive lawn, sloping down to the town and castle, and finely screened and backed with umbrageous woods, which form great embellishments to this part of the Island. The house was built in the year 1618, by Sir Richard Bulkeley, a distinguished character in the reign of James I, but it has since that period been very much altered and improved. The grounds surrounding this charming residence are richly diversified by nature, and variegated by art; the lawns, groves and bridges are finely dispersed, and the numerous walks and rides judiciously laid out. But the view from the hill far surpasses all, and is justly the boast of the Island;—

> " Now, Muse, ascend the sylvan summits gay,
> That tower above the town—the valley—bay,
> Where now unheeded lie the heap of stones,
> The altar's ruin, and the mouldering bones:
> The soil once softened by contrition's eyes,
> On all that's mortal of St. Mougan lies,
> Who blindly thought that pains inflictive rod
> Would lead the lonely hermit up to God. "

The spot chosen for investing the bards and other successful candidates with the medals, was the terrace in front of the building. The musical arrangements were under the direction of Mr. John Parry. The veteran harper, Roberts, occupied a distinguished post; and upon the entry of their Royal Highnesses, attended by Sir Richard and Lady Bulkeley, struck up the national air, "God save the King". Mr. Parry sung the following additional stanza, to the national song of "Mewn awen fwyn lawen", written by himself.

> Far, far from the pomp and the splendour of court,
> To Cambria's sweet valleys the Royal resort;
> Oh ! let us our love and our gratitude shew,
> To those who such honour on Wallia bestow.
> Ye bards and ye minstrels your voices combine,
> To welcome a Princess of Tudor's famed line.
> *Gogoniant a moliant i'r Seren lwys gain.*

The Rev. John Blackwell was the first called and was invested with the silver gilt medal by their Royal Highnesses jointly.

Miss Angharad Llwyd was next invested, and had also the honour to be formally presented to their Royal Highnesses, who were pleased to speak in highly complimentary terms of the distinguished talents of this fair daughter of Cambria.

The successful competitor for the silver harp, John Williams of Oswestry, was next brought forward.

The Rev. W. Williams, of Caernarvon, was the next to receive his honours. The rest of the successful candidates were invested in the order in which they had gained their prizes. Their names are as follows:—Aneurin Owen Pughe, Esq., Mr. Edward Parry, Chester; Rev. D. Williams, Clynnog; Robert Davies, Nantglyn; William Edwards, Ysgeifiog; Mr. T. Lloyd Jones, Holywell; Mr. Richard Roberts, Carnarvon; Rev. J. Jones, Holyhead.

At the conclusion of the ceremony, their Royal Highnesses retired, and shortly afterwards sat down to dinner in a capacious room, erected for the occasion. At the table her Royal Highness the Princess Victoria sat on the right of her parent; Lady Bulkeley on the right of the Princess Victoria, and Sir Richard Bulkeley on the left of the Duchess of Kent. The Honourable E. Mostyn Lloyd was at the head of the table, and Brice Pierce, Esq. at the bottom. Many distinguished individuals were present; among then were Lord and Lady Robert Grosvenor. About seven o'clock their Royal Highnesses took their departure for Plas Newydd.

History makes us acquainted with an interesting anecdote of one of Sir R. Bulkeley's predecessors in the time of Queen Elizabeth, and we may without impropriety introduce it here. An attempt was made to have him accused upon false evidence of treason; and the Earl of Leicester informed her Majesty that the council had been examining him, and that they found him a dangerous person; that he dwelt in a *suspicious corner* of the world, and should be committed to the tower. "What! Sir Richard Bulkeley!" said the Queen; "he never intended us any harm; we have brought him up from a boy, and have had special trial of his fidelity; ye shall not commit him!" "We have the care of your Majesty's person", said the Earl, "and see more and hear more of the man than you do; he is of an aspiring mind, and lives in a remote place." "Before God", replied the Queen, "we will be sworn upon the Holy Evangelists he never intended any harm; and then her Majesty ran to the Bible, and kissing it said, "you shall not commit him; we have brought him up from a boy". Subsequently Sir Richard proved the accusation against him to be founded on forged testimony.

THE ROTHSAY CASTLE.

We must not forget to record that while their Royal Highnesses were at Baron Hill, they were presented with a set of engravings, beautifully bound in morocco and gold, illustrative of a circumstantial Narrative of the Wreck of the Rothsay Castle, which is about to be published. The author of this interesting little work, is a gentleman of the most kindly feelings and happened to be at Beaumaris at the time of the melancholy event; he had taken his passage in the ill-fated vessel, but most fortunately, departed in another, and arrived before the wreck; by which accident, or as he calls it, providential interference, he was spared the fate of those whose misfortunes he has carefully portrayed. Mr. Adshead was a great comforter to the survivors, as well as to the friends and relatives of those who were lost, and we believe he has interested himself more than any other person with all the particulars in any way connected with the melancholy event. Many little grave-stones in Beaumaris churchyard attest his anxious and kindly feelings; and we record with much pleasure the few hours passed in his company at Beaumaris last week. During the Eisteddfod he picked up several relics belonging to a most amiable lady, Miss Selwyn, who perished in the wreck; and among other things was a common prayer book, and a pair of jet black ear-rings, which had been washed ashore. The Prayer Book was once splendidly bound in morocco; the name of the owner is written upon a blank leaf, but almost obliterated by the action of the waves; and although every leaf was loosened and the cover detached, yet not the smallest portion of the book was deficient and therefore might be easily rebound. Mr. Adshead's narrative is to be embellished with several engravings, which will convey to the world a most vivid picture of the distressing scene. One of them which we noticed, in an unfinished state, was a plate representing Mrs. Payne, floating upon the paddle-box, supporting with her hand the dead body of her husband, which was dangling in the dark blue sea beneath. This affecting incident will be best understood by the following brief narrative which we received from the lips of Mr. Adshead, his eyes bright with glistening tears at the time. "When the danger of the vessel became apparent, Mr. Payne took refuge with his wife upon the paddle-box, and tied himself to her, saying 'dear, if we must die, we will perish together'. In a few minutes an angry wave swept the paddle-box into the surge below, and soon after Mr. Payne sunk from exhaustion. As he fell, his distressed and affectionate wife seized him by the pocket of his trowsers, and held him in that manner for several hours, for when rescued from her situation in the morning, she was found nearly blind and almost insensible, but still supporting the lifeless body of her partner. The boatmen were about to take her off the box, when she is said to have exclaimed 'Lord save me, or I perish', and it was then that the sailors perceived the body of Mr. Payne, as depicted by the plate, we have endeavoured to describe." There are several other plates in Mr. Adshead's work, which we have promised ourselves the melancholy pleasure of noticing at some future time.

THE BALL.

The ball in the evening was honoured by the company of two hundred and fifty individuals, comprising not only a great portion of the nobility and gentry of North Wales, but a galaxy of youth and beauty, which it would be difficult to equal in this or any other part of the King's dominions. The company did not separate till the hour of three in the morning.

THURSDAY.

Perhaps no part of the festival excited such lively sensations of pleasure as the Regatta, the first of which was fixed for this day. The preceding night had been occasionally wet and stormy, but the early morn gave symptoms of a bright and sunny day. The wind blew fresh from the N.N.W. and by 10 o'-clock, the beach and its beautiful bay, with the magnificent environs, presented a most picturesque and animated scene. The promenade, which is a large and convenient velvet-like green, was crowded with carriages, and covered by a galaxy of fashion and beauty; and whilst the water was studded with sailing boats, pleasure boats, yachts and steamers, all dressed in their nautical finery, the lofty range of Snowdonian mountains in the back were enveloped in clouds, and frowned with majestic grandeur upon the picture below. It would, indeed, require the poet's fancy and the painter's pencil to convey an idea of any thing like that which we witnessed. The *Menai* was moored in the middle of the strait, and by the royal standard which floated in the breeze, it was obvious that the royal party were on board. High water was at one o'clock, and the signal guns gave intimation of the coming tug of war.

The rowing boats had to round a buoy moored near Puffin Island, about one mile and a half from the starting place. The sailing vessels had to round the Island, making the entire distance about six miles. The following is a correct account of the result:

1.—For a Gold Cup, presented by the Duchess of Kent; for Yachts not exceeding 70 tons. Eleven entered, five started.

	Yachts' name		Tons		Owners
1	Zephyr Cutter	....	42	.....	James Watson, Esq.
2	Eliza Cutter	....	41	.....	J. C. Ewart, Esq.
3	Peri Cutter	....	26	.....	Henry Molony, Esq.

2.—For four-oared boats of every description. First boat, 15 sovereigns. Second boat, 7 ditto. Seven started.

1	Fairy Queen, Chester	....	Mr. Walker
2	Water Witch, Chester	....	Mr. E. W. Lloyd
3	Jack's Alive	....	Mr. John Jones

At starting the Fairy Queen was twice fouled, and much retarded by the accident, yet she came home, dancing like a sylph over the waves, and won cleverly.

3.—For sailing boats, not exceeding 18 feet on the keel. First boat, five sovereigns; second boat, two ditto.

1	Royal Antelope	....	Hugh Jones
2	Resolute	....	Evan Thomas

4.—For a Cup, value 30 sovereigns, for six-oared boats, to be rowed and steered by gentlemen amateurs.

1	Diable Boiteux	....	Sir R. B. W. Bulkeley, Bart.
2	Water Witch, Liverpool	....	C. Moulson, Esq.

5.—For a Cup, value 20 sovereigns, to be sailed for by yachts not exceeding 20 tons.

1	Peri Cutter	....	26	.....	Henry Molony, Esq.
2	Dicky Sam Cutter	.....	19	.....	J. C. Shaw, Esq.
3	Tickler Cutter	....	15	.....	Jonathan Grindrod, Esq,

6.—For six-oar boats, to be rowed and steered by residents of Anglesey or Caernarvon. Heats. First boat, £15, second ditto, £7.

1	Jack's Alive	....	Mr. John Jones
2	Snowdon Ranger	....	Mr. Owen Owens
3	Princess Victoria	....	Mr. John Williams

The Regatta terminated about five o'clock, and certainly no one could have wished for a happier day. The Royal Party proceeded up the straits to the Menai Bridge, that wonderful and enchanting structure, which as the Rev. J. H. Bransby says, in his delightful little History of Caernarvon Castle, almost realizes the vision of the divine Spenser:—

> Then did I see a bridge made all of golde,
> Over the sea from one to th' other side,
> Withouten prop or pillour it to upholde,
> But like the coloured rain-bowe arched wide;
> Not that great arche which Trajan edifide,
> To be a wonder to all age ensuing,
> Was matchable to this in equal viewing.

A large body of people had assembled from Bangor and the neighbourhood, to greet them with a welcome, and were somewhat disappointed at their not landing. They were received from the steamer into a pleasure yacht, which conveyed them to Plasnewydd.

CONCERT.

The Concert of this evening though not quite so numerously attended as that of Tuesday, was honoured by all the nobility and gentry of the neighbourhood, and a very brilliant company of youth, fashion, and beauty. The performances went off exceedingly well, and drew from the audience the most rapturous applause. The vocal and instrumental performers were the same as on the former night, with the addition of Mr. E. Thomas, a native of Wales, and a pupil of Spagnoletti, who played a Concerto on the violin, which was rewarded with much approbation by the audience.

FRIDAY.

The entertainments this day, were a Public Breakfast, a Regatta, and in the evening a Ball. The Breakfast, which was held at Mrs. Bicknell's beautiful hotel, to be known in future by the title of the Royal Victoria, was but tolerably attended. It was not so with the regatta; for the weather being beautifully fine, a most brilliant and numerous company were induced to assemble upon the green to enjoy the aquatic sports. The animated appearance of the bay, surrounded as it was by the most magnificent scenery, called forth the admiration of every one present, and contributed greatly to the pleasures of the day. The following is a correct account of the sailing and rowing matches:

1.—For a Cup, value £40 for yachts not exceeding 50 tons. Six started.

1	Zephyr Cutter	 42	.....	James Watson, Esq.
2	Ariel Cutter	 29	.....	John Mc Cracken, Esq.
3	Crusader Cutter	 46	.....	John Patterson, Esq.

2.—For a Cup, value £20 for four-oar boats, rowed and steered by gentlemen amateurs.

1	Water Witch, Liverpool	....	Charles Moulson, Esq.
2	Fairy Queen	....	Mr. T. Walker

There was no race for this prize, as the Fairy Queen withdrew.

3.—For four-oar boats, to be steered by residents in Anglesey or Caernarvon.
First boat, £8, second ditto, £4.

1	Jack's Alive	....	Mr. John Jones
2	Snowdon Ranger	....	Mr. Owen Owens
3	Princess Victoria	....	Mr. John Williams

4.—For a Cup, value £10, to be sailed for by yachts not exceeding 15 tons. Eleven started.

1	Tickler Cutter	 15	......	Jonathan Grindrod, Esq.
2	Royal Eagle	 12	......	Thomas Goddard, Esq.
3	Pearl Cutter	 15	......	Thomas Jervis, Esq.
4	Maria Cutter	 15	......	Thomas Farnell, Esq.

5.—For six-oared boats. First boat, £20, second ditto, £10. Eight started.

1	Water Witch	....	Mr. E. W. Lloyd
2	Templar	....	Captain Wright
3	Liver	....	Mr. Richard Parry
4	Lark	....	Mr. Walker
5	Diable Boiteux	....	Sir R. B. W. Bulkeley, Bart.

The buoy was rounded in the following order:—Lark, first; Water Witch, second; Liver, third. The Water Witch then fouled the Lark and broke her yoke, by which accident, as she could not steer, she went a quarter of a mile out of her course. The Lark claimed the prize, and it was determined that she was entitled either to the £20, or the £10. We have not yet heard which of the two she is to receive. In consequence of this occurrence, Sir R.W. Bulkeley, in the most handsome manner, gave £10, and called it Lady Bulkeley's Cup, for the Lark, Templar, and Diable Boiteux. A very capital race ensued, which was won cleverly by the Lark of Chester.

6.—Given by the Duchess of Kent, for six-oared boats, to be steered by boatmen of Anglesey or Caernarvonshire. First boats, £15, second, £7, and third £3.

1	Jack's Alive	....	Mr. John Jones
2	Snowdon Ranger	....	Mr. Owen Owens
3	Princess Victoria	....	Mr. John Williams

7.—For a Ladies' Cup, value £20, for six-oared boats, by gentlemen amateurs.

Water Witch	....	Charles Moulson, Esq.
Diable Boiteux	....	Sir R. B. W. Bulkeley, Bart.

On Saturday, a match took place between the Water Witch, four-oared boat, of Liverpool, and the Chester Fairy Queen, each rowed by fishermen. The Sconces in the Fairy Queen won in admirable style.

THE BALL.

The Ball room in the evening at the Royal Victoria was crowded as before by fashion, youth, and beauty; and many tripped it on the light fantastic toe, till "bright Aurora tinged the morn".

Thus has terminated the proceedings of the Royal Eisteddfod at Beaumaris, and although it was not so numerously attended as that of Denbigh in 1828, a circumstance which may be explained by taking into consideration the prevalence of the Cholera, yet we are assured by competent judges, that as regards nobility, rank, and fashion, it was honoured above all others. Before we conclude, we must congratulate the friends of Welsh literature upon a resolution passed by the committee before they left Beaumaris, namely, "that the surplus money shall not be diverted from the main object of the institution, but be strictly applied to Cambrian literary purposes". This resolution has given much satisfaction, and already induced several gentlemen to come forward with subscriptions, who before, had some peculiar feelings upon the subject; among them we mention Lord Mostyn and the Hon. E. M. Ll. Mostyn, who have given twenty-five pounds each. The committee have likewise determined to publish the successful compositions without delay; and to reward the secretary Mr. W. Jones, with some mark of their approbation, for his unwearied and valuable services.

BISHOP HEBER'S SPEECH.

On the celebration of the bardic meeting at Wrexham, in the year 1820, Reginald Heber, afterwards Bishop of Calcutta, made the following admirable speech, which I shall transcribe into these pages, as the most appropriate conclusion to my account of the last Royal Eisteddfod.

———————

" Sir Watkin and Gentlemen ! As I am certainly taken a little by surprize, you will, I trust, excuse me if I express my gratitude less fluently than you have been usually addressed on such occasions.—I cannot however refrain from offering you my warmest thanks for the honour which you have been pleased to confer on me—an honour, to which I am well aware I have no pretensions, though I will say that I give place to none in my good wishes for the welfare of the principality, to which on this, as well as on former, and still more interesting occasions of my life, I consider myself as deeply indebted. And in proportion to my zeal for the prosperity of Wales, my anxiety must be naturally great for the permanence and extension of an Institution, which like that of the Eisteddfodau, is devoted to the revival, the preservation, and encouragement of the ancient literature, the ancient language, and the existing talent, and mental cultivation of your country.

"Though not myself a Welshman, and though I have not the good fortune to be able to appreciate, any otherwise than through the medium of translation, the treasures of our elder Bards, I cannot at all forget that it is from them, Gray and Southey have borrowed some of the most striking poetry which my own language contains, or that the British tongue had already attained a high degree of cultivation. Nor can I forget that in the pedigree of almost all existing tongues, and in the history of all civilized nations, a knowledge of your antiquities is necessary to a certain extent, whether to the Philologist, or the Antiquary; inasmuch as they were your ancestors who first colonized the widest and fairest regions of Europe, and who have left behind them, intermixed with the languages of their successors, and impressed on the most striking features of nature from Caucasus to Denmark, the traces of their previous occupancy.

" But even if the language of the Cymry were less ancient, or its stores less valuable, yet so long as it is the living language of half a million of our fellow christians, and fellow subjects, it must richly deserve, and abundantly repay whatever labour, or encouragment may be bestowed on its cultivation. It is evident to all, who consider the subject with attention, that as every man thinks in his mother tongue, so whoever is compelled to express himself in a language different from that in which his conceptions are formed, is however unconsciously, compelled to the act of translation.

But we all of us know from a comparison of those classic writers which we read in the original, with even the best translations which modern talent and learning can supply, how much is lost in the course of such a transfusion; how much of fire, how much of originality evaporates, and how greatly the sharp touches of genius are effaced from each succeeding impression.

" If then we discourage, or degrade, or neglect the language of any nation soever, we neglect, or degrade, or discourage, we cripple and fetter, and so far as in us lies, we extinguish the native genius of that people. And feeling this so forcibly as I do, I can never look back without sorrow, and shame too, I will not say the cold neglect, but the systematic and persevering hostility, of which, on the part of your English Rulers, the Welsh Language was for many years the object. It is needless and it would be painful to go back to the causes of that hostility, or to the manner in which it was carried on, but it is to the credit of your ancestors and yourselves that its effects were not successful. They must have succeeded with a people of less simple manners, less warmly attached to the memory and institutions of their forefathers, and who had not those forefathers recalled so frequently to their recollection and veneration by the names and associations of the majestic natural objects, by which you are surrounded.

"The present meeting, the mass of talent, of learning, landed wealth, and of ancient aristocracy which I see before me embarked, in the same good cause, is an omen, I trust, that these evil days are now gone by for ever. And I would venture to exhort those who hear me, to continue and extend their patriotic exertions till they have compensated for ages of past depression, or indifference. Saxon, as I am myself, and proud of my nation, I am certainly very far from blaming, I am naturally disposed to rejoice in the pains which *we* have taken to preserve and illustrate the most remote, and barren of the Gothic Dialects. But I cannot perceive why the *Mabinogion*, and the *Gododin*, do not call for editions equally splendid with those of the Icelandic Sagas, and why there should not be a Welsh, as well as an Anglo-Saxon Professor, in one or both of our Universities.

" I can only conclude by wishing you abundant success in your present objects, and that these objects may extend and prosper in proportion as your means are extended.—These objects I repeat are every way worthy of an ancient, a wise, and a generous people, nor can they be pursued under better auspices than the auspices of those 'blazoned Eaglets', whose influence in war or peace has been at all times propitious to the military renown, and domestic improvement of their native country. Gentlemen, I again offer you my best thanks for the honour conferred on me. "

In the delivery of this address, the learned and eloquent gentleman was several times interrupted by the plaudits of the company, and when he concluded they were continued for a considerable time.

THE END.

INDEX.